PAKISTAN

POLITICAL ROOTS AND
DEVELOPMENT
1947–1999

PAKISTAN
POLITICAL ROOTS AND DEVELOPMENT
1947–1999

Safdar Mahmood

OXFORD

UNIVERSITY PRESS

Great Clarendon Street, Oxford OX2 6DP

Oxford University Press is a department of the University of Oxford.
It furthers the University's objective of excellence in research, scholarship,
and education by publishing worldwide in

Oxford New York

Athens Auckland Bangkok Bogotá Buenos Aires Calcutta
Cape Town Chennai Dar es Salaam Delhi Florence Hong Kong Istanbul
Karachi Kuala Lumpur Madrid Melbourne Mexico City Mumbai
Nairobi Paris São Paulo Singapore Taipei Tokyo Toronto Warsaw

with associated companies in Berlin Ibadan

Oxford is a registered trade mark of Oxford University Press
in the UK and in certain other countries

ISBN 0 19 579373 0

Second Impression 2000

Printed in Pakistan at
Asian Packages (Pvt) Ltd., Karachi.
Published by
Ameena Saiyid, Oxford University Press
5-Bangalore Town, Sharae Faisal
PO Box 13033, Karachi-75350, Pakistan.

CONTENTS

PREFACE

Pakistan's political history is marked with unnecessary delay in constitution-making, breakdowns of constitutional order, political instability, military rule, and extra-parliamentary pressure, and agitation for political change. Pakistan had three 'regular' constitutions (1956, 1962, and 1973), last of which was drastically changed by the military regime in 1985, two 'interim' constitutions (1947, 1972), and three country-wide martial laws and military rules (1958–62, 1969–72, and 1977–85). During the years of parliamentary rule, the political leaders and the political parties often violated the spirit of the constitution and democracy. They got engaged in a ruthless struggle for power, and regional and narrow partisan interests and priorities superseded the needs of political consensus-building and shared decision-making. In the fifties, Pakistan suffered from a serious problem of political instability and confusion. The elected governments often resorted to authoritarian ways, using the state apparatus to suppress dissent. These tendencies were reinforced during military rule. Pakistan returned to democratic path in 1985 after a very long period of martial law. Though this transition was commendable, the performance of different elected governments since then was far from satisfactory, raising doubts about institutionalization of the democratic process.

It is important to understand the dynamics and causes of these developments. Why could Pakistan not evolve viable political institutions and faced serious problems of political and economic management? Why were the bureaucracy and the military able to expand their role and become important power wielders? There are a host of issues about military rule in Pakistan: the establishment of military rule, the policies of military governments and their impact on the political process, the country's return to civilian rule, and the military's role in the post-withdrawal period. Pakistan's return to democracy and its slow democratic transition is another important aspect of the country's politics and history. What is the nature and direction of this transition? What are the future prospects of constitutionalism, democracy, and political stability?

This book endeavours to answer these questions with historical and analytical perspectives so as to untangle the complexities of Pakistani politics. The book opens with a chapter on the historical roots of Pakistan, analysing the factors and political circumstances that shaped the Muslim perspective on politics and society in British India in the post-1857 period and how and why the Muslims demanded, first, constitutional protection for their socio-cultural and political identity and interests, and later, the establishment of a separate state for themselves. The chapter notes the highlights and turning points in the struggle for the establishment of Pakistan, especially the opposition the Muslims had to face at the hands of the Congress Party and the British Indian government.

The book's central focus is on Pakistan's political process. It offers a thorough overview of the making and abolition of different constitutions and the performance of various political parties and their leaders. Pakistan began with the first interim constitution of 1947 which was an adapted version of the Government of India Act, 1935, and then spent almost nine years to frame a constitution. The study provides insights on the stages in constitution-making and outlines the characteristic features of various constitutions and why and how these did not work effectively. It also examines the working of the military governments of Ayub Khan, Yahya Khan, and Ziaul Haq, and the post-withdrawal elected governments of Benazir Bhutto and Nawaz Sharif. It provides data and analysis on the leading political parties with a focus on the organizational problems, their leadership and political programmes and alliance amongst these parties for pursuing their political goals.

The poor track record of democracy has been explained with reference to the crisis of leadership after the demise of the father of the nation, Quaid-i-Azam Muhammad Ali Jinnah; lack of leadership qualities among the political leaders who followed him; decline and degeneration of the Muslim League, the party that had led the independence movement, weak and disorganized political parties with programmes that failed to inspire people; domination of the political process by the feudal and other traditional elite who had little faith in democracy; unnecessary intervention of the head of state in the day-to-day affairs of the state; the rise of the bureaucracy and the military to power; imposition of martial law; absence of fair and free elections; inter-provincial rivalries; misuse of state authority for personal and party interests, and serious economic problems. The leaders deliberately neglected the interests and welfare of the common people who themselves were not provided with sufficient and fair opportunities for political participation.

The chapter on foreign policy provides a review of Pakistan's interaction with the international community with a focus on geographic, political, and economic factors. It also reviews the impact of global and regional environment on the country's foreign policy, and the problems of a small state in the neighbourhood of a powerful and ambitious adversary. India-Pakistan relations, including the Kashmir problem, rightly get a lengthy treatment, pointing out India's hegemonic agenda and Pakistan's efforts to maintain its foreign policy options. Other aspects of foreign policy include, *inter alia*, relations with the major powers and the Muslim world, especially Afghanistan, Central Asia and the Gulf region. Pakistan's efforts to cope with the post-Cold war international and regional environment have also been examined, thereby providing the readers with a comprehensive perspective on all major aspects of Pakistan's foreign policy.

It can be safely claimed that this book captures the highlights of Pakistan's political history up to 1999 and endeavours to understand the dynamic factors shaping this history. The same can be said about the study of Pakistan's foreign policy. The book is useful not only for researchers and students but also serves as a valuable reference for general readers who are looking for a single volume with comprehensive overview of Pakistan's history, politics, and foreign policy.

Dr Safdar Mahmood
12, Golf Road,
GOR-I,
Lahore

1

PAKISTAN MOVEMENT:
THE HISTORICAL PERSPECTIVE

After the demise of Aurangzeb, the edifice of the Mughal empire
in India had begun to crumble and eventually the very survival
of the Muslim polity in India was threatened by the rising tide
of Jats, Rajputs, Sikhs, and Marathas. Shah Waliullah, a religious
scholar and reformer, clearly foresaw the danger. He approached
several Muslim notables to organize themselves to face the threat
looming large on the horizon. He himself started a movement to
encourage the Muslim masses to channelize their energies into
a cohesive and unified force for the protection and glorification
of Islam in India. His movement was meant to purify the Muslim
society by eliminating corruption which was rampant at that
time and to revive the spirit of *Jihad*. It was the first mass
movement of its kind in India. It rekindled the spirit of Islam,
aroused the Muslim mass-consciousness and organized the
Muslims to meet the challenge of powerful adversaries. The
movement, after a while, and with the advent of the British in
the country, went underground only to re-surface subsequently
through the 'War of Independence' of 1857.[1]

The British, of course, saw it as a 'sepoy mutiny' aimed at
'the extinction' of British authority.[2] They crushed it ruthlessly.
The result was that the last vestige of the Muslim rule was
erased from the throne of Delhi and power was transferred from
East India Company to the British Government in London. This
was a great setback to the Muslims. The new rulers were
naturally suspicious of the Muslims from whom they had
captured power. W.W. Hunter reflected the feelings of the

British rulers when he remarked in 1871 that 'the Mussalmans of India are, and have been for many years, a source of chronic danger to the British Power in India'.[3] The British did all they could to suppress the Muslims. They were convinced that 'the only course left to them for the expansion of the new power and its continuance'[4] was to destroy them. While the Muslims suffered, the Hindus accepted the new order without any hesitation because for them it meant only 'a change of masters'. As one writer described it: 'Hindus poured into official life with a joy which knew no bounds and hailed the British as their great benefactors.'[5] They extended complete support to the new rulers in their efforts to suppress the Muslims. The Muslims lost everything.

Indeed, according to one estimate, the Muslims 'were subjected to ruthless punishment and merciless vengeance. In every department of life where government patronage was essential, the doors were closed on Muslims. The Muslims were hounded out of employment and opportunities.'[6] The government was not only indifferent, it bluntly discouraged the Muslims; this injustice was evident when a number of vacancies in the office of the Commissioner of Sunderban were advertised with a supplementary note that only Hindus were to be appointed.

There was scarcely a government office where a Muslim could get any job other than that of a porter or a carrier. Actually, this repressive policy originated from the Company days. As far back as 1842, Lord Ellenborough had written to the Duke of Wellington that the Muslims were fundamentally hostile towards the British and that their enmity towards the government was an established fact.[7] But the collapse of the 'War of Independence' in 1857, with its storm-centres in the Muslim areas of Delhi and Oudh, further darkened the Muslims' prospects.

Being the victims of the repressive attitude of the British, the Muslims became insolent and desperate, and boycotted the Anglo-Indian schools and the new educational system. They also believed that the English system of education would impair their faith. As Hunter described it: 'No young man passes through our Anglo-Indian schools without learning to disbelieve the faith of his fathers.'[8] There was no denying that the Muslim community had fallen into an abyss of despair.

In fact, the Muslims went through one crisis after another till Sir Syed Ahmad Khan rose like a star above the storm to guide them out of their distressful situation. He appealed to the Muslims to break with the past and the 'old method'. He called it 'a broom of which the string binding the twigs has been broken, so that they have all fallen apart, and cannot be re-united unless a fresh cord is provided'.[9] He was convinced that if the Anglo-Muslim relations continued to be tense and the Muslims kept themselves aloof from modern education, there could be no hope of regeneration of the Muslim community. So, he undertook the formidable task of improving the condition of the Muslims, and, suggested:

1. that the distrust prevailing between the British and the Muslims should be removed and an atmosphere of understanding and cordiality should be created between the two communities; and
2. that the Muslims should be equipped with modern education.

With this end in view, Sir Syed wrote *Asbab-i-Baghawat-i-Hind* (The Causes of the Indian Revolt) in 1858 in which he gave a historical survey of the factors which led to this 'Revolt'. The purpose was to show that the uprising was not a planned affair, and that the Muslim share in it was not greater than that of the Hindus. In this booklet, Sir Syed enumerated many causes responsible for the turn of events but, according to him, the most important cause was the non-admission of Indians into the legislative council. 'If some sons of the soil had been included in the legislative council, they would have kept the rulers informed of the trends of public opinion.'[10] In this way, Sir Syed partially blamed the East India Company Government for the eventual developments.

Sir Syed also published a series of pamphlets, including *The Loyal Mohammadans of India,* which gave the names of those Muslim families who had saved British lives during the events of 1857. Again, the purpose was to prove that the Muslims did not participate in the events as a community. In addition, he also wrote a book pointing out some affinities between Islam and Christianity. The idea was to create religious harmony between the Muslims and the British by showing 'that both these faiths are two harmonious phases of the religious ideal, and as such, can and ought to influence the human mind in the same direction.'[11]

In 1864, Sir Syed founded the Scientific Society at Ghazipur which sought to introduce Western knowledge in India. It also provided a platform where the Indians and the British could meet and discuss subjects of their mutual interest. A school was founded at Aligarh in 1875; it became a college two years later, and was ultimately converted into the Aligarh Muslim University.

During this period, several forces came to the fore which went on to determine the future course of Hindu-Muslim relations. Urdu-Hindi controversy surfaced in 1867 to replace Urdu by Hindi as the court language because the Hindus regarded Urdu as a language of Muslim origin representing Muslim culture. It laid bare the real Hindu mentality. 'This development caused deep disappointment to Sir Syed as it manifested a sectional spirit to divide the Hindu and Muslim communities permanently.'[12] It was the first time that Sir Syed got suspicious of the majority community. He thought that 'it would be difficult for Hindus and Muslims to go together as a nation.'[13] This explains why he advised the Muslims to keep aloof from the Indian National Congress when it was established in 1885. He could foresee that the Muslims were bound to be under the domination of the Hindu majority community as a result of the demand for the introduction of a representative government in India. His point of view was that 'so long as differences of races and creed and distinctions of caste form an important element in the socio-political life of India, and influence her inhabitants in matters connected, with the administration and welfare of the country at large, the system of elections, pure and simple, cannot be safely adopted. The larger community would totally override the interests of the smaller community.'[14]

Sir Syed knew that the Congress was virtually controlled by the Hindus; the Muslims, therefore, would not be in a position to play any significant role in it and, indeed, on the contrary, would run the risk of being exploited. He was also afraid that the tragedy of 1857 might be repeated. In these circumstances, Sir Syed could give no better advice to the Muslims than to refrain from joining the Congress. His apprehensions about this party were based on realities, and subsequently proved true when the Congress took part in the anti-Urdu and anti-Partition of Bengal movements. The subsequent events clearly showed that the Congress was altogether a Hindu body and was determined to establish Hindu rule under the cover of representative institutions.

The rise and role of the Congress, in fact, changed the outlook of Muslim leaders on Indian political life. They soon came to reckon the need for a separate political organization 'in order to protect their rights.'[15] Step by step, they moved towards their separate party. Sir Syed himself provided the lead by founding the Mohammadan Anglo-Oriental Defence Association in 1893, which was meant to protect the political rights of the Muslims and to provide a forum to them to discuss their problems. Gradually, political problems also came up for discussion along with educational issues. Muslims increasingly became involved with politics and political developments.

During the lifetime of Sir Syed, the need for a political party of the Muslims was not fully realized, but his death created a great vacuum in the political and social life of the community. As long as he lived, Sir Syed successfully performed the functions of an institution. Now the mantle of Muslim leadership fell upon his successors who had to lead a distressed and distraught community.

Nawab Mohsinul Mulk urged the need for a separate political organization of the Muslims at a meeting of Urdu Defence Association held in 1900. Nawab Viqarul Mulk reinforced the idea by the end of 1901. The same spirit inspired Nawab Salimullah to form the 'Mohammadan Provincial Union' in Bengal in October 1905. But 1906 proved to be an eventful year, for it marked the crystallization of the efforts of the Indian Muslims towards their destiny. A deputation of about thirty-five selected Muslim leaders, led by Sir Aga Khan, called upon the Viceroy of India, Lord Minto, at Simla, on 1 October 1906. The deputation demanded separate electorates on the basis of different and distinct religion, culture, and traditions. The Viceroy did not promise anything substantial to the deputation for the fear of offending other communities. But he assured the Muslims that 'their political rights and interests as a community will be safeguarded by an administrative reorganization.'[16] The Simla Deputation, as it came to be known eventually, proved to be a stepping stone in the struggle of Indian Muslims because, by acceding to this principle, the British recognized the Muslims as a separate 'nation'. The demand for separate electorates was understandable. The members elected by joint electorates could not be true representatives of the Muslims. But once they were recognized as a separate political entity, it was but only natural to found a political organization for the promotion and protection of their rights.

Some writers have argued that the recognition of separate electorates was a deliberate attempt of the British to sow the seeds of conflict between the Hindus and the Muslims. But all evidence goes on to suggest that the British Government at that time regarded India as a subcontinent inhabited by a number of 'nations' and, therefore, there was no question of dividing any so-called 'Indian nation'. Lord Morley's letter to Lord Minto proves the point beyond any shadow of doubt. He wrote: 'Not one whit more than you do I think it desirable or possible, or even conceivable, to adopt English political institutions to the nations who inhabit India.'[17] Besides it must be pointed that the British did not exclusively grant the right of separate electorates to the Muslims. It was granted to other minority communities too, such as, the Anglo-Indians, Indian Christians, Sikhs, and Europeans as well as commercial and industrial classes and landowners. This was more in line with the Indian 'conditions' than the British.[18]

The desire of the Indian Muslims for a separate political organization of their own was strengthened by the encouraging results of the Simla Deputation. The Muslim leaders, therefore, held a meeting on 30 December 1906 in Dacca (now Dhaka), to discuss the matter at some length. Nawab Viqarul Mulk presided over this meeting. In his presidential address, he noted: 'The Muslims are only one-fifth of the population of India. It is obvious that if at any time the British Government ceases to exist in India, the nation which is four times numerous will rule the country.'[19] It was resolved after great deliberation that 'this meeting, composed of Muslims from all parts of India assembled at Dacca, decides that a political association be formed, styled the All-India Muslim League.'[20] The long-aspired objective of the Indian Muslims took a concrete shape with the emergence of the All-India Muslim League on the political scene.

The aims and objects of the Muslim League were as follows:

1. 'To promote among the Mussulmans of India feelings of loyalty to the British Government...;
2. 'To protect and advance the political rights and interests of the Mussulmans of India...; and
3. 'To prevent the rise among the Mussulmans of any feeling of hostility towards other communities...'[21]

The first objective of the Muslim League, namely, 'to promote feelings of loyalty', was criticized by the Hindus on the ground that the Muslim League was created 'not to safeguard Muslim interests but to strengthen the British rule in India.' The critics, however, forgot that the Congress too started off with a reaffirmation of loyalty to the British Crown. The Muslim League changed its creed after a few years, and emerged as the sword-arm of the Indian Muslims in their political struggle. Of course, the Congress was not pleased with its progress. Its leaders did not like the Muslims to organize themselves politically and thereby challenge the prospects of Hindu-majority rule in India.

The establishment of the Muslim League marked the emergence of Muslim nationalism in India in an organized form. The League became the main vehicle of Muslim demands and interests. Its first regular session was held on 29–30 December 1907 in Karachi. The objectives of the League were redefined in the constitution adopted at this session. On 18 March 1908, the League met at Aligarh. This meeting launched the League fully and finally in Indian politics. It was at the Aligarh session that a resolution was passed to impress upon the government the demand 'to accept the Muslim demands as incorporated in the Simla Deputation Address.'[22]

The decade following Morley-Minto Reforms of 1909 is an important era in the political history of India. During this period, a number of developments alienated the Muslims from the British which, in turn, brought them closer to the Hindus. This was in spite of fact that the 1909 reforms were encouraging for the Muslims. They felt secure because their demand for separate electorates had been accepted. But the sudden annulment of the Partition of Bengal in 1911 'came as a shock to their faith in Government and was rightly looked upon as a gross betrayal.'[23] The year 1912 witnessed the Balkans War which ended the Turkish rule over the Balkans. It sent a wave of anger among the Muslims. The Muslim press, led by the *Zamindar*, *Al-Hilal* and *Comrade*, published fiery articles and helped 'to swell the mighty current in favour of political consciousness, and this rapidly growing consciousness amongst Muslims was finding an expression in day-to-day meetings.'[24] In 1913, two further developments caused a great deal of frustration among the Muslims against the British Government, and, thus, paved the way for a closer collaboration with the Congress. One, the government refused to raise the status of the Aligarh college to a university. Two, a portion of a mosque in Kanpur was demolished by the municipality.

It was against this background that the League leadership thought of changing its creed and amended its constitution at its Lucknow Session held on 23 March 1913. It adopted its new objective as 'the attainment, under the aegis of British Crown, of a system of self-government *suitable* to India.'[25] This change in the objectives of the Muslim League was welcomed all over the country and it brought the League closer to the Congress. It also indicated that the League was moving away from its traditional path and that 'liberal' forces were becoming influential in Muslim politics.

The need for creating a united front of Hindus and Muslims was already being suggested by all political quarters, because the government was expected to introduce important reforms after the First World War, aimed at broadening the base of democracy. The British actions against Turkey had already caused great resentment in Muslim India. Maulana Mohammad Ali and his brother, Maulana Shaukat Ali, had been interned under the Defence of India Rules. 'Thus, this current bitter feeling against the British enabled Jinnah and Mazharul Haq to persuade the Muslim League to think in terms of coming to a long-term settlement with the Congress.[26] A committee was, therefore, formed under Quaid-i-Azam Muhammad Ali Jinnah whose subsequent efforts won him the title of the 'Ambassador of Hindu-Muslim Unity', to prepare a plan for future reforms. The scheme prepared by this committee was approved both by the Congress and the Muslim League in Lucknow in December 1916. The Congress and the League entered into the famous 'Lucknow Pact' in their joint session. According to this Pact, the Hindus accepted the principle of separate electorates for the Muslims. In addition, the Muslims were promised one-third seats in the central council. It was for the first (and also for the last) time that the two communities agreed upon one constitutional draft. Autonomy for provinces and a responsible self-government at the centre became the common demand of both the parties.

But the Montagu-Chelmsford Reforms, introduced in 1919, did not reflect the aspirations of the Congress and the League.

Described as 'Dyarchy', it envisaged two categories of subjects: 'Transferred' and 'Reserved'. The ministers could make laws only regarding the subjects enumerated in the first list. The second list was reserved for the Governor and his Executive Council. The result was that there was hardly any progress on the realization of responsible self-government, even in the provinces. The reforms, however, extended the right of separate electorates to all minorities in India and provided a central legislature with a majority of elected members.

The Rowlatt Act was passed after the War and was strongly resented by the Indians. This Act was the outcome of two bills introduced in the Imperial Legislative Council based on the Rowlatt Committee's recommendation, termed as 'Black Bills'. Under the Act, the provincial government could arrest a person without warrant, and imprison him, without any right of appeal. The passage of the Rowlatt Act led to a series of country-wide agitations and *hartals* (strikes). Jinnah had made a strong speech against the bills in the Imperial Legislative Council. He was sure that 'no civilized government' could 'ever dream of putting those recommendations in the form of laws'.[27] As a protest, he also resigned from the Council. M.K. Gandhi, a prominent leader of the Congress, started a 'civil disobedience' movement, *Satyagraha*, which soon led to large-scale violence and bloodshed. Eventually, the campaign was called off on 18 April 1919, after Gandhi admitted that he had made a 'Himalayan miscalculation' in launching 'Civil disobedience prematurely'.[28]

The political climate of India was charged with emotions when the Jallianwala tragedy took place and the trust of people in the British Government was completely shaken. On 13 April 1919, General Dyer fired on an open public meeting which was being held in Jallianwala Bagh, Amritsar. The sustained firing into the unarmed crowd resulted in 1516 casualties.[29] The news of this massacre sent a wave of great indignation throughout India. This and other related events made the people realize that their life, religion, and future were not safe under the British rule.

The feelings of outrage had not yet subsided when the treatment meted out to Turkey by the victorious Allies further embittered the Indian Muslims against the British rulers. Despite the assurances given by the British Premier, the allied forces occupied the Arab dominions. It was obvious that the great Turkish empire would be disintegrated and the institution of Caliphate would come to an end. The Indian Muslims had great respect for the Turkish Caliph. Alarmed and apprehensive of the fate of the Caliph and his dominions, they started the Khilafat movement. A deputation led by Maulana Mohammad Ali was sent to England. Gandhi, to show his sympathy for the movement, launched his 'non-cooperation' movement which aimed at renouncing titles, boycotting councils, and refusing government service. The feeling against the British was so high that a complete *hartal* was observed when the Prince of Wales came to visit India on 17 November 1921.

It is important to note that Gandhi was in the forefront of the Khilafat movement, for he wanted to use it as a weapon for establishing his leadership and for uniting Hindus and Muslims against the British. But this effort at Hindu-Muslim unity was obviously not based on firm foundations. It was primarily an alliance between 'bed-fellows in adversity.'[30] The myth of unity soon exploded when the Hindus started movements like *shuddhi* which aimed at reconverting the relatively poorer Muslims to Hinduism. Communal clashes became frequent. It was the incident at Chauri Chaura, a village in the United Provinces, where a mob set fire to a police station and twenty-two constables lost their lives, that led Gandhi to call off civil disobedience. Gandhi was arrested after the Chauri Chaura incident. The concept of Hindu-Muslim unity and all the desired goals were shattered. *Swaraj* (freedom) was not achieved and the Khilafat movement had failed to save the Caliph or his dominions.

In 1927, the British Government decided to send a constitutional commission to India, headed by Sir John Simon, to evaluate the political situation and propose a constitution for India. Since no Indian member was included in the commission, the Indians felt slighted, and decided to boycott it. The Congress invited an all-parties conference to draft its version of the constitution. The conference which was held in February 1928, decided to form a committee under Motilal Nehru. The committee published a report known as the Nehru Report.

The Report completely ignored the Muslim demands. Even those principles which had been agreed upon in the Lucknow Pact of 1916 were set aside. The Report recommended the abolition of separate electorates and demanded a unitary form of government for India. It further widened the gulf between the Hindus and the Muslims. Jinnah described it as 'the parting of ways'.[31] Expressing his apprehensions about the domination of the Hindu majority community, he noted: 'Majorities are apt to be oppressive and tyrannical and minorities always dread and fear that their interests and rights, unless clearly safeguarded by statutory provisions, would suffer and be prejudiced.'[32] The Report also frustrated Maulana Mohammad Ali who turned away from the Congress, never to return.

Earlier, in 1927, the Muslim League had split on the issue of co-operating with the Simon Commission, into two groups, one led by Sir Shafi and the other under Jinnah. The two groups held separate meetings, at Lahore and Calcutta, respectively. The 'Jinnah League' decided to boycott the Commission. It appointed a committee to negotiate with the Congress in order to draft a constitution for India. Jinnah was hopeful, till then, that some solution of the communal problem would be found, but in vain. The negative attitude of the Congress disappointed him.

In March 1929, Sir Shafi and Jinnah met at Delhi and agreed to unite the two groups of the Muslim League. Jinnah issued a statement to the League Council that the Nehru Report was not acceptable to the Muslims. He put forward his own scheme regarding the demands of the Muslims in his famous 'Fourteen Points' which provided a programme of political action for the Muslims. The major objectives were to both increase the number of Muslim-majority provinces and to demand more provincial autonomy. This was the united demand of all the Muslims. It has, therefore, been rightly remarked that one important result of the Nehru Report was to help unite the hitherto divided Muslims.

The British Government decided to hold a Round Table Conference of the British and Indian leaders of all shades of opinion when all their efforts to find a solution of the constitutional problem failed. The first Round Table Conference was held on 12 November 1930. A vast majority of Indian leaders were present, except the Congress, which had refused to participate and had started its 'civil disobedience movement'. Nothing substantial could be achieved at the Conference.

Meanwhile, the annual session of the Muslim League was held at Allahabad on 29 December 1930. It was at this session that Allama Muhammad Iqbal presented his historic presidential address in which he proposed and promoted the destiny of Indian Muslims. He said: 'The units of Indian society were not territorial as in European countries. India is a continent of human groups belonging to different religions. The Muslim demand for the creation of a Muslim India is, therefore, perfectly justified.' He, therefore, proposed: 'I would like to see Punjab, NWFP, Sind and Baluchistan amalgamated into a single state. Self-government within the British Empire or without the British Empire, the formation of a consolidated north-west Indian Muslim state, appears to me to be the final destiny of the Muslims.'[33] Iqbal thus emerged as the philosopher-guide of the Pakistan Movement in the subsequent years, under the able and dynamic leadership of Jinnah.

The second Round Table Conference held in 1931 failed to make any progress either. Gandhi, who attended the Conference as the sole representative of the Congress, refused to accommodate the Muslim demands and interests. He even opposed the already settled issue of separate electorates for the Muslims. The result was that no final agreement could be reached. Subsequently, the Government announced its own scheme on 16 August 1932, known as the 'Communal Award'. The Award maintained the principle of separate electorates, which was resented by the Hindus. But it was rejected by the

Muslims, because they continued to lose their statutory majorities in Bengal and Punjab. Thus, the 'Communal Award' failed to serve any useful purpose. The third Round Table Conference which was convened in November 1932, did not contribute anything at all. In March 1933, the Government issued a White Paper containing proposals for constitutional reform in India. In August 1935, the Government of India Act, 1935 was passed, which opened a new chapter in the Indian politics.

The 1935 Act abolished 'Dyarchy' which was introduced in 1919. It provided for bicameral federal legislature and responsible governments in the provinces. It also provided three lists of subjects: Federal, Provincial, and Concurrent. The Federal legislature was given exclusive jurisdiction over the federal list and provincial legislatures over the provincial list. Both the legislatures could make laws regarding subjects included in the third list, but, in case of inconsistency, the federal law was to prevail. But the Act did not establish a federation instantly. It had to come into operation after the acceptance of the Indian States, which did not happen. However, the Act helped the cause of representative and responsible government in the provinces.[34] Each province was provided with a Council of Ministers which was to be responsible to the legislature. Provincial leaders were 'to govern, so to speak on their own'.[35]

The 1935 Act thus represented a definite advance over the previous constitutional arrangements but it fell far short of the expectations of the people. Since it did not concede full self-government at the Centre and had many other shortcomings, it was described as 'thoroughly rotten, fundamentally bad and totally unacceptable' by Jinnah.[36] However, both the Muslim League and the Congress decided to accept the provincial part of the Act and contest the provincial elections in due course of time.

The new reforms under the 1935 Act helped to enlarge the scope of politics. The Act invested the provinces with executive and legislative powers in their own right. The number of general seats in the legislatures were increased. Franchise was expanded to include more than thirty million voters. The Muslims, therefore, felt that they should reorganize themselves to take advantage of the increased opportunities. Liaquat Ali Khan and many other Muslim leaders requested Jinnah to come back from London, where he was in a self-imposed exile since 1932, to lead the Muslims. Jinnah responded positively and returned in early 1934. A combined meeting of all sections of the Muslim League was held in March 1934 which elected Jinnah as the President of the party. The Muslim League was by no means a well-organized party at that time. Jinnah had to make all possible efforts to infuse a new life and vigour in the party.

The Congress, on the other hand, was a better organized party. It had an effective propaganda machinery and sound financial backing. The Congress, therefore, claimed that it was the sole representative body of the Indians. In Calcutta, Jawaharlal Nehru declared that there were only two parties in India, namely, the Government and the Congress. But Jinnah could not agree. He thundered: 'There is a third party in the country and that is Muslim India. We are not going to be dictated by anybody.'[37]

Elections were scheduled to be held in 1936–37, and political parties were hard-pressed to try their best in the election campaigns. The All-India Muslim League formed a Parliamentary Board on 12 April 1936 and issued an election manifesto. In its manifesto, the League expressed its determination to protect the rights of the Muslims and to work for their betterment. The League also stated categorically that it would strive for the replacement of the Act of 1935 by full self-government. Unfortunately, the League could not do well in the elections, mainly because of 'its small membership and extremely limited appeal' among the voters.[38] The Congress secured a clear majority in seven provinces out of eleven. The election results, however, indicated that Congress victories were secured mainly in Hindu constituencies. It had to form coalition ministries in Assam and Sindh. Only Punjab and Bengal remained under a non-Congress rule.

The bitter experience of two-and-a-half years of Congress rule (1937–39) was an eye-opener for the Muslims. Until then

Jinnah and many other Muslim leaders had been thinking in terms of 'coalitions', 'safeguards', 'concessions', and 'special responsibilities'. But now they were convinced that the so-called constitutional devices were no help at all. With the passage of time, the Muslims came to realize that 'appeals to patriotism or fairplay and topics of virtues of moderation and humanity which are so familiar to the eloquence of the weak, always excite rather than change the dark designs or check the aggression of the stronger.'[39] During its rule, the Congress cared little for the minorities. The inexorable logic of the majority principle was employed to exclude the Muslim League from the governments of the Hindu-majority provinces.

The Congress refused to give any share to the League in the provincial ministries, though the latter had captured a fairly good number of seats. Instead of taking the nominees of the League into cabinets, the Congress selected Independent Muslim members who could best serve its purpose. The Congress deliberately subjected the Muslims to hardships. They were refused due share in the public services. Muslim children were compelled to study Hindi at schools. Attempts were made to re-mould the educational system through *Vidyamandir* scheme. The textbooks extolled the virtues of Hindu culture and portrayed Hindu leaders as 'national' heroes. In addition, the policies and pronouncements of the Congress ministries made the situation worse. The recitation of 'Bande Mataram' before the opening session of the Assembly proved to be the last straw on the proverbial camel's back.[40]

Jinnah exposed the designs of Hindu leaders in his speech at Patna session of the Muslim League, held in December 1938. He pointed out: 'They talk of national government but they mean only Hindu government... Muslim children must accept 'Bande Mataram' as their national song, no matter whether their religious beliefs permit them to do so or not. It is idolatrous and worse—a hymn of hatred for Muslims.'[41]

The Muslim League could not make the Congress see reason. The resultant bitterness increased to such an extent that there was no hope of reconciliation. The political situation was best explained by Allama Iqbal in his letter of 28 May 1937 to Jinnah. Describing the political position of the Indian Muslims, and emphasizing the need for transforming the Muslim League into a mass party, he said:

> The problem of bread is becoming more and more acute. The Muslim has begun to feel that he had been going down and down during the last 200 years. Ordinarily, he believes that his poverty is due to Hindu money-lending or capitalism. The perception that it is equally due to foreign rule has not yet fully come to him. But it is bound to come... The question, therefore, is: How is it possible to solve the problem of Muslim poverty? And the whole future of the League depends on the League's ability to solve this question... Happily there is a solution in the enforcement of the Law of Islam and its further development in the light of modern ideas... But the enforcement and development of Shariat of Islam is impossible in this country without a free Muslim state or states. This has been my honest conviction for many years and I still believe this to be the only way to solve the problem of bread for Muslims as well as to secure a peaceful India.

He further maintained:

> For Islam the acceptance of social democracy in some suitable form and consistent with the legal principles of Islam is not a revolution but a return to the original purity of Islam... But, as I have said above, in order to make it possible for Muslim India to solve the problems, it is necessary to redistribute the country and to provide one or more Muslim states with absolute majorities. Don't you think that the time for such a demand has already arrived?[42]

Jinnah was moved.

The Muslim League held its twenty-fifth session in Lucknow from 15 to 18 October 1937. It was at this session that the Muslim League made a historic decision and resolved that the Muslim politics should be re-ordered. This session attracted a more representative gathering of the Indian Muslims than had ever been seen during the last twenty years. A new constitution was adopted which demanded, among other things, 'the establishment of full independence, in the form of federation, or free democratic states, in which full safeguards for Muslims and other minorities will be secured.'[43] Commenting on the new objectives of the Muslims League, the weekly *Paisa Akhbar* wrote: 'League has become a freedom-loving party that stands for independence of the motherland and protection of Muslims' rights.'[44]

The 'Jinnah-Sikandar Pact' was another important outcome of this session. Strictly speaking, it was not a Pact because it was neither signed nor given the shape of a pact. Its significance lay in the fact that it gave the Muslim League a more representative character. Though its terms were far from satisfactory, it was accepted by Jinnah because it gave the Muslim League a foothold in Punjab, a Muslim-majority province. Jinnah needed the support of Punjab, the 'cornerstone of Pakistan,' as he subsequently called it.[45] The Lucknow session thus helped a great deal 'in creating a sense of self-defence in the Muslims and they realized the importance of uniting their forces.'[46] It opened a new chapter in the history of Muslim politics.

One-and-a-half years had passed since the promulgation of the 1935 Act, and the Muslim League had not achieved much except for mobilizing some support against the rising Hindu influence and authority in the Indian political life. Sensing the gravity of the situation, the Muslim League, for the first time, at its Patna session in December 1938, authorized its Working Committee to decide upon launching 'Direct Action' to safeguard the Muslim interests and rights, if and when necessary. It was a hard time for the Muslims. They were passing through a very critical phase and had to make difficult decisions about their future. 'Muslim leaders were opposed to the continuance of British rule but before they would commit themselves to drastic action, they wanted to know what would replace it. The result was a policy that was a double negative against Congress before being against the British.'[47]

The Second World War broke out on 1 September 1939. The Muslim League empowered Jinnah to 'assure Great Britain on behalf of the Indian Muslims of their support in the War, provided they were assured the acceptance of their demands.'[48] But, on the other hand, the Congress Working Committee decided on 22 October 1939 'to ask Congress Ministries to resign as a mark of protest against the Government attitude.'[49] The Congress had reacted against the non-acceptance of their demand to establish a representative legislative body to decide the future of India and to frame the constitution. Jinnah availed himself this opportunity to appeal to the Muslims 'to observe the Deliverance Day on 22 December in all the Congress-ruled Provinces, as a mark of redress from the oppressive rule of the Congress.'[50] Jinnah emphasized that the day was simply meant to convey Muslim relief at the end of Congress rule.

The Viceroy invited Jinnah, Gandhi, and Rajendra Prasad to discuss the new situation, especially as it impacted upon the on-going War. The Viceroy was keen to expand his Council to help mobilize the Indian support. He met them on 1 November and 4 November, but nothing was agreed upon, and on 5 November the failure of these negotiations was announced.

The year 1939 concluded with dim prospects of Hindu-Muslim unity. The Hindus and the Muslims stood poles apart. The gulf between the two communities was wider than ever. As one writer put it: 'It was necessary that one of them should conquer the other. To hope both could remain equal was to desire the impossible and inconceivable.'[51] Gradually, the Muslims were driven to the conclusion that the only alternative left to them was to demand a separate homeland in which they could live according to their own ideals and way of life. They were a separate nation by any standard. Their culture, civilization, religion, even their food and clothing, were different from those of the Hindus. 'The theory of nationality is imbedded in the democratic theory of sovereignty of the will of the people. This means that 'the demand by a nationality for a national state does not require to be supported by any list of grievances. The will of the people is enough to justify it. But if grievances must be cited in support of their claims, the Muslims have them in plenty.'[52]

A resolution passed by the Sindh Muslim League in 1938 gave an instance of the way the minds of the League leaders were working during that period. The resolution said that differences between the Hindus and the Muslims had arisen on account of acute differences of religion, language, script, culture, etc. 'For the first time Hindus and Muslims were described officially by the League as two distinct nations.'[53]

These developments led Jinnah to agree with Allama Iqbal that 'the English parliamentary form of government, with its emphasis on the majority rule would permanently subject the Muslims to the Congress rule and, therefore, was not suitable to India.' Jinnah had come to realize that the idea of a separate homeland for the Muslims was inevitable. He was now convinced that there were two nations in India. He made this absolutely clear in the article he wrote in *Time and Tide* of London on 19 January 1940. Hindus and Muslims, he asserted, 'are in fact two different nations' with their own 'definite social codes which govern not so much man's relation with God, as man's relation with his neighbour'.[54]

Punjab, being a Muslim-majority province, occupied a significant position in the Muslim politics. It was necessary for the Muslim League to secure full support of this province, so that the cause of the Indian Muslims could be reinforced. The Muslim League leaders were of the view that the 'Declaration' for a separate homeland should be made from a province where the Muslims were in majority. They chose Punjab in view of the favourable attitude of its Premier, Sir Sikandar Hayat. Finally, the city of Lahore, the heart of Punjab, was selected for holding the next session of the Muslim League in March 1940, and for adopting the now famous 'Lahore Resolution'.

A committee, known as the 'The Punjab Committee', was sent to Lahore to examine the situation and report to the Council of Muslim League whether the circumstances for holding a League session were favourable or not. The Punjab Committee gave a favourable report, and, thus, it was finally decided that the historic session would be held there on 22–24 March.

In his presidential address on 22 March to a large gathering of Muslims drawn from all over India, Jinnah set the stage for the Muslim demand of a separate homeland, comprising Muslim-majority areas of India. As he explained it:

> The Hindus and Muslims belong to two different philosophies, social customs, literatures. They neither intermarry nor interdine together and, indeed, they belong to two different civilizations which are based mainly on conflicting ideas and conceptions. Their concepts on life are different. They have different epics, different heroes, and different episodes. Very often the hero of one is the foe of the other and, likewise, their victories and defeats overlap. To yoke together two such nations under a single state, one as a numerical minority and the other as a majority, must lead to growing discontent... Mussalamans are a nation according to any definition of nation, and they must have their homeland, their territory and their state.[55]

The Muslim League responded enthusiastically to Jinnah's call on 23 March, and in a Resolution adopted on 24 March declared:

> No constitutional plan would be workable in this country or acceptable to the Muslims unless it is designed on the following basic principles, viz., that geographically contiguous units are demarcated into regions which should be so constituted with such territorial readjustments as may be necessary, that the areas in which the Muslims are numerically in a majority, as in the North-Western and Eastern zones of India, should be grouped to constitute 'Independent States' in which the constituent units shall be autonomous and sovereign.[56]

The historical significance of this session of the Muslim League lies in the fact that it determined the destiny of the Indian Muslims. Once a goal was decided, the energies of the whole Muslim nation were directed towards its achievement. The demand for a separate homeland infused a new spirit in the Muslim nation and united it under the banner of the Muslim

League. So far, the League did not have deep roots among Muslim masses. After the passage of the Lahore Resolution, it was increasingly transformed into a mass organization.

It is interesting to note that the word 'Pakistan' was neither used by any speaker nor was it contained in the body of the Resolution but the Hindu press obliged the Muslims by giving it the name of 'Pakistan Resolution'. As one prominent League leader put it: 'It would have taken long for the Muslim leaders to explain Lahore Resolution and convey its real meaning and significance. Years of labour of the Muslim leaders to propagate its full import amongst the masses was shortened by the Hindu press in naming the resolution the "Pakistan Resolution".'[57] The Congress leaders criticized and rejected the Resolution. They claimed that partition was nothing more than a 'wild card proposal'. But the day eventually came when Nehru was forced to say that the League might take its Pakistan but not those parts of India which were unwilling to join Pakistan. The British did not approve of the Lahore Resolution either. Lord Linlithgow, the Viceroy, and Lord Zetland, the Secretary of State, exchanged letters ridiculing the demand for a Muslim homeland. Zetland even went on to argue that 'to create a number of ulsters in India' would mean 'the wrecking of all that we have been working for a number of years past.'[58]

The British Government was disturbed by the initial setbacks suffered during the War. By February 1942, the Japanese forces were knocking at the doors of India. Forced by circumstances as well as because of the pressure from the United States, the British Prime Minister despatched Sir Stafford Cripps to India[59] to find a constitutional solution. He held meetings with the Indian leaders from 23 to 29 March 1942, and discussed a whole range of issues of immediate concern. Finally, he prepared his proposals which were published on 30 March. These proposals, known as Cripps Proposals, envisaged the setting up of a Constituent Assembly to frame the constitution after the War. It was to be elected by the Provincial Legislatures through proportional representation. Any province, if it so desired, could retain its independence.

There was an implicit recognition of the principle of Pakistan in the Proposals. However, Jinnah expressed grave apprehensions about them, because Pakistan 'which was a matter of life and death for Muslim India', found only 'veiled recognition in the document.' The Muslim League had before it an elaborate scheme for the partition of India and could not accept any plan which did not clearly spell out the outline of a separate Muslim homeland. The League, therefore, rejected the Proposals. 'It could not compel the Muslims', said the League Resolution, 'to enter such a constitution-making body whose main object is the creation of a new Indian Union.' The Congress Working Committee did not accept the Proposals either. Thus, both the Muslim League and the Congress rejected the Cripps Proposals, though for different reasons. The Muslim League rejected the Proposals because they did not present any clear recognition of the Pakistan scheme. It was not accepted by the Congress because it thought that the Proposals were a 'severe blow to the conception of Indian Unity.'[60] On 14 April, Jinnah in a press interview, declared that the Muslim League was prepared to reach a compromise only if 'the scheme of Pakistan was acceptable to all parties.'[61] The Congress Working Committee met at Wardha from 6 to 14 July and passed the well-known resolution which laid down that the 'Communal problem would not be settled until the British leave India in the hands of Indians who would settle the issue by mutual agreements.'[62]

Gandhi's stance, 'British withdrawal first, communal settlement afterwards', was embodied in this resolution. Gandhi, indeed, moved to launch a 'civil disobedience movement' to press his demand for the British withdrawal. This was severely criticized by the Muslim League. Jinnah condemned the move, and appealed to the Muslims to keep aloof. He said: 'Congress aimed at enforcing demands at the point of bayonet. If these demands were conceded, that would amount to the surrender of Muslim rights to Hindus.'[63] Jinnah explained: 'I will, myself, lead the movement for India's independence and be the first to go to prison along with Gandhi if the Congress arrives at an immediate settlement with the Muslim League.'[64] The British Prime Minister, Sir Winston Churchill, had his own reservations about the Congress claim to represent the whole of India. In a statement on 10 September, he noted: 'The Indian Congress Party does not represent all Indians. Outside that party and fundamentally opposed to it are ninety million Muslims in India who have their rights of self-expression. Congress cannot claim to represent depressed classes, Sikhs and Christians and the Government cannot ignore this basic data.'[65]

The 'Quit India' movement of the Congress, which started in August 1942, put the British Government in a difficult situation. However, the Government acted swiftly and arrested Congress leaders in large numbers, including Gandhi. It was followed by massive demonstrations resulting in the disruption of communications and serious damage to public property. India was thrown in a state of chaos. But the Government adopted strong measures and suppressed the movement with force. The result was that by the end of the year the movement was virtually over.[66]

At this point in time, the policy of the British Government was favourable to the Muslims but there was no guarantee that the British would stick to it. The Government shifted its patronage from Congress to the League and vice versa in keeping with their own interests. Since there was no consistency in its policy, the Muslims had to be very careful. However, as a counterblast to the Congress movement, Jinnah coined a new phrase—'Divide and Quit'—in the Delhi session of the Muslim League.[67]

There was a notable change in the position of the Muslim League by 1943. Taking advantage of the Congress ministries' resignations during the War years, it formed ministries in the NWFP, Sindh, Bengal, and Assam. By virtue of the Jinnah-Sikandar Pact, the Punjab Ministry was also representing the Muslim League. Now the League was in a position to claim that it was the only representative party of the Indian Muslims. In its meeting on 14–15 November 1943, the Muslim League Council discussed the question of formulating a common policy for the five Muslim provinces.[68] The premiers of Bengal, Punjab, Sindh, and NWFP, were personally present at the meeting, while the Premier of Assam sent a deputy to represent him. Leaders of the Muslim-majority provinces had come to yield to the all-India character and role of the League.

After his release in May 1944, Gandhi reckoned that the Muslim League had become an effective political organization and that, without its cooperation, no headway could be made towards the goal of independence. Gandhi, therefore, wrote to Jinnah on 17 July 1944, asking him to meet and discuss the political situation with him. The two leaders met from 9 to 27 September 1944, to consider the formula presented by C. Rajagopalachari (CR). The CR Formula, as it was popularly known, envisaged the appointment of a commission which was to hold a plebiscite in the districts where the Muslims were in majority. The issue of separation from India was to be decided by the majority of the inhabitants of those areas. In the very first meeting, Jinnah tried to persuade Gandhi to accept the basic and fundamental principles embodied in the Lahore Resolution. Gandhi stressed the importance of the unity of India. Showing his disapproval of the Lahore Resolution, he remarked, 'There was an ocean between him and Jinnah.' Gandhi expressed his opinion that in implementing such a Resolution, he could see nothing but ruin for the whole of India. For Jinnah, it was the question of self-determination for ninety million Muslims who sought their own freedom. No wonder, the talks ended in complete failure, but they helped in establishing the image of Jinnah as the sole representative leader of Muslim India.[69] The Muslim League regarded the failure of Jinnah-Gandhi talks as the starting point of a renewed effort to secure freedom for the Muslims. For the first time, it was publicly recognized in India and abroad that the political deadlock could not be resolved without the co-operation and consent of Jinnah.

The Simla Conference, held on 25 June 1945 was another significant event in the history of Indian constitutional development which helped in determining the future of the Indian Muslims. The Viceroy, Lord Wavell, convened the

Conference to bring about an understanding between the Congress and the League, so that the two parties might participate in the formation of an Interim Government at the Centre. The Muslim League subsequently rejected the Wavell Plan, for it did not give the League the sole right to nominate the Muslim members to the Executive Council. The Congress was not prepared to concede this right because it expected to win some Muslim members on their quota. The disagreement led to the failure of the Simla Conference. Maulana Azad rightly remarked that the Simla Conference marked a watershed in Indian political history.[70] Now the Congress started realizing that the achievement of independence was not an easy affair. It was not simply a matter of forcing the British to quit. There was another party also, that is, the Muslim League, without whose approval the Indian deadlock could not be resolved.

India was still facing chaos when the second general elections under the 1935 Act were announced. These were scheduled in 1945–46. This opened the next phase of political activities in the country. The elections were to determine the fate of the Muslim League and Pakistan. It was for the League now to prove that it was the only organization which could represent the Muslims. The League contested these elections on the basis of the demand for Pakistan and returned victorious against all opposition. In the Central Assembly, the Muslim League won all the thirty Muslim seats, while in provincial legislatures it got 446 seats out of 495 seats allotted to the Muslim community and thus secured about 88 per cent of the Muslim votes.[71] The results of the elections demonstrated the solidarity of the Muslims. The victory was celebrated on 11 January 1946, throughout India. Subsequently, in April 1946, a convention of the newly elected League legislators was held in Delhi. The convention passed a resolution demanding a sovereign independent state 'where the safety and security, and the salvation and destiny of the Muslim Nation, inhabiting the subcontinent of India lies.'[72] The legislators also took a solemn oath pledging to undergo any danger, trial, or sacrifice for the attainment of the cherished goal of Pakistan.

In February 1946, Lord Pethick-Lawrence, Secretary of State for India, announced in the House of Lords that the British Government had decided to send a Cabinet Mission to India to evolve some agreement between the two communities on the future of India. The Mission reached New Delhi on 24 March. The talks started with the Indian leaders on 26 March, which continued till 11 September 1946. The Commission gave Jinnah the choice to accept a 'truncated' but sovereign Pakistan or to have Pakistan with undivided provinces, not completely sovereign. Jinnah chose the latter. The League, in a resolution, asked for the setting up of the Constituent Assembly for the six Muslim-majority provinces which would constitute one group. This group was to enjoy complete autonomy in internal affairs. Other subjects like foreign affairs, defence, and communications were to be entrusted to the Union Government.

On the other hand, the scheme presented by the Congress placed more subjects under the Union Government. It also proposed that the constitution-making assembly should be elected and its meeting held before the formation of this group of provinces. The scheme was not acceptable to the League. So the negotiations failed.

On 16 May 1946, the Cabinet Mission announced its own Plan which was a curious blend of the positions taken by the League and the Congress. The salient futures of the Plan were as follows:

1. Establishment of a machinery to evolve a Union of India including both British India and the Indian States;
2. Setting up of an Interim Government at the Centre;
3. Formation of Three Groups of Provinces;
4. Setting up of a Constituent Assembly;
5. The Union Government should deal only with Foreign Affairs, Defence, Communications and Finance; and
6. All residuary powers should be vested in the Provinces.[73]

The Muslim League accepted the Plan because it thought that the compulsory grouping of provinces would eventually lead to the emergence of Pakistan. This was inspite of the fact that Jinnah identified at least nine areas in which the Plan violated the fundamental interests of the Muslims. Jinnah was in particular critical of the fact that the Plan did not concede two constitution-making bodies.[74] Nehru maintained that the congress was willing only to join the Constituent Assembly but it would not accept any condition laid down by the cabinet mission for constitutional and political arrangements. This practically meant rejection of the cabinet mission plan.

In pursuance of the Proposals, the Government had to set up an Interim Government. The Viceroy, Lord Wavell, named six Congressmen and five Leaguers for the new Executive Council. The League accepted the proposal, but the Congress rejected it, because the name of a nationalist Muslim was not included in the list. Hence, the League expected that Wavell would go ahead with the formation of the Interim Government, but he backed out. He did so in spite of his personal assurance that the British 'do not make to propose any discrimination in the treatment of either party; and that we shall go ahead with the plan laid down in our statement...'[75] Jinnah was utterly disappointed. He rejected the Cabinet Mission Plan, and called for 'Direct Action' to achieve Pakistan. Jinnah called it 'a most historic decision.'[76] Direct Action Day was observed on 16 August.

In the meanwhile, on 6 August 1946, Lord Wavell invited Nehru to form an Interim Government. The partisan spirit shown by the British authorities was evident from the fact that Wavell refused to form the government when the Congress rejected the Plan.[77] But, when the League hesitated, Wavell not only requested Nehru to form the government but also authorized him to nominate some non-Leaguer Muslims to the Council. Soon, however, Wavell realized that the deteriorating political situation could not be handled without the participation of the Muslim League.[78] The League, too, realized that it would be disastrous to leave the field open for the Congress to work out its political agenda unchallenged. Thus, after negotiations, with Wavell, the League joined the Viceroy's Executive Council on 25 October.

With the two hostile parties, the concept of collective responsibility could not materialize, and the Government could not work smoothly. The Cabinet was divided, and its members quarrelled over petty issues. The Congress wanted Nehru to be recognized as the leader of the Cabinet. But Liaquat Ali Khan made it clear that Nehru was 'nobody else's leader except of the Congress'.[79] Even Wavell could not help recognize that there were clearly 'two blocks in the Cabinet.'[80]

There was a serious deadlock by the end of 1946, when the League refused to attend the Constituent Assembly. It would not attend the Assembly unless the Congress accepted the Cabinet Mission Plan by adhering to its grouping provisions. The British leaders invited the representatives of the League and the Congress to London for talks. Although the meeting could not resolve the deadlock, it gave a sense of victory and moral support to the League. During the meeting, the British Government endorsed the League's stand regarding the grouping of provinces in the Cabinet Mission Plan.

The Constituent Assembly started functioning in January 1947. The Muslim League demanded its dissolution on the basis that the British Government's interpretation of the Plan was not accepted by the Sikhs and the Scheduled Castes, and that the sessions and proceedings of the Assembly were invalid. In fact, a resolution of the League Working Committee on 31 January 1947 termed the proceedings of the Constituent Assembly as 'ultra vires'.[81]

Meanwhile, the country was in the grip of a civil war. Communal riots had become a daily feature of the Indian scene and the law and order situation was fast deteriorating. In the light of these circumstances, Lord Attlee, the British Prime Minister, decided that a definite date for the transfer of power should be fixed. The 'present state of uncertainty is fraught with danger and cannot be indefinitely prolonged.'[82] On 20 February, he announced his Government's intention to effect the transfer of power by a date not later than June 1948.

In March 1947, Lord Mountbatten was appointed the Viceroy of India. Soon after his arrival, he developed personal friendship with Nehru and began to take his advice in drawing up his plans for the transfer of power. Eventually, Mountbatten formulated the plan for partition of India and went to London for its approval by the British Government. There is concrete evidence to suggest that he had the approval of Nehru before leaving for England.[83] 'At no time does it seem to have occurred to Mountbatten that his behaviour, in showing the plan to only one of the two Indian parties concerned and amending it to suit the wishes of that party, was not befitting a British Viceroy whose mandate...was impartiality.'[84]

Mountbatten came back in May and started consultations with the Indian leaders, including Jinnah. Formal announcement of the plan was scheduled on 3 June. Jinnah asked for time to seek opinion of the League Council. But Mountbatten refused and threatened that in that case 'he might lose his Pakistan'.[85] Jinnah was not to be intimidated: 'what must be, must be', was his only reaction...'[86] On 3 June, Jinnah, Nehru and Baldev Singh broadcast their acceptance of the plan. The League Council approved it a few days later.

The Partition Plan provided for the partition of Punjab and Bengal if the legislative assemblies of these provinces voted for it. The Sindh Legislative Assembly was also given a choice to join the new Constituent Assembly. A referendum was to be held in the NWFP and Sylhet, to decide their future. The date for the transfer of power was fixed on 14 August 1947, instead of June 1948.

Consequently, the Assemblies of Bengal and Punjab supported the idea of partition in their meetings on 20 and 23 June, respectively, which was later effected by the Boundary Commission. According to the principles of partition, the Muslim-majority districts of Punjab and Bengal were to become part of Pakistan, but all the canons of justice and fair play were set aside while demarcating the boundaries of Pakistan. The Muslim-majority districts like Amritsar and Jullundur were handed over to India to provide her a route to Kashmir. The states of Hyderabad and Junagadh were forcibly occupied by the Indian Army despite their declaration to join Pakistan. The

Sindh Assembly, at its special meeting on 26 June, decided in favour of Pakistan. Sylhet and the NWFP also decided to join Pakistan. On 7 August, Jinnah left Delhi for Karachi. He addressed the Constituent Assembly of Pakistan on 11 August, and declared that the partition of India and the creation of Pakistan was the only 'solution' of the problem in India. 'Any idea of a United India could never have worked and, in my judgement, it would have led us to teriffic disaster.'[87] On 14 August, Pakistan emerged as an independent Muslim state and on 15 August, Jinnah was sworn in as its first Governor-General. Thus came into being the State of Pakistan. The long and demanding struggle of the Muslims had finally achieved its ultimate goal and objective of a separate homeland.

NOTES AND REFERENCES

1. Safdar Mahmood and Javaid Zafar, *Founders of Pakistan*, Lahore: Publishers United, 1968, p. 9.
2. Thomas Metcalf, *The Aftermath of Revolt*, Princeton: University Press, 1962, p. 298.
3. W.W. Hunter, *The Indian Mussalmans*, Calcutta: Comrade Publishers, 1945, p. 3.
4. Altaf Hussain Hali, *Hayat-i-Javed*, Lahore: Academy Punjab, 1957, p. 145.
5. Ram Gopal, *Indian Muslims: A Political History*, Bombay: Asia Publishing House, 1959, p. 16.
6. Ishtiaq Husain Qureshi, *The Struggle for Pakistan*, Karachi: University of Karachi, 1965, pp. 15–16.
7. Amin Zuberi, *Siyasat-i-Milliyah*, Agra: Azizi Press, 1941, p. 5.
8. Hunter, *The Indian Mussalmans*, p. 172.
9. Sir Syed Ahmad, *The Present State of Indian Politics: Speeches and Letters*, Intr. Farman Fathepuri, Lahore, 1982, p. 93.
10. I.H. Qureshi, *A Short History of Pakistan*, book four, Karachi: University of Karachi, 1967, p. 147.
11. Ibid., p. 148.
12. Ibid., p. 150.
13. Hali, *Hayat-i-Javed*, p. 194.
14. Ibid., pp. 320–21.

15. Muhammad Noman, *Muslim India: Rise and Growth of the All-India Muslim League,* Allahabad: Kitabistan, 1942, p. 67.
16. Mary, Countess of Minto, *India: Minto and Morley, 1905-1910,* London: Macmillan, 1934, pp. 45–46.
17. Cited in Khalid bin Sayeed, *Pakistan: The Formative Phase, 1858-1947,* London: Oxford University Press, 1968, p. 30.
18. Reginald Coupland, *India: A Re-Statement,* London: Oxford University Press, 1945, p. 106.
19. Noman, *Muslim India,* p. 78.
20. *A History of the Freedom Movement,* Karachi: Pakistan Historical Society, 1963, p. 37.
21. Syed Sharifuddin Pirzada, *Foundations of Pakistan: All-India Muslim League Documents, 1906-1947,* vol. 1, Karachi: National Publishing House, 1969, p. 6.
22. *A History of the Freedom Movement,* p. 38.
23. *Report on Indian Constitutional Reforms,* Montagu-Chelmsford Report, 1918, pp. 14–18.
24. Rajendra Prasad, *India Divided,* Bombay: Hind Kitab, 1946, p. 112.
25. Pirzada, *Foundations of Pakistan,* vol. 1, p. 279.
26. Sayeed, *Pakistan,* p. 39.
27. M. Rafique Afzal, ed., *Selected Speeches and Statements of the Quaid-i-Azam Mohammad Ali Jinnah,* Lahore: Research Society of Pakistan, 1966, p. 141.
28. M.K. Gandhi, *An Autobiography,* London: Penguin, 1982, pp. 423–4.
29. *Pakistan, Twenty Years of Pakistan,* Islamabad: Ministry of Information, 1967, p. 42.
30. Abdul Hamid, *Muslim Separatism in India,* Lahore: Oxford University Press, 1967, p. 147.
31. Qureshi, *A Short History of Pakistan,* book four, p. 202.
32. Rafique Afzal, *Selected Speeches and Statements of the Quaid-i-Azam,* p. 289.
33. Shamloo, ed., *Speeches and Statements of Iqbal,* Lahore: Al-Manar Academy, 1944, p. 12.
34. Waheed Ahmad, *Road to Indian Freedom: The Formation of the Government of India Act, 1935,* Lahore: Caravan Book House, 1979, pp. 266–67.
35. Coupland, *India,* p. 113.
36. Jamil-ud-Din Ahmad, ed., *Speeches and Writings of Mr. Jinnah,* vol. 1, Lahore: Sh. Muhammad Ashraf, 1968, p. 20.
37. *Star of India,* 4 January 1937.
38. Z.H. Zaidi, 'Aspects of the Development of Muslim League Policy, 1937-47', in C.H. Philips and Mary Doreen Wainwright, eds., *The Partition of India: Policies and Perspectives, 1937-1947,* London: George Allen and Unwin, 1970, p. 274.

39. A. Aziz, *Discovery of Pakistan,* Lahore: Ghulam Ali, 1957, p. 296.
40. For details *see* Pirpur Committee Report, Delhi, 1938. Also *see* 'Muslim Sufferings under Congress Rule', Calcutta: 1939. Cited in K. K. Aziz, *Muslims under Congress Rule, 1937-39,* vol. 1, Islamabad: National Commission on Historical and Cultural Research, 1978, part ix, pp. 307–86 and 388–419.
41. Syed Sharifuddin Pirzada, *Foundations of Pakistan*: All-India Muslim League Documents, 1906-1947, vol. 2, Karachi: National Publishing House, 1969, p. 305.
42. *Letters of Iqbal to Jinnah,* Lahore: Sh. Muhammad Ashraf, 1968. See the letter dated 28 May 1937.
43. *The Civil & Military Gazette,* 15 October 1937.
44. *Paisa Akhbar* (Weekly), 18 November 1937.
45. Ahmad, *Speeches and Writings of Mr. Jinnah,* vol. 1, p. 494.
46. *Paisa Akhbar,* 23 December 1937.
47. Keith Callard, *Pakistan: A Political Study,* London: George Allen and Unwin, 1957, p. 12.
48. *Keesing's Contemporary Archives,* 11–18 November, 1939, p. 3806.
49. Ibid., 4–11 November 1939, p. 3787.
50. Ahmad, *Speeches and Writings of Mr. Jinnah,* vol. 1, p. 104.
51. Richard Symonds, *The Making of Pakistan,* London: Faber and Faber, 1957, p. 31.
52. B.R. Ambedkar, *Pakistan or The Partition of India,* Bombay: Thacker and Co., 1946, p. 24.
53. Khalid bin Sayeed, *The Political System of Pakistan,* Karachi: Oxford University Press, 1967, p. 107.
54. See the full text in Waheed Ahmad, *Quaid-i-Azam Mohammad Ali Jinnah*: *The Nation's Voice, Speeches and Statements, March 1935-March 1940,* Karachi: Quaid-i-Azam Academy, 1996, pp. 473–79.
55. Ahmad, *Speeches and Writings of Mr. Jinnah,* vol. 1, pp. 160–62.
56. Pirzada, *Foundations of Pakistan,* vol. 2, p. 341.
57. Chaudhry Khaliquzzaman, *Pathway to Pakistan,* Lahore: Longmans, 1961, p. 237.
58. Cited in Waheed-uz-Zaman, *Quaid-i-Azam Mohammad Ali Jinnah: Myth and Reality,* Islamabad: Committee for Birth Centenary Celebrations of Quaid-i-Azam Mohammad Ali Jinnah, 1976, p. 60.
59. Pirzada, *Foundations of Pakistan,* vol. 2, p. 388.
60. Cited in Sayeed, *The Political System of Pakistan,* p. 119.
61. *The Civil & Military Gazette,* 15 April 1942.
62. Ibid., 16 July 1942.
63. *The Eastern Times,* 20 August 1942.
64. Ibid.
65. Ibid., 12 September 1942.

66. Nicholas Mansergh and E.W.R. Lumby, eds., *Constitutional Relations between Britain and India: The Transfer of Power, 1942-47*, vol. 2, London: Her Majesty's Stationery Office, 1971, p. 1003.
67. *The Eastern Times*, 24–26 April 1943.
68. *The Civil & Military Gazette*, 16 November 1943.
69. *Twenty Years of Pakistan*, p. 61.
70. Cited in Sayeed, *The Formative Phase*, p. 133.
71. Chaudhri Muhammad Ali, *The Emergence of Pakistan*, New York: Columbia University Press, 1967, p. 48.
72. Pirzada, *Foundations of Pakistan*, vol. 2, pp. 522–23.
73. For details of the Plan see, Mansergh, *Transfer of Power*, vol. 7, 'The Cabinet Mission', especially pp. 582–91.
74. Ahmad, *Speeches and Writings of Mr. Jinnah*, vol. 2, Lahore: Sh. Muhammad Ashraf, 1976, pp. 295–96.
75. Mansergh, *Transfer of Power*, vol. 7, p. 785.
76. Pirzada, *Foundations of Pakistan*, vol. 2, p. 561.
77. Jamil-ud-Din Ahmad, *The Final Phase of the Struggle for Pakistan*, 2nd edn., Lahore: Publishers United, 1968, p. 51.
78. Mansergh, *Transfer of Power*, vol. 8, p. 311.
79. Muhammad Ashraf, *Cabinet Mission and After*, Lahore: Sh. Muhammad Ashraf, 1946, p. 430.
80. Mansergh, *Transfer of Power*, vol. 8, p. 842.
81. Mansergh, *Transfer of Power*, vol. 9, p. 586.
82. Full text of the Statement in V.P. Menon, *Transfer of Power in India*, Princeton: University Press, 1957, pp. 506–9.
83. Leonard Mosley, *Last Days of British Raj*, cited in *Twenty Years of Pakistan*, p. 69.
84. Muhammad Ali, *The Emergence of Pakistan*, p. 139.
85. *Twenty Years of Pakistan*, p. 70.
86. Allan Campbell-Johnson, *Mission with Mountbatten*, London: Hamish Hamilton, 1951, pp. 102–3.
87. Ahmad, *Speeches and Writings of Mr. Jinnah*, vol. 2, p. 402.

2

CHASING THE CONSTITUTION

One of the major problems which bedevilled Pakistan's politics was the unnecessary delay in the framing of a constitution. At the time of independence, Pakistan had no constitution of its own. Under section 8 of the Indian Independence Act of 1947, the Government of India Act 1935, coupled with some amendments was adopted as the working constitution. But since this old Act did not contain all that was required for the constitutional government of an independent state, a new Constituent Assembly was established for framing the new constitution. This Constituent Assembly which held its first meeting on 11 August 1947, i.e., four days before the independence, was assigned the dual responsibility of framing a constitution and serving as the national legislature for ordinary law making.

The first year of independence was spent mainly in setting up the hitherto non-existent structure of administration and in tackling the refugee problem. But barely a year after its emergence as an independent state, Pakistan became orphan; its founder, Quaid-i-Azam Muhammad Ali Jinnah, died on 11 September 1948. The responsibility of constitution-making, therefore, devolved on the first Prime Minister, Liaquat Ali Khan. The framing of a constitution even in the most favourable circumstances is always a stupendous task. Since it is intended to accommodate diverse political perspectives, constitution-making is often faced with conflicts of ideology, clash of interests, and sometimes linguistic and ethnic questions. The study of some other constitutions in the world would fully bear this out. Nevertheless, Pakistan took the longest time in resolving its constitutional dilemma.

The post-Independence history reveals that the problems and difficulties which the framers of Pakistan's constitution had to face were numerous, diverse, and most complex. Some of the most intractable problem that hindered the progress of constitution-making and complicated constitutional development in Pakistan included:

1. The character of the proposed constitution, and especially the place which Islam should occupy in it.
2. Geographical division of the country and the question of quantum of representation in federal legislature.
3. Distribution or allocation of powers between the federal government and the provinces; the question of autonomy for the provinces.
4. The national language issue.
5. The question of relationship between the executive and the legislature, that is, whether Pakistan should adopt a parliamentary or presidential form of government.
6. Most important, the provincial and parochial power tussles.

The Constituent Assembly passed the 'Objectives Resolution'[1] in March 1949, stating the broad objectives and goals of the future constitution of Pakistan. It was described by Liaquat Ali Khan as 'the most important occasion in the life of this country, next in importance only to the achievement of Independence.' The Resolution provided, *inter alia*, that the principles of democracy, freedom, equality, and social justice as enunciated by Islam would be fully observed and that the Muslims should be enabled to order their lives in accordance with the teachings and requirements of Islam. It also recognized the rights of minorities to freely profess and practise their religions and develop their cultures. In addition, it stipulated that the exercise of fundamental rights shall be fully guaranteed. The resolution also provided for the independence of Judiciary and for the organization of the state on a federal pattern.

Moreover, it clearly laid down that sovereignty over the entire universe belonged to God and the authority delegated by Him to the people of Pakistan was only a sacred trust.

The Objectives Resolution was discussed in five successive meetings of the Constituent Assembly. The Pakistan National Congress, which was the main opposition party in the Constituent Assembly, objected to it on the plea that it mixed politics with religion and that it would reduce the minority communities to the status of serfs. Among the Muslim members, with the solitary exception of Mian Iftikharuddin, all upheld the resolution. Mian Sahib was of the opinion that unless radical changes were brought safeguarding of political liberty was useless. The non-Muslims were definitely dissatisfied with the resolution. They expressed apprehensions that it would allow the state to interfere in the personal lives of the citizens. The leader of the Congress party, S.C. Chattopadhyaya, protested that the resolution would make the non-Muslims in Pakistan 'drawers of water and hewers of wood'.[2] Strange as it is, some of the orthodox Ulama were also not satisfied with the resolution on the ground that it laid too great emphasis on the rights of non-Muslims.

But this resolution was not the entire constitution as it simply laid down the fundamental principles of the future constitution. Having done this, the Constituent Assembly, like any other legislature, set up several committees and subcommittees to carry out the task of framing the constitution. Among these, the Basic Principles Committee was the most important. It was appointed on 12 March 1949, after the passage of the Objectives Resolution was passed by the Constituent Assembly, and all political parties were represented on it. It was charged with the duty of charting out, as early as possible, the main principles on which the future constitution was finally to be based. On its part, the Basic Principles Committee set up three subcommittees to examine separately certain important issues.

On 28 September 1950, an Interim Report of the Basic Principles Committee (also called the first report) was presented to the Constituent Assembly. The Report recommended a bicameral federal legislature with equal powers vested in both the houses. The Upper House, known as House of Units, was to consist of an equal number of representatives from all provinces, while the Lower House was expected to give representation on basis of population.

The Head of the State was to be elected by both Houses. His tenure was five years but he could be removed by the two-third majority of the central legislature. He was to be assisted by a Cabinet headed by the Prime Minister, who was, along with his Ministers, to be responsible to both the Houses of Parliament.

The same pattern was to be adopted in provinces, except that they were provided with a single House. In case of inconsistency between the federal law and the provincial law, the federal law was to prevail.

The Report caused great disappointment amongst the people and was subjected to severe criticism. It was argued that it provided an incomplete constitutional structure. First, it was rejected on the basis that it did not have Islamic character as envisaged by the Objectives Resolution. Secondly, the East Pakistani leaders contended that their majority was being reduced to a minority. In East Pakistan, the publication of the Report sparked off full-scale agitation causing a split between the Centre and the province.[3] Thirdly, the Report declared Urdu to be the only national language which created great resentment in East Pakistan. In view of an all-round criticism and public demand, Liaquat Ali Khan moved the House to postpone its consideration and asked the Committee to review the report in the light of the criticism and suggestions made by the members and others.

While the Basic Principles Committee was reviewing the report, Liaquat Ali Khan was assassinated at Rawalpindi on 16 October 1951. Although he was instantaneously replaced by Khwaja Nazimuddin, who stepped down from the office of Governor-General to become the Prime Minister, the finalization of the Report was considerably delayed for more than one reason.

Notwithstanding the great sacrifices Liaquat Ali made for the achievement of Pakistan, he cannot escape the criticism that there was a waste of time and neglect on his part in the process of framing the constitution. There was, no doubt, heavy pressure of governmental business in the early days of Pakistan, but no amount of administrative preoccupation could justify the neglect to which constitution-making was subjected. During his rule of four and a half years, he even failed to prepare the basic framework of the future constitution.

The task of constitution-making left incomplete by Liaquat Ali Khan was taken up by Khwaja Nazimuddin on his assumption of the office of Prime Minister. He presented the consolidated report of the Basic Principles Committee (also called the second or revised report) on 22 December 1952. Its chief recommendations were as follow:

The Head of the State shall be a Muslim. He shall be elected by the joint session of both the Houses of the central legislature but will not be a member of the legislature and hence not responsible to it. His term of office shall be for five years and during this term no action shall be taken against him in any court of law. The central legislature shall consist of two Houses: the House of Units and the House of People, the former shall consist of 120 members, and the latter 400 members, both giving equal representation to the two wings of the country. The share of West Pakistan was to be further divided amongst its provinces according to population. The term of each House shall be fixed at five years. Both shall have equal powers but Money Bills shall originate only in the Lower House. The ministry shall be responsible to the Lower House but could address both the Houses. The constitution shall be amended with the agreement of both the central and provincial legislatures, subject, however, to certain conditions, at the time of its adoption. Three lists of subjects were drawn up for the division of powers between the Federation and the Units. The Centre was to be strong with residuary powers given to it. Adult franchise was to be introduced.

The most important recommendation of the committee pertained to the setting up of the Boards of Ulama, both by the

Head of the State and the Provincial Governors, consisting of persons well-versed in Islamic law. All proposed legislations were to be referred to these Boards to ensure that nothing against the teachings of the Qur'an and the Sunnah was enacted. In a way, a provision had been made whereby the Ulama were to have a virtual veto on the working of the legislature. There was to be a Supreme Court consisting of a Chief Justice who was to be appointed by the Head of the State and could be removed by him on the advice and report of a bench of judges. Similarly, the judges of the High Courts were to be appointed by the Governors and could be removed by them after a reference to the Supreme Court.

Like the first report, this report faced opposition from many political quarters. It gave rise to an unending controversy and generated bitterness between East and West Pakistan. First, a controversy regarding the federal structure of the constitution, particularly the quantum of representation in the federal legislature, arose.[4] In the Report, the position of East Pakistan in the central legislature was brought at par, with regard to the number of seats, with the combined strength of all the units and area comprising West Pakistan. This was called the 'Parity Proposal'. Against all recognized principles of federation, the Report provided that in the House of People there should be 200 members from East and 200 from the nine units of West Pakistan. Even in the so-called House of Units, it was provided that there should be sixty from the East Wing and sixty from all the units of the West Wing. The arrangement was tantamount to partitioning the country between East and West.[5]

The principle of parity, as incorporated in the Report, was not acceptable to the people of East Pakistan. They thought injustice was being done to them by ignoring their numerical majority and giving them equal representation. Parity between East and West Pakistan as regards seats in the central legislature violated the federal principle. This had been done in utter disregard of the social, linguistic, cultural, economic, and climatic divergences; disequilibrium in population; and lack of geographical contiguity between the two Wings. This part of the Report was, therefore, widely criticized by the Punjabi and the Bengali groups.[6] The Punjabi group feared that East Pakistan had been given a position of complete domination over the West, which was already divided into nine units, against one unified unit of East Pakistan.[7] Owing to these and other differences, the Basic Principles Committee Report was popularly known as the 'Bengali-Punjabi Crisis Report'.

The greatest drawback of the Parity Proposal was that it diverted people's thinking into provincial grooves, as if the people had never been part of the mainstream of the Pakistan movement and that they had only agreed to federate the provinces of East and West into the new State of Pakistan.[8]

The second recommendation of the Basic Principles Committee Report, which invited scathing criticism, was the one relating to the appointment of the Boards of Ulama to review the central and provincial legislation.[9] These Boards sought to give sweeping powers to a handful of persons who could monopolize the right to interpret the Qur'an. This part of the Report appeared to be motivated by extreme religiosity. According to Khwaja Nazimuddin himself, the Report had been the result of long discussions held by two or three members of his Cabinet with the Ulama. Khwaja Nazimuddin's alliance with the orthodox Ulama in providing in the constitution 'a Board of Ulama' outside the Parliament which could veto any legislation in the light of whether or not it was Islamic, created new dangers. He conceived the image of an Islamic state in terms of the revival of some laws and practices without any notion of the dictates of the contemporary world.

Another controversial issue between East and West Pakistan, which also contributed to the delay in constitution-making, pertained to the distribution of powers between the federal and provincial governments. The Objectives Resolution passed by the Constituent Assembly in March 1949, had laid down that Pakistan shall be a federation. This decision has been regarded as the 'Dictate of Geography'. The Basic Principles Committee Report had also recommended a federal structure of the state.

As stated above, three lists of subjects were drawn up for the division of powers between the federation and the units. The Centre was to be strong with residuary powers given to it. But along with other recommendations of the Basic Principles Committee Report, the federal form of government proposed by it also gave rise to conflict. With the lapse of years, two groups emerged, one advocating a strong Centre and the other championing the cause of maximum autonomy for the Provinces. Strangely enough, though East Pakistan was the largest unit, the demand for maximum provincial autonomy came initially from that Wing. The makers of the Constitution, therefore, took pains to steer a course midway between these two groups. Matters were further complicated by the lack of understanding and mutual trust between the people and the leaders of two Wings.

Despite the defects inherent in the Report, Khwaja Nazimuddin commended it to the nation as a document representing the 'maximum agreement'. He described it as 'the first golden ray of the sun which illumines the sky'.[10] In his opinion, the recommendations reflected not only the aspirations of Pakistanis but also their genius and needs. Notwithstanding his being sanguine that the proposals would take the country towards the destined goal, he was utterly dismayed; a final agreement proved to be elusive. It came to be known later that only sixteen of the original twenty-nine members of the Committee had signed the Report. Many of the prominent leaders of Punjab who were members of the Committee, including Mian Mumtaz Muhammad Khan Daultana, then Chief Minister of Punjab; M.A. Gurmani, then Central Minister of the Interior; and Chaudhri Nazir Ahmad; dissociated themselves from the Report and did not put their signatures to it. There was a deadlock in the process of constitution-making. The political stalemate was ultimately resolved after the dismissal of Khwaja Nazimuddin by the Governor-General on 16 April 1953, and with the appointment of Muhammad Ali Bogra as the new Prime Minister who was till then the Ambassador of Pakistan in the United States of America.

The Governor-General's decision to replace Khwaja Nazimuddin with Muhammad Ali Bogra was endorsed by the ruling party, i.e., the Muslim League, by electing Bogra as its leader. On 7 October 1953, that is, within less than six months of his acceptance of office as Prime Minster, Muhammad Ali Bogra announced his constitutional formula in the Constituent Assembly which, according to him, was acceptable to the representatives of both the Wings. The proposals embodied his formula were as follows:

The central legislature was to have two Houses, Upper and Lower. In the former, the total membership was fifty, distributed equally among the five units of Pakistan of which East Pakistan was one. That meant that the four West Pakistani units were to have forty members (ten each) and East Pakistan was given ten. The second House would comprise 300 seats, divided among these five units on the basis of population. East Pakistan was allocated 165 seats and the four units of West Pakistan were given 135 seats. When the two house met together, both the wings had equal representatives: East Pakistan 10+165= 175; West Pakistan 40+135= 175. In this way, despite acceptance of the population principle for the lower house, the principle of parity applied to the legislature as a whole. The allocation of seats[11] in the central legislature was to be as follows:

Units	upper house	Lower house	Total
1. East Pakistan	10	165	175
2. The Pubjab	10	75	85
3. NWFP and tribal Areas	10	24	34
4. Sind and Khairpur	10	19	29
5. Baluchistan, Baluchistan states Union, Bahawalpur and Karachi	10	17	27
	30	300	350

The powers of the two Houses were to be equal and a Ministry was to be responsible to both the Houses. In case of a conflict between the two chambers, there was a provision for a joint session. But in case of serious disagreement on matters of exceptional importance, the Head of the State was competent to dissolve them and order fresh elections. A provision was also made that if the Head of the State was from West Pakistan, the Prime Minister shall be from East Pakistan and vice versa.[12] In this new arrangement, hope was expressed that there would be no permanent domination by any Wing.

Another significant change made in these proposals was that in place of the Board of Ulama which had to ensure that no law repugnant to the Qur'an and the Sunnah was passed, the function was assigned to the Supreme Court. It was a step definitely in the right direction.

These suggestions, popularly known as the Prime Minister's formula or Muhammad Ali's formula, were generally hailed by almost all sections of public opinion. It was thought that these would lead to closer integration and co-operation between the two wings, giving a crippling blow to centrifugal tendencies.

These suggestions were considered by the Constituent Assembly for thirteen days in the month of October and again on 14 November 1953. A drafting committee was appointed to write down the provisions as approved by the Assembly. For this purpose, the services of an eminent British constitutional expert, Sir Ivor Jennings, were also secured. Some headway had been made in the drafting of the constitution when the Constituent Assembly was dissolved by the Governor-General in October 1954.

The story of constitution-making will remain incomplete without examining the factors and circumstances leading to the dissolution of the Constituent Assembly.

As already stated, the Constituent Assembly of Pakistan, having been set up in August 1947, was assigned with two functions, namely, to prepare the Constitution, and to act as the Federal Legislative Assembly or Parliament until the constitution was enacted. While its performance as a legislature was far from satisfactory, more conspicuous was its failure as a constitution-making body. Its go-slow mood was in evidence from the very beginning, even during the lifetime of Liaquat Ali Khan. From 14 August 1947, to 16 October 1951, when Liaquat Ali Khan fell a victim to the assassin's bullet, the entire progress made in the constitution-making process was confined to the Objectives Resolution. The first Basic Principles Committee Report did not secure popular approval, but more disheartening was the fact that Liaquat Ali Khan refrained from making further effort in the framing of the constitution. Khwaja Nazimuddin who succeeded him after his death, took a year and a quarter to produce the second Basic Principles Committee Report. It not only got a cold reception, as did the first Basic Principles Committee Report, but it also divided the nation by its Parity Proposal. After another eighteen months of the Bogra regime, constitution-making was still incomplete. It was during this regime that the Muslim League was defeated in the general election in East Pakistan (March 1954). Its authority to frame the constitution was, therefore, later challenged by the United Front. In West Pakistan also, the people were equally frustrated with the role of the Muslim League. With opposition mounting in both the Wings, the Muslim League's efforts to proceed with constitution-making only added to bitterness, suspicion, and distrust.

In the first place the Public Representative Officers Disqualification Act (PRODA) of 1948–49, which empowered the government to bring corrupt ministers and politicians to book, was replaced by the Constituent Assembly; this was on 20 September 1954. A day later, the Assembly revoked sections 9, 10, 10-A, 10-B of the Government of India Act 1935, by virtue of which the Governor-General could dissolve the Cabinet. The amendment was designed to curtail the powers of the Governor-General to dismiss the Cabinet as Ghulam Muhammad had done in the past when he dismissed the Nazimuddin Ministry. All this was done without the previous knowledge of the Governor-General and at a time when he was away from the Capital. This amendment was rushed through in a single day and published in the *Gazette of Pakistan* the day it was passed in the House. This action was taken in a spirit of vindictiveness and revenge. The whole atmosphere reeked of a conspiratorial hush-hush. The Governor-General returned to Karachi immediately and, taking advantage of the public opinion, retaliated against the actions of the Assembly. He issued a Proclamation declaring a state of emergency throughout Pakistan and dissolved the Constituent Assembly on 24 October 1954, as it had obviously lost the confidence of the people. The climax had been reached. All previous attempts at framing the constitution and the entire spadework done in this connection was brought to naught by a sweep of the pen of the highest executive authority in the country.[13] This was the second drastic action taken by Ghulam Muhammad in the short span of eighteen months; earlier, he had dismissed the Nazimuddin Ministry. Both these steps retarded the growth of parliamentary democracy in Pakistan.

The sovereign authority of the Constituent Assembly was thought to be invulnerable and perpetual. Its dissolution, therefore, led to court proceedings against the Governor-General and his Cabinet. The late Maulvi Tamizuddin, President and Speaker of the dissolved Assembly, challenged the order of the Governor-General and filed a petition[14] before the Sindh High Court on the ground that no assent of the Governor-General was needed for legislation under subsection (1) of section 8 of the Indian Independence Act of 1947,[15] and as such the dissolution of the Constituent Assembly was unconstitutional and illegal. The full bench of the Sindh High Court unanimously upheld the plaint of the plaintiff (Maulvi Tamizuddin) and gave the verdict that the dissolution of the Constituent Assembly was illegal. Thereupon, the Federation of Pakistan appealed to the Federal Court. A long drawn-out hearing took place. Finally, the Federal Court gave its ruling in favour of the Governor-General.

The Sindh High Court gave a unanimous decision in favour of Maulvi Tamizuddin[16] declaring that the Constituent Assembly was a sovereign body and could not be dissolved unless it had completed the task for which it had been set up. The argument of the Federal Court in upholding the Governor-General's action was that the Constituent Assembly had failed to frame a constitution and had become unrepresentative in the course of time. Moreover, it had assumed the form of a perpetual legislature. The Federal Court, therefore, set aside the judgement of the Sindh High Court and declared that the Governor-General was legally empowered to dissolve it[17] under the Indian Independence Act 1947.

After the dissolution of the Constituent Assembly, the Governor-General again invited Muhammad Ali Bogra to form a new Cabinet. The reconstituted Cabinet consisted of some new Ministers like General Muhammad Ayub Khan, Major-General Iskandar Mirza and Dr Khan Sahib, subsequently, Huseyn Shaheed Suhrawardy also became a member of this Cabinet which was not responsible to anybody except Ghulam Muhammad. For the first time, the Commander-in-Chief of the Army, General Ayub Khan, was included in the Cabinet, paving way for the involvement of army in politics.

The second Constituent Assembly had eighty members, divided equally between East and West Pakistan; the seats of West Pakistan were further divided among its constituent units. The following table gives the details of seats allocation in the second Constituent Assembly:

East Pakistan	40 seats (nine for non-Muslims)
Punjab	21 seats (one for non-Muslims)
NWFP	4 seats
Sindh	5 seats (one for non-Muslims)
Other Areas	10 seats

Ten Members from Baluchistan, Frontier States, Tribal Areas, Khairpur State, Bahawalpur State, and Karachi were to be nominated by the Governor-General, and from other areas, they were elected by the provincial assemblies.[18]

The Muslim League had a comfortable majority in the first Constituent Assembly but it lost this position in the second Constituent Assembly because it had lost badly in the East Pakistan Provincial Assembly elections in 1954. Therefore, it lost a large number of seats to other parties in that province;

this reduced its strength, although it was still the largest party in the Constituent Assembly. The party position in the 1955 Constituent Assembly elections was:

Muslim League	25	Pakistan Congress	4
United Front	16	Scheduled Caste federation	3
Awami League	12	United Progressive Party	2
Noon Group	3	Other	6
Independent Muslim	1		

As no party was in majority in the new House, a coalition ministry was sworn in with Chaudhri Muhammad Ali as the Prime Minister. The Cabinet had the support of the Muslim League and the United Front. Muhammad Ali Bogra went back to his old job as Pakistan's Ambassador to the United States.[19]

The experience of constitution-making suggested that the non-contiguity of the two wings of Pakistan and the division of West Pakistan into different administrative units were the major obstacles to finding satisfactory solution to the question of providing representation to the provinces in the central legislature; the two wings could not be placed on equal footing. Chaudhri Muhammad Ali addressed this after becoming the Prime Minister by integrating various provinces and administrative units in West Pakistan into one integrated province of West Pakistan. This change, called the One Unit, was passed by the Constituent Assembly on 30 September 1955 and implemented on 15 October 1955. This simplified the issue of representation in the central legislature, because Pakistan now had two provinces—East and West Pakistan.

Chaudhri Muhammad Ali worked day and night and produced a draft Constitution which was presented to the Constituent Assembly on 8 January 1956. Finally adopted on 29 February, it secured the Governor-General's assent on 2 March 1956. On 23 March, Pakistan was declared an Islamic Republic. This ended an era of constitutional confusion and public frustration in Pakistan, at least, for the time being. The Constitution envisaged federal and parliamentary form of government based on Islamic principles.

A summary of the first Constitution of Pakistan is given below.

THE CONSTITUTION OF 1956

The President: Under the 1956 Constitution, the President was the executive and symbolic Head of the State. He was to be elected by members of both the National Assembly and Provincial Legislatures with majority votes.

Three qualifications were laid down for the President. He should be a Muslim citizen of not less than forty years of age, and qualified to be a member of the National Assembly. His tenure was for five years and he could not serve for more than two terms.

The President could be removed through impeachment for gross misconduct or violation of the Constitution. The notice for impeachment was required to be signed by, at least, one-third members of the National Assembly. After the expiry of fourteen days, a resolution could be moved. The resolution was considered to be carried if supported by three-fourth members of the National Assembly.[20] In this case, the President had to vacate his office and the Speaker of the National Assembly was to act as President till a new President was elected.

The President's most important function was to appoint a Prime Minister who commanded the support of majority in the National Assembly. Apart from it, he was the appointing authority of Governors, Judges of the Supreme Court, Auditor-General and Advocate-General. He could also appoint an Inter-Provincial Council for the purpose of national integration and promoting understanding between the provinces.

The President could summon, prorogue, and dissolve the National Assembly.[21] The President could withhold his assent to the bills, except Money Bills, passed by the National Assembly, but the Assembly could override him by two-third majority.

The Bills concerning Federal Court and Federal Public Service Commission could not be introduced in the Assembly without his previous consent. The President could also issue ordinances. No financial bill involving expenditure could be introduced in the Assembly without his prior approval.

The President could issue a proclamation of emergency if he was convinced that the country's existence was in danger due to an internal, economic, or external threat.[22] He could assume all executive powers and suspend fundamental rights in any province during an emergency.

He had the power to grant pardon, reprieve, or reduce punishments or sentences awarded by any court of law in Pakistan. Most of these presidential powers were to be exercised on the advice of the Prime Minister.

The Prime Minister: In the parliamentary form of government, power tends to concentrate in the Prime Minister who is said to represent the people. As a result, the President exercises his powers on the advice of the Prime Minister, making the latter a pivot around which the whole machinery of the government revolves.

According to the 1956 Constitution, the President invites the person who, in his opinion, had the support of the majority to form the government. Other members of the Cabinet were selected by the Prime Minister. The Prime Minister could hold office during the pleasure of the President, but the President could not dismiss the Prime Minister as long as he was supported by the majority. The Cabinet was collectively responsible to the National Assembly. It implied that the ministers were not only to be appointed with the consent of the Prime Minister but could also be dismissed if he desired. The number of Cabinet ministers was not fixed. A minister had to be a member of the National Assembly. A non-member could be appointed minister but he had to be elected as a member within six months of his appointment. In case of dissolution of the Assembly, the Cabinet was to continue in office.[23]

The Prime Minister was supposed to furnish such information as the President might call for and, if required by him,[24] to submit any matter before the Cabinet on which a decision had been taken by the Prime Minister without the consideration of the Cabinet.

The National Assembly: The unicameral central legislature—the National Assembly—consisted of 300 members of whom 150 were to be elected from each Wing. Thus, parity was maintained between East and West Pakistan. Ten seats, equally divided between the two provinces, were reserved for women for ten years only.

The Constitution provided three lists of subjects for legislation, namely, Federal List, Concurrent List, and Provincial List. The National Assembly had exclusive jurisdiction over the Federal List. Both the Provincial and National assemblies were empowered to legislate in respect of the Concurrent List of subjects. In case there was an inconsistency between the Federal law and the Provincial law, the Federal law was to prevail. The Provincial Assembly could also request the National Assembly to legislate for it. The National Assembly was empowered to make laws for the implementation of any treaty or convention with any country. During an emergency, it was competent to make laws regarding any subject for the area which was under emergency.

The National Assembly had complete control over the finances of the country. No expenditure could be incurred or tax levied without the authority of an Act passed by the Assembly.[25] Financial measures could only be introduced by the ministers. The Budget had to be approved by the National Assembly.

The Governor: The Governor was appointed by the President and served during his pleasure. Like the President in the Centre, the Governor was entrusted with the responsibility of appointing the Chief Minister who, in his opinion, commanded the support of the majority in the Provincial Assembly.

In the field of legislative powers, he performed more or less the same duties in the province as were discharged by the President at the federal level.

The Provincial Assembly: The provincial legislature, called the Provincial Assembly, had 300 members. Ten seats were reserved for women.

The provincial legislature was empowered to make laws regarding the subjects enumerated in the Provincial List and the Concurrent List. But if there was a conflict between the Federal law and the Provincial law, the former was to prevail. Its other powers in the financial and executive fields were the same as given to the National Assembly.

The Judicial Administration: A unified judicial system was provided for the whole country with the Supreme Court at the top as the final court, which comprised a Chief Justice and other judges.

The Chief Justice was appointed by the President and other Judges were appointed by him in consultation with the Chief Justice. A Judge could be removed only by the President after an address to the National Assembly, with two-thirds of its members concurring.[26]

The Supreme Court had original jurisdiction in the cases pertaining to disputes between the Central Government and a Province or between the Provinces themselves, provided this disagreement was regarding the interpretation of some constitutional provision. It was empowered to issue writs for the enforcement of fundamental rights. The Supreme Court was also to hear appeals against the decisions of High Courts or any other court. The Supreme Court enjoyed advisory jurisdiction. The President could refer any matter of public importance, involving interpretation of law, to the Supreme Court for advice.

The judgements of the Supreme Court were binding on all subordinate courts. It could also issue orders, decrees, or directions to implement its judgements and orders.

The High Court: Each province was provided with a High Court which consisted of a Chief Justice and other judges. They were appointed by the President after consultation with the Chief Justice of the Supreme Court and the Governor of the concerned province.

The High Court had original jurisdiction in cases concerning fundamental rights. As an Appellate Court, appeals against the lower courts were to be heard in the High Court. The High Court also had to look after the administration of District and Sessions Judge Courts and Civil Courts.

* * *

The Constitution was enforced on 23 March 1956, amidst great happiness and celebrations. After nine years the nation had, at last, framed a constitution for itself. But, by this time, politics had already degenerated. New elections were promised but this promise was not fulfilled. Had general elections been held earlier at regular intervals, the country might have been spared the drama of politics which was enacted by self-seeking leaders. After the integration of West Pakistan, the Republican Party led by Dr Khan Sahib[27] won the support of the majority of the members of West Pakistan Assembly and formed its government with Dr Khan Sahib as its leader. The Republican Party did not have any roots among the masses. It was not in a position to contest against Muslim League in a general election but through political manoeuvres and extension of patronage, it won over many legislators who were elected on the League ticket.

In the Centre, none of the parties had a majority. Thus, there was no choice but to form coalition ministries which tended to be weak governments. The Muslim League had only twenty-five seats out of the total of eighty seats in the National Assembly. Chaudhri Muhammad Ali remained the Prime Minister till 9 September 1956, but had to resign due to the betrayal of his supporters. The League Ministry was succeeded by a coalition ministry of the Awami League and the Republican Party. But even this Ministry could not remain in power for more than a year. Then followed a spell of political instability. Politicians changed loyalties overnight. Floor-crossing became so frequent that no ministry could stay in office for any reasonable length of time. Political uncertainties not only hampered developmental activities but also impaired the law and order situation. Demonstrations against 'One Unit' and in favour of regional autonomy became a recurring feature. The atmosphere of national politics was charged with emotions.[28] The greatest misfortune of the country was that there was no popular leadership of high calibre to control the situation.

So Martial Law was declared in the country on 7 October 1958. Muhammad Ayub Khan, Commander-in-Chief of the Pakistan Army, took over the government as the Chief Martial Law Administrator, and then, on 27 October, assumed Presidency.

President Ayub Khan appointed a Constitution Commission in February 1960 which was headed by Justice Shahabuddin. After considerable deliberations, the Commission submitted its report on 6 May 1961. It attributed the failure of parliament government to the absence of popular and sincere leadership. According to the findings of the Commission, the lack of leadership which, in turn, resulted in the lack of well-organized and disciplined parties, and the general lack of integrity among the politicians, were chiefly responsible for the debacle of democracy.[29]

The report of the Commission was examined by several committees. In the light of its recommendations, a new Constitution was framed by a body of men appointed by the President for this purpose. They were neither elected representatives nor did they enjoy popular support. The Constitution was framed in an atmosphere of secrecy and was then imposed on the people. Contrary to the democratic traditions and practices, it was never placed before the people to obtain their opinion. In France, the Constitution was framed on similar lines but it was put to general referendum for approval. To the people of Pakistan, the Constitution was handed down from above as a 'gift' of the military regime of Ayub Khan. It was implemented on 8 June 1962, when martial law was withdrawn.

THE CONSTITUTION OF 1962

The President: The Constitution of 1962 introduced a powerful presidential system. The head of state, called the President, performed ceremonial as well as executive functions and was solely responsible for the country's administration. Any thirty-five year old Muslim citizen of Pakistan, eligible to be a member of the National Assembly, could contest for the office of the President.[30] However, the President could not be a member of the legislature. The President was elected indirectly by 80,000 (enhanced to 1,20,000) Basic Democrats, elected on the basis of adult franchise. The President could be removed only by the National Assembly. One-third of the total number of MNAs could move a resolution of impeachment and vote three-fourths for conviction. If less than half of the total number of members of the National Assembly supported the resolution, the initiators of impeachment were to lose their membership.[31]

Being the Head of the State, the President was responsible for the executive powers of the Federation of Pakistan. He was constitutionally all-powerful in the appointment and dismissal of governors, ministers, and members of various administrative commissions. All civil appointments were made in his name. His appointees, except the judges of the High Courts and Supreme Court, were directly responsible to him. The President was the Chief of the Defence Services of Pakistan. He had the final say in Pakistan's external relations. The President promulgated and enforced the adopted laws and could recommend new laws to the legislature through his Council of Ministers or by way of presenting an advisable line of action in his casual addresses to the legislature. The President exercised strong veto power overriding the passage of a measure with two-third majority of the National Assembly and subsequent assent of the majority of the members of the Electoral College.

Besides these indirect powers, the President enjoyed positive legislative powers. He was empowered to issue Ordinances having the force of the Act of the central legislature. He had the power of summoning, of proroguing[32] (when he had summoned), and (except under certain conditions) of dissolving the National Assembly. However, in case of dissolution, he himself was to lose his office. Pakistan's Budget was divided constitutionally between Committed and New Expenditures. The President had an unfettered control over the Committed Expenditures. In the National Assembly, 'financial measures' were exclusively Government measures. The President was the sole authority to declare a 'state of emergency' in the country. Emergency, when formally declared, entitled the President to issue Ordinances,[33] having the force of the Acts of the central legislature. These Ordinances were enforceable as long as the 'emergency' existed. Besides these specific powers, the President exercised many miscellaneous powers, which enabled him to command the country with authority.

The President appointed a number of officials to be the members of his Council of Ministers. The Ministers were eligible to take part in the deliberations of the National Assembly. However, they had no right to vote. Governmental measures were introduced in the House by the Ministers. The Ministers were responsible only to the President who could dismiss them. The Council of Ministers as a collective body was a mere advisory board, the President was not obliged to agree with its recommendations.

The National Assembly: The central legislature, according to the new Constitution, consisted of the President and the National Assembly. The National Assembly was composed of 156 members. Six seats were reserved for women. All the seats were equally distributed between the two Wings. The normal term of the Assembly was five years.[34] A constitutional amendment raised the strength of the National Assembly to 218 (200 elected seats, ten reserved for intellectuals and eight reserved for women). This change was to be effected from the general elections in 1970, but a year before this, Ayub Khan was forced out of office, and martial law was imposed.

The National Assembly was empowered to legislate for the Central subjects of Pakistan. It could also legislate on matters falling under provincial jurisdiction, if so desired. In case of inconsistency between the Central and Provincial legislation, the former prevailed.[35] Any legislative matter pertaining to preventive detention could be taken up only with the prior permission of the President.

The authority for levying taxes rested solely with the centre legislature. However, the introduction of financial measures and the recommendations for enhancement of any grant could be made only by a government official. The Annual Budget and the Supplementary Budget (if any), placed before the Assembly, consisted of the expenditure to be met from the Central Consolidated Fund and the New Expenditure. The Central Consolidated Fund, which could be debated but not voted in the Assembly, included remuneration, the administrative expenses of the offices connected with the National Assembly, and any debt incurred by the Central Government. The 'New Expenditure', which was subject to the assent of the House, included that much of the expenditure which exceeded by more than 10 per cent of the expenditure already approved by the Assembly; any other non-recurring expenditure; recurring expenditure for which there was no provision in previous years' Authorised Expenditure; and recurring expenditure that exceeded 10 per cent of the previous allocation.[36]

Besides these two types of expenditures, there was an 'Unexpected Expenditure' chargeable by the President on his discretion from the Central Consolidated Fund. The President was obliged to lay before the Assembly a report relating to this expenditure which could be discussed but not voted by the Assembly. After presenting Annual and Supplementary Budgets, the government could present an 'Excess Budget' if more amount was needed from the Central Consolidated Fund during the same financial year.

The National Assembly was to sit as a court when a resolution of impeachment, conviction, or one declaring the President as incapacitated, was before the House.

The National Assembly was empowered to pass by a two-third majority an 'Amendment Bill' seeking amendment to the Constitution. To override the Presidential veto, the Assembly had to pass the measure with a three-fourth majority. The President might still withhold his assent and refer the matter to the Electoral College. If a majority of the Electoral College passed the measure, the Constitution could be amended, notwithstanding the Presidential assent.

The Governor: The provincial governments were considerably dependent upon the President. The Governor—the provincial chief executive, was the President's nominee. He could be removed by the President's order at any time. He also ceased to hold office once the President, who nominated him, was changed.[37] The Governor, too, could relinquish the charge by resignation.[38]

The Governor exercised exactly the same executive, legislative, financial, and miscellaneous powers in the Province as did the President in the Central Government. However, the Governor was responsible for his acts to the President.

The Provincial Council of Ministers was appointed by the Governor with the consent of the President. The Governor was authorized to remove any of the ministers at any time. Moreover, if he found a minister guilty of gross misconduct, he could punish the minister authenticating his action by a special tribunal appointed by him in consultation with the Chief Justice of the High Court. The convicted minister was disqualified from holding any public office for five years.

The principles regulating the relations of the Central Council of Ministers, the President, and the National Assembly also applied to the Provincial Council of Ministers, the Governor, and the Provincial Assembly.

The Provincial Legislature: The Governor and the Provincial Assembly constituted the provincial legislature in each province. There were 150 general seats and five exclusive seats for women in the Assembly. According to a subsequent amendment in the Constitution, the Provincial Assembly was to consist of 218 members, of which ten seats were reserved for the intellectuals nominated by government. The normal term for a Provincial Assembly was five years. However, it could be dissolved by the concurrence of the National Assembly and the President on the recommendation of the Governor or the Speaker of the Provincial Assembly.[39]

The National and Provincial assemblies had identical rules of procedure, role of the Speaker, and the legislative business of the House. The role of the President in dealing with the National Assembly was assumed by the Governor in the Provincial Assembly. In case of any inconsistency between the Central and the provincial legislation, the former prevailed.

The Constitution of 1956 was chiefly based on the Government of India Act of 1935. Though it envisaged a parliamentary form of government, it did not combine the form and spirit of the system, and created a conflict between the President and the Prime Minister. In contrast, the Constitution of 1962 introduced a centralized and Presidential system. It vested dictatorial powers in the President who virtually commanded the political system. The National Assembly had limited powers. The ministers were appointed and dismissed by the President at his discretion, who also had to power to dissolve the National Assembly.

* * *

Popular dissatisfaction against the 1962 Constitution and authoritarian governance by Ayub Khan led to countrywide street agitation in the last quarter of 1968 while the Ayub regime was busy celebrating the ten years of Ayub's rule as the Decade of Development. The major political parties demanded, *inter alia*, resignation of Ayub Khan, abrogation of the 1962

Constitution, and restoration of the parliamentary system of government. They also demanded the dismemberment of the 'One Unit' and restoration of four provinces in West Pakistan. From East Pakistan came the old demand for provincial autonomy and representation on population basis in the national legislature. Agitations created political chaos in the country and no compromise formula could be evolved to overcome the crisis. In view of the street agitation and deteriorating law and order situation, Ayub Khan resigned from the office and handed over power to the Army Chief, General Yahya Khan, who abrogated the constitution and declared martial law on 25 March 1969.

There was a sharp disagreement amongst the leaders over the shape of the future constitution. Twenty-two years after the Independence, the country was again faced with a constitutional dilemma. The basic issues such as maximum provincial autonomy, disintegration of the 'One-Unit', and representation on the basis of population, were again revived. These were the major obstacles in constitution-making during the period 1947 to 1956, and delayed the framing of the 1956 Constitution. When the Constitution was enforced in 1956, people thought that constitutional differences had been resolved for ever. But now the leaders were up against the old problems.

Taking advantage of his powerful position, Yahya Khan decided that 'One Unit' be dissolved and the old provinces of Punjab, NWFP, Sindh and Baluchistan be revived. These provinces became fully operative by July 1970. The principle of one-man-one-vote was also accepted, putting an end to the principle of parity. All these fundamental issues were settled by an unrepresentative authority who had no mandate from the people.

According to General Yahya Khan's constitutional formula,[40] the National Assembly was to consist of 313 members, 169 members were to be elected from East Pakistan, the remaining 144 from West Pakistan. General elections held in December 1970, revealed that the Awami League had won 167 seats, all from East Pakistan, and the Pakistan People's Party emerged as the majority party in West Pakistan with eighty-six seats to its credit.

After the separation of East Pakistan in December 1971, Yahya Khan resigned and handed over the government to Zulfikar Ali Bhutto, Chairman of the Pakistan People's Party. Apart from repairing the broken ship of state, the most important task before the new government was to frame a constitution for Pakistan. The National Assembly approved an Interim Constitution on 12 April 1972, which replaced martial law on 21 April. Earlier, on 17 April, the National Assembly appointed a committee of its members, representing the major political parties, to prepare a draft of the new constitution. The committee finalized its report by 31 December, and the draft constitution was presented to the National Assembly on 2 February 1973. It was debated and discussed in the Assembly till the government and the Opposition agreed on the draft which was passed unanimously and assented to the President on 12 April 1973. The Constitution was inaugurated on 14 August 1973, and the new Cabinet headed by the Prime Minister was sworn in.

The Constitution reflected the aspirations of the people and presented an improvement on the previous constitutions. It envisaged parliamentary form of government. The salient features of the 1973 Constitution are discussed below:

THE CONSTITUTION OF 1973

The President: The 1973 Constitution, in its original shape, envisaged the President only as a figurehead because almost all the executive powers were vested in the office of the Prime Minister. The President was the symbolic head of the state and represented the unity of the Islamic Republic of Pakistan.

The President, who must be a Muslim, is elected in a joint sitting of the two Houses (the Senate and the National Assembly) of Parliament by a majority vote.

The term of the President is five years from the day he assumes office. However, he remains in the office until his successor assumes the office. According to Article 44 (2), a person cannot hold the office of President for more than two consecutive terms.

The President can be removed from office through impeachment on the following grounds:

1. for physical or mental incapacity,
2. for violation of the Constitution, and
3. for gross misconduct.

According to the procedure laid down in the Constitution, not less than one-half of the total number of members of any of the House of Parliament may notify in writing to the Speaker or the Chairman of the Senate, as the case may be, a resolution recommending the removal of the President. The resolution so submitted must contain the charges against the President on account of which he is to be removed.

The resolution of impeachment is deemed to have been passed resulting into automatic removal of the President, if it is supported at least by two-third majority of the total number of members of Parliament.

According to Article 48 of the Constitution as it originally stood, the President was bound, by the advice of the Prime Minister in the performance of his duties. The Constitution specifically stated that all orders issued by the President must bear the signature of the Prime Minister in order to be effective. Thus, the President was reduced to a state of helplessness.

Practically, it is inadvisable to divide the powers between the President and the Prime Minister because, in this situation, the possibility of a conflict or a tug-of-war between the two cannot be ruled out, which may eventually erode the authority of the Constitution. However, the President must be equipped with powers to deal with the emergencies such as continuous agitation, civil war, etc., so that constitutional means are available to change the government when it becomes indispensable. The absence of such a provision contributed to the imposition of martial law in July 1977.

Under Article 54 of the Constitution, the President can summon the sessions of the National Assembly and the Senate or a joint session of both the houses. The President can also address any House of Parliament and can dissolve the National Assembly only on the advice of the Prime Minister.

If the Prime Minister's advice to dissolve the National Assembly is not accepted by the President, the Assembly automatically stands dissolved after forty-eight hours of the advice of the Prime Minister.

In the field of legislation, the President enjoys limited power. According to the Constitution, each bill passed by the Parliament has to be assented by the President within seven days. If the President fails to give his assent to a bill within this period, that bill is deemed to have been assented to by the President and becomes law.

However, the President's decision is final in case there is a difference of opinion as to whether or not a particular subject belongs to Part I of the Federal Legislative List.

The President appoints the Governors, Attorney-General, Chief Election Commissioner, Chief Justice, and Chief of Staff of the Army, the Navy and the Air Force. He is also the Supreme Commander of the armed forces.

Under Article 232, the President is empowered to issue a proclamation of emergency in the country if he is satisfied that a grave situation threatening peace and tranquillity in the country exists, or that the security of the country is being threatened by internal strife or foreign aggression, or that the financial stability or economic life is threatened, or a provincial government has failed to maintain the law and order. However, the declaration of a state of emergency has to be approved by a joint session of Parliament within thirty days of its imposition. The President can also suspend the basic rights or a part of an article or a part of the Constitution except the part which falls within the purview of the High Court during the period of emergency. But this action of the President has to be approved by the Parliament as in the case of the declaration of emergency.

If the President is satisfied that a provincial government has failed to run the administration of the Province, or the Parliament passes a resolution to that effect, the President can himself assume the executive powers of that Province or may direct the Governor of the Province to act on his (President's) behalf. In a separate order, the President can also transfer the authority and duties of the Provincial Assembly to the Parliament.

During the state of emergency, the legislative powers of the Provincial Assembly are vested in the Parliament which may authorize the President to use these powers. But any such legislation is valid only for six months.

The Prime Minister: In a parliamentary form of government, the Prime Minister is considered to be the fountainhead of executive authority. His position is sometimes compared with a moon in a galaxy of stars.

According to Article 90 of the Constitution, the Federal Government of Pakistan is composed of the Prime Minister and the members of his cabinet. The Prime Minister is the head of the executive, though executive decisions are taken in the name of the President. The Prime Minister and his Cabinet are collectively responsible to the National Assembly.

The President calls the session of the National Assembly in order to elect the Prime Minister, after thirty days have elapsed since the general elections. In order to be elected as Prime Minister, the Constitution requires the candidate to poll the votes of the majority of the total number of members of the National Assembly. In case, none of the candidates fulfils this requirement, a second round of election is held in which only two candidates with the highest number of votes in the first round are allowed to contest. The one who polls the majority of the votes of the members present at the time of voting is declared elected as the Prime Minister.

The Prime Minister then forms his Cabinet from amongst the Members of Parliament. Here the Constitution has placed another restriction—the number of Cabinet ministers chosen from the Senate shall not exceed one-fourth of the total number of ministers. This condition reflects the importance of the National Assembly.

The essence of the concept of collective responsibility is that the Prime Minister is empowered to appoint and dismiss the members of his Cabinet. According to this Constitution of Pakistan, the Prime Minister has the power to remove any Minister from the Cabinet whenever he so desires.

The Prime Minister can tender his resignation to the President. His resignation means the resignation of all the ministers of his Cabinet. Nevertheless, he may ask any minister of his Cabinet to take charge of the office of the Prime Minister as long as the National Assembly does not elect a new Prime Minister.

The following procedure has been laid down in the Constitution to pass a vote of no-confidence against the Prime Minister.

1. The resolution proposing a vote of no-confidence cannot be moved in the National Assembly unless it specifies the name of a successor to the Prime Minister already in the office.
2. The resolution proposing a vote of no-confidence in the Prime Minister cannot be placed before the National Assembly during the Budget session.
3. Once the motion of no-confidence has been moved in the National Assembly, it cannot be voted upon for first three days. It also cannot be voted upon after seven days have passed. If the vote of no-confidence is not passed during these days, it is considered to have been lost.
4. If the majority of the total number of members of the National Assembly supports the move of no-confidence, it is carried and the Prime Minister stands removed from his office. In this case, the President calls upon the person whose name has been proposed in the resolution to assume the office of Prime Minister.
5. Freedom of the members of the National Assembly to vote on a resolution of no-confidence has been circumscribed for ten years by the provision which states that for a period of ten years until the holding of the second general elections,

whichever occurs later, the vote of a member of a certain political party cast in support of the no-confidence move will be disregarded if majority of the members of the same party cast their votes against the move.[41] This provision, though novel, has been included in the Constitution to maintain party discipline and to create an atmosphere of political stability. This provision is also intended to check the activities of the deserters.

6. The vote of no-confidence cannot be moved for the second time in the Assembly unless a period of six months has passed.

The executive authority of the Federation is exercised by the Federal Government which is headed by the Prime Minister who is described by the Constitution as the chief executive of the Federation. The authority of the Federal Government extends over the subjects on which the Parliament has the power to legislate. Practically, it is the Prime Minister who exercises this authority because he leads the majority in the National Assembly.

As regards the functions of the Prime Minister, his most important duty is to run the administration of the country, particularly that of the Federal Government. The Cabinet is, of course, there to assist him in the execution of his functions and duties. Each minister heads a ministry or a division and is individually responsible to the Prime Minister. The Prime Minister takes important decisions after discussing them with his colleagues in the Cabinet. According to the Constitution, he can act through his ministers or directly. Moreover, each minister holds office during his pleasure. This indicates how powerful the Prime Minister is.

Article 90 (clause 3) of the Constitution lays down the concept of collective responsibility. According to this clause, the Prime Minister and his Cabinet is collectively responsible to the National Assembly. The concept of collective responsibility is based on the principle that the Prime Minister should be empowered to appoint and dismiss a Minister of his Cabinet. If it were not so, a divided Cabinet cannot be collectively responsible.

Clause 2 of Article 93 lays down that the Prime Minister and his Cabinet shall remain in office even when the National Assembly stands dissolved. In such a situation, the Federal Government can meet its expenditure for four months from the Federal Consolidated Fund.

A bill or an amendment which if enacted, would involve expenditure from the Federal Consolidated Fund or withdrawal from the Public Account or affect the currency, cannot be introduced in the National Assembly without the consent of the Federal Government as preparation of the annual budget statement and placing it before the National Assembly is the responsibility of the Federal Government. This also applies to a demand for a grant.

The 1956 Constitution had laid down that the President was to act on the advice of the Prime Minister. This Constitution has gone a step further by stating that the advice of the Prime Minister is binding on the President. The President's hands have been further tied down by a provision in the Constitution that the advice given by the Prime Minister to the President cannot be investigated or questioned in a court of law. Moreover, an order issued by the President is not valid unless it also carries the signature of the Prime Minister. It may be cited here, as an example, that the Presidential Order suspending the Fundamental Rights issued by the President of Pakistan, Chaudhry Fazal Elahi, bore the signature of the former Prime Minister, because the Constitution specifically states that orders of the President without the counter signature of the Prime Minister shall not be valid and lawful.

The Prime Minister also happens to be the Chairman of the National Economic Council and the Council of Common Interests. Both the Councils, appointed by the President, play an important role in formulating and planning the economic policies of the country.

Although the President appoints the Chiefs of Staff of the armed forces and also grants commissions to the officers of the armed forces, the power to control the armed forces is vested in the Federal Government which is headed by the Prime Minister. In contrast to the 1956 Constitution, wherein power to declare war was vested in the President, the present Constitution has empowered to defend the country in case of foreign aggression. It can also order the armed forces to come to the aid of civil administration. In practice, therefore, the power to declare war also rests with the Prime Minister who is the chief of the Federal Government. Another function of the Prime Minister is to keep the President informed of the legislative activities and internal and external affairs of the country. Although the President has the power to dissolve the National Assembly, he exercises this power only when advised so by the Prime Minister. In other words, the Prime Minister also has the power to dissolve the National Assembly.

According to Article 248 of the Constitution, in the performance of his duties and functions, the Prime Minister is not answerable to any court of law.

Parliament: The Parliament is the most important institution in a democracy, as sovereignty of the people is reposed and expressed through the Parliament. It reflects their 'general will' and aspirations. The executive, the Prime Minister and his Cabinet derive their powers from the Parliament and are also answerable to it. In the United Kingdom, the Parliament can make any law. In Pakistan, the Parliament does not enjoy complete freedom in the legislative field because it can legislate only on the subjects which have been specified in the Federal List. This, in any case, does not reduce the importance of Parliament because in a federation, legislative powers have to be divided between the Centre and provinces. Division of powers is the basic principle of the federal system. Legislative, Federal and Provincial lists, have been provided in the constitutions of India and the USA in the same manner.

In principle, a federal constitution should provide for two houses of Parliament. The 1956 Constitution of Pakistan, though federal in nature, established a single-house National Assembly.

In the same manner, the 1962 Constitution, though federal, provided for a single House, also called the National Assembly. The 1973 Constitution, however, changed this by providing two Houses of Parliament; the National Assembly (lower house) and the Senate (upper house).

It is for the first time that Pakistan has a bicameral legislature. A bicameral legislature has several advantages. First, a bill can he thoroughly debated and discussed in the two Houses before it becomes a law. Secondly, if the National Assembly passes a law in the heat of emotions, the Senate can act as a brake and might take a more realistic view of the situation and implications of the bill. In the meantime, tempers may cool down and a clearer picture of the public opinion may become available to the law-makers. Thirdly, talented and well-known personalities of national stature, who otherwise do not like to indulge in practical politics, can easily be elected to the Senate. In this way their experience and talent can be utilized in the service of the nation. In this regard, the election of Mr Aziz Ahmad, former Minister of State for Defence and Foreign Affairs to Senate, can be cited as an example. Nevertheless, the type of persons elected to the Senate mostly depends upon the majority party in the National Assembly. Fourthly, a bicameral legislature, in a federal system of government, also imparts a sense of participation in the national affairs and equality of status to smaller units as the Upper House is constituted on the basis of equal representation to each province.

However, of the two Houses of the Parliament of Pakistan, the National Assembly enjoys more powers than the Senate.

The National Assembly: Under the 1973 Constitution, the National Assembly of Pakistan consists of 200 members who are elected by direct adult franchise. A person cannot be elected to the Parliament unless:

(i) He is a citizen of Pakistan,
(ii) His age is not less than twenty-five years, and he is enrolled as a voter in any electoral roll for election to that Assembly; and

(iii) He possesses other qualifications as may be prescribed by an Act of the Parliament.

The seats have been allocated in the National Assembly for each province, the Federal Capital and Federally Administered Tribal Areas. As is the case in other federal systems, these seats have been allocated on the basis of the population of each province.

Ten seats have been reserved for women in the National Assembly for a period of ten years from the commencing day or until the second general elections, whichever occurs later. These ten seats are divided among the four provinces on the basis of their population. The National Assembly members belonging to each province separately constitute the electoral college to elect the women representatives. It has been left to the President to decide the mode of election of the representatives from the Federally Administered and Tribal Areas.

In the present constitution of Pakistan, the term of the National Assembly is fixed for five years unless it is dissolved earlier. This term begins from the first meeting of the National Assembly and after five years it would stand dissolved automatically.

Like the last constitution of Pakistan, the present constitution has also provided that the National Assembly must hold, at least two sessions in one year and the interval between these two sessions must not exceed 120 days. It has also been provided that the Assembly shall meet for, at least, 130 days in one year.

All the decisions in the National Assembly are taken by the majority vote of the members present. The Speaker or the Deputy Speaker, whosoever is presiding, cannot cast his vote unless the number of votes in favour and against the motion are equal. One-fourth of the total number of members of the Assembly form the quorum.

Like the last constitution, the present constitution has also empowered the Prime Minister, a Federal Minister, a Minister of State, and the Attorney-General to address and take part in the proceedings of a House of Parliament or a joint sitting. The

Attorney-General can also speak and take part in the proceedings of a committee of which he has been nominated a member. However, he is not entitled to vote by virtue of Article 57.

If the Prime Minister advises the President to dissolve the Assembly, the Assembly automatically stands dissolved at the expiration of forty-eight hours after tendering the advice by the Prime Minister, even if the President does not do so.[42] According to the last constitution of Pakistan (1956), the Prime Minister could advise the President to dissolve the Assembly, but the condition that the Assembly would automatically stand dissolved after a specified period, was not provided.

The Speaker: Under Article 53 of the Constitution, the National Assembly elects from amongst its members a Speaker and a Deputy Speaker after the general election. Whenever the office of the Speaker falls vacant, the Assembly immediately meets to fill up that vacancy. The Speaker vacates his office if he is unseated from his membership in the Assembly. The Assembly, by the majority of the total members, can also pass a vote of no-confidence against the Speaker.

Under clause 8 of Article 53, in case of dissolution of the Assembly, the Speaker remains in office as long as his successor is not elected by the next Assembly. This provision also existed in the 1956 constitution.[43]

The most important function of the Speaker is to preside over the meetings of the Assembly, maintaining discipline and decorum in the House. No member of the Assembly can speak or raise a question or move an adjournment motion without his permission. Moreover, all members of the Assembly, while speaking in the House, must address and speak through the Chair.

The Speaker also has the power to decide whether or not a bill is a money bill. In this case, his decision is final.[44] Consequently, a money bill passed by the Parliament, carries a certificate to that effect under the signature of the Speaker before it is presented to the President for his assent.[45]

The Senate: The upper house of the Parliament is known as the Senate in the 1973 Constitution. The Senate consists of sixty-three members representing the four provinces of Pakistan, Tribal Areas, and the Federal Capital.

In accordance with Article 59, the Senate is constituted as under:

1. Each Provincial Assembly elects fourteen members to the Senate;
2. Members of the National Assembly representing Federally Administered Tribal Areas elect five members to the Senate, and
3. Two members of the Senate from the Federal Capital are to be elected in a manner prescribed by the President.

Provincial assemblies conduct the election for the Senate in accordance with the system of proportional representation by means of the single transferable vote.

Under clause 3 of Article 59, the Senate cannot be dissolved. The term of office of its members is four years; half the number of members retiring after every two years. Of the five members from the Federally Administered Tribal Areas, three will retire after the expiry of the first two years, while other two members will retire after the expiry of the next two years.

The members of the Senate elect from amongst them a Chairman and a Deputy Chairman at the first meeting of the Senate. The term of the office of Chairman and Deputy Chairman is two years.

A majority of the total number of members of the Senate can remove the Chairman or the Deputy Chairman from their office by passing a resolution to the effect. Seven days' notice is required for such a resolution.

All members enjoy complete freedom in the Parliament. A member of the Parliament cannot be proceeded against in a court of law in respect of his speech and vote cast in Parliament or a publication, paper, report, or proceedings of the Parliament. For a certain number of days before and after the session and during the session, a member of Parliament is not liable to appear before a court of law.

The Parliament, being a sovereign body conduct of its members can neither be challenged in a court of law nor interfered with. Similarly, the Speaker and the Deputy Speaker are not answerable to any court of law with respect to the performance of their function in the Parliament.[46]

If a government servant interferes with the performance of a member's duties or insults him, the member can move a privilege motion in the Parliament. The Parliament or its Privileges Committee can recommend action against the involved government servant.

The Parliament has the privilege to make laws for the punishment of a person or to empower the court to punish a person who refuses to give evidence or refuses to produce documentary proof required of him by the Chairman of a Committee of the House. This provision is, however, subject to a Presidential Order, safeguarding confidential papers and matters from disclosure. This privilege has been further qualified by another provision which states that this article shall apply to persons who have the right to speak and take part in the proceedings of the Parliament.

The Parliament has the power to decide by law its own powers, immunities, and privileges under Article 66 (2) of the Constitution. Under Article 67(1), the House frames its own rules regulating its procedure and conduct of its business, while under Article 69(1), validity of any proceedings in the Parliament cannot be questioned on the ground of any irregularity of the procedure.

The Constitution has divided the legislative powers into two lists: One is called the Federal Legislative List while the other is known as the Concurrent Legislative List. In order to avoid any confusion, nearly all legislative subjects have been clearly defined in these lists and the power to legislate on these subjects have been divided between the Parliament and the Provincial Assembly.

The Parliament has exclusive power to legislate on the subjects included in the Federal Legislative List. Parliament as well as a Provincial Assembly can legislate on the subjects enumerated in the Concurrent List. However, if an Act passed by a Provincial Assembly is repugnant to an Act or any provision of an Act of Parliament then the Act of Parliament prevails while the Act passed by the Provincial Assembly becomes void to the extent of its inconsistency with the Act passed by the Parliament.

A Provincial Assembly has exclusive power to legislate on the subjects not included in any of the legislative lists whereas the Parliament has exclusive right to legislate on subjects not included in any of the legislative lists for such areas in the Federation which do not fall in the jurisdiction of a province.

The Federal Legislative List is further divided into two parts—Part I and Part II. The Constitution provides that a bill pertaining to Part I of the Federal Legislative List must originate in the National Assembly. After the National Assembly has passed it by a majority vote, that bill is transmitted to the Senate for consideration. The Senate must pass it within ninety days of its receipt without amendment, or it may amend or reject the said bill and send it back to the National Assembly for its consideration. But, in case the Senate does not reject or amend the bill, the bill is deemed to have been passed by the Parliament after ninety days.

If the Senate rejects a bill, it is sent back to the National Assembly for reconsideration. If the National Assembly again approves the bill as it was originally approved by it or with amendment as proposed by the Senate, the bill is presented to the President for his assent.

The President's assent is a mere formality. When a bill is presented to him for assent, he gives his assent in seven days. If he fails to do so, the bill is deemed to have been assented to after the passage of seven days.[47] If there is any confusion as to whether or not a bill pertains to Part I of the Federal Legislative List, the President's decision in this regard is final.

A bill pertaining to a subject enumerated in Part II of the Federal Legislative list may originate in any of the two Houses of Parliament. After it has been passed in one House, it is sent to the other House of Parliament. If the other House also passes this bill, the Bill is sent to the President for his assent. But, in case the other House refuses to give its approval to the bill and sends it back to the House where it originated, the House where the bill had originated can request for a joint sitting of the two Houses to reconsider it. The joint sitting is summoned by the President; and if a majority of the total membership of the two Houses approves the bill, it is passed.

Any Provincial Assembly can request the Parliament, by passing a resolution, to enact a certain law. In that case, the Parliament will have the power to enact a law on the subject mentioned in the resolution, while a Provincial Assembly will have the power to amend that law in order to meet its requirements, within the province.

When the Federal Government declares a state of emergency in a Province, the legislative powers of that Provincial Assembly are vested in the Parliament. But the laws enacted by the Parliament during the period of emergency become void after six months of the withdrawal of the emergency. Nevertheless, actions taken under these laws do not become void.

When a state of emergency has been declared in the country, the Parliament has the power to extend the term of the National Assembly but such an extension cannot be for a period of more than one year and cannot last for more than six months after the state of emergency has been withdrawn.

The declaration of the state of emergency is placed before a joint sitting of the Parliament within thirty days from the day on which the declaration is made by the President. The President summons such a sitting of the Parliament.

The Parliament can also enact laws to meet the losses incurred during the state of emergency. Under Article 237, the Parliament has the power to enact a law providing for indemnity to any person in the service of the Federal or Provincial Government, or any other person, in respect of any act done in connection with the performance of his duty for maintenance of law and order in any area of the country.

The Parliament's most important power lies in its control over the finances of the country. As the state exchequer is formed by the taxes paid by the people, justice requires that people's representatives should have control over the financial matters of the country. This is in accordance with the spirit of democracy.

Under Article 73 of the Constitution, all bills pertaining to financial matters must originate in the National Assembly. After the Assembly has passed it, the bill is directly presented to the President for his assent. The Senate has no say on a Money Bill.

Under Article 80, the Federal Government places an annual Budget Statement for every financial year before the National Assembly. The Budget Statement shows the sum required to meet the expenditure charged upon the Federal Consolidated Fund and the sum required to meet other expenditures proposed to be made from the Federal Consolidated Fund.

The expenditure charged upon the Federal Consolidated Fund cannot be voted upon in the National Assembly. However, when it is placed before the Assembly, the members can debate and discuss this expenditure. The fund mostly consists of the salaries of the President, Judges, Election Commission, Auditor-General, etc.

The second part of the Budget Statement is submitted to the National Assembly in the form of 'Demand for Grants' and the National Assembly has the power to assent to, or refuse to assent to any such demand, or assent to a reduced grant However, the Constitution provides that this part of the Budget Statement will be deemed to have been assented without any reduction of the amount mentioned in a Demand for Grant for a period of ten years or the holding of the second general elections, whichever occurs later. Nevertheless, a majority of the total membership of the Assembly can refuse or give assent to an amount specified in a Demand for Grant.

No demand for a grant can be made without the recommendation of the Federal Government. Under Article 83 of the Constitution, the Prime Minister must authenticate by his signature the Annual Budget Statement in the form of a schedule. The schedule shall not exceed in any case the sum shown in the Budget Statement. The schedule authenticated by the Prime Minister is laid before the National Assembly but is not open to discussion or vote thereon.[48] The Federal Government cannot make any other expenditure except that which is included in the schedule. However, if the Federal Government later on finds that the sums authorized to be expended in the schedule are not sufficient, it can authorize expenditure from the Federal Consolidated Fund and can lay a statement before the National Assembly in the form of a supplementary Budget Statement setting out the amount of that expenditure.[49]

The National Assembly can also make any grant in advance in respect of the estimated expenditure for a part of any financial year not exceeding four months pending completion of the procedure prescribed in Article 82.

Similarly, According to Article 82 when the National Assembly stands dissolved, the Federal Government can authorize expenditure from the Federal Consolidated Fund for a period not exceeding four months in any financial year.

The Parliament also keeps a close eye on the administration of the country. The Prime Minister and his Cabinet members are responsible to the Parliament. They have to explain their administrative actions and policies before the Parliament. The Parliament also, like other democratic countries, controls and checks the administration by asking questions, moving adjournment motions, passing resolutions, and vote of no-confidence.

The Provincial Governors: Each of the four provinces of Pakistan is headed by a Governor who is appointed by the President on the advice of the Prime Minister. Constitutionally, the Governor is a representative of the President and is answerable to him. The Governor's political and executive position in the province is similar to that of the President at the Centre. On account of the non-partisan nature of his office, a

Governor has also to resign, like the President, from his seat in the Parliament or the Provincial Assembly.

The Governor is appointed by the President in whom this power has been vested under Article 110 of the Constitution. The Governor holds his office during the pleasure of the President.

The Chief Justice of the High Court administers the oath of office to the Governor. The text of the oath, given in the Third Schedule of the Constitution, shows that whereas it is imperative for the President and the Prime Minister of Pakistan to be a Muslim who believes in the Oneness of Almighty Allah; the Books of Allah, the Holy Qur'an being the last of them, the prophethood of Muhammad (PBUH) as the last of the prophets, that there can be no prophet after him; the Day of Judgement, and all the requirements and teachings of the Holy Qur'an and the Sunnah, it is not necessary that a Governor, Speaker or a minister should also be a Muslim.

The duties and functions of the Governor in his Province are very much akin to those of the President at the Centre. He is a figurehead of the Province because the real source of executive powers in the Province is the Chief Minister and his Cabinet. The Article 105 of the Constitution provides that the Governor is to act on the advice of the Chief Minister whose advice is binding upon the Governor.

If the Chief Minister advises the Governor to dissolve the Provincial Assembly, the Governor has to do so within forty-eight hours.

Under Article 116 of the Constitution, the Governor gives assent to a bill passed by the Provincial Assembly within seven days. However, if he fails to do so, the bill is deemed to have been assented to by the Governor after the specified period.

The Governor can issue an ordinance. An ordinance issued by the Governor becomes void after three months if the Provincial Assembly does not approve it.

The Governor appoints the Advocate-General of the province who holds his office during the pleasure of the Governor. Judges of High Court are appointed by the President in consultation with the Governor.

The Chief Minister: The Provincial Government is composed of the Chief Minister and his Cabinet. It performs its functions and duties through the Chief Minister. Although, executive actions and decisions are taken in the name of the Governor, the actual source of these decisions is the Provincial Government, that is, the Chief Minister. Within his province, a Chief Minister enjoys a status similar to the Prime Minister in the Federal Government.

Under the 1956 Constitution, the Governor appointed a Chief Minister. The 1973 Constitution changed this by providing that the Provincial Assembly would elect the Chief Minister in the same manner as the Prime Minister was elected by the National Assembly.

The Provincial Assembly can pass a resolution for a vote of no-confidence against the Chief Minister in the same manner and within the same limits as are provided in the case of Prime Minister.

The Chief Minister is responsible for the administration of the whole province. He divides his responsibilities by assigning the charge of different departments to his Cabinet members. The decisions are mostly taken in the Cabinet by mutual discussion and consultation but the Chief Minister has the final say. The Chief Minister also controls the exchequer of the Province. Although, the Budget of the province is prepared and placed before the Assembly by the Finance Minister, it is finalized in the Cabinet meeting.

The Constitution also provides that only those actions of the Provincial Government will have the authority which are carried out in accordance with law.

The Provincial Assemblies: Whereas the Parliament frames laws for the whole of the country, the provincial assemblies have the power to legislate for their provinces within the limits laid down in the Constitution. As pointed out earlier, the

Constitution provides two lists for the purposes of legislation. One list is called the Federal Legislative List and the other is known as the Concurrent Legislative List. The parliament can frame a law on any subject included in the two lists, whereas a Provincial Assembly can legislate on those subjects which are included in the concurrent Legislative List. Apart from that, it can also legislate on the subjects which are not included in any of the two lists.

There are four provinces which constitute the Federation of Pakistan. Each province has a Provincial Assembly. The number of members in each Assembly is as follows:

Baluchistan - 48
NWFP   - 80
Punjab   - 240
Sindh   - 100

The members of the assemblies are elected directly by the people on the basis of universal adult franchise. In addition to the above-mentioned seats, the religious minorities have been provided with separate seats in order to ensure their representation in all provincial assemblies. The following seats have been reserved for Christians, Hindus, Sikhs, Buddhists and Parsis and Ahmadis in the Provincial Assemblies:

Baluchistan - 1
NWFP   - 1
Punjab   - 3
Sindh   - 2

Moreover, for ten years or until the second general election is held, whichever occurs later, five seats for women have been reserved in each Provincial Assembly. The members of a Provincial Assembly form the electoral college for election of women to these reserved seats.

Under the Constitution, a Provincial Assembly enjoys a five-year term which begins from the date of its first meeting. After five years, a Provincial Assembly is automatically dissolved. Each Provincial Assembly elects a Speaker and a Deputy Speaker at its first meeting. The Advocate-General can address the Assembly and can also participate in the committees of the Assembly without being entitled to vote.

The Governor can dissolve the Provincial Assembly on the advice of the Chief Minister. The advice of the Chief Minister is binding on the Governor. If the Governor fails to dissolve the Assembly on the advice of the Chief Minister, it is deemed to have been dissolved within forty-eight hours of tendering such advice. However, the Governor is not bound by the advice of a Chief Minister against whom a resolution of no-confidence has been moved in the Assembly.

A Provincial Assembly must hold, at least, two sessions in one year for a total number of 130 days. The interval between the two sessions must not exceed 120 days.

If one-fourth of the total membership of an Assembly demands that a meeting of the Assembly shall be called, it is binding upon the Speaker to call the meeting within fourteen days. The decisions in the Provincial Assembly are taken by majority vote.

The members of Provincial Assembly enjoy the same privileges and immunities as are provided to the members of the National Assembly. They enjoy complete freedom on the floor of the House and proceedings cannot be instituted against them for speech or an act performed in the Provincial Assembly.

In order to ensure control on finances, it is provided in the Constitution that a Money Bill can be placed before the legislature only by the Government. The same provision was made in the 1956 Constitution of Pakistan. Under Article 155 of the Constitution, only a Provincial Government can place a Money Bill before a Provincial Assembly. Moreover, a Provincial Government alone can move a Money Bill relating to the Provincial Consolidated Fund or Provincial Public Account. A bill cannot be called a Money Bill unless it relates to the following:

1. Imposition of a tax, any decrease in its rate, or change in a regulation connected with the tax;
2. Raising a loan or a security or an amendment thereto, which is included in the functions of a Provincial Government;
3. Supervision of the Provincial Consolidated Fund and withdrawal and receipts therefrom;
4. A demand on the Provincial Consolidated Fund or a change in such a demand;
5. Supervision, withdrawal, and receipt from the Provincial Public Account; and
6. Any other matter connected with the above subjects.

It has also been clarified in the Constitution that a bill relating to the imposition of a fine, or a fee, or a tax imposed by a local government authority does not fall within the definition of a Money Bill. However, if a difference of opinion arises, whether a bill is a Money Bill or not, the Speaker's decision is final. The Constitution also provides that a Money Bill passed by a Provincial Assembly shall carry the signatures of the Speaker certifying that the bill is a Money Bill before it is presented to the Governor for his assent. The same procedure was provided in the 1956 Constitution of Pakistan.

Under Article 116, all bills passed by a Provincial Assembly are presented to the Governor for his assent. The Governor gives his assent within seven days of the receipt of a bill, after which it becomes a law. However, if the Governor fails to give his assent within the prescribed period, the bill is deemed to have been assented to by the Governor and automatically becomes a law. In other words, the presentation of the bill to the Governor and his assent is more or less a ceremonial function.

According to the 1956 Constitution of Pakistan, the Governor could withhold his assent to a bill. In that case, if the bill was again passed by the two-third majority of the members present and voting, the Governor was bound to give his assent. The present Constitution has simplified the procedure.

The Provincial Government prepares the budget and places it before the Assembly. Under Article 118 of the Constitution, all revenues collected by the Provincial Government, loans raised by it, and all the money received by it in repayment of a loan, would form the Provincial Consolidated Fund. All other collections by a Provincial Government or its agencies, including the fees deposited in the High Court, form the Provincial Public Account. All matters concerning control, payments, and withdrawals from the Provincial Consolidated Fund and Public Account are regulated by the law passed by the Provincial Assembly.

The expenditure relating to salaries of the Governor, Judges, Speaker, etc., met by the Provincial Consolidated Fund, can be discussed and debated in the Provincial Assembly but cannot be voted upon.

All other expenditure is placed before the Assembly in the form of Demands for Grant. The Assembly has the power to slash, raise, or reject a demand for grant, or pass it as presented by the government.

Apart from legislation, the Provincial Assembly also has the power to keep an eye on the executive of the province which is responsible to the Assembly under the present Constitution. The Assembly can adopt the following methods to keep its control over the executive:

(1)   Questions
(2)   Resolutions
(3)   Adjournment Motion
(4)   Move for a vote of No-Confidence

The Judiciary: An independent judiciary is one of the most important pillars of democracy. Only a strong and independent judiciary can guarantee fundamental rights by dispensing justice to the people and protecting them from the high-handedness of the executive.

Pakistan is a federation of four provinces. The Constitution has clearly laid down the functions and powers of the provinces and the Federal Government. Yet, there is always a possibility of misunderstanding or a dispute between different provinces or between a Province and the Federal Government. In such a situation, only the Supreme Court can settle the dispute. This gives the judiciary added importance in a Federal Constitution.

The importance and status of judiciary in a country reflects the freedom available to the people. The more the judiciary is independent, the more the people of that country are free and secure. It is for this reason that in all democratic countries the judiciary enjoys independence from the executive. The Constitution of Pakistan also provides that the judiciary will be separated from the executive within three years after the promulgation of this Constitution. This is certainly a progressive step in the right direction.

In most Federal systems, the judiciary is generally divided into two parts; one for the Federation and the other for the Provinces. The most important quality of Pakistan's judicial system is that the judiciary is knit in an effective single system for the whole country under the guidance and command of the Supreme Court of Pakistan.

The Supreme Court: The Article 175 of the 1973 Constitution provides that the Supreme Court shall have jurisdiction over the whole of the country, though each province will have its separate High Court. The jurisdiction of these courts has been defined by the Constitution and law.

The Supreme Court consists of a Chief Justice and other judges whose number is determined by the President until the Parliament fixes their number. The Chief Justice is appointed by the President. Each of the other Judges of the Supreme Court are also appointed by the President, but after consultation with the Chief Justice. A person who is a Judge of the Supreme Court must fulfil the following qualifications:

1. Shall be a citizen of Pakistan;
2. Shall have served as judge of a High Court for, at least, five

years or should have worked as an advocate in a High Court for fifteen years.

Under Article 184, the Supreme Court has the original jurisdiction to hear and determine appeals regarding judgement, decrees, final orders, or sentences of a High Court. However, such an appeal in the Supreme Court can be filed only in the following circumstances:

(a) If the High Court has on appeal reversed an order of acquittal of an accused person and sentenced him to death or to transportation for life or imprisonment for life; or, on revision, has enhanced to a sentence as aforesaid; or

(b) If the High Court has withdrawn for trial before itself any case from any court subordinate to it and has in such trial convicted the accused person and sentenced him as aforesaid; or

(c) If the High Court has imposed any punishment on any person for contempt of the High Court; or

(d) If the amount or value of the subject-matter of the dispute in the court of first instance was, and also in dispute an appeal is, not less than fifty thousand rupees or such other sum as may be specified in that behalf by an act of the Parliament and the judgement, decree, or final order appealed from has varied or set aside the judgement, decree, or final order of the court immediately below; or

(e) If the judgement, decree, or final order involves directly or indirectly some claim or question respecting property of the like amount or value and the judgment, decree or final order appealed from has varied or set aside the judgement, decree, or final order of the court immediately below; or

(f) If the High Court certifies that the case involves a substantial question of law as to the interpretation of the Constitution.

In all other cases, not mentioned above, an appeal in the Supreme Court can be filed only with the permission of the Supreme Court. Under Article 187, the Supreme Court can issue such orders and guidelines which are necessary for the justiciable dispensation of a case. In this connection it can direct a person to appear before it. It can also direct that a document may be placed before it for examination. The Supreme Court has also the power to revise its own decision if a law passed by the Parliament or the Supreme Court's own procedures does not stand in the way of such a revision. All decisions given by the Supreme Court on a substantial question of law or an explanation of it are binding upon the lower courts. All judicial and executive authorities of Pakistan function as subsidiary to the Supreme Court. The Supreme Court can also lay down its own procedure.

One of the functions of the Supreme Court is to give its advice to the President on a legal matter of public importance on which the President may ask the Supreme Court to give its opinion.

The High Court: Each province has been provided with a High Court consisting of a Chief Justice and other Judges whose number is fixed by the President, until it is determined by law. Generally, the jurisdiction of a High Court extends only to the limits of the province for which it is constituted, but under clause 5 of Article 192, the Parliament has the power to extend the jurisdiction of a High Court to any other area or region.

Under Article 193 of the 1973 Constitution, the Chief Justice of a High Court is appointed by the President in consultation with the Chief Justice of Pakistan and the Governor of the province concerned. Other Judges of a High Court are appointed by the President on the advice of the Chief Justice of Pakistan, the Chief Justice of the High Court, and the Governor of the province concerned.

A Judge of High Court must fulfil the following qualifications:

(1) Shall be a citizen of Pakistan;
(2) Shall not be less than forty years of age;
(3) Shall have worked for, at least, ten years in the capacity of an advocate in a High Court; or

(4) Shall have served for ten yearn in the civil service of Pakistan and as a District Judge for, at least, three years; or

(5) Shall have held for ten years a judicial office in Pakistan.

Under Article 199, if a High Court is satisfied that no other adequate remedy is provided by law, it can issue the following orders on the application of any aggrieved party:

(i) It can ask a person in the service of Pakistan or a legal authority to refrain from or take an action which the High Court considers unlawful or may direct him to carry out a certain function which the High Court considers necessary under the law.

(ii) The High Court can declare as void and unlawful an action taken by a person functioning for the Federal, Provincial, or local authority for which he is not legally authorized.

(iii) It can issue at the request of any person a writ of *habeas corpus* to satisfy itself that a person under detention has been detained under the law and that he is being treated according to the law.

(iv) It can direct a person in the service of Pakistan to explain under which authority he has occupied a certain position in the service of Pakistan.

(v) It can direct any person or authority of the government within its jurisdiction to protect the fundamental rights of a person when such rights have been contravened.

The Constitution provides that the authority of the High Court for protecting the fundamental rights cannot be circumscribed. It shows that whenever fundamental rights of a person are contravened, he can seek redress from the High Court. A limitation on the fundamental rights can only be imposed by amending the Constitution. Consequently, if the Parliament frames a law which contravenes fundamental rights, the High Court can declare that law void and infructuous.

However, the above-mentioned protection provided for fundamental rights does not cover the armed forces of Pakistan.

The High Court cannot make an order in relation to a member of the armed forces in respect of his terms and conditions of service or in respect of any action taken against him as a member of the armed forces.

The High Court cannot issue an interim order when such an interim order may prejudice or interfere with the assessment or collection of public revenue, or carrying out of a public work, or may be harmful to public interest. Moreover, before making an interim order, the High Court shall provide opportunity to the prescribed law officer (that is, Advocate-General, his representative, or that of a public corporation, or Federal or Provincial Governments) to be heard.

The President can transfer a judge of the High Court but not against the wish of the judge. The President has also to consult the Chief Justice of Pakistan and the Chief Justices of the two High Courts involved in the transfer of a judge.

Under Article 201, a decision given by the High Court on a substantial question of law is binding on the lower courts. In order that the High Court may supervise and control the dispensation of justice within its jurisdiction, the Article 201 of the Constitution has empowered the High Court to control and supervise the lower courts.

Under Article 204, the High Court and the Supreme Court can punish a person who:

1. Interferes in the work of the court, misuses the procedure of the court, or refuses to implement the decisions of the court; or
2. Brings into disrepute the name of the court, or commits an action which may spread hatred against a judge or make him the target of insult, ridicule, or contempt; or
3. Commits an action which prejudices the proceedings of a case being heard by the court; or
4. Commits an action which may be considered, under the law, contempt of court.

However, it has been explained that a review based on good intention or public interest will not be considered a contempt of the court.

The Article 207 of the 1973 Constitution stipulates that a judge of the Supreme Court or of a High Court cannot hold any other office of profit in the service of Pakistan, excepting such quasi-judicial office as Chief Election Commissioner, Chairman or Member of Law Commission or Council of Islamic Ideology, before the expiration of two years after his retirement. Moreover, a retired (permanent) Judge of the Supreme Court cannot plead before any court or authority in Pakistan. A retired judge of High Courts of the present provinces of Pakistan as well as of West Pakistan High Court or its permanent Bench cannot plead in any court or authority within the jurisdiction of the court, from which he has retired. The purpose of this Article is to maintain the dignity of the high office of a judge and the judicature.

Supreme Judicial Council: Under Article 209 of the 1973 Constitution, a Supreme Judicial Council, consisting of the following persons, has been established in Pakistan.

1. The Chief Justice of Pakistan.
2. The two next senior-most Judges of the Supreme Court.
3. The two senior-most Chief Justices of High Courts.

If, in the opinion of the President, informed by the Council or by any other source, a judge of the Supreme Court or of a High Court may have been guilty of misconduct or may have become incapable of performing his duties due to physical or mental incapacity, the President may ask the Council to enquire into the matter and submit a report to the President. If the Council, after enquiring into the matter, finds the judge guilty of misconduct or incapable of performing his duties, and recommends by majority vote that he may be removed from his office, the President may remove the judge from his office.

Another duty of the Council is to issue a code of conduct to be observed by all the judges of the Supreme Court and of High Courts.

In the 1956 Constitution of Pakistan, the President had the power to remove a judge of the Supreme Court after informing the National Assembly. The President could remove the judge of a High Court at the recommendations of the Supreme Court. In the 1962 Constitution, a Supreme Judicial Council was provided.

* * *

The 1973 Constitution reflected the consensus of all the provinces of Pakistan and was accepted by almost all the political parties having representation in the National Assembly. Its enforcement from 14 August 1973, heralded a new era of democracy and political stability in Pakistan. A written constitution is an important document for a nation. However, what matters most is how it is actually implemented and how far it is respected in letter and spirit. Unfortunately, the working of the 1973 Constitution during August 1973 and July 1977 was far from satisfactory.

The government, headed by the Pakistan People's Party, was accused of making fundamental amendments in the Constitution. The major charge against the government was that it did not allow the provincial governments of Baluchistan and NWFP to function properly within the framework of provincial autonomy as provided in the Constitution. In the beginning, the Central Government unnecessarily interfered in provincial matters and then removed the Government of Baluchistan. This was followed by the resignation of the NWFP Ministry as a protest. Thus, both the provinces were placed under governors' rule causing great disillusionment to the people. Emergency remained in force for a longer period than required, depriving the people of their fundamental rights. The sanctity of the Parliament was violated when members of the Opposition were thrown out of the House.

The first general elections under the new Constitution were held in March 1977. The rigging of the election by the ruling party sparked off a country-wide agitation which posed a serious threat to the internal security of the country. All the political parties demanded fresh general elections but the government refused to accept the demand. The continuous populist agitation and inflexible attitude of the government plunged the country into a serious constitutional crisis of unprecedented nature. It was the first real test of the Constitution.

Unfortunately, the Constitution did not contain any appropriate solution to this problem as all the powers were vested in the Prime Minister. The President who could save the situation by acting in such emergencies, had no effective powers. It was, therefore, realized that the Constitution must provide for reasonable division of powers between the Prime Minister and the President to ensure its successful operation. The President should have the power to dissolve the National Assembly and to order a fresh election in such an eventuality so that a constitutional breakdown could be averted.

The street agitation in the aftermath of the 1977 general elections paralysed the government of Zulfikar Ali Bhutto. The government and the Opposition could not come to a concrete understanding for resolving their sharp political differences. The Army decided to break the deadlock by assuming power. General Ziaul Haq, Chief of the Army Staff, overthrew the Bhutto government on 5 July 1977. The 1973 Constitution was suspended (not abrogated) and martial law was imposed in the country, Nusrat Bhutto, wife of the ousted Prime Minister, Zulfikar Ali Bhutto, challenged the legality of the imposition of martial law in the Supreme Court. In its judgement on 10 November 1977, the Supreme Court held that the imposition of martial law was covered by the law of necessity and declared that General Zia's administration was the de facto government. During the hearing of the case, the Attorney General assured the court on behalf of the military government that elections would soon be held. The Supreme Court considered this as a pledge by the Martial Law regime and it was said in the judgement that the court expects the General to redeem his pledge.

The Martial Law regime started with the assurance to hold the elections and to keep the Constitution intact—that the Constitution had only been suspended and put in abeyance for the time being. The political circles expressed their apprehensions that the military regime might abrogate it, which would have 'disastrous consequences for the country.' It was said that 'the 1973 Constitution was prepared with great difficulty and was endorsed by the elected representatives of the four provinces including the Opposition. It [would] not be possible to obtain their agreement in future.'[50] Moreover, 'abrogation of the Constitution would pose a serious threat to the unity of the country.'[51] Such fears were set aside when General Ziaul Haq announced that 'the Constitution will not be abrogated, but necessary amendments will be made to pave way for the establishment of an Islamic society.'[52]

The martial law government gradually introduced changes in the Constitution. For example, in 1979, a new Article 22-A was added by Presidential Order to provide for military courts and tribunals for the trial of offences punishable under Martial Law Regulations. The order debarred the jurisdiction of regular courts.[53] Bar associations took exception to this order and demanded restoration of the constitution in toto as well as the holding of general elections in the country because the continued suspension of the basic rights, indefinite postponement of elections and ban on political activities had landed the country in a critical situation.[54]

In March 1981, the martial law government introduced the Provisional Constitutional Order (PCO) which replaced what was left of the 1973 Constitution. It provided for setting up a nominated Federal Council as an advisory body. The PCO provided that the political parties that had registered with the Election Commission by 30 September 1979, could function whenever the President granted them permission to engage in political activities.[55] Unregistered parties stood dissolved and their properties were to be forfeited to the Federal Government.

No political party could be formed without prior permission of the Chief Election Commissioner. The President could dissolve a political party in consultation with the Chief Election Commissioner if he was convinced that a party was formed or was operating in a manner prejudicial to the Islamic ideology or the sovereignty, integrity, or security of Pakistan.[56]

The PCO validated all Presidential orders, orders of the CMLA, martial law regulations, martial law orders, and all laws made on or after 5 July 1977, notwithstanding any judgement of any court, to have been validly made and shall not be called in question in any court on any ground whatsoever.

The Judges of the High Courts and the Supreme Court were required to take oath under the PCO. Many judges, including Chief Justice Anwarul Haq, refused to take oath. Consequently they lost their jobs.

MAJOR CHANGES IN THE 1973 CONSTITUTION

President Zia continued serving as the sole fountain of constitutional, political, and administrative powers from 1977 to 1983. Though he tried to keep up the facade of consultative process by holding conventions of different sections of society, the need for an advisory forum having a semblance of a parliament was felt in 1982. In order to fill the political vacuum, even in an artificial manner, a Majlis-e-Shoora (Federal Council) was set up. It consisted of 350 members representing all sections of society but nominated by the government on the basis of their own merits such as personal character, reputation, influence, and background. It was basically an advisory body but subsequently, on 19 April 1982, the President declared that it would function as a legislative assembly till the election of a parliament. The Majlis-e-Shoora was dissolved soon after the 1985 general elections.

Mounting political pressure including the growing demands for restoration of democracy led the military government to decide that the power be transferred to an elected government.

First, even the process of transfer was prolonged over a period of more than eighteen months and, secondly, the arrangement proposed by the President visualised the sharing of power instead of its transfer. In order to implement the power sharing plan, some fundamental changes were proposed in the 1973 Constitution. Whether the proposed changes altered the basic character of the Constitution or not, it was the minimum price that the nation had to pay for the transfer of power from the army to the civil. Against this background, the President placed the following proposals before the nation for handing over power. These were:

1. There will be no new role for the armed forces in the Constitution.
2. The 1973 Constitution will be restored after incorporating certain amendments.
3. General elections will be held on adult franchise basis in two phases; first, local bodies, then the national and provincial assemblies and the Senate. The entire process will be completed by 23 March 1985, and thereafter Martial Law will be lifted.
4. The President will be the Supreme Commander of the armed forces, empowered to appoint the Chairman of the Joint Chiefs of Staff Committee and three services chiefs.
5. The President will appoint the Prime Minister who will seek a vote of confidence within sixty days.
6. The President will have the power to dissolve the National Assembly if in his opinion the Prime Minister had ceased to enjoy the support of the majority in the National Assembly and order fresh elections within seventy-five days;
7. The President will have the power to send back a bill to the National Assembly for reconsideration.
8. The President will not declare emergency in the country without consulting the National Security Council whose composition and number of members will be announced later.

9. The President will appoint the Provincial Governors and the Chief Election Commissioner.[57]

The most important link in the chain of power transfer was President Zia's own continuance and survival for which he did not intend to depend on the newly elected assemblies. He was determined to keep his grip tight on power politics like a powerful political commander. After all, what he had conceded after ruling the country for about eight years was not transfer of power but sharing of power with the elected representatives. Hence, the Presidential order, called 'The Referendum Order 1984', was issued on 1 December 1984, which provided for a national referendum for his election as President after the restoration of civilian rule.

The referendum did not seek approval for Ziaul Haq's continuation as President. Rather, it asked the people if they supported Islamization and the steps for transfer of power, as initiated by the Zia government. The referendum question put to vote was:

Whether the people of Pakistan endorse the process initiated by General Muhammad Ziaul Haq, the President of Pakistan, for bringing laws in Pakistan in conformity with the injunctions of Islam as laid down in the Holy Qur'an and Sunnah of the Holy Prophet (peace be upon him) and for the preservation of the ideology of Pakistan, for the continuation and consolidation of that process and for the smooth and orderly transfer of power to the elected representatives of the people?

The voters were given a choice to answer the question in 'No' or 'Yes'. But the question was deliberately framed in such a way as to leave little scope for dissent or 'No'. Though, the question was silent about the election of Zia as President, the referendum order maintained that the majority affirmative vote would mean that the people of Pakistan had elected General Ziaul Haq as the President for a term of five years from the day the Parliament holds its first joint session.[58] As designed and expected, the referendum held on 19 December 1984, showed

97.71 per cent votes in affirmative, out of 62.2 per cent cast.[59] The referendum results reflected efficiency of the administration more than the popularity of General Zia or the political process initiated by him.

After having secured himself, President Zia arranged election to the National Assembly and the Provincial Assemblies on 25 and 28 February 1985, respectively. Before the newly elected assemblies could meet, the President promulgated an order on 2 March for the revival of the 1973 Constitution, incorporating some key amendments with a view to redefine the President-Prime Minister relationship, and to create the National Security Council consisting of eleven members to deal with emergencies. The Presidential Order amending the Constitution was called the Revival of the Constitution Order (RCO) 1985.

The amended Constitution formalized President Zia's election for the next five years with a provision that a future president would be elected by an electoral college consisting of four provincial assemblies and two houses of the federal parliament. The Objectives Resolution of 1949 was inserted into the body of the Constitution and the question of revival of political parties was left to the National Assembly. The President was given wide discretionary powers such as:

1. The President will appoint the Prime Minister from amongst the members of Parliament who will seek a vote of confidence of the House within sixty days.
2. The President, either on the advice of the Prime Minister or on his own, can order a national referendum on any issue of national importance.
3. The President can dissolve the National Assembly on the advice of the Prime Minister or on his own, followed by a general election in hundred days and appoint a caretaker government for the interim period.
4. The President will have the power to appoint Governors, Chairman of the Joint Chiefs of Staff Committee, Chiefs of the three armed forces.

5. The President will have powers to appoint provincial ministers; ministers of state and advisors, in consultation with the Prime Minister. The President was to be the Supreme Commander of the Armed Forces.

The order increased the life of the Senate from four to six years, one-third of its strength rotating every two years. For constitutional amendments, besides two-third majority in the National Assembly, the Provincial Assemblies were also required to back it to make it effective. A no-confidence vote could be brought against the Prime Minister by at least 20 per cent of the House but not during the Budget session. The Chief Ministers were to be appointed by the Governors in consultation with the President. The President was required to give assent to a bill passed by the Parliament in forty-five days. The President could refer it back to the Parliament for reconsideration and then was bound to give his assent. However, provisions relating to the provincial autonomy were not disturbed.

Another amendment gave protection to all those laws enacted during the past eight years relating to the judicial system, including the laws relating to the contempt of Court.[60]

These amendments were not received well by the political circles and these were described 'as a modified rule of Martial Law... destroying the very basis of the 1973 Constitution.'[61] 'The net result of these will be to whittle down the Prime Minister's status to practically that of a senior minister in the cabinet, plus the likelihood that the members of Parliament as well as those in the Cabinet will look to the President as the principal distributor of official munificence.'[62] Precisely, the general reaction was hostile as these amendments, instead of establishing a balance between the President and the Prime Minister, indicated a clear tilt in favour of the President who was given vital powers.

The President promulgated another order on 10 March 1985, enforcing all but 27 Articles of the amended 1973 Constitution, setting the stage for the induction of newly elected National and Provincial Assemblies. The Articles left suspended related to fundamental rights, appointment of Governors, Chief Election Commissioner, Election Commission, and writ jurisdiction of High Courts. Another Article held in abeyance described the abrogation; the 1973 Constitution was revived excepting 27 Articles.

The joint session of the National Assembly and the Senate was held on 23 March 1985, where General Zia took oath as the President of Pakistan for the next five years. He nominated Muhammad Khan Junejo as Prime Minister who took oath on the same day. Finally, the eight-and-a-half-year-old Martial Law was lifted on 30 December 1985.

THE EIGHTH AMENDMENT

The changes made in the 1973 Constitution by the military regime, especially those introduced in March 1985 under the RCO were presented to the newly elected Parliament for approval on 6 September 1985, packaged as the Eighth Amendment. This also provided for a blanket indemnity and legal and constitutional protection to all orders, actions, decisions, and policy measures adopted by the martial law authorities, including the judgements of the military courts, at any level.[63]

In spite of the governmental efforts to achieve consensus, the introduction of the Eighth Constitution Amendment Bill was strongly resented by the Independent Parliamentary Group (IPG). It vehemently criticized the Bill and described it as 'a calculated attempt to perpetuate Martial Law in the country in civilian guise'.[64] Haji Saifullah, leader of the IPG, rightly remarked that the Indemnity Bill introduced by the government was different from the amendments made in the Constitution to give protection to the orders of Yahya Khan. That was a temporary validation and accorded protection only for two years after which the Assembly was empowered to amend or change them by a simple majority; whereas the eighth amendment accorded permanent protection to all the acts of the President and CMLA which otherwise could be amended by two-third majority.[65] This contention is also supported by history because even after the first Martial Law in 1953, only the actions taken in good faith were indemnified and mala fide actions were open to judicial review.[66]

Generally, the proposed amendment was criticized *in toto* and it created a cleavage even amongst the ranks of Official Parliamentary Group (OPG). The specific resentment was against the provisions relating to the validation of all acts and actions of the Martial Law regime as well as against the President's power to dissolve the National Assembly at his own discretion and to appoint the Prime Minister. Most of the members of Parliament felt that these provisions jeopardized the sovereignty of Parliament. Senator Professor Khurshid Ahmad commented that Article 270 A, intended to indemnify all actions of the Martial Law regime, was an abominal piece of legislation.[67]

In order to develop a consensus on the provisions of the Eighth Amendment, the Prime Minister opened a dialogue with the Independent Parliamentary Group (IPG). Furthermore, there were differences within the OPG which needed to be sorted out. A joint committee was formed to review the Bill. Meanwhile, the Prime Minister announced on 29 September, in the presence of President Zia, that the proposal regarding the National Security Council had been dropped on the unanimous demand of the Official Parliamentary Group.[68] As the Joint Committee deliberated on the differences, the Prime Minister made it clear to the members on 6 October that the passage of the amendment would facilitate an early end to Martial Law.[69] He further said that some of the suggestions offered by the IPG and others were being incorporated in the bill to make it more acceptable. He was of the view that the imposition of limits on the powers of the President to remove the Prime Minister and the dropping of the National Security Council were no small achievements.[70]

The members of the IPG wanted to introduce more changes, especially to reduce the powers of the President. Mr Bhindara, an IPG member, moved an amendment on 15 October which provided that the 'question of dissolution of National Assembly should be decided through referendum.'[71] While addressing the Assembly, he said: 'Had such a provision existed, the nation would have neither seen the dissolution of the Constituent Assembly at the hands of Ghulam Muhammad, nor would it have suffered another Martial Law in 1977.[72] Another IPG member, Haji Saifullah, said: 'Vesting powers in the hands of one individual to dissolve the National Assembly will lead to dire consequences. President Iskandar Mirza dissolved the Assembly in 1958, though he had no power to do so under the 1956 Constitution.[73] They were opposed by the Federal Minister of Justice on the basis that all precautions had been taken and lacunas removed. The irony of the history is that it repeats itself yet we do not learn from it. Once again apprehensions turned out to be solid reality. When the moment for decision arrived, President Zia dissolved the National Assembly on 29 May 1988, by using his discretion under section 58(2B) of the Constitution. This was for the third time that the National Assembly was dissolved in Pakistan during the forty-one years of its total life.

Finally negotiations between the two groups of the National Assembly led to an accord on 16 October which paved the way for almost a unanimous passage of the Eighth Amendment Bill. Taking credit for the efforts of the IGP, Haji Saifullah said that now the President could not dissolve the National Assembly using his own discretion. The amended bill had also restricted the power of the President regarding appointment of Governors who could now be appointed in consultation with the Prime Minister. Another major achievement of the group was to remove constitutional protection from the Political Parties Act which would now be an ordinary law.[74]

After the passage of the revised Eighth Amendment by the National Assembly, it was approved without any change by the Senate on 14 November 1985. Thus, the stage was set for the lifting of the longest Martial Law from the country on 30 December 1985.

The Eighth Amendment introduced major changes in the 1973 Constitution which cannot be properly understood and appreciated unless each amended Article is discussed with reference to its original position. It is explained as under.

Article 48: The original Article envisaged that the President was to act in accordance with the advice of the Prime Minister in the performance of his Presidential functions and that the Prime Minister's advice was binding on him. Advice tendered by the Prime Minister to the President was immune from enquiry by a court. The President's orders required the signatures of the Prime Minister for their validity, that is, every order issued by the President was required to be countersigned by the Prime Minister. The procedure for authentication of such orders or instruments had been prescribed in Article 99 of the Constitution.

The amendments made in 1985 by the Eighth Amendment, however, have tilted the balance of power in favour of the President. The Article, as amended, envisaged that the President would act in accordance with the advice of the Prime Minister or the cabinet in performance of his duties. The President, however, has been invested with power to require the Cabinet or the Prime Minister to reconsider the advice tendered either generally or otherwise. The President is to act in accordance with the advice tendered after reconsideration. Sub-Article (2) of the Article empowers the President to act in his discretion in respect of any matter for which he is empowered by the Constitution. The validity of any act done by the President in the exercise of his discretion cannot be enquired into by any court, tribunal, or authority. Any advice tendered to the President by the Cabinet, the Prime Minister, or any Minister cannot be called in question on any ground.

When the President has dissolved the National Assembly, he would in his discretion appoint a date not later than ninety days from the date of dissolution, for the holding of general elections to the National Assembly and would also appoint a caretaker cabinet. When the President in his discretion, or on the advice of the Prime Minister, considers that any matter of national importance should be referred to a referendum in the form of a question that is capable of being answered either by 'Yes' or 'No', he can do so. The Parliament has been empowered to lay down the procedure for the holding of such a referendum and the compiling and consideration of the result of that referendum.

The President's discretion relates to fixing a date within ninety days from the date of dissolution of the National Assembly for holding of a general election. This article has to be read with Article 58 which empowers the President to dissolve the National Assembly either on the advice of the Prime Minister which is binding, or at his discretion under two situations: One, when a vote of no-confidence has been passed by the National Assembly and no other member is likely to command the major support in the National Assembly. Two, when he is of the firm view that a situation has developed in which the federal government cannot be carried on in accordance with the provision of the Constitution and an appeal to the electorate is necessary. (See below for Article 58).

Article 51: Before the amendment, a person not less than eighteen years of age was entitled to vote. Now the age of voter has been raised to twenty-one years. Proviso to Sub-Article (2) which provided that for the purpose of first general elections or for bye-election to a vacant seat before holding of second general elections, the age of voter shall be construed to be twenty-one years of age, has now been omitted. It has in effect become redundant.

Prior to the amendment, the National Assembly was to consist of 200 members to be elected by direct and free vote. Now the general seats have been enhanced to 207. In addition to this, ten seats have been reserved for religious minorities like Christians, Hindus, Sikhs, Buddhists and the Qadianis or the Lahori group. Twenty seats have now been reserved in the National Assembly for women instead of ten seats for a specified period of time. The members belonging to minority communities are now to be elected on the basis of separate electorates, i.e., the registered voters of each community electing their representatives. Under the old system these members were elected by the members of the National Assembly. Women members are elected by the provincial assemblies.

Article 56: Sub-Articles (2) to (4) have been newly added to Article 56 which empowers the President to send messages to either House with respect to a bill pending in the Parliament or otherwise, and the House where such a message has been sent is required to take the matter into consideration as required by the message. The President has also been empowered to address the first session after each general election and every first session of each year. The President shall address both the Houses, i.e. the Parliament and the Senate.

Article 58: The Eighth Amendment has authorized the President to dissolve the National Assembly in his discretion under these circumstances:

1. Where a vote of no-confidence having been passed against the Prime Minister, no other member of the National Assembly is likely to command the confidence of the majority of the members;
2. Where a situation has arisen in which the Federal Government cannot be carried on in accordance with the provisions of the Constitution and an appeal to the electorate is necessary.

The dissolution power under the second situation was used by the President to dissolve the National Assembly in 1988, 1990, 1993, and 1996. In April 1997, the Thirteenth Amendment in the Constitution did away with this power. (See also the commentary on Article 48).

Article 59: The changes brought about in this article by the Eighth Amendment Bill are as follows: The number of Senate seats has been enhanced from sixty-three to eighty-seven. Eight senators are to be elected from the Federally Administered Tribal Areas against five prior to the amendment. From the Federal capital area, three instead of two are now to be elected. Five additional seats have been allocated to the Ulama, technocrats, or other professionals from each province to be elected by the concerned Provincial Assembly. Half of the members of each category are to retire after every three years. Previously the term was for two years.

Article 60: The only change brought about in this Article is about the term of office of the Chairman and Deputy Chairman of the Senate. The term of office has been extended from two years to three years.

Article 75: Prior to the amendment, the President was required to give his assent to a bill within seven days after it had been presented to him. If he failed to do so, he was deemed to have assented thereto. The amended article requires the President to give his assent to the bill within thirty days. He is also empowered to return a bill other than a Money Bill to the Parliament for reconsideration of the whole or a part of the bill. If the Parliament, in a joint sitting, again passes the bill, the President cannot withhold his assent.

Article 90: Before the Eighth Amendment, the executive authority of the Federation was to be exercised in the name of the President by the Federal Government consisting of the Prime Minister and the Federal Ministers, which was required to act through the Prime Minister. After the amendment, the executive authority has been vested in the President who is required to exercise it either directly or through officers subordinate to him, in accordance with the Constitution. These powers, however, have been qualified to the extent that the function conferred to any existing law on the government of any province or other authority would not be deemed to have been transferred to the President. The Parliament could confer by law such functions on authorities other than the President. The gist of the Article is that even under this Article, the executive authority of the

Federation has to be exercised by the Parliament through its Cabinet in the name of the President.

Article 91: Before the Eighth Amendment, the requirement of the Article was that the National Assembly by a majority vote of the total membership was empowered to elect the Prime Minister, and if no member secured such a majority in the first poll, the second poll was to be held between two candidates securing the largest number of votes.

Under the amended Article, the President has been empowered at his discretion to appoint from amongst the members of the National Assembly, a Prime Minister who, in his opinion, is most likely to command the confidence of the majority of the Members of the National Assembly. This power is available to the President till a specified date namely, 20 March 1990. After this date, the Prime Minister is to be elected by the National Assembly.

Another important amendment effected in this Article is that the Prime Minister is to hold office during the pleasure of the President, but the President has been debarred to exercise his power in this respect unless he is satisfied that the Prime Minister does not command the confidence of the majority of Members of the National Assembly, in which case he would summon the National Assembly and require the Prime Minister to obtain a vote of confidence from the Assembly.

Article 101: There is no substantial change in this Article. Before the amendment, the Governor was to be appointed by the President. After the amendment, the Governor is to be appointed by the President in consultation with the Prime Minister.

Article 105: Before the Eighth Amendment, the Governor of a province was required to act on and in accordance with the advice of the Chief Minister, and such advice was binding on him. After the amendment, the Governor still has to act on the advice of the Chief Minister, but he can ask the Chief Minister and the cabinet to reconsider the advice. The Governor is required to act in accordance with the advice tendered after reconsideration.

The other amendment in this Article is to the effect that after the dissolution of the Provincial Assembly, the Governor shall appoint a caretaker government at his discretion, but with prior approval of the President.

Article 106: No substantial change has been effected in this Article. In sub-clause (4) of the Article, instead of the word 'second', the word 'third' has been inserted. The powers conferred on the Governor by virtue of the Eighth Amendment, for dissolution of a Provincial Assembly are similar to those conferred on the President for the dissolution of the National Assembly under Article 58.

Article 116: The powers of the Governor are similar in nature as the powers of the President under Article 75. It envisages that the Governor is to give his assent to a bill within thirty days of the passing of the bill by the Provincial Assembly. The Governor can send back a bill except a Money Bill to the Assembly for reconsideration. The Governor has to give his assent to the bill after it has been reconsidered by the Assembly.

Article 130: The powers conferred on the Governor by this Article are similar to those exercisable by the President under Article 91. This Article empowers the Governor to appoint at his discretion any member of the Provincial Assembly to be the Chief Minister till the specified date, that is, 20 March 1988. After that, date the Provincial Assembly shall be empowered to elect the Chief Minister by a majority vote. (For further details see commentary under Article 91).

Article 152-A: This Article which was introduced by the President's Order No. 14 of 1985, regarding the National Security Council, has been omitted by the eighth amendment. It may, however, be mentioned that this Article did not exist in the Constitution as originally framed.

Article 270-A: This Article indemnifies all the President's Orders, Ordinances, Martial Law Regulations, Martial Law Orders including the Referendum Order made between 5 July 1977, and 13 September 1985. After that date, the President's Orders, Martial Law Regulations, Martial Law Orders are to be confined only to making such provisions as are to facilitate or incidental to the revocation of the Proclamation of 5 July 1977. A list of above-mentioned secured enactments, made immune from the jurisdiction of courts after the withdrawal of martial law has been provided in the amended Constitution. In this way, a blanket indemnity and constitutional cover was provided to all the actions and orders of the military government of Ziaul Haq from 5 July 1977 to 30 December 1985.

THE WORKING OF THE AMENDED CONSTITUTION OF 1973

With the withdrawal of martial law on 30 December 1985, the amended 1973 Constitutional became fully operational. It had tilted the balance of power in favour of the President in such a decisive manner that the Prime Minister could not become an autonomous centre of power. In a situation of difference of opinions between the Prime Minister and the President, the latter had enough power to enforce his will. The concept of a powerful President compromised the parliamentary character of the Constitution. The Presidential powers were criticized by the political circles. The Presidential power to dissolve the National Assembly at his discretion was criticized most severely.

Those supporting the President's powers to dissolve the National Assembly and call for new elections at his discretion maintained that if a serious political deadlock paralysed the government, the President could exercise this power to resolve the deadlock by calling for new elections, thereby blocking the prospects of a change being forced through extra-constitutional means. This clause was, therefore, considered to be a safety valve and preventive device against the military intervention.[75]

The President dissolved the National Assembly and dismissed the Prime Minister and the cabinet in May 1988, August 1990, April 1993, and November 1996. These Presidential actions were challenged in the superior courts, sometimes successfully and sometimes unsuccessfully. The National Assembly and the Prime Minister were restored by the Supreme Court only once, i.e., in 1993. However, these court judgements placed some check on the discretionary powers of the President by underlining the need of providing credible evidence of the circumstances that had made the smooth functioning of the government impossible.

THIRTEENTH AMENDMENT

Four general elections were held after the passing of the Eighth Amendment and the elected governments often talked of curtailing the powers of the President as enhanced by the Eighth Amendment. However, no effort was made to do that as the government and the Opposition could not develop consensus on this and other contentious issues.

In February 1997, the Muslim League, led by Nawaz Sharif swept the general elections by winning a comfortable majority which crossed the figure of two-third majority after the establishment of post-elections alliances with other parties. No previous Pakistani government since 1985 had such a massive support in the house. Taking advantage of such strong support in the Parliament, the government got a new amendment (Thirteenth Amendment) passed by the parliament on 1 April 1997, curtailing the powers of the President and enhancing the powers of the Prime Minister. The President's power under Article 58-2-b which empowered him to dissolve the National Assembly in his discretion was omitted. This amendment had great significance for the political set-up in the country as the

President was stripped off the powers to dissolve the National Assembly at his discretion. He could dissolve the Assembly only on the advice of the Prime Minister as envisaged in the original 1973 Constitution, or do the same when, after the vote of no-confidence no other leader could command a majority in the National Assembly. While this amendment had a wholesome effect on the members of the National Assembly as the fear of dissolution of Assembly under which they constantly lived was removed, the darker side of the picture was that in the absence of this option, any breakdown of the constitutional machinery could lead to military's direct or indirect intervention, as had happened in July 1977.

The Thirteenth amendment also amended the Constitution to the extent that the Governor, like the President, was also deprived of the power to dissolve the Provincial Assembly at his discretion. Another important provision of the Thirteenth Amendment was that the words 'after consultation with' occurring in clause (1) of Article 101 of the Constitution were substituted with the words 'on the advice of'. This amendment related to the appointment of Governors of the Provinces by the President which now reads as under: 'There shall be a Governor for each Province which shall be appointed by the President on the advice of the Prime Minister.' This change has brought the authority of appointment of Governor of a Province within the ambit of power of the Prime Minister.

Another change of great significance brought about by this amendment is the omission of words 'at his discretion' from Article 243. This omission has further weakened the authority of the President and has enhanced the position of the Prime Minister for the appointment of Chairman Joint Chiefs of Staff Committee, the Chief of the Army Staff, the Chief of the Naval Staff, and the Chief of Air Staff, and in determining their salaries and allowances. This has obviously strengthened the position of Prime Minister in relation to Armed Forces.

FOURTEENTH AMENDMENT

On 3 July 1997 the Parliament approved the Fourteenth Amendment, to introduce a new Article 63-A in the Constitution. The object of insertion of this Article was to add one more item in the long list of disqualifications for membership of the Parliament, already existing in the form of the Article 63. The new Article was intended to eliminate the malpractice of changing party loyalties by the elected members of the Parliament and the provincial assemblies for personal gains and other ulterior motives. This practice of defecting from one party to another is known in common parlance as indulging in 'horse-trading' and had been one of the major factors contributing to political instability in the past. This new Article comprehensively defines the term 'defection' and exhaustively explains the procedure to be followed in case of defection by a member of the Parliament or Provincial Assembly and thoroughly lays down the consequences which are to follow from such defection.

The new Article, 63-A, adopted unanimously[76], provides that if a member of a Parliamentary party defects, he may, by means of a notice in writing by the head of the concerned political party, be called upon to explain his action within seven days that why not the prescribed penalty for defection be imposed on him. The act of defection from a party has been elaborately defined in the explanation provided in the Article which, briefly states that if a member of a House having been elected as a candidate or nominee of a political party, or under a symbol of political party or having been elected otherwise than as a candidate or nominee of a political party, and having become member of a political party after such election by means of a declaration in writing, commits a breach of a party discipline, that is, violation of the party constitution, code of conduct and its declared policies, or votes contrary to any direction issued by the parliamentary party to which he belongs, or abstains from voting in the House against party policy in relation to any Bill, will constitute defection.

In clause (2) of the Article, the procedure for action against a member charged with an act of defection is provided. It lays down that where action is proposed to be taken against a member, the disciplinary committee of the party, on a reference by the head of the party, shall decide the matter, after giving personal hearing to the member within seven days. In case the decision is against the member proceeded against, he can file an appeal within seven days before the head of the party whose decision shall be final. The decision shall be conveyed to the Presiding Officer of the House concerned by the head of the political party. The Presiding Officer shall, within two days, send the decision to the Chief Election Commissioner who shall give effect to such decision within seven days from the date of receipt of such intimation by declaring the seat vacant. Another important aspect of this Amendment is bar and ouster of jurisdiction of the Supreme Court and High Courts in clause (6) of this Amendment Act by providing that notwithstanding anything contained in the Constitution, no court including the Supreme Court and a High Court, shall entertain any legal proceedings, exercise any jurisdiction, or make any order in relation to the action taken under the present Article.

Naturally there was great uproar in the political circles of the country against this Amendment. The opposition in the Parliament decried and disparaged the Amendment alleging that the Article 63-A is violative of Fundamental Rights guaranteed in the Constitution and expressly conflicts with various Articles of the Constitution and that the new Article is not against defection but is against dissent. It was argued that this Article will make it extremely difficult for the members of various legislatures to express their views freely on any matter of national importance, that this will promote the dictatorship of the party leader who has been made the sole and final judge of act of defection, with no right of appeal to the accused to any court of law. It was said that 'in a culture of dictatorial leadership within political parties, such a bill which institutionalizes enhanced power of the party leader virtually without any checks may, in fact, further strengthen one-man rule within political parties.'[77]

This issue has two aspects. Firstly, the amendment was passed by the Parliament without dissent. Secondly, this was not the first time in the legislative history of Pakistan that the law against defection or floor-crossing was passed. In fact attempt was made as far back as 5 September 1958 to seek a legislation on the question of defection, but before any progress could be made, the country was placed under Martial Law on 7 October 1958, resulting in the dissolution of assemblies and abrogation of the 1956 Constitution. However, the first legislative measure dealing with the problem of defection or floor-crossing by elected members of a political party was introduced when the Political Parties Act 1962 was passed on 15 July 1962. Section 8(2) of the said Act provided as under:

> If a person having been elected to the National or a Provincial Assembly as a candidate or nominee of a political party, withdraws himself from it, he shall, from the date of such withdrawal, be disqualified from being a member of the Assembly for the unexpired period of his term.

The above sub-section (2) of section 8 of the Political Parties Act 1962 held the field until it was omitted with retrospective effect from 8 May 1974 by Act XXI of 1975. Hence, there was no comprehensive law on defection except clause (5) of Article 96 of the Constitution which remained operative till it was omitted by President Ziaul Haq on 2 March 1985. After omission of Article 96 of the Constitution, there was no law in the field dealing with floor-crossing or defection by the elected members of the assemblies belonging to a political party. To fill this gap section 8-B was introduced in the Political Parties Act on 24 December 1985 which was more or less on the same lines as the newly added Article 63-A of the Constitution. Some amendments were made in Section 8-B of the Political Parties Act through an Ordinance but since this Ordinance was not placed before the Assembly as required by Article 89 of the Constitution, it stood repealed on the expiry of four months.

The validity of Article 63-A was, however, challenged in the Supreme Court by 'Wukala Mohaz Barai Tahafaz Dastoor' on the grounds, *inter alia*, that it is violative of basic structure of the Constitution, and is also against tenets of Islam. The Court, after giving full consideration to the contentions for and against the validity of the Article, came to the conclusion that Article 63-A was not violative of any of the three basic structures of the Constitution, namely, representative form of government, Islamic concept of democracy, and independence of judiciary. The Supreme Court was of the view that the Article 63-A, on the other hand, would tend to eradicate the cancerous vice of defection and floor-crossing and will thus bring stability in the polity of the country.

> Historically, defection of members of political parties has been instrumental to the dissolution of more than one elected assemblies in the past. Floor-crossing and horse-trading, as the practice has been nick-named by the people, has generally been criticized as a highly immoral practice eroding the foundations of democratic institutions. The basic object of this newly inserted Article was to strengthen the party discipline by imposing legal ban on the changing of party loyalty. The anti-defection bill was also expected to 'contribute towards a shift from individualized self-interest driven politics to issue-based politics.[78]

It was the considered view of the Supreme Court that the new Article would help the democratic system to run smoothly and successfully. There is no restriction on the party members to express their views and ventilate their feelings on a controversial issue. However, once a decision is taken by the majority of party members, it shall bind all of them. Resultantly, the Supreme Court held that Article 63-A of the constitution is *intra vires* with this clarification that a member of a House can be disqualified for a breach of party discipline provided the breach occurred within the House. The Court further clarified its order by observing that paragraph (a) of explanation to clause

(1) of Article 63-A is to be construed in such a way that it should preserve the freedom of speech of a member in the House, subject to reasonable restrictions as are envisaged in Article 66 read with Article 19 of the Constitution. In the backdrop of various apprehensions expressed by the political analysts, this interpretation of the Court is likely to provide adequate protection to the freedom of expression available to the members of the Parliament.

Pakistan has been moving on the democratic and constitutional path since 1985. It has made significant gains in this respect. Some amendments have been made in the Constitution to adapt to the changing and evolving political conditions. This process will continue. This is how democracy takes roots and constitutionalism stabilizes.

NOTES AND REFERENCES

1. For the Resolution, see Appendix.
2. Constituent Assembly of Pakistan, *Debates*, 1949, vol. 5, no. 5, p. 66.
3. *Pakistan Observer*, Dacca, 1 October 1950.
4. *The Pakistan Times*, 12 January 1953.
5. Ibid.
6. Ibid., 11 and 12 January 1953.
7. Ibid.
8. Z.A. Suleri, *Politicians and Ayub*, Rawalpindi: Capital Law and General Book Depot, 1964, pp. 53–54.
9. *The Pakistan Times*, 12 January 1953.
10. Quoted in H. Feldman, *A Constitution for Pakistan,* Karachi: Oxford University Press, 1955, p. 35.
11. *The Pakistan Times*, 8 October 1953.
12. Ibid.
13. G.W. Choudhury, *Constitutional Development in Pakistan,* London: Longman, 1957, p. 141.
14. Writ Petition No. 43 of 1954.
15. Government of India Act 1935, with Indian Independence Act 1947, as adapted in Pakistan by (Provisional Constitution) Order 1947, and amended up to April 1955.
16. Feldman, *A Constitution for Pakistan,* p. 70.
17. Ibid., p. 75.

18. Choudhury, *Constitutional Development*, p. 155.
19. Ibid., p. 157.
20. *The Constitution of Islamic Republic of Pakistan,* Government of Pakistan, 1956, Article 222, p. 122, Article 35, p. 10.
21. Ibid., Article 50, p. 17.
22. Ibid., Article 191, p. 70.
23. Ibid., Article 37 (a), p. 13.
24. Choudhury, *Constitutional Development*, p. 216.
25. *The Constitution of Islamic Republic of Pakistan, 1956*, Article 60.
26. Ibid., Article 151.
27. Brother of Khan Abdul Ghaffar Khan, and Chief Minister of West Pakistan in 1956.
28. Sayeed, *The Political System of Pakistan,* pp. 60–92.
29. M. Ayub Khan, *Friends Not Masters,* New York: Oxford University Press, 1967, p. 212.
30. *The Constitution of Pakistan, 1962*, Article 10.
31. Ibid., Article 11.
32. Ibid., Article 22.
33. Ibid., Article 23.
34. Ibid., p.141.
35. Ibid., pp. 152–53.
36. Ibid., p. 155.
37. *The Constitution of Pakistan, 1962*, Article 118 (3).
38. Ibid., Article 111 (2).
39. Ibid., Article 74.
40. Legal Framework Order. See Appendix also.
41. Article 96 (5).
42. Article 58.
43. Article 54, *Constitution of the Islamic Republic of Pakistan, 1956.*
44. Article 73 (4), *Constitution of the Islamic Republic of Pakistan, 1973.*
45. Ibid., Article 73 (5)
46. Article 66 (4).
47. Article 75.
48. Article 83 (2).
49. Article 84.
50. *Nawa-i-Waqt,* 16 October 1979.
51. *Sadaqat,* 17 October 1979.
52. See editorial, *Nawa-i-Waqt,* 7 July 1980.
53. *The Muslim,* 17 October 1979.
54. *Dawn,* 20 November 1979.
55. *Pakistan Times,* 25 March 1981.
56. Ibid.
57. Rafique Akhtar, ed., *Pakistan Year Book 1987-88*, Karachi: East and West Publishing Company, 1988, Karachi, p. 234.

58. Ibid.
59. Ibid., p. 235.
60. *The Muslim,* 3 March 1985.
61. Ibid., 5 March 1985
62. Ibid., See editorial.
63. Ibid., 9 September 1985.
64. Ibid., 11 September 1985.
65. Ibid.
66. Ibid., 16 October 1985. See article by Professor Khurshid Ahmad.
67. Ibid.
68. Ibid., 30 September 1985.
69. Ibid., 7 October 1985.
70. Ibid.
71. Ibid., 16 October 1985.
72. Ibid.
73. Ibid.
74. Ibid., 18 October 1985.
75. 'Supreme Court upholds Eighth Amendment', *Dawn,* 13 January 1997. Also see 'Pakistan Acts to Cut Power of President', *New York Times,* 2 April 1997.
76. *Frontier Post,* 1 and 2 July 1997.
77. Nasim Zehra, *The News,* 2 July 1997.
78. Ibid.

3

THE POLITICAL PARTIES

Political parties are integral to the democratic process. No democracy can function effectively without political parties. However, the mere presence of political parties does not ensure smooth functioning of democracy. The quality of political leadership and how the political parties discharge their tasks go a long way to shape the nature and direction of the political system. Unless the political parties engage in interest articulation and aggregation, electoral exercise and governance within a democratic framework, and respect the democratic and constitutional norms, these [political parties] may adversely affect governance and political and economic management.

Pakistan began with a dominant party system. The Muslim League was the dominant party in the early years of independence while several small parties existed in the legislature and the outside. Subsequently, it gradually changed into a multi-party system with the attendant problems of this system. Most of these parties having weak organizational structures, often fall victim to internal dissension and conflicts. Invariably, there is a strong imprint of the leadership on these parties who run these with the help of a small group of loyalists, often in a personalized manner. These political parties have also suffered due to periodic disruption of the democratic process by the imposition of martial laws when the political parties are either disallowed to function, or severe restrictions are imposed on their activities. Pakistan's return to democracy in 1985 has provided yet another opportunity to the political parties and the, leaders to perform their role in strengthening democracy and consolidating the national identity. It is reassuring that despite difficulties and problems these political parties have stayed on the democratic course. However, there is a need to improve their performance. The following discussion provides a historical sketch of the major political parties and how these have performed in the political domain over time.

PAKISTAN MUSLIM LEAGUE

The Muslim League, founded in 1906, is the oldest political party in Pakistan. It waged the Muslim struggle for independence, changed the political map of the subcontinent, and created Pakistan. Therefore, it enjoyed a unique position in Pakistan and was the natural heir to state power at the time of independence. The Muslims had great emotional attachment with the Muslim League, because its name was synonymous with the Muslim liberation movement. This phenomenon had an impact on post-independence politics; several political parties which emerged on the political scene in Pakistan used the word 'Muslim League' in their names. Among them were: the Jinnah Muslim League, the Awami (Muslim) League, the Qayyum Muslim League, and the Quaid-i-Azam Muslim League.

After independence, the Muslim League formed governments at the centre and in the provinces. During its long spell of power (1947–54), it enjoyed undisputed supremacy in politics.[1] However, it could not evolve a viable and comprehensive programme for the amelioration of the lot of the masses. Most of its leaders were interested more in capturing offices than serving the nation. They indulged in petty intrigues against one another and were largely responsible for damaging the prestige of the party and the democratic process in the country. Their differences and rivalries undermined the organization and discipline of the party and caused its fragmentation; some of its members left the party to set up new parties that challenged its pre-eminent position.

The Pakistan Muslim League (PML) came into being when the All-India Muslim League council, in its last session at

Karachi in December 1947, decided to bifurcate the party into two parties: one for Pakistan and the other for the Indian Union. In February the following year, the PML council adopted a party constitution which debarred ministers from holding any office in the party organization. When Jinnah's name was proposed for the office of president, he declined to accept the offer because as head of the state, he observed, he would have to keep the balance among all the parties. As a result, the PML could not benefit from the Quaid's leadership. Chaudhri Khaliquzzaman was elected the chief organizer and was assigned the responsibility of organizing the party at the primary, city, district, and provincial levels.[2] He launched an enrolment campaign, established a party machine, and managed elections of new office-bearers, who, in turn, elected Khaliquzzaman as the president of the PML. He lacked the Quaid-i-Azam's stature. He 'was not even his pale shadow,'[3] and was unable to run the party as a coherent and effective machine. He patronized his supporters in the provinces and became a party to their intrigues and feuds. As internal divisions sharpened, the PML began to lose its momentum. This poor state of affairs climaxed in his unceremonious resignation from the presidentship after a demonstration by the refugees in front of his residence in Karachi.

After Khaliquzzaman's exit, the PML amended the party constitution to pave way for the election of Liaquat Ali Khan, first prime minister of Pakistan, as its president. The amendment was a smooth affair; he was easily elected president in October 1950.[4] But even Liaquat Ali Khan could not retrieve the PML's stature and prestige. Several reasons accounted for this. First, he was too busy in governmental affairs to pay much attention to party affairs. Second, he was exposed to criticism as prime minister which he had to own as the PML president.[5] Third, the unification of the party's high command with the government brought to an end the separate identity of the party and made it 'a handmaiden of the government'.[6] Fourth, Liaquat Ali Khan encouraged factional intrigues in the provinces by supporting his friends against their rivals who were known for their devotion and loyalty to the organization. For instance, he patronized Mian Mumtaz Daultana in Punjab and Khan Abdul Qayyum Khan in the NWFP, which resulted in the exit of sincere workers like Iftikhar Husain Khan of Mamdot, Pir Aminul Hasanat of Manki Sharif and others from the party. They formed their own parties. Such divisions in the party adversely affected its popularity and reduced its political support-base.

After the assassination of Liaquat Ali Khan, Khwaja Nazimuddin succeeded him as the prime minister. He was later elected president of the PML after an amendment in the party constitution to facilitate his election. Nazimuddin was essentially a weak person who showed little interest in running the League. He did not even nominate all the members of its Working Committee for a long time. Besides, the party was never properly consulted on national affairs. Gradually, it became so weak that when Governor-General Ghulam Muhammad dismissed the Nazimuddin ministry in 1953 and appointed Muhammad Ali Bogra as prime minister, the latter was readily accepted by the PML as its leader. This exposed the hollowness of the party organization and shook the confidence of the people in its capabilities.

In January 1956, the PML council again amended the party constitution to re-introduce the clause debarring ministers from holding party offices. Sardar Abdur Rub Nishtar was elected its president. A trusted lieutenant of the Quaid, he was widely respected for his integrity and devotion to the national cause. He restored the authority of the party and its president; he would often remind the League ministers that 'the people and the party were the real fountainhead of power'.[7] On his death, Khan Abdul Qayyum Khan succeeded him as the PML president. Once in that office, Qayyum Khan lived up to his reputation as a strong man. He kept up a firm control on the activities of the PML members in the assemblies,[8] and brought the PML parliamentary groups firmly under the control of the party organization. Infused with a new spirit, the party regained much of its lost popularity. Qayyum was still the League president when martial law was declared in October 1958, imposing a ban on the political parties.

After the lifting of martial law and the enactment of the Political Parties Act in July 1962, the political parties were revived. The PML was split up into two parties in the process of revival; the pro-Ayub leaders of the Muslim League held a party convention in Karachi to revive the Muslim League, later known as the Convention Muslim League (ConML). The Leaguers who opposed Ayub Khan and his presidential system summoned the meeting of the council of the Muslim League at Dhaka to revive the party. This party was later known as the Council Muslim League (CML). Both claimed to be the real PML and adopted constitutions modelled on the 1948 party constitution.

Convention Muslim League: Chaudhri Khaliquzzaman, who was appointed chief organizer of the Convention Muslim League (ConML), organized the party throughout the country. By the time it was formally organized, Ayub Khan decided to assume its presidentship which he did in December 1963 and held that office till December 1970. The ConML was actually his handmaiden and revolved around his personality and policies. Although it had regular party branches and offices in wards, cities, districts, divisions, and provinces, it could not evoke popular support. But, aided by the Basic Democrats, landlords, and industrialists, and patronized by the government, it wielded comfortable majorities in the National Assembly and the two assemblies of East and West Pakistan till Ayub Khan's downfall. A large number of its leaders and activists were self-seekers interested only in political power and material rewards; there was hardly any commitment to ideology or democracy except in rhetoric. The Ayub regime made sure that they were kept happy by making state patronage available to the members of the National and Provincial assemblies and other supporters. Some of the common material rewards included, *inter alia*, route permits for running inter-city transport, industrial and commercial licences, contracts for government projects, and recruitment to government jobs on their recommendations.

The ConML had no constructive programme of its own for the welfare of the people. Its basic goal was to extend unconditional support to Ayub Khan's dictatorial system. As the 'King's Party', it projected and praised the government policies; in fact, it took decisions after consulting the government. Its weak support-base was exposed when the public revolted against the Ayub regime and the whole country was engulfed in agitation in the last quarter of 1968. Massive street demonstrations against the constitution, the system of Basic Democracies, Ayub's dictatorial rule and economic policies led to breakdown of the law and order machinery. The ConML was unable to neutralize the agitation; its leaders and activists were the targets of the public wrath and others disowned their links with the party.

With Ayub Khan's exit from power in March 1969, the ConML's fortunes fell sharply. Many of its leaders and workers left the party and those who stayed were divided among themselves. It could neither evolve a new attractive political programme nor present a charismatic leadership. Its identification with Ayub Khan, which was once a source of strength, became its main liability. Finally, Ayub Khan resigned from the presidentship. Fazlul Qadir Chaudhury, a former Bengali federal minister and Speaker of the National Assembly, succeeded him first as a nominated and then as its elected president. Under his leadership, the party actively participated in the December 1970 general elections. The salient features of its manifesto were: a federal system of government with defence, currency, foreign affairs, foreign trade, and inter-wing communications as the central subjects; decentralization of economic structure and provincial autonomy; nationalization of basic industries, banks, and insurance companies; and fixation of ceiling on landholding at 250 acres.

It put up thirty-one and ninety-three candidates from West and East Pakistan respectively for the National Assembly but it could win only two seats, both in Punjab. Fazlul Qadir Chaudhury himself was defeated. After the military crackdown in East Pakistan, its Bengali leadership co-operated with the martial law regime and later, after the establishment of Bangladesh, suffered at the hands of the Mukti Bahini for their support to Pakistan. In (West) Pakistan, it stayed with the Opposition till it was merged with the CML to form a broader party.

Council Muslim League: Like the ConML, the CML claimed to be the real PML. To be fair to its claims, the council meeting at Dhaka in 1962, at which it was formally launched, was more representative of the League opinion than the Leaguers' convention in Karachi. More League councillors and prominent Muslim Leaguers, including the veterans of the independence movement, participated in the council's Dhaka meeting than the Karachi convention. Khwaja Nazimuddin, a Leaguer of long standing and a former prime minister, was elected the CML president who led the party till his death in October 1964. Sayyid Muhammad Afzal, a Leaguer from East Pakistan, succeeded him in that office. Mian Mumtaz Daultana took over as president in 1967. During the 1970 election campaign, he submitted his resignation as president on health grounds more than once but was persuaded to withdraw his resignation. The party manifesto for the 1970 general elections advocated enforcement of the 1956 Constitution with a bicameral legislature at the Centre; maximum provincial autonomy with parity between the two wings; social and economic justice based on Islamic principles; nationalization of banks, insurance institutions, and basic industries such as iron and steel, machine tools, chemical, and fertilizers; fixation of land ceiling at 250 irrigated acres and 500 non-irrigated acres; enforcement of Quranic laws; independent foreign policy; and withdrawal from the defence pacts, namely the SEATO and CENTO. The performance of CML in the elections was as bad as that of the other Leagues. It put up fifty and sixty-nine candidates for the National Assembly from East and West Pakistan, respectively, but it could capture only seven seats. All these seven seats were in Punjab, including that of Mumtaz Daultana who defeated a PPP candidate by a small margin.

Qayyum Muslim League: The Qayyum Muslim League (QML) was one of the splinter groups of the PML. The problem with the PML was that after the death of the Quaid-i-Azam, it could not keep so many 'strong leaders' in its fold. Mutual jealousies, desire to build personal support-base in the party and grab the top slot in the party at any cost made it impossible for them to work in harmony with one another. Some of them left the party to set up their own political organizations.

A senior leader of the Muslim League, Abdul Qayyum Khan, established his own faction during the course of the anti-Ayub agitation (1968–69). This came to be known as the Qayyum Muslim League (QML). He had been in the vanguard of the freedom struggle and, in the post-independence period, had served as the chief minister of the NWFP (1947–53) and then as a minister in the federal cabinet (1953–54). When martial law was proclaimed in 1958, he was president of the PML, and suffered imprisonment under Ayub Khan's government. As the Ayub regime weakened, he again became active in politics.

The QML participated in the 1970 elections and its manifesto demanded: nationalization of heavy industries; a truly democratic constitution, providing safeguards against any violation of its provisions and ensuring complete democracy and its continuity; provision of basic necessities of life, i.e., food, clothes, shelter, medical facilities, and education to all Pakistanis; rationalization of the structure and management of public sector enterprises; check on the multiplication of ownership in the industrial sector; review of land ceilings; compulsory education; ban on the use of alcohol by Muslims; and giving due share to minorities; etc.

The QML put up 132 candidates for the National Assembly from all over the country, out of which only nine were elected; seven of them, including Qayyum Khan and Yusuf Khattak, were from the NWFP. When the Pakistan People's Party (PPP) assumed power in December 1971, Qayyum Khan joined Bhutto's cabinet as the Interior Minister, which eclipsed his political image and relegated him and his party into a role secondary to that of the PPP. However, before the general elections of 1977, Qayyum Khan dissociated himself from the cabinet. The QML put up thirty-seven candidates for the National Assembly seats, out of which only one got elected. Its programme for these elections was similar to that of 1970. However, the QML became insignificant as the election campaign focused on two forces, the PPP and the Pakistan National Alliance (PNA).

The QML derived its strength from its founder and mentor, Qayyum Khan. After his death, it was pushed to the background.

MERGERS AND SPLITS IN THE MUSLIM LEAGUE

After the assumption of power by the PPP in December 1971, Mumtaz Daultana (CML leader) accepted the post of Pakistan's ambassador in England, excluding himself from active politics. Many other prominent CML members also aligned with the PPP or became inactive. Meanwhile, in 1972, the CML and the ConML decided to merge into one party with Hasan A. Sheikh as president and Malik Muhammad Qasim as general secretary. Mumtaz Daultana and Sardar Shaukat Hayat disagreed with this decision and kept themselves aloof from the new party. By 1973, in a bid to revitalize the reunited PML, the Pir of Pagaro was elected as its president. He activated the party and vehemently opposed the PPP government led by Zulfikar Ali Bhutto. It could not develop a strong popular base because of the feudal base of the key leaders and the policy of the PPP government to place curbs on political activities. However, it enjoyed the support of landlords and some well-known politicians.

In the 1977 elections, the PML led by the Pir of Pagaro joined the nine-party electoral alliance, Pakistan National Alliance (PNA), and played an important role in the PNA protest movement against the rigging in the elections and in forcing Bhutto to negotiate with the Opposition; this role has been discussed below in a separate section. After Bhutto's exit from power and assumption of power by General Ziaul Haq, the PML

(Pagaro Group) co-operated with the martial law regime. This perspective was not shared by all Muslim Leaguers. One group of the PML, led by Khwaja Khairuddin, opposed any co-operation with General Zia's military government. This group, called the Muslim League (Khairuddin), joined the Movement for the Restoration of Democracy (MRD), a broad-based alliance of different political parties, including the PPP, Tehrik-i-Istaqlal, National Democratic Party (NDP), and Pakistan Democratic Party (PDP), demanding the removal of martial law and the holding of general elections for setting up representative government.

In 1985, President Ziaul Haq decided to restore democratic order by holding non-party elections to the National and Provincial assemblies in February. Although the candidates were neither allowed to use party symbols nor could they announce their party affiliations, they did severe their party links. Before the convening of the assemblies, President Zia issued the Revival of the Constitution Order 1985, which introduced a large number of changes in the 1973 Constitution which was gradually restored. The elected civilian governments began to function from 23 March 1985, but martial law was not withdrawn until 30 December 1985. General Zia nominated Mohammad Khan Junejo as the prime minister who subsequently took a vote of confidence from the National Assembly. When the National Assembly and the Senate began to function, the two houses automatically divided into an official group, headed by Junejo, and a non-official group, which acted as the Opposition. Now, restoration of political parties became imperative because a parliamentary system could not function without them. Since the official group mostly consisted of the Muslim Leaguers, Junejo co-opted the PML (Pagaro) as the official political party. Junejo became its leader. The example set at the Centre was followed in the provinces; the four chief ministers came to lead PML parties in the provincial assemblies. Thus, the PML came into power indirectly, claiming majorities at the Centre and in the provinces. Its leaders spread its political tentacles all over the country. Party offices were opened and members were enrolled followed by party elections. Despite sincere efforts, the PML could not form a solid political base at the mass level except in Punjab, although it had an egalitarian five-point programme. Other factions of the PML stayed away. Later, the Pir of Pagaro decided to revive his faction again as a separate entity.

The PML led by Junejo rightly deserves credit for the withdrawal of martial law and emergency as well as restoration of fundamental rights and the 1973 Constitution. A new democratic era re-started in Pakistan from January 1986, after the lifting of martial law in the country. Civil liberties were restored and freedom of expression was ensured. The Junejo government attached great importance to developmental activities such as construction of roads, hospitals, schools, and rural development. Its record on this front is quite impressive. It made a useful contribution to national political life in another area. It introduced a good number of young and energetic leaders who proved a better substitute for the old League leadership. This group was headed by Mian Nawaz Sharif, then chief minister of Punjab.

President Zia dismissed the Junejo government in May 1988. The provincial governments were also dismissed and replaced with the Zia loyalists. Zia launched a systematic propaganda campaign against the ousted PML government to justify his action. His move to demolish the democratic system that he had himself created was considered the 'most unkindest cut of all'. His action divided the PML into two groups: PML (Junejo Group) that sympathized with the dismissed prime minister while PML (Fida Group), headed by Fida Muhammad Khan and supported by Mian Nawaz Sharif, sided with Zia. A total break-up of the party was temporarily averted by Zia's sudden death in an air crash on 17 August 1988. After his death, both the factions united and elected Junejo as the PML president to participate in the general elections under an electoral alliance with a couple of other parties, called the Islami Jamhoori Ittehad (IJI). In its 1988 manifesto, the PML called for the creation of justice; ensuring equal opportunities for all citizens; provincial autonomy consistent with national integrity; rural development; eradication of poverty and illiteracy; distribution of evacuee land among the landless cultivators; incentives leading to industrialization; creation of job opportunities; provision of energy, better communications and simpler tax system; provision of plots to the homeless and small income groups; independent foreign policy; and strong defence for the country.

The major set-back in the October 1988 elections was the defeat of its President, Junejo, its former president; Pir of Pagaro; and its general secretary, Iqbal Ahmad Khan. However, out of the total number of seats won by the IJI, the PML had the largest number of seats. Its poor performance was partly because of its identification with Zia and Punjab as against the PPP's appeal to Sindhi nationalism, its identification with Bhutto, and its long struggle against the Zia regime. But soon PML posed a serious challenge to the PPP and emerged as a major contender for political power. Its campaign against the PPP government, whose performance was very poor, resulted in the dismissal of Benazir government and the convening of new elections. The PML had learnt its lessons and made the IJI more cohesive. In the 1990 elections, it worked for adjustments on seats within the IJI as well as with parties outside the alliance to ensure that the anti-PPP vote was not divided. The result was that the IJI had the largest number of seats in the National Assembly. Within the IJI, the PML was the dominant party, and its Punjab chief, Mian Nawaz Sharif, was elected the leader of the IJI parliamentary party and asked to form the government at the federal level. His performance as the chief minister, especially in the economic field, was better than his predecessor.

In 1990 general elections, the IJI was able to defeat the PPP and win a majority in the National Assembly, enabling Nawaz Sharif to become the prime minister in November 1990. During Nawaz Sharif's prime ministership, the PML intra-party differences re-surfaced. However, an open rift was avoided in Junejo's life-time, but on his death in March 1993, the pro-Junejo Leaguers not only criticized Nawaz Sharif's style of governance but also began to side with his opponents. Later on, they played a critical role in bringing down the Nawaz Sharif government by siding with President Ghulam Ishaq Khan. The PML then broke up into two parties: PML (Nawaz or N); and PML (Junejo or J). In the 1993 elections, the former party fielded its own candidates and made some electoral adjustments with other parties, while the latter party aligned with the PPP. After the elections, the PML (J) leaders joined the Benazir-headed government at the Centre, and one of its members, Mian Manzoor Wattoo, formed the PML (J)-PPP coalition government in Punjab. The PML (N) in co-operation with the ANP could form a coalition ministry only in the NWFP, which was headed by Pir Sabir Shah, a Muslim Leaguer, but even that was brought down in 1994 by the PPP through questionable means.

The PML (N) now decided to consolidate its base under Nawaz Sharif's leadership. After a long time, it was re-organized methodically at the grass roots throughout the country. Its leaders negated the impression that they could not survive in the Opposition. They were willing to undergo suffering. Many of them were detained on cooked up charges and were maltreated under detention. Among those who suffered were Nawaz Sharif's father, his two brothers, and a nephew. Besides, more than 140 cases were instituted against him and his family. In response, the party launched a massive movement against the Benazir government, including the *Karwan-i-Nijat* (deliverance march), in which its leaders and workers faced severe repression. Although the movement did not bring about any immediate positive results, it solidified the party ranks and discredited the PPP and its government. The PML (N) took full advantage of the PPP leadership's incompetence and mistakes. The corruption in the PPP government at the top was fully exploited and widely publicized in and outside the country. The PML (N) broadened its support-base and worked for co-operative relationships with smaller parties in various regions. When President Farooq Leghari finally dismissed the Benazir government, the PML (N) was ready to face the elections.

In the 1997 elections, the PML (N) fielded its own candidates to the National Assembly and the provincial assemblies. It swept the polls to the National Assembly, winning 134 seats; and to the Punjab assembly, securing 211 seats. It was the largest party in the NWFP, and it improved upon its past performance in Sindh and Baluchistan. The PML (J) was virtually wiped out of the political scene. After the elections, Mian Nawaz Sharif formed the government at the Centre, and Mian Shahbaz Sharif, Sardar Mehtab Khan Abbasi and Liaquat Ali Jatoi, the PML (N) leaders, formed governments in Punjab, the NWFP and Sindh respectively. In Baluchistan, Sardar Akhtar Mengal initially formed the coalition ministry in which the PML (N) members were his partners. Recently, a PML (N) leader, Jan Muhammad Jamali, has succeeded him as chief minister. Soon after assumption of office, the Nawaz Sharif government repealed clause 58(2)B of the constitution under which the presidents had dismissed various governments and dissolved the assemblies. Another important legislation passed by the National Assembly was designed to prevent floor crossing.

The PML (N) government re-emerged as a political force with roots in all the provinces of Pakistan. Some other factions of the PML persisted but their electoral support was minimal.

PAKISTAN DEMOCRATIC PARTY

The Pakistan Democratic Party (PDP) came into existence in June 1969 after the merger of four political parties, namely the Nizam-i-Islam Party, the Awami League (Nawabzada Nasrullah Group), the National Democratic Front (NDF), and the Justice Party. At the time of merger, these parties were headed by Chaudhri Muhammad Ali, Nawabzada Nasrullah Khan, Nurul Amin, and Air Marshal (Retd.) Asghar Khan respectively. They were noted for their moderate views and a strong belief in the unity and solidarity of Pakistan. Its first convention elected Nurul Amin as the president and Nasim Hasan as secretary-general. Later on, Nawabzada Nasrullah Khan succeeded Nurul Amin as its President. The PDP aimed at creating a democratic social order based on Islamic values and principles of justice, equity, freedom, universal brotherhood and human dignity in conformity with the Holy Qur'an and Sunnah.[9]

The PDP had a good start but it soon ran into difficulties as some of the founding leaders fell apart. In November 1969, Chaudhri Muhammad Ali retired from politics on health grounds, and on 2 December 1969, Asghar Khan announced his withdrawal from politics because, according to him, the purpose for which he had entered politics had been achieved, although he soon launched another organization, the Tehrik-i-Istaqlal. Some other leaders and workers also left the PDP which weakened it even before it could show its strength in any electoral exercise.

The PDP maintained a national outlook at a time when several other parties had adopted regional approach to national problems. It was a broad-based party with a liberal political perspective and its membership was drawn mostly from lawyers, old political workers, and ex-servicemen. In its 1970 election manifesto, the party called for the grant of fundamental rights, acceptance of the 1956 Constitution with certain modifications, pursuance of an independent foreign policy, separation of the judiciary from the executive, withdrawal from the SEATO and CENTO, compulsory teaching of the Holy Qur'an and Islamiat to Muslim children, elimination of social and economic disparities, nationalization of all big industries, abolition of the *jagirdari* (feudal) system, and fixation of land ceiling at 150 acres of irrigated land. It nominated eighty-one and twenty-one candidates for the National Assembly seats from East and West Pakistan respectively, but only one of its leader, Nurul Amin, could win his seat from East Pakistan.

During 1971–77, the PDP under the leadership of Nawabzada Nasrullah Khan, played an active role in the Opposition ranks. It was extremely critical of the PPP government's undemocratic and authoritarian political management. The real asset of the party was the stature of its leaders, especially that of Nawabzada Nasrullah Khan, who enjoyed much respect both among the leaders and the masses. However, its electoral support was always very limited. The PDP joined the PNA for the 1977 general elections. Its leaders were in the forefront of the election campaign. When the PNA refused to accept the election results due to the charge of rigging of the elections by the ruling party, it took active part in the agitation against the Bhutto government demanding fresh elections. Its leader, Nawabzada Nasrullah Khan, played an important role in the movement and the subsequent negotiations between the government and the PNA for resolving the political crisis.

After the imposition of martial law by General Ziaul Haq, the PNA joined the government and the PDP got representation in the federal cabinet. Later, the PDP left the government and distanced itself from the martial law authorities. Subsequently, the PDP joined the anti-Zia political alliance, called the Movement for the Restoration of Democracy (MRD) and Nawabzada Nasrullah Khan was arrested while participating in the MRD agitation against the military government.

After President Zia's death, the PDP actively participated in the 1988 elections. Its manifesto called for a welfare society based on the teachings of the Qur'an; provincial autonomy, fundamental rights for all citizens, equal opportunities for women, complete freedom of the press, non-aligned foreign policy, support to the cause of Palestinian Muslims, and a tension-free South Asia. But, as in the past, it did not perform well in the elections. It could win only one seat in the National Assembly, that of its president, Nawabzada Nasrullah Khan whose success was due to his personal influence in his ancestral area. In the provincial elections, it could secure only two seats in Punjab. Nawabzada Nasrullah Khan contested the presidential elections (December 1988) against Ghulam Ishaq Khan, but was defeated.

The PDP could not enhance its influence in the subsequent elections. When the PML (N) coalition came to power after the 1990 elections, the PDP campaigned against the government from the platforms of the National Democratic Alliance (NDA) and the All Parties Conference. In the 1993 elections, the NDA co-operated with the PPP. It put up eight candidates to the National Assembly, twelve to the Punjab Assembly, and one each to the NWFP assembly and Baluchistan assembly. It could secure only one seat in the National Assembly and two seats in the Punjab assembly, all of whom belonged to the PDP. For the first time, Nawabzada Nasrullah Khan accepted an official assignment in the PPP government; it was the chairmanship of the Kashmir Committee with the status of a federal minister. In that capacity, he undertook foreign tours for mobilization of international support for Pakistan's case on the Kashmir dispute. The Opposition led by Nawaz Sharif was critical of his performance. In the February 1997 elections, the PDP could win only one seat to the Punjab assembly. Since then, with the Opposition in complete disarray, the PDP has not been able to carve out a role for itself. The party continues to survive because of Nawabzada Nasrullah.

TEHRIK-I-ISTAQLAL

Air Marshal (Retd.) Muhammad Asghar Khan, former chief of Pakistan air force and Pakistan International Airlines (PIA), is the founder-president of the Tehrik-i-Istaqlal. He had commanded the Pakistan air force from 1957 to 1965 and was considered largely responsible for developing it into an effective striking power. He was respected in the military circles and in public for his integrity, professionalism, and clean record.

Asghar Khan was shrewd enough to enter politics at the most appropriate time. In October 1968, the movement against Ayub Khan was gradually picking up pace. The student and labour agitation and demonstrations against the government had become a regular feature. Bhutto was leading this countrywide agitation; his arrest on 13 November 1968, under the emergency regulations, created a political vacuum. The old political leadership, with whom the people were generally disillusioned, failed to take the initiative. Against this political backdrop, Asghar Khan entered politics. Announcing his decision to enter politics at a press conference in Lahore on 17 November, he observed that he had been watching the deteriorating political, social, and economic conditions of the country for some time. Graft, corruption, nepotism, and administrative incompetence had influenced the lives of millions of his countrymen. The increasing social inequality and economic disparity had widened the gap between the rich and the poor. Freedom of speech and press had been suppressed.

Asghar Khan's decision was hailed both in East and West Pakistan. He went on a fifteen-day tour of Punjab and the NWFP, followed by an eleven-day tour of East Pakistan. He was accorded a warm welcome everywhere. His entry into politics accelerated the tempo of the movement against Ayub Khan, which finally forced him to surrender before public pressure. The round table conference, to which all the major politicians including Asghar Khan were invited, could not arrive at any agreement for the transfer of power and Ayub Khan had to quit the office of president. The anti-Ayub movement, according to the *Newsweek,* suddenly raised Asghar Khan to the status of a national hero. He was hailed as the 'president-in-waiting'. Even the government-controlled press viewed him as a possible successor to Ayub Khan.[10] Subsequently, he was unable to maintain this 'overnight' popularity because he lacked political skill, training, and ability to consolidate his initial success and build on it.

Asghar Khan launched his own political party, the Justice Party, on 13 March 1969. Declining to describe it as a rightist or a leftist party, he commented that 'its main aims would be to achieve unity of the people in working towards the achievement of Islamic values and the creation of a society in which the poorer classes could live honourably with their basic human needs fulfilled'. Justifying the need for a new political party, he observed: 'There are difficulties with [every] existing party. You have to defend its past which is difficult in Pakistan. You have to believe in its programme and no party in Pakistan has ever made any effort to implement its programme.'[11]

After the fall of Ayub Khan, four political parties including the Justice Party, decided to merge themselves into a new party, the PDP. Asghar Khan chaired the manifesto committee of the new party. The PDP, at its first convention, elected Nurul Amin as president and Nasim Hasan as secretary-general. Asghar Khan, who felt sidelined by the first convention of the party and was frustrated by its performance, decided to quit politics on 2 December 1969, observing that the objective for which he had entered politics had been achieved after Yahya's announcement calling for general elections in October 1970. But he could not stay away from politics for too long. He was young, ambitious, energetic with a desire to make his mark in the political field. He once again returned to politics and formed a new political party, the Tehrik-i-Istaqlal, which vowed to uphold democratic and Islamic values. He toured the country extensively to establish contacts at the mass level. An energetic and untiring person, he addressed numerous political meetings and succeeded in extending the Tehrik's tentacles in the masses. Unlike many other political parties, the Tehrik opened its offices all over the country and organized party elections. But despite his excellent start and popular image, Asghar Khan was defeated by a PPP candidate in the 1970 general elections from a constituency in Rawalpindi.

During Bhutto's rule (1971–77), the Tehrik-i-Istaqlal was in the forefront of the Opposition. None of the ex-military men who ventured into politics 'survived the breaking in period.' Their 'disciplinarian training' was 'responsible for their early disenchantment from politics which needs a patient understanding of the public demands.'[12] Asghar Khan was an exception; he persevered. He challenged Bhutto's authoritarianism and criticized the Bhutto government's policies at a time when one had to pay a heavy cost for such acts. By doing so, he acquired the reputation of being a 'brave and bold' politician. The dissension in the PPP ranks further helped him, because the disillusioned PPP politicians joined the Tehrik after resigning from the PPP. Among them were such figures as Mahmud Ali Qasuri, J.A. Rahim, and Aitzaz Ahsan who were all known for their calibre. In fact, all the progressive politicians perceived in the Tehrik an alternative to the PPP, because of its democratic, socialistic, and progressive posture.

Ideologically, a left-of-the-centre party, the Tehrik gathered in its ranks various ideological-cum-political elements comprising technical socialists, moderates, rightists, and former bureaucrats. In its programme, the party advocated economic amelioration, fair distribution of wealth, Islamic justice and social order, and independent foreign policy. During the 1977 elections, it joined the PNA against the PPP. It played an important role in the PNA election campaign and the subsequent protest movement against rigging. The PNA-PPP tussle ended in a military takeover. When General Ziaul Haq constituted a federal cabinet representing the armed forces and the PNA, the Tehrik-i-Istaqlal refused to join it and withdrew from the PNA. The Tehrik resumed its role in the Opposition when President Zia did not honour his promise to hold elections in November 1979. It demanded withdrawal of martial law, fresh general elections, and restoration of the 1973 Constitution. The Tehrik joined the MRD and fully participated in its activities, although Asghar remained under house arrest for several years.

The Tehrik boycotted the 1985 non-party elections in pursuance of the decision by the MRD, but actively participated in the 1988 elections. In its manifesto, the Tehrik promised the abolition of the *jagirdari* system, allotment of land to landless tenants, fixation of land ceiling at 125 acres of irrigated land, inexpensive justice, religious freedom, free press, elimination of corruption, self-reliance, unemployment allowance, and non-aligned foreign policy. Unexpectedly, the Tehrik did not fare well on the election front in spite of its long history of political struggle and well-organized party structure. In developing countries, charismatic leadership, influential candidates and undue exploitation of political issues play more important part than party manifestoes in the elections. The Tehrik, perhaps, lacked these qualities. It could not win any seat in the National Assembly or any of the provincial assemblies; thus, it failed to enter the parliamentary arena. However, Asghar Khan reiterated his resolve to continue his struggle outside the assemblies.

In the 1990 elections, the Tehrik came closer to the PPP for electoral purposes. Asghar Khan himself was pitted against

Nawaz Sharif in a constituency from Lahore. But the party could not win a single seat. The Tehrik remained with the Opposition (PPP) and participated in the long march that was organized against the Nawaz Sharif government in November 1992. However, it soon moved away from the PPP, and when Benazir co-operated with President Ghulam Ishaq Khan in the dismissal of Prime Minister Nawaz Sharif, there was a total break with the PPP. It then sought co-operation with the PML (N). However, in the 1993 elections as well, its performance was bad. It won only two seats in the Punjab assembly. It did not take part in the 1997 elections, Asghar Khan calling on the caretaker government to hold a referendum on the issue of election or accountability first. Although it is now part of the Pakistan National Conference, its role in politics, electoral or otherwise, is very limited. It is too much identified with the personality of Asghar Khan and has never made any serious effort to organize itself at the grassroots. Keeping in view its past performance and its present state, it is not expected to make much impact on the course of politics in Pakistan.

PAKISTAN PEOPLE'S PARTY

The Pakistan People's Party (PPP) was founded by Zulfikar Ali Bhutto in Lahore in November 1967. Bhutto had held ministerial positions in the Ayub regime; as foreign minister, he was largely responsible for the establishment of friendly relations with the Peoples Republic of China. After his exit from Ayub's cabinet in 1966, he spent some time in thinking about his future strategy and then decided to launch his independent political career. Being unsatisfied with the programmes and performance of the existing political parties, Bhutto decided to set up a new party called the Pakistan People's Party, often called the People's Party.

The PPP is a left-of-the-centre party with a socialistic socio-economic programme and greater emphasis on participatory governance. Initially, despite Bhutto's charismatic personality, it could not attract membership of high calibre and good repute. But its young devoted workers opened offices and introduced its programme in cities and towns all over the country. Its programme of food, clothing, and shelter for everyone; Islamic equality; and nationalization of basic industries and lands; had a mass appeal. Being innovative in popular mobilization and using strong rhetoric promising social transformation, the PPP built popular support in a short period and outstripped the older political parties. It drew strength basically from labourers, workers, students, peasants, and the urban poor.

The PPP's *Foundation Documents* and the manifesto for the 1970 elections talked of transforming Pakistani economy on socialistic lines, emphasizing that only socialism, the highest expression of democracy,[13] could create equal opportunities for all, protect people from exploitation, remove the barrier of class distinctions and privileges, and establish economic and social justice. It promised nationalization of banks, insurance companies and all major industries including sources of supply of energy and means of public transport; land reforms with elimination of exploitation of the cultivators, and strengthening of trade unions. Full fruits of nationalization were to go to the industrial labour and peasants as producers of national income. It wanted an egalitarian democracy wherein all Pakistanis would enjoy equal rights in every sphere of activity. In his television address on the eve of the 1970 general elections, Bhutto promised to wipe out poverty, exploitation, and unemployment, and vowed to integrate the nation which 'is ripped up by dices'. He observed: 'Our ideology is inspiring and Islam, our religion, is the final message of Allah to man. In other words, we certainly possess the wherewithal to overcome the lingering crisis.'[14] In response to the Opposition claim that the PPP was making false promises, he declared: 'These are no empty boasts. I am not making tall promises to capture votes. Such radical changes have taken place in other countries and they can take place in Pakistan as well.'[15]

The PPP put up 119 candidates for the National Assembly from West Pakistan where it secured eighty-eight seats out of

144 seats allocated to Western Pakistan. In the provinces, it won a large majority in Punjab with 113 seats out of 184, and a relatively smaller majority in Sindh with thirty-two seats out of sixty-two. On the whole, it secured approximately 39 per cent of the total votes cast in Punjab and Sindh and 14 per cent and 2 per cent of the total votes polled in the NWFP and Baluchistan respectively. Its unexpected victory was due to its economic programme, loud promises, articulation of the demands of the masses and its dynamic leader, Bhutto, who was well-versed in the art of demagogy. Bhutto had already attracted popular support in the course of his movement against Ayub Khan's dictatorship (1968–69). Furthermore, his tough stand on the Kashmir issue and his expression of identification with the poor made him a popular figure. The PPP successfully created the impression that given the political polarization within Pakistan between the wings, i.e., East and West Pakistan, only Bhutto could deal with Mujib and protect the interests of West Pakistan. Another factor was that the people were completely disillusioned with the old leadership who had ruled the country for a long time but had not solved even the basic problems of the common man. Moreover, PPP's main rivals, the right-wing political parties and groups, were divided among themselves. In comparison, the PPP offered a new, young, and dynamic leadership which stood united behind Bhutto who was making the first bid for power through popular mobilization.

The PPP assumed power on 20 December 1971, when General Yahya Khan resigned after Pakistan lost the war to India. Initially, Bhutto exercised power as the chief martial law administrator (CMLA) and president and on 21 April 1972, when an interim constitution was enforced; martial law was withdrawn, he continued only as president. On 14 August 1973, Bhutto became the prime minister under the 1973 Constitution, which introduced the parliamentary system of government. He served in that capacity till 5 July 1977, when his government was dislodged by an army takeover led by General Ziaul Haq after a widespread street agitation against Bhutto. During the years of Bhutto's power, his media people boasted quite loudly of the commendable achievement of his government but, as a matter of fact, many of these 'achievements' had a 'hollow sound'.[16] The PPP government nationalized banks, insurance companies, and important industries, except textiles, as promised in its election manifesto. These reforms were bound to fail in the absence of trained staff with managerial skills and economic infrastructure. The result was a decline in production and confusion in the economic sector. Private investors were frightened; this adversely affected the industrialization process and led to the draining of capital from the country. Land, labour, and industrial reforms, according to impartial studies of these 'achievements', neither improved the lot of the workers and the common man nor proved beneficial for the government or the country.

The PPP government's greatest achievements were that it inspired confidence in the nation after Pakistan's disintegration in 1971, gave a democratic constitution, and imparted political consciousness and a sense of elation to the common man. But a constitutional document is not sufficient by itself; institutions and processes reflecting the true spirit of the principles underlying the constitution have to be created and allowed to mature. The PPP government failed in this respect because it did not strengthen the political institutions and gradually compromised on the democratic principles of the constitution. For most of the time, the PPP ruled the country under the state of emergency and the people were denied fundamental rights. The control apparatus of state was often used to harass the Opposition leaders and a couple of them were killed by unknown gunmen. The non-PPP provincial governments in Baluchistan and the NWFP were forced out of the office in 1973. Provincial autonomy provided in the constitution was denied to the provinces. There was 'virtually no freedom for the Press.'[17] Even the sanctity of the legislature was violated when the Opposition members were thrown out of the National Assembly by the Federal Security Force and a constitutional amendment was adopted in their absence.[18] Gradually, the traditional leadership consisting of the feudal landlords crept into the party, diluting its revolutionary image. The growing influence of the feudal landlords and other traditionally powerful elite was highly resented by genuine and sincere party workers. As a result, the party suffered from serious internal dissension; different factions got engaged in struggle against each other. In some districts, the competing factions resorted to violence. All this undermined the party organization and performance.

The PPP claimed to be a democratic party but it never held elections of its various tiers. Bhutto nominated its office-bearers and kept a tight control on the party affairs. He himself served as the fountainhead of all powers, appointing and dismissing office-bearers at will. As a result, the party could neither function properly nor develop on democratic lines. There were charges of corruption against the party officials. Even responsible party leaders acknowledged that party men were making money through illegal practices. During a party convention in Sindh on 1 December 1973, it was openly alleged that the PPP ministers were involved in corruption.[19] Such charges seriously damaged the image of the party among the masses.

But Bhutto did not lose faith in the party's potential. He was sure that it could win the next elections. Therefore, on 7 January 1977, he announced the elections to the National and Provincial assemblies to be held in March. The PPP put up 191 candidates for 200 National Assembly seats. The election results indicated a landslide victory for the PPP which won 155 seats against thirty-six seats won by the Opposition alliance, the PNA. The PNA refused to accept the results, alleging that there had been a large-scale rigging, and started a movement against Bhutto and his government. The climax was the removal of the PPP government by the Commander-in-Chief of the Pakistan Army, General Ziaul Haq, who declared martial law in the country. Subsequently, Bhutto was arrested on the charge of murder of a political opponent. He was tried in a regular court of law which convicted him and awarded death sentence which was carried out on 4 April 1979.

After Bhutto's death, the PPP was led by his wife, Nusrat Bhutto, and daughter, Benazir Bhutto. They challenged the martial law government and expressed their determination to take revenge. Despite various instances of defection from the party, it still remained a political force with its support-base intact. Some of the leaders who left the party in eighties included Mumtaz Bhutto, Hafeez Pirzada, and Ghulam Mustafa Jatoi. The PPP leadership launched an Opposition alliance, the Movement for Restoration of Democracy (MRD) in 1981, demanding the holding of elections and restoration of a representative government. However, its efforts were adversely affected by the hijacking of a PIA aircraft by the activists of an underground terrorist organization, Al-Zulfikar, led by two sons of Bhutto. This group was also engaged in a number of other terrorist activities, including killing of some pro-Zia political leaders. Though the PPP tried to distance itself from the activities of this group, but, as Bhutto's sons were running it, the PPP's reputation was adversely affected; it also lost some political support.

The MRD's agitation against the military regime gained momentum in August 1983, but it did not succeed in dislodging the government. This failure created a difficult situation for the PPP; there was a sense of demoralization in the party. Some of the allied parties were also critical of the behaviour of the PPP leadership. The military government was also building a lot of pressure on the Bhutto ladies. Therefore, both Nusrat and Benazir, left the country and did not return till 10 April 1986. On her return, Benazir was accorded a historically enthusiastic welcome in Lahore which demonstrated the party strength. Soon after, the PPP started an agitation to press the demand for mid-term elections, but the movement fizzled out. This failure proved a turning point in its history; thereafter, the party gave up the politics of violence and adopted a long-term strategy for electoral politics.

After the dismissal of Prime Minister Junejo in May 1988 and death of President Zia in an air crash in August 1988, the PPP prepared itself for participating in the general elections. It issued a manifesto which promised to eliminate discrimination, exploitation, corruption, poverty, illiteracy, and social injustice. It supported provincial autonomy, democratic process, self-reliance, and a system of check and balances leading to accountability. It stood for strong defence and free press, and promised to offer material compensation to its workers who had suffered under the Zia regime. Discarding the policy of nationalization as it was implemented in the early 1970s, the 1988 party manifesto recognized the role of the private sector, promising not to nationalize any industry in future. In the elections held in November 1988, it got 37.63 per cent of the total votes polled. Although it managed a majority at the Centre, it could not secure that in any of the provincial assemblies except in Sindh. Subsequently, it was able to form a coalition government in the NWFP. Punjab had an IJI government and Baluchistan had a coalition government which remained hostile to the PPP. At the Centre, PPP formed a coalition government. At the provincial level, it established its own government in Sindh and a coalition government in the NWFP. The PPP coalition governments had to face difficulties in sustaining the partnership with other parties.

The exit of senior members and Benazir's 'uncles' from the party created room for young enthusiasts like Aitzaz Ahsan, Jahangir Badar, Farooq Leghari, and Faisal Saleh Hayat. The press described their style of politics as a game by an 'under-nineteen' team. Their inexperience and immaturity was quite conspicuous in their performance as senior members of the government. The PPP began to exert for complete control in every sphere of governance. This policy was resisted by the provincial governments in Punjab and Baluchistan which were controlled by PPP adversaries. It faced no problem in the NWFP and Sindh which were controlled by the PPP. It appointed its own governor in the NWFP, contrary to its understanding with the Awami National Party (ANP), and clipped the powers of the ANP ministers in the provincial cabinet. The ANP resented this and in protest broke away from the PPP and joined hands with the Opposition. The PPP partners in Sindh, the Mohajir Qaumi

Movement (MQM), was disappointed with the PPP policies regarding the repatriation of the Biharis from Bangladesh to Pakistan and the quota system. The climax was the Pucca Qila firing in Hyderabad; as a result, the MQM also joined the Opposition. Besides, the PPP alienated the bureaucracy, the judiciary, the army, and the president in its bid for complete control. Its tussle with these institutions culminated in the dismissal of the Benazir government by President Ghulam Ishaq Khan on 6 August 1993. Benazir filed a petition against the dismissal of her government, which was turned down by the Supreme Court.

The PPP could not perform well in the 1990 elections partly because it faced a fairly united opposition. The PPP-supported Pakistan Democratic Alliance could win only about four-dozen seats in the National Assembly; and its performance in the provincial elections, except in Sindh, was dismal. It alleged rigging in the elections and harped on that theme for quite some time. Later, it tried to mend fences with smaller parties to organize a broad movement against the Nawaz Sharif government. Its long march in November 1992, had the support of the Tehrik-i-Istaqlal, Jamiat-ul-Ulema-i-Islam (Fazlur Rahman Group/JUI-F), PDP, and several other small parties. It improved its relations with the army and the US. Its biggest climb down was the understanding that it developed with President Ishaq Khan after the latter developed differences with Nawaz Sharif in the first quarter of 1993. Although this irreparably damaged the PPP's popular image, it succeeded in getting the PML (N)-led coalition removed from power. In the 1993 elections, it sought accommodation with the smaller parties to win more seats than the PML (N) in the National Assembly. This policy was successful. After the elections, it formed governments at the Centre and in Sindh, and a PML (J)-PPP coalition government in Punjab. In the presidential election in November 1993, Farooq Ahmad Khan Leghari, one of the PPP leaders, was elected to the office of the president. In March-April 1994, the elected PPP managed to oust the PML (N)-ANP government in the NWFP through a vote of no-confidence.

Benazir began her second tenure as the prime minister with greater confidence and apparently more experience. But she repeated the mistakes of her earlier term. The Opposition was completely alienated because of unnecessary harassment and victimization. Her own brother, Murtaza Bhutto, who had come back to Pakistan and headed the PPP (Shaheed Bhutto Group), was not reconciled. The bureaucracy, the judiciary, the army, and even the president were estranged by her actions. Contrary to Benazir's expectations that PML (N) leadership would submit before repression, the latter mobilized the opposition parties against the government. The climax was reached with the killing of Murtaza Bhutto in police firing in Karachi in September 1996. Since her government remained unable to cope with the political and economic problems, and the law and order situation further deteriorated, it was dismissed by President Leghari on 5 November 1996 on the charges of corruption and incompetence. Her husband, Asif Ali Zardari, was detained for his alleged involvement in the killing of her brother. The overall disappointing performance of the PPP in the 1997 elections, except in Sindh, has brought it down to the status of a small party. With its leadership facing charges of corruption in several cases, the party is in complete disarray and its re-organization presents a formidable task.

NATIONAL AWAMI PARTY, NATIONAL DEMOCRATIC PARTY, AWAMI NATIONAL PARTY

The National Awami Party (NAP) was established on 25 July 1957, as a result of a rift in the Awami League. Maulana Abdul Hamid Bhashani, the East Pakistan chief of the Awami League, differed with the party president, Huseyn Shaheed Suhrawardy, and left the party along with his supporters. At a democratic workers' convention held in Dhaka in July 1957, the NAP was formally launched with Bhashani as the head of its organizing committee. The West Pakistan-based Pakistan National Party (PNP) merged into NAP; the PNP itself was a merger of six minor parties: Azad Pakistan Party, Red Shirts, Sindh Awami Mahaz, Sindh Hari Committee, Wrore Pakhtun, and Ustaman Gal.

The NAP's main objectives were the break-up of One Unit in West Pakistan, introduction of land reforms, regional autonomy, abrogation of defence pacts with the West, and adoption of an independent foreign policy.[20] Its prominent leaders were Khan Abdul Ghaffar Khan, Abdus Samad Achakzai, Prince Abdul Karim, G.M. Syed, and Maulana Bhashani. Among these leaders, Maulana Bhashani had prominently participated in the Pakistan movement. He was respected for his memorable role in the Sylhet referendum which was held to decide whether that area should join Pakistan or India. He had founded the Awami League in East Pakistan and his exit from it was essentially a clash of personalities. He and Suhrawardy apparently differed on two issues: regional autonomy and foreign policy. Although both of them favoured provincial autonomy, Bhashani was dissatisfied with its quantum in the 1956 Constitution. In foreign policy, he wanted immediate withdrawal of Pakistan from the defence pacts. A socialist in his views, he reflected pro-China leanings in international politics. Suhrawardy, leader of the Awami League, was pro-West in his views. The Suez Canal crisis sharpened their differences in 1956, when Suhrawardy did not show much enthusiasm for the Arab cause which, in fact, was indirectly a reflection of his pro-West views.

The NAP had some well-known politicians like Ghaffar Khan, Abdul Samad Achakzai, and Prince Abdul Karim, who had never subscribed to the Muslim League policies. In fact, they had opposed the demand for Pakistan and sided with the Congress in the freedom struggle. Since they had worked actively for a united India, they naturally had problems finding a role in Pakistan's national politics. Another leader, G.M. Syed, a former Muslim Leaguer, was now working for a vague plan of Sindhu Desh, an independent state for Sindhis. All these leaders enjoyed some support in their areas. Over time, they carved out a role for themselves in the post-independence politics by championing the cause of provincial autonomy, and at times clamoured for the establishment of 'Pakhtunistan' for the Pathans, 'Sindhu Desh' for the Sindhis, and 'Baluchistan' for the Baluchis. They were among those who fanned the idea of provincialism in Pakistan. Mian Iftikharuddin once an active Muslim Leaguer from Punjab, also joined them. He was at one time president of the Punjab Muslim League (1948) and a minister in the Mamdot cabinet (1947). Known for his leftist views, he propagated socialism despite the fact that he himself was a big landlord. Thus, the NAP, a forum of regionalist, and socialists, was rightly described as a 'union of malcontents' who were always in the opposition.[21] It stood for the abolition of feudalism, better peasant-proprietor relationship, withdrawal from the defence pacts, and 'reconstruction of the economy through encouragement of national enterprise, and securing the rights of the working class through state intervention'.[22]

The NAP leadership was divided in its approach to various issues. While Bhashani laid more emphasis on the rights of the labourers and peasants, Ghaffar Khan, G.M. Syed, and Achakzai were primarily interested in the dissolution of One Unit. As a result, this patchwork could not continue for long. The party splintered into different factions. One faction was led by Ghaffar Khan who passed on its leadership to his son, Abdul Wali Khan; that faction came to be known as the NAP (Wali). The other faction was called the NAP (Bhashani). These two factions operated as two separate parties. The NAP (Wali) had support in the NWFP and Baluchistan, but it was neither properly organized nor enjoyed popular support in other areas of Pakistan. Its 1970 election manifesto called for socialism, democracy, nationalization of industries, a welfare state, and an independent foreign policy, along with friendly relations with India. These elections brought the NAP to the forefront as an opposition party. During the campaign, Wali Khan tried to mobilize support from the landowning class as well as from the petty bourgeoisie, particularly in areas like Peshawar and Mardan divisions by stressing NWFP's 'under-development at the hands of the Punjab-dominated centre.'[23] His appeal was purely on the basis of Pakhtun culture. Qayyum Khan, NWFP's non-Pakhtun leader and former chief minister, who was alleged to be an agent of the Centre by Wali Khan. Despite this, the NAP could not win a majority of seats in the NWFP or Baluchistan. One analysis revealed that apart from the Peshawar and Mardan divisions, it was unable 'to establish itself as a clear majority party.'[24] It contested sixty-four seats for the National Assembly from both the Wings and six of its candidates, including Wali Khan, were elected from the NWFP and Baluchistan. In the provincial elections, it won thirteen seats in the NWFP and eight seats in Baluchistan. Its success in these provinces was not due to its programme or organization but largely due to its leaders' regionalist stance.

Wali Khan enjoyed considerable support in some areas of the NWFP because of his family contacts and political standing. But he and his colleagues were known for their regional approach in politics, and they concentrated on the problems of their respective areas and conspicuously ignored the national issues. They showed little interest in expanding the party base beyond their regions, which perhaps gradually became their political necessity. Their complete identification with provincial causes aroused doubts about their credentials in other provinces. Hence, despite his long political career and struggle for democracy, Wali Khan was unable to acquire the stature of a national leader.

The PPP won the elections in the Punjab and Sindh while the NAP had a stronghold in the other two provinces of West Pakistan. Both the parties believed in socialism and were expected to arrive at some sort of a broad agreement after 1971, but these prospects were marred by a clash of personalities between Wali Khan and Bhutto. After assuming power, Bhutto offered two seats to the NAP in the central cabinet, but Wali Khan declined the offer and chose to sit on the Opposition benches. Wali Khan was elected the Leader of Opposition in the National Assembly and he discharged his responsibilities gracefully. He led the onslaught of criticism against the undemocratic policies of the PPP. In April 1972, the NAP and the JUI formed coalition governments in the NWFP and

Baluchistan which reflected a broad understanding and general agreement between them. Qayyum Khan had joined the central cabinet as Interior Minister. As Wali and Qayyum were traditional adversaries in the NWFP politics, the relations between the Centre and the NAP governments in the NWFP and Baluchistan were strained.[25] A series of charges and counter-charges followed.[26] The central government accused Wali Khan of engaging in anti-Pakistan activities through an alleged 'London Plan' which he was accused to have chartered in London for the disintegration of Pakistan. Wali Khan refuted these allegations and retaliated by suggesting that 'Bhutto and Pakistan [could not] go together'. This exchange of charges and counter-charges between the PPP government at the federal level and the NAP governments in the NWFP and Baluchistan went on for quite some time. The discovery of an arms cache in the Iraqi embassy in Islamabad, allegedly for transfer to Baluchistan, gave the federal government an excuse to dismiss the NAP-JUI ministry in Baluchistan in February 1973; the NWFP ministry resigned in protest. There were other reasons behind these developments. The general impression was that Bhutto was eager to extend his party's influence in these two provinces; this had precipitated the action against the Baluchistan government. The governors of Baluchistan and the NWFP were also replaced. This situation provided justification to the NAP to spearhead a movement for regional autonomy and to criticize the Punjabi-dominated Centre for its high-handedness.

The period following the removal of the NAP-JUI government witnessed bitterness and polarization between the NAP and PPP. They levelled all sorts of allegations against each other. The NAP public meeting in Liaquat Bagh, Rawalpindi, in March 1973, was attacked and disrupted by the law enforcing agencies and the PPP supporters. The firing resulted in casualties. After this incident, Ajmal Khattak, a close associate of Wali Khan and secretary-general of the NAP, crossed over to Kabul where he unleashed a propaganda campaign against Pakistan and demanded the establishment of an independent 'Pakhtunistan'. The opposition parties in

Pakistan, including the NAP, criticized Bhutto for his undemocratic policies and the use of the Federal Security Force for harassing and victimizing the Opposition. The sense of insecurity, created by the provocative acts of the Bhutto government, led to the formation of an eight-party alliance, the United Democratic Front (UDF), consisting of the NAP, the PML, the JUP, the JUI, the Jamaat-i-Islami, the PDP, the Khaksars, and the Independents.[27] The UDF aimed at evolving ways and means to restore democracy, check dictatorship, and work for an Islamic and parliamentary constitution, and the release of political prisoners.[28]

In February 1975, Hayat Muhammad Sherpao, a PPP leader in NWFP, was killed in a bomb explosion; this provided enough reason to Bhutto to ban the NAP. Thus the NAP was banned and sixty of its top leaders, including Wali Khan, were arrested. Along with the ban, an organized propaganda campaign was unleashed against the NAP, and the official media was also used for this purpose. After the ban, the Political Parties Act of 1962 was amended to authorize the government to declare any foreign-aided political party as an unlawful organization. The ban was referred to the Supreme Court which upheld the action of the government. Subsequently, Wali Khan and fifty-two others were charged with high treason and tried by a specially constituted tribunal known as the Hyderabad Tribunal. They remained in jail till they were released by Ziaul Haq in January 1978.

After the banning of the ANP in 1975, some of its activists organized a new party, the National Democratic Party (NDP), with Sardar Sherbaz Khan Mazari, a former member of the National Assembly, as its leader. The NDP served as a new forum for the NAP workers who immediately joined it. The lead was given by Begum Nasim Wali Khan who filled the vacuum created by her husband's detention. She began to address public meetings which attracted large crowds. The NDP supported non-alignment and a democratic system. In the beginning, the movement was anti-Pakhtunistan and criticized Kabul's interference in the internal affairs of Pakistan. Perhaps such views were deliberately projected to allay apprehensions of the Punjabis. The NDP continued its campaign against Bhutto throughout his rule.

The NDP, as a component party of the Pakistan National Alliance (PNA), played an important role in the 1977 elections and the movement against rigging. When the PNA joined Zia's cabinet in 1978, the NDP dissociated itself from the PNA. Its leadership felt that any co-operation with the military government would undermine its credentials as a democratic party. It came out openly against the military government of Ziaul Haq, and demanded restoration of the 1973 constitution and holding of general elections. It stood for fundamental rights of the people, freedom of the press, and non-alignment in external affairs. In 1981, the NDP joined the Opposition alliance, the MRD, to achieve these objectives. However, its lukewarm attitude towards the Russian invasion of Afghanistan aroused suspicions among many of its supporters. Then, differences between Mazari and Wali Khan led to the formation of the Awami National Party (ANP), headed by Wali Khan, and the NDP was gradually eased out of the political scene. Wali Khan's support of Moscow on the Afghan issue and his leanings towards India thwarted his attempts to extend his party's influence to Punjab. It thus remained limited to a few areas in the NWFP.

The Awami National Party (ANP) actively participated in the 1988 elections. Its manifesto promised full provincial autonomy to all the constituent units of the federation, except in matters of defence, foreign affairs, currency, and communications. It promised not to legislate against the Qur'an and the Sunnah. It advocated revolutionary changes in the agricultural system, establishment of heavy industries in the private sector, protection of tenants' rights, and an independent foreign policy. One family, according to its manifesto, would not own more than fifty acres of irrigated land. It wanted close collaboration with the socialist countries. In the elections the party secured thirteen seats in the NWFP assembly and three seats in the National Assembly. Unlike the 1970 elections, it failed to get any seat in Baluchistan. Its strength in that province was swayed by local

Pakhtun and Baluch ethnic parties like the Pakhtunkhwa Milli Awami Party (PKMAP), the Baluchistan National Party (BNP), and the Baluchistan National Movement (BNM). These minor parties were established by former NAP and ANP leaders. However, the ANP was able to preserve its strength in the NWFP. It co-operated with the PPP in the 1988 elections and joined the coalition government in the NWFP.

The co-operation with the PPP did not last for long. The two parties soon developed differences on the appointment of the NWFP governor and over the powers of the ANP ministers. The differences turned into open hostilities which brought the alliance between the two parties to an end. The ANP then joined hands with the PML (N) and put up candidates in the 1990 elections by mutual adjustments with PML (N). The ANP benefited from this co-operation. It secured seven seats in the National Assembly and twenty-two seats in the NWFP assembly. Besides, it won four seats in the Senate. A PML (N)-ANP coalition government, headed by Mir Afzal Khan, remained in power in the NWFP till the removal of the Nawaz Sharif government and the dissolution of the assemblies in 1993. The ANP again co-operated with the PML (N) in the 1993 elections. It secured three seats in the National Assembly and twenty-one seats in the NWFP assembly. After the elections, it joined the PML (N) to form a coalition ministry in the NWFP, but that ministry could stay in power for just two months.

The ANP participated in the Opposition movement against the Benazir government which led to its dismissal. In the 1997 elections, it won nine seats in the National Assembly and twenty-seven in the NWFP assembly. When representative governments were installed, it got its share in the federal and the NWFP government. Its repeated successes revived its parochial tendencies. When the Nawaz Sharif government was besieged in its conflict with the judiciary, the party thought it fit to pressurize the beleaguered prime minister to change the name of the NWFP to 'Pakhtunkhwa'. But because of pressure from within the PML (N), Nawaz Sharif refused to accept this demand; this led to the break-up of the nine-year-long PML

(N)-ANP co-operation. The ANP is now struggling to define its autonomous role in the politics of Pakistan.

JAMAAT-I-ISLAMI

Founded in 1941 by Maulana Syed Abul A'la Maududi, the Jamaat-i-Islami is the most well-organized party in Pakistan. Originally, it was established to revive Islamic values and to implement Islam as a practical code of life for the Muslims. Its object, as explained at its first convention in 1941, was to give Islam the shape of a practical movement.[29] Its founders asserted that it was not a religious or a political party but an ideological movement covering all aspects of life.[30] As a matter of principle, the Jamaat did not confine its activities to one nation or country; it aimed at 'changing the moral, political, economic, and social system of the whole world'.[31]

The Jamaat did not support the movement for the creation of Pakistan because its leaders thought that the All-India Muslim League would not establish an Islamic state since the Leaguers were not true Muslims and they lacked a proper understanding of the Islamic spirit. When Pakistan was established, the Jamaat changed its position and decided to work for the establishment of an Islamic government in Pakistan.[32] In the beginning, the Jamaat concentrated its energies on social and educational work. It established small libraries, travelling dispensaries, and educational institutions, and issued magazines for the religious training of the people. Although its membership was restricted, it became an effective body. Unlike other political parties of Pakistan, it never tried to grow into a mass organization. It set a very high standard for its adherents to qualify as members.

Till 1957, the Jamaat did not take active part in politics except that it tried to raise consciousness about various constitutional and religious issues among the people. It put up just a few candidates in Punjab in the 1951 elections, but in 1958 it entered the political arena with a bang, and captured more than a dozen seats in the elections to the Karachi Metropolitan Corporation.

In January 1964, the Ayub Khan government banned the Jamaat. The ban was, however, removed by the Supreme Court in September 1964, but the Jamaat could not find sufficient time to re-organize itself for the Basic Democracy elections which were held in November 1964. The Jamaat alleged that the government had resorted to corrupt practices in these elections. For the 1964–65 presidential elections the Jamaat, as one of the components of the Combined Opposition Parties (COP), supported Miss Fatima Jinnah against Ayub Khan. The Jamaat fully participated in the general elections of 1970. Its manifesto described the Holy Qur'an and the Sunnah as the basic sources of law. Other major themes set out in the manifesto included provincial autonomy, separation of the judiciary from the executive, complete religious freedom for the minorities, foreign policy to conform to Pakistan's ideological needs, opposition to all forms of imperialism, and closer relations with the Muslim world. It opposed 'economic inequality' and advocated 'economic justice'. The basic objectives of its economic policy were to achieve equitable distribution of wealth, create equal opportunities for all citizens, and eliminate poverty. It opposed fixing of any land ceiling permanently but only as a temporary measure; a ceiling on landholding was to be fixed between 100 and 200 acres with a view to achieving economic justice. It also opposed nationalization and restriction on the ownership of personal property. It supported the right of the workers and labourers to go on strike. It strongly favoured the system of proportional representation for Pakistan. The Jamaat put up 148 candidates for the National Assembly elections from both the wings and captured only four seats; all from West Pakistan. Being a close-knit party, it lacked the germs to develop into a mass organization which was essential to win elections. However, it possessed a solid political base in Karachi, Lahore, and a few other cities. The Jamaat holds party elections regularly. Maulana Maududi was succeeded by Maulana Tufail Muhammad as its *Amir* (leader).

During the PPP rule, the Jamaat opposed Bhutto's dictatorial policies as well as his economic policies including the policy of nationalization. Backed by its intellectuals and its powerful publicity machine, it posed a serious challenge to the PPP in and outside the assemblies. Against the PPP's ideology of socialism, the Jamaat strongly advocated the ideology of Islam. This contributed to polarization in politics. The Jamaat had to pay a heavy price for its opposition to Bhutto's rule. Its leaders and workers were intimidated, threatened, and imprisoned by the government. Dr Nazir Ahmad, one of its prominent leaders and a member of the National Assembly, was shot dead. However, the Jamaat remained steadfast and undaunted. During the 1977 elections, it joined the PNA for participation in the elections and then played an active role in the movement against Bhutto.

After the imposition of martial law in July 1977, the Jamaat extended support to President Zia's military regime and his programme for Islamization. It joined the cabinet in 1978. Though the Jamaat resigned from the cabinet along with other parties of the PNA in 1979, it maintained a close relationship with the military government. However, some of its leaders like Professor Abdul Ghafoor Ahmad questioned the Jamaat's links with General Zia and openly criticized the military government.

The Jamaat allowed its members to participate in the 1985 non-party elections as individuals. It contested the 1988 elections as part of the IJI, but before joining the IJI, it issued a manifesto which demanded the supremacy of the Holy Qur'an and Sunnah, the separation of the judiciary from the executive, complete provincial autonomy, the adoption of a simple lifestyle, the elimination of corruption, an interest-free economy, separate universities for women, industrialization with self reliance, labours' share in the industrial income, and a non-aligned independent foreign policy with special relations with the Muslim world.

However, the Jamaat was able to capture only a few seats in the National and Provincial assemblies. In the 1990 elections, it again participated from the platform of the IJI; eight of its candidates were elected to the National Assembly. When the IJI came to power, the Jamaat co-operated with its government but declined to take any ministry. It gradually moved away from the PML (N), accusing the government of deviating from the IJI manifesto. Later, it left the IJI and the PML (N). In the 1993 elections, its *Amir*, Qazi Husain Ahmad, floated the Pakistan Islamic Front (PIF) to contest the elections. The PIF attracted large gatherings in the election campaign but it could not win a respectable number of seats. It secured only three seats in the National Assembly; two of these were in Karachi where the MQM had boycotted the national elections. In the provincial elections it won only two seats in the NWFP assembly.

After these elections, the Jamaat, under Qazi Husain Ahmad's leadership, decided not to join any alliance in the future. Maintaining an independent stance, it opposed the policies of the Benazir government. It held protest demonstrations against the government, in one of which three of its workers were killed in police firing, contributed to the weakening of her government and its eventual dismissal by President Leghari with whom Qazi Husain Ahmad had developed cordial relations. The Jamaat demanded strict accountability of the politicians (especially the ousted Benazir government) before new elections were held, and enforcement of clauses 62 and 63 of the 1973 Constitution for scrutiny of the candidates to various assemblies. When these demands were not accepted and the interim government decided to hold elections in the constitutional stipulated time of three months, the Jamaat boycotted the elections and organized *dharnas* (sit-ins) to stop the voters from polling. Its campaign partially contributed to the low turnout in the elections. Since then it has been campaigning for accountability of the political leaders and fresh elections under the 1973 Constitution, after applying its clauses 62 and 63 on the candidates.

JAMIAT-UL-ULEMA-I-ISLAM

During the Pakistan movement, as a result of general dissatisfaction with the pro-Congress policy of the Jamiat-ul-Ulema-i-Hind, the pro-Muslim League decided to set up the

Jamiat-ul-Ulema-i Islam (JUI) to support the demand for Pakistan.[33] Its formation was announced at a largely attended meeting in Calcutta on 22–29 October 1945. Maulana Shabbir Ahmad Usmani was elected its first president. The JUI was hastily organized throughout the subcontinent and it made a significant contribution to the Muslim League victory in the 1945–46 elections. It also helped the Muslim League in winning the referendums in the NWFP and Sylhet in 1947. Its services were gratefully acknowledged by the Muslim League leadership.

After independence, the JUI was formally re-organized in December 1947, with its office at Maulana Ihteshamul Haq Thanvi's residence in Karachi, and was headed by Maulana Shabbir Ahmad Usmani who, as a member of the Constituent Assembly of Pakistan, wielded considerable influence. The party was identified with the Deobandi school of religious thought. After Maulana Usmani's death, it was headed by Sayyid Suleman Nadvi, another well-known religious scholar. The JUI strongly advocated an Islamic constitution for Pakistan. On its initiative, a conference of thirty-one ulema belonging to various parties including the JUP, the Jamaat-i-Islami and the Jamiat-i-Ahli-Hadith, was held at Karachi in 1951. This conference unanimously formulated twenty-two principles of an Islamic state which served as a guideline for the framers of the constitution. Initially the JUI was better organized in East Pakistan than in West Pakistan and participated in the East Pakistan provincial elections of 1954 by sponsoring another organization under the title of Nizam-i-Islam Party.

In 1956, at a big JUI convention, some Ahrar and Deobandi ulema, including Mufti Mahmood and Maulana Ghulam Ghaus Hazarvi, joined the party. Maulana Ahmad Ali was elected its president. This development disillusioned the pro-Muslim League ulema who dissociated themselves from the party. During the Ayub regime, Mufti Mahmud and Maulana Hazarvi represented the party in the National Assembly and the West Pakistan assembly. It participated in the 1970 elections and won seven National Assembly seats from the districts of Kohat, Bannu, and Dera Ismail Khan of the NWFP and Baluchistan; its general secretary, Mufti Mahmud, defeated Bhutto in a constituency from Dera Ismail Khan. In the 1977 elections, it improved upon its performance in these areas. In response to Bhutto's socialism, Mufti Mahmud propagated, *Socialism Kufr Hey* (Socialism is un-Islamic); yet, in 1972, the JUI aligned with the NAP, another socialist party, to form coalition governments in the NWFP and Baluchistan. Mufti Mahmud headed the coalition government in the NWFP, which introduced various reform measures including a ban on drinking. As stated earlier, due to differences with the PPP, the coalition government of Baluchistan was dismissed, and the NWFP government resigned in protest.

The JUI was a component party of the Pakistan National Alliance (PNA) in the 1977 elections. Its leader, Mufti Mahmud, played an important role in the PNA agitation against Bhutto and served on the PNA team that negotiated with Bhutto and his team. After the death of Mufti Mahmud in 1980, his son, Maulana Fazlur Rehman, was elected the general secretary and Maulana Abdullah Darkhwasti its *Amir*. During the martial law, the party was split into two groups: JUI (F) led by Maulana Fazlur Rehman, and JUI (S) led by Maulana Samiul Haq. The former opposed Zia and generally supported the PPP, and the latter sided with the military regime. The JUI (S) won four seats in the National Assembly in the 1985 non-party elections, and repeated this performance in the 1988 elections. It secured two seats in the Senate. In the 1990 elections, it secured one seat in the National Assembly and two in the Punjab assembly. In the next general elections in 1990, it again won one seat in the National Assembly and one in the Punjab assembly. Its primary objective was to seek enforcement of the Islamic law and for that, it struggled for legislation in the Parliament. Gradually, within the ranks of JUI (S) developed an extremely orthodox and militant group, the Sipah-i-Sahaba-i-Pakistan (SSP), which broke apart from the party and played up sensitive Islamic-sectarian issues; this adversely affected the inter-sectarian relations in Pakistan, often resulting in acute violence and killings.

The JUI (F) has performed better than the JUI (S). It boycotted the 1985 non-party elections. But it took part in the 1988 elections and secured six seats in the National Assembly and two in the NWFP assembly. Although it had been associated with the PPP in the MRD, it did not join the government. In the 1990 elections, although Fazlur Rehman himself was defeated, the party secured four seats in the National Assembly, two in the NWFP assembly and six in the Baluchistan assembly. Its members joined the coalition government in Baluchistan but remained in the Opposition in the NWFP. In 1993, it won four seats in the National Assembly, and Fazlur Rehman served as the chairman of the Foreign Relations Committee, with the status of a minister. The following year, Maulana Darkhwasti died, and Maulana Muhammad Ajmal Khan was elected his successor. In the 1997 elections, the party secured two seats in the National Assembly, one seat in the NWFP assembly, and five in the Baluchistan assembly. During these years, a couple of attempts were made to unite the two groups of the JUI, but these did not succeed.

JAMIAT-UL-ULEMA-I-PAKISTAN

The Jamiat-ul-Ulema-i-Pakistan (JUP) was set up by the ulema of the Barelvi school of thought in 1948, with Maulana Abdul Hamid Badauni as its president. It wanted an Islamic system for Pakistan. It enjoyed the support of the *Pirs* and *mashaikh*, a section of the religious groups and some members of the landed elite. Its first direct participation in the elections was in 1970, when it was able to win a few seats. Its leader, Maulana Shah Ahmad Noorani, advocated legislation in accordance with Islamic teachings. During the 1977 elections, it joined the Pakistan National Alliance (PNA) and introduced the slogan of *Nizam-i-Mustafa* (Islamic system), a slogan which became popular in the agitation against Bhutto's government.

In 1978, when the PNA joined Zia's cabinet, the JUP dissociated itself from the alliance. After that, it struggled for the lifting of martial law and restoration of democracy under the 1973 Constitution, but did not join the MRD which had been set up with similar objectives. The JUP did not take part in the 1985 non-party elections, but it participated in the 1988 elections. In its manifesto, it advocated enforcement of the *Nizam-i-Mustafa*, equality of rights for all the citizens, assurance of basic needs to everyone, land to landless, plots to shelterless families, industrialization in the private sector, self-sufficiency in defence, independent judiciary, and non-aligned foreign policy with special attention to the unity of the Muslim world. In co-operation with the Tehrik-i-Istaqlal and the PML (J), it formed an alliance, the Pakistan People's Alliance, but the exit of the PML (J) from the alliance soon after its formation damaged its electoral prospects. However, the JUP did win three seats in the National Assembly and two seats in the Punjab assembly. Maulana Abdus Sattar Niazi, General (Retd.) M.H. Ansari, and Dr Sher Afgan were elected to the National Assembly on its tickets. After the elections, Dr Sher Afgan joined the PPP cabinet without resigning from the party.

The JUP has remained divided into two groups: JUP (Niazi), led by Maulana Abdus Sattar Khan Niazi; and JUP (Noorani), led by Maulana Shah Ahmad Noorani. The JUP (Niazi) has been siding with the PML (N) and the latter has generally followed an independent policy. Both support the introduction of an Islamic system. Unlike the JUP (Noorani), the JUP (Niazi) has been represented in the assemblies where it has voiced its demand for the enforcement of Shariat law in Pakistan. Maulana Niazi was the one who moved the 'Tauhin-i-Risalat Bill' which was adopted by the Parliament. The electoral support of both the factions has remained limited, although the Niazi faction has made some gains by associating with the PML (N).

ELECTORAL POLITICS

(I) THE 1977 ELECTIONS (PNA VS. PPP): Electoral politics under the 1973 Constitution began in January 1977, when Bhutto announced general elections in the country. By that time, he had succeeded in establishing an authoritarian government by suppressing the Opposition, curbing the freedom of the press, and removing the dissidents from the PPP. He was confident that the PPP would win the support of various sections of the society, for he had introduced many reforms during the short period of his rule to transform the Pakistani society. He was proud of his successes in the field of foreign policy and his achievements on the domestic front. He could have continued without election for another year because the five-year term of the National Assembly had started from August 1973 after the promulgation of the constitution. His announcement for holding the general elections on 7 January 1977 was meant to overshadow the announcement to that effect made by Indira Gandhi in India. He wanted a fresh mandate to consolidate his reforms and his power. He had no doubts about his victory. Before this announcement, on 4 January, he had announced labour reforms, and the following day, he brought in another package of land reforms.

The Opposition saw in his move a threat to their existence. They believed that ' this was more than an election; it was a question of Bhutto's or their survival', and that in case of Bhutto's victory, Pakistan would be unceremoniously transformed into a 'one-party state or a no-party state'.[34] Fears generated by these perceptions and increasingly undemocratic attitude of the PPP chairman, led the Opposition parties to forge an electoral coalition, the Pakistan National Alliance (PNA), which included nine political parties: the Tehrik-i-Istaqlal, PML, Jamaat-i-Islami, PDP, NDP, JUI, JUP, All-Jammu and Kashmir Muslim Conference, and the Khaksars. Mufti Mahmud of JUI and Rafiq Bajwa of JUP were elected as its president and secretary-general respectively. The emergence of the PNA was a major development which was absolutely against Bhutto's expectations. The PPP was now faced with a united Opposition, unlike the 1970 elections when these parties had separate platforms. It was not easy to unite these disparate parties with several inter-party differences and deep-rooted inter-personal rivalries between their leaders. The most important motivating force behind this alliance was the fear of Bhutto's authoritarianism.

The PPP manifesto, issued in January, began with a promise to teach the Qur'an and Holy Prophet's (PBUH) *Seerat* (life) as compulsory subjects in educational institutions, and to propagate Islam in other countries. These introductory remarks were designed to take the wind out of the sails of the rightist parties. Apart from attracting the religious sections of the society, these were meant to dispel the general feeling against the PPP's programme of socialism which was considered to be un-Islamic. The manifesto called for increase in the wages of working classes, keeping in view the production and performance of the industrial sector; allocation of 20,000 residential plots free of cost to the industrial workers every year; attainment of self-sufficiency in food and oil in five years; and grant of one million plots in rural areas and 0.75 million plots in urban areas were to those without shelter. The party still favoured to shape economic policy on socialism within the framework of Islam in order to remove social inequalities. Due importance was to be given to the private sector. Steps were to be taken against waterlogging and salinity. The party promised to improve the system of communication. Efforts were to be made to achieve the right of self-determination for the people of Kashmir. Defence was to be strengthened through special measures like expansion and modernization of the arms industry, leading to less dependence on other countries. In the field of foreign affairs, the PPP stood for closer relations with the Muslim world and Third World countries. Bhutto promised to carry forward the task of building a more prosperous Pakistan, and requested the people to support the PPP to face the challenge of the future.[35] In short, the manifesto was a well-prepared document, covering all aspects and promising a brighter future to all sections of the society.

The PNA took some time to issue a manifesto; the PPP ridiculed the delay, and when the PNA finally issued its manifesto on 8 February, Bhutto castigated it as having 'no philosophy, no ideology, and no rationale'. The manifesto was divided into various sections such as economic system, general economic reforms, national health, agriculture, rights of the low-income groups, state laws, press, radio and television, education, public administration, the constitution, defence, and foreign policy. Recounting the PPP's failure to 'fulfil the promises made to the people of Pakistan', it resolved 'to give the people their rightful place in society after obliterating unlawful restrictions, economic depression, and social inequities'.[36] It promised to enforce the Holy Qur'an and the Sunnah; to establish a just system; to destroy all modes of exploitation; to bring the prices within the reach of the common man; to guarantee provision of food, clothing, accommodation, education, and medical care to everyone; to guarantee rights to women; to promote friendly relations among the Muslim countries with a view to achieve unity; to realize the right of self-determination for the people of Kashmir; to extend assistance for the uplift of Azad Kashmir, Gilgit, and Baltistan; to give right to the people of tribal areas to elect their own representatives; and to establish a truly democratic regime in Pakistan.[37]

The manifesto emphasized the creation of a free society by assuring fundamental rights to the citizens and by declaring all such constitutional 'amendments null and void which had affected the basic rights of the citizens'. It called for provincial autonomy, restrictions on the unlimited powers of the prime minister and chief ministers; full protection to the minorities; withdrawal of emergency; abrogation of the Defence of Pakistan Rules; complete ban on drinking, adultery, horse racing, obscenity, nudity and other evils; abolition of interest; dissolution of the National Press Trust; freedom to radio and television; provision of constitutional security to government servants; elimination of corruption and red-tapism; and improvement of pay structure of government servants.[38] Its manifesto envisaged a 'clear-cut industrial policy giving protection to both the labour and the capital, an agricultural policy ensuring sufficiency in food, participation of workers in the administration and profit, new taxation system, distribution of cultivable land among the landless, encouragement to cottage industry, a national health policy, modernization of army and compulsory military training', etc.[39]

As compared to the PPP manifesto, the PNA manifesto was vague on a number of issues. It reflected a number of compromises in view of the fact that the PNA constituent parties lacked ideological harmony. Both manifestos contained high-sounding promises, economic strategies, and sophisticated expressions. But the election campaign soon degenerated into unsophisticated personalized attacks and strong polemics. Bhutto remarked that Asghar Khan, who once could not travel by air, was now living on the doles of capitalists. Asghar Khan in retaliation dubbed Bhutto a rat from Larkana.

The PNA focused on the undemocratic policies and repressive measures of the Bhutto government and the un-Islamic steps of his party in which corruption, moral as well as financial, was rampant. However, its major attack was directed against Bhutto's role in the disintegration of the country in 1971. The PNA promised to release the Hamoodur Rehman Commission Report after coming to power. The anti-Bhutto sentiments were articulated by highlighting the conspicuous failures of the government as reflected in price hike, squandering of national wealth, failure of economic policies, excessive expenditure on empire building, corruption, misuse of power, and creation of the Federal Security Force to suppress the Opposition. The PNA offensive was so powerful that it kept Bhutto on the defensive from the beginning.[40]

The aggressive personal attacks against Bhutto drew him out of his calm demeanour. Now he realized that what he had thought would be an easy victory was a hazardous exercise. He resorted to his usual rhetoric and condemned the PNA as enemies of Pakistan, who had opposed the Quaid-i-Azam and the creation of Pakistan. He held them responsible for turmoil in Baluchistan and asserted that some of them were still working against the unity of the country. He described them as a band of capitalists whose exploitation would be eliminated by the PPP sword.

Both the sides laid emphasis on Islamization. The PNA raised the slogan of *Nizam-i-Mustafa* thus trying 'to pre-empt the PPP's socio-economic plank', whereas the PPP leadership counted a number of its outstanding services to the cause of Islam and 'dropped all direct references to socialism, replacing it by Musawaat-e-Muhammadi'.[41] However, personal attacks continued to be the conspicuous note of the election speeches. Approximately 44 per cent of all speeches of PPP leaders were devoted to scathing criticism of the Opposition leaders, their past affiliations, their 'subversive' role and their 'future designs'; in contrast, about 75 per cent of the campaign speeches of the PNA leaders were directed against Bhutto.[42] As the campaign entered its final phase, large processions were organized by both the groups to demonstrate their strength and following.

The elections to the National and Provincial assemblies were held on 7 and 10 March, respectively. The PPP won 155 seats out of 200, including nineteen seats where its candidates were elected unopposed. The PNA could capture only thirty-six seats. The election results sent a wave of indignation and triggered a protest movement against the PPP. Although PPP's victory was anticipated, but the practical elimination of the Opposition bewildered everyone. The PNA was quick to charge the PPP with massive rigging of the polls. Asghar Khan, in a press conference on 8 March, described the polls a fraud with the nation, and announced the PNA decision to boycott the elections to the provincial assemblies.

Bhutto denied the rigging charges but the PNA succeeded in producing concrete evidence in support of their claim; even the chief election commissioner conceded that 'hair-raising' malpractices had been committed.[43] In fact, the people had become suspicious when the radio and television announced results of the far-flung areas before the results of big cities. While there were clear instances of rigging, the fact was that these were greatly magnified by the PNA as well. The PNA launched a movement against the PPP government which was unprecedented in its intensity in the history of Pakistan. From March to July, the nation was gripped by a frenzy leading to demonstrations, protest processions, and *hartals* (strikes) almost everyday. In April, the movement picked up tempo. The turning point arrived on 9 April when the police opened fire on demonstrators in Lahore, who were marching towards the assembly building to prevent the convening of the new assembly. The police firing resulted in many casualties and the angry mob burnt banks and other government buildings.[44] Demonstrations and processions became a daily feature almost in all the cities, putting great strain on the economy. Meanwhile, the newly elected Opposition members of the National Assembly started submitting resignations; the PPP members joined them with the passage of time. Due to the mishandling of the situation, both politically and administratively, the movement went out of control. It appeared as if the PPP regime was going to crumble down. Law and order situation in the five big cities deteriorated to such an extent that the army had to be called in to restore order.

At last, Bhutto agreed to negotiate with the PNA leaders. The PPP government team consisted of Bhutto himself, Hafeez Pirzada, and Maulana Kausar Niazi; whereas the PNA team comprised Mufti Mahmud, Nawabzada Nasrullah Khan, and Professor Ghafoor Ahmad. The negotiations which began in June, eased the political tension in the streets. After several rounds of talks, the two sides agreed to hold fresh elections under the supervision of the army and the judiciary. For the implementation of the agreement, a joint implementation council was to be constituted consisting of five representatives of each side. While the agreement was being given final touches, Bhutto left for a foreign tour. His absence from the country at such a critical juncture created suspicions as to the genuineness of Bhutto's desire to settle the issue with the Opposition. When the dialogue was resumed on his return, the PNA insisted that the Implementation Council should be the supreme body, whereas Bhutto was reluctant to accept a super government. On 2 July, the official circles announced that an agreement had been concluded, but the PNA central council immediately rejected it.[45] Talks were resumed, but again these reached a deadlock.

General Ziaul Haq, the army chief, had prepared a contingency plan for such an eventuality. On 5 July 1977, he imposed martial law in the country and became Chief Martial Law Administrator (CMLA). The following year, he assumed the office of president as well. Thus, once again, differences among the politicians paved the way for army rule, and the nation had to suffer under it till 1985. Zia did not hold general elections as he had initially promised. Instead, he not only postponed the elections indefinitely but also banned the political parties.

(II) THE 1985 NON-PARTY ELECTIONS: In February 1981, the political parties opposed to the martial law and supportive of the revival of a democratic order under the 1973 Constitution established the MRD. These parties included the PPP, the Tehrik-i-Istaqlal, the PML (Khairuddin Group), the PDP, and the NDP. Although the MRD led a forceful movement especially in Sindh in August 1983, but it was President Zia who on his own initiative took steps to revive a democratic order. At first, he held a presidential referendum in December 1984 to attain the position of an elected president for the next five years. Then, he held non-party elections to the National and Provincial assemblies in the last week of February 1985. The MRD parties boycotted these non-party elections. Before the elected assemblies met, Zia issued the Revival of the Constitution Order (RCO), which restored the 1973 Constitution in a drastically amended form. Exercising powers under the RCO, President Zia nominated Muhammad Khan Junejo, a former Muslim Leaguer and West Pakistan minister, as the prime minister. Junejo managed to pass the RCO with some modifications as the Eighth Amendment to the 1973 Constitution in the National Assembly in return for the lifting of martial law on 30 December 1985.

Soon after, Junejo, as the prime minister and the PML president, began to assert his authority which brought him in conflict with Zia. Their differences were fostered by policy conflict on such issues as the Geneva Accords on Afghanistan and the Ojhri Camp blast. The climax was the unceremonious dismissal of Prime Minister Junejo on 29 May 1988 by Ziaul Haq who invoked the article 58(2)b of the amended constitution for this action.

(III) THE 1988 ELECTIONS: Zia announced plans to hold new general elections. While he was settling the modalities for the elections, he died in a mysterious plane crash on 17 August 1988. The acting President, Ghulam Ishaq Khan, decided to hold the elections as announced by the late president. When the Supreme Court, on a writ petition, ruled in favour of party-based elections, the interim government accepted that ruling and announced the dates for the general elections, to the National Assembly on 7 November, and to the Provincial assemblies on 17 November.

The political parties formed new alliances. The major one was the nine-party alliance, the Islami Jamhoori Ittehad (IJI), which included the PML (Fida Group), Jamaat-i-Islami, National People's Party (NPP) headed by Ghulam Mustafa Jatoi, JUP (Dastoori group) and Jamiat-i-Ahli Hadith. Another was a three-party alliance, the Pakistan Awami Ittehad (PAI), consisting of the PML (Junejo), the Tehrik-i Istaqlal, and the JUP (Noorani), with Maulana Shah Ahmad Noorani as the convener. The PML (Junejo) soon reunited with the other faction of the PML and joined the IJI; this step weakened the PAI. The subsequent IJI-PAI understanding for adjustments of seats further undermined the PAI. The MRD could have been another strong electoral alliance, but the PPP disengaged itself from that alliance when differences arose over the distribution of tickets. Still the PPP it announced that it will not put up candidates against the heads of the MRD parties. There were several other parties that participated in the elections, but the major contestants were the IJI and the PPP.

The IJI, in its seven-point manifesto, called for the supremacy of the Qur'an and the Sunnah; equal economic opportunities for all sections of the society including traders, peasants, and students; inexpensive justice for all, without discrimination; participation of women in national life and protection of their rights; full support to the Afghan Jihad; preservation of the atomic energy programme and its use for development; participation in the non-aligned movement; support to the cause of the Palestinians and Kashmiris, and co-operation with the Third World. The PPP, in its manifesto, demanded the abolition of National Press Trust, freedom of the Associated Press of Pakistan from the government's control; safe return for all political exiles; release of political prisoners and restoration of their property and jobs; and building of monuments for the martyrs of democracy. It promised to uphold the ideals of Islam; to unite the nation; to restore democratic rule; to safeguard provincial autonomy; to eliminate poverty; to make the atmosphere conducive for economic growth; to ensure economic justice; to expand education including vocational, scientific, technical, and university education; and to induct and aid the private sector in the economic field.[46]

The PPP emerged as the largest party in the National Assembly, winning ninety-two seats. The IJI was the next in strength, securing fifty-four seats. The remaining seats were distributed among several parties: MQM thirteen, JUI (F) seven, ANP three, PAI three, NPP (Khar Group) two, BNA (Baluchistan National Alliance) two, PDP one, JUI (Darkhwasti Group) one, and the Independents forty. The IJI was the majority party in the Punjab assembly; the PPP gained majority in Sindh and in the NWFP. The party-position in the Baluchistan assembly was mixed. Ghulam Ishaq Khan was elected president of the country, securing 348 votes against ninety-one of his rival candidate, Nawabzada Nasrullah; both the IJI and the PPP supported Ghulam Ishaq Khan. Benazir was nominated as the prime minister; she formed the government at the Centre by aligning with the MQM. Mian Nawaz Sharif (IJI) formed the government in Punjab, Sayyid Qaim Ali Shah (PPP) in Sindh, Aftab Ahmad Khan Sherpao (PPP) in the NWFP, and Sardar Zafrullah Khan Jamali (IJI) in Baluchistan.

(IV) **THE 1990 ELECTIONS (IJI VS. PDA):** The Benazir government had an inauspicious start. A few days after her swearing in as the prime minister, Chief Minister Zafrullah Jamali dissolved the Baluchistan assembly, which led to a series of accusations and counter-accusations. Although the Baluchistan assembly was restored by the Baluchistan High Court and a new chief minister was subsequently elected, this incident seriously damaged the government's reputation. The new ministry in Baluchistan was not friendly towards Benazir. She faced hostile governments in the Punjab and Baluchistan, which were opposed to her government's policies especially the People's Works Programme. The PPP focused on its charges of election rigging; it wanted Chief Minister Nawaz Sharif's removal to capture power in Punjab at all costs. The IJI, in retaliation, brought in a no-confidence motion against her government. Although she survived in power, this move further intensified IJI-PPP hostility. Another factor that led to the PPP government's downfall was its failure to keep up its agreement with the MQM. Differences arose over repatriation of Biharis to Pakistan; abolition of the Placement Bureau and provincial quota in services, with the result that the MQM dissociated from the PPP and joined hands with the IJI.[47] Benazir Bhutto's inexperience, incompetence, corruption, and ambition to assume powers in every area brought her in conflict with the judiciary, the army and the president. This led to the dismissal of her government on 6 August 1990 by President Ghulam Ishaq Khan.

Benazir's fierce outbursts against her dismissal further antagonized those who represented these institutions. Besides, she did not fully concentrate on preparing for the elections. She represented to the Supreme Court for the restoration of her government, arguing that her government had been unlawfully dismissed. Her supporters wasted valuable time in the hope of a favourable decision, but the Supreme Court ruled against her contention. When Benazir began the election campaign, she was on the defensive, defending the performance of her government. Contrary to the PPP policy in 1988, when it was anxious to campaign alone, it was now keen to have partners and formed an alliance, the Peoples Democratic Alliance (PDA). On the other hand, the IJI, with a friendly administration, was on the offensive, deriding the performance of its opponents. It was more judicious in the distribution of tickets, and meticulously worked for adjustments among the IJI constituent parties and other like-minded parties to select winning candidates. Nawaz Sharif emphasized that the contest was between the IJI and the PPP, and that there was no third force.

The IJI strategy paid dividends in the elections. The voter turnout at the national level was 44.9 per cent, the IJI secured 37. 27 votes with 105 seats and the PPP-supported PDA gained 36.65 per cent of the total votes polled with only forty-five seats. The remaining seats were secured by other parties: MQM fifteen, ANP six, JUI (F) six, JUP (Noorani) three, JWP (Jamhoori Watan Party) two, PNP two, PKMAP one, and Independents thirteen. In the elections to the Punjab assembly, the IJI won 216 seats out of a total of 240 seats and the PDA ten seats; in the Sindh assembly, the PDA secured forty-six seats out of a total of hundred seats and the IJI six seats; in the NWFP assembly, the IJI won twenty-nine out of a total eighty seats and the PDA eight seats; and in the Baluchistan assembly, the IJI won seven seats out of a total of thirty-two seats, and the PDA one seat. After the elections, the IJI parliamentary leader, Mian Nawaz Sharif, formed the government at the Centre. He made a good start, and with an apparently supportive bureaucracy and army, he was expected to complete his term of office. He was able to resolve some long-standing contentious inter-province issues which were incorporated in the Indus Waters Award and the National Finance Commission's Award. His impressive agenda included disinvestments and privatization, exchange deregulation and incentive for private sector investment. But he also ran into trouble with the army chief and the president.

Nawaz Sharif's differences with the army chief, General Mirza Aslam Beg, emerged over policies towards the law and order problem in urban Sindh, the Gulf War, and appointments in the Intelligence services and the army.[48] These continued with Beg's successor, General Asif Nawaz Janjua. Nawaz Sharif also developed differences with the president, which were aggravated with General Asif Nawaz's sudden death, and the selection of his successor against the president's wishes in January 1993. Several of Nawaz Sharif's IJI partners, who felt that he had not implemented the IJI manifesto and was not giving them due importance, also deserted him. Among them were the JUI (S), the Jamaat-i-Islami and the MQM. He thought that his problems would end if the Eighth Amendment was repealed. Strangely enough, he looked toward the PPP for co-operation in this regard. With his tacit consent, Benazir was elected chairperson of the Parliamentary Committee of Foreign Affairs. But she had her own plans; she was anxious to avenge her dismissal and return to power. The president initiated the demolition process. He engineered defections in the IJI, as a result federal ministers began to resign. Using this and Nawaz Sharif's performance as a pretext, the president dismissed the government on 18 April 1993, after Benazir presented him the resignations of her party MNAs. The crisis deepened with the prime minister's dismissal. Instead of accepting the dismissal decision, he challenged it in the Supreme Court which restored his government in the last week of May. The president-prime minister conflict continued, with Benazir now threatening a long march in Islamabad in July. Finally, a settlement was reached through the army chief in which both the prime minister and the president resigned. Fresh elections were to be held, for the National Assembly on 6 October and the provincial assemblies on 9 October.[49] Waseem Sajjad, chairman of the Senate, took over as president and Moin Qureshi, a Pakistani-American who had served the World Bank in a senior position, was sworn in as the caretaker prime minister.

(v) THE 1993 ELECTIONS (PML [N] vs. PPP): The main contestants in these elections were the PML (N) and the PPP. Both had allied parties with which they co-operated in the election campaign and the distribution of tickets. They sought cooperative relationship rather than broad alliances with smaller, region-based parties for adjustment of seats. For this purpose, the PML (N) worked closely with the ANP, MQM, PML (Functional), Pakhtunkhwa Milli Awami Party (PKMAP), and others. It had a more independent posture in these elections than the earlier ones. As compared with the PML (N), the PPP had to carry a larger baggage. A number of parties and alliances, which formed part of the APC (All Parties Conference), had supported its movement against the Nawaz Sharif government. It had to accommodate component parties of the NDA, PDA, PML (J), JUI (F), and others. The Jamaat-i-Islami, under Qazi Husain Ahmad's leadership thought that it could perform better by leading the Islamic forces than by aligning with other parties. It floated the PIF and contested the elections from its platform.

The manifestos of the two main contestants, PML (N) and the PPP, had some common items. Both called for privatization, population planning, eradication of drug production and trade, reforms in labour laws, job opportunities for the unemployed, land to landless peasants, electricity to far-flung area, improvement of educational facilities, female literacy, primary education, health for all, freedom of the press, legislation against floor-crossing, improvement in the investment climate, development of small-scale industries, revival of the reserved seats for women in assemblies, friendly relations with the US, China, and the Muslim world, and resolution of the problems of Kashmir, Palestine, and Bosnia. They differed in their advocacy of Islamic themes. While the PML (N) advocated separate electorates, the PPP stressed the need for joint electorates. The former advocated industrialization and overall development, recounting its performance in power, while the latter was more interested in the agricultural development and proposed structural changes including a vague scheme of a new social contract.[50]

The PML (N) was partially defensive in its campaign and defended various developmental schemes and policies that its government had launched during its tenure, particularly the Motorway and the Yellow Cab schemes. The disclosure of the government's financial mismanagement and corruption lent support to the PPP propaganda in this regard.[51] The PML (N) campaign was influenced by veiled and open references to the involvement of the Nawaz government in the sudden death of General Asif Nawaz. On the other hand, the PPP was embarrassed by Murtaza Bhutto's criticism of Asif Zardari's interference in party affairs. Murtaza Bhutto had turned down all overtures of reconciliation with Benazir. Besides, the PPP leadership had to respond to charges of its having Zionist links and doubts about its commitment to Pakistan's nuclear programme.[52]

The election results showed that the PPP and PML (N) were the two major parties in Pakistan and that the country was moving towards a two-party system. The PPP secured eighty-six out of 202 National Assembly seats while the PML (N) won seventy-three seats. In terms of percentage, the PPP got 37.86 per cent of votes while the PML (N) secured 39.86 per cent votes. The remaining seats were distributed among twelve minor parties and the Independents: PML (J) six, IJM (Islami Jamhoori Mahaz) four, ANP three, PIF three, BNM (Baluchistan National Movement) (Haye Group) one, BNM (Mengal Group) one, JWP two, MDM (Mutahidda Dini Mahaz) two, NDA one, NPP one, PKMAP three, PKQP one, and Independents fifteen. In the Punjab assembly, the PML (N) was the largest party with 106 seats while the PPP secured ninety-four and PML (J) twenty-two seats; in the Sindh assembly, the PPP was the majority party with PML (N) eight seats and MQM twenty-seven seats; in the NWFP assembly, the PPP had twenty-two seats, the ANP twenty-one seats and the PML (N) fifteen seats; and in the Baluchistan assembly, the seats were distributed among eleven parties and nine Independents.[53] In the presidential elections in November, Sardar Farooq Ahmad Khan Leghari (PPP) received 274 out of 446 valid polled votes against 168 of Waseem Sajjad [PML (N)].[54]

The National Assembly elected Benazir Bhutto as the prime minister by 121 votes against Nawaz Sharif's seventy-two votes. In Punjab, the PPP-PML (J) nominee, Mian Manzoor Ahmad Wattoo, was elected chief minister, defeating Mian Shahbaz

Sharif; in Sindh, Sayyid Abdullah Shah (PPP) was elected chief minister, defeating Dr Farooq Sattar (MQM); in the NWFP, the PML (N)-ANP nominee, Pir Sabir Shah, was elected chief minister, defeating Aftab Sherpao; and in Baluchistan, an independent-Muslim Leaguer, Zulfikar Ali Magsi, was elected chief minister by defeating Akhtar Mengal of BNM (M).

Benazir's performance in her second tenure was worse than the first one. She completely alienated the Opposition by her actions. The first step that her government took was to bring down the PML (N)-ANP Government in the NWFP by a no-confidence motion, using highly dubious means. Then, more than 140 cases were instituted against Nawaz Sharif and his family. The fact that the cases were dismissed by the higher court strengthened the impression of victimization. Prominent Leaguers were put under detention on trumped-up charges. Many of them were manhandled inside the National Assembly building by the PPP political workers. The Opposition strongly protested against these high-handed measures and launched the *Karwan-i Nijat* and a nation-wide strike in September 1994, which damaged the image of the Benazir government. More serious was the impact of the police firing on a procession of Jamaat-i-Islami at Rawalpindi, in which three persons were killed.

Benazir government's relations with the judiciary also deteriorated. She criticized the Supreme Court for restoring the National Assembly and Nawaz Sharif's government while her government was not restored although it had been dismissed on similar grounds. Soon after, she appointed a junior judge, Justice Sayyid Sajjad Ali Shah, as the Chief Justice of the Supreme Court. Justice Shah was the only dissenting Judge when the Supreme Court had ruled in favour of Nawaz Sharif's contention. The appointment of twenty additional judges to the Lahore High Court in 1994, which included some PPP activists, became the subject of public debate and criticism. Another cause of conflict was the Supreme Court rulings for the separation of judiciary from the executive by 23 March 1994. The PPP government allegedly put pressure on the Chief Justice and his family members to get this decision amended. Then, on 20

March 1996, the Supreme Court overturned the appointment of eleven judges to the higher judiciary.

The law and order situation in Karachi was controlled, according to the MQM, by custodial killings and extra-judicial killings during fake police encounters. President Farooq Leghari felt that he had been relegated to a secondary role and his relations with the Benazir's government did not remain cordial. He openly differed with the government over several issues including the appointment of judges, and developed close contacts with the Opposition and the armed forces. The stories of corruption in the government were rampant and appeared in the media in and outside the country. The most scandalous was the alleged purchase of a mansion in Surrey (UK) by Benazir and her husband, Asif Zardari. The climax was the death of Benazir's brother, Murtaza Bhutto, on 20 September, in a police encounter in Karachi. Ghinwa Bhutto, Murtaza's wife, and many others accused Asif Zardari of involvement in this murder.[55] Now the dismissal of Benazir government was a mere formality; on 5 November, President Leghari dissolved the National Assembly, dismissed the Benazir government, and announced elections to the National Assembly on 3 February 1997. Within two weeks, the governors also dissolved the provincial assemblies and fresh elections to these assemblies were scheduled to be held on the same date. Meraj Khalid, an estranged PPP leader, was installed as the caretaker prime minister.

(vi) THE 1997 ELECTIONS (PML [N] vs. PPP): Again the main contestants were the PML (N) and the PPP, although for a while Imran Khan, with his newly formed party, the Tehrik-i-Insaf, gave the impression of a newly emerging force, but he was soon silenced by the wide publicity of his sex scandals. Qazi Husain Ahmad, the Jamaat-i-Islami chief, advocated a boycott of the elections unless the candidates were screened out according to clauses 62 and 63 of the constitution.

The PML (N), in its election manifesto, advocated an ideal welfare state based on social justice, equal rights for all the sections of the society, provision of basic facilities by modernization of the economy to double the GDP in ten years, higher priority to hydro-electricity to bring down the cost of electricity, greater self-reliance by reducing dependence on foreign loans; balancing of budget, liberalization of laws relating to trade and industry, rationalization of general sales tax, overhauling of tax collection machinery, increase in agricultural production, realization of overdue bank loans, reforms in the financial institutions, autonomy to the State Bank of Pakistan, transparency and acceleration of the privatization process, expansion of the network of highways and motorways, and modernization of the ports and shipping facilities.[56]

The PPP manifesto focused more on the 'achievements' of the Benazir's ousted government, especially in the field of foreign policy. It highlighted its efforts to project the Kashmir issue at the international level and to maintain cordial relations with the US, China, and the Muslim countries. On the domestic front, its emphasis was on its commitment to improve the status of women in the country.[57]

The PML (N) soon emerged as the front-runner in the election campaign, partly by hard work and partly by default. It selected its candidates carefully and made adjustments on seats with the ANP, MQM, and others in various regions. It focused on its performance during its first tenure (1990–93), and denounced the Benazir government's repressive policies, corruption, and disappointing performance. The PPP started campaigning rather late; it was waiting for the Supreme Court to decide the case filed by Benazir against dissolution of her government. It also toyed with the idea of boycotting the elections for some time. It focused on the injustice done by President Farooq Leghari who was christened as 'Farooqul Haq'. But this kind of campaigning could not change the general atmosphere against the party and its leader.

The PML (N) scored a landslide victory. It won 134 out of 204 seats in the National Assembly, while the PPP could win only eighteen seats. The remaining seats were shared by various parties, some of which were allies of the PML (N). MQM (Altaf

Group) got twelve seats, ANP nine, JUI (F) two, BNP three, JWP two, NPP one, PPP (Shaheed Bhutto Group) one, Independents twenty-two.[58] The PML (N) swept the polls to the Punjab assembly, securing 211 seats, while the PPP could win only two seats. In the NWFP also the PML (N) was the leading party with thirty-one seats and its coalescing partner ANP with twenty-seven seats, while the PPP could secure only one seat. In Sindh, the seats were distributed among three parties: the PML (N) fifteen; its coalescing partner MQM (A) twenty-six; PPP thirty-four, and Independents fourteen. In Baluchistan, like the earlier elections, seats were divided among several parties: PML (N) four, BNP nine, JWP six, JUI (F) five, BNM two, PKMAP two, PPP one.[59]

GENERAL OBSERVATIONS

Political parties are the core institution of the democratic process. Their significance for Pakistan is immense because the country itself is the product of the political and constitutional struggle of a political party. Pakistan's chequered political history has hindered the harmonious development of political parties. But except for the period of first martial law, they have maintained their presence on the political scene, even when they were officially banned.

Political parties in Pakistan do not have any scientific method of maintaining their organizations or training their workers in democratic values. One mechanism that is common with parties in Pakistan and other South Asian countries is the enrolment of members and party elections at various tiers. Most of the parties do not perform these functions properly. The enrolment is not done at regular intervals and whenever it is undertaken, it is very faulty. Membership forms are distributed through influential individuals who enrol their supporters and loyalists or enter fictitious names and deposit membership fees from their own pockets. Thus, they manoeuvre to secure party offices for themselves or their nominees, and the party can claim high-sounding membership figures which may not actually be true. The political parties generally avoid elections; some hold it periodically, often adopting dubious methods. If and when party election are held these bring out latent intra-party tensions and conflict. Therefore, those who are in control of the party organization avoid party elections. This policy engenders unhealthy political trends within the party, which are reflected in its performance if it comes to power.

Parties have mushroomed in Pakistan, especially at the time of elections. Many political parties have similar political agenda but they still want to maintain their separate identity. This phenomenon justifies the remark that Pakistan has more political parties than there are shades of opinion. Petty personality differences dissuade the leaders from merging smaller parties into broader parties with uniformity of views. This directly affects electoral politics, and often disables parties to have clear majorities in the elections. The coalition governments that result from such a political situation often find it difficult to govern effectively. These coalition governments spend more energy in keeping the coalition intact than in governing effectively. Material rewards and other benefits are offered to individuals to sustain the support.

This interrupted political process and lack of proper elections within parties have not only resulted in an unnecessary proliferation of political parties, but have also impeded the emergence of responsible political leadership with a national outlook. As a result, the leaders prefer to lead smaller parties with parochial, regional, and sectarian agendas rather than be part of a bigger and broader national programme. They lack confidence in their own party and programme. Therefore, instead of being engaged in a positive projection of their own standpoints, they indulge in negative tactics. Undue derision and character assassination of the rivals are the major weapons, especially in the election campaign. Such an attitude generates intolerance and hinders the development of a stable party system and a healthy polity.

These political parties often offer high sounding and unrealistic programmes and promises to attract voters. They use slogans of a topical nature to charm the politically uneducated masses to their ranks. Religious and economic issues are commonly exploited in an environment of poverty and illiteracy. The policy statements and speeches of the leaders hardly reflect any deep and serious understanding of the socio-economic problems and the ways and means to cope with these problems. It is important that the political parties develop a mature and articulate approach to the socio-economic problems and engage in popular mobilization in a realistic manner. The stabilization and success of the democratic process depends mainly on the quality of the political leadership and how the political parties discharge their primary responsibilities in the polity.

NOTES AND REFERENCES

1. For a detailed study, see Safdar Mahmood, *Muslim League ka Daur-e-Hakumat, 1947-54* (Urdu), Lahore: 1972.
2. *Dawn,* 20 February 1948.
3. Mushtaq Ahmad, *Government and Politics in Pakistan,* Karachi: 1978, p. 138.
4. *Dawn,* 9 October 1950.
5. Ibid.
6. *Nawa-i-Waqt,* 13 August 1950.
7. Proceedings of the Pakistan Muslim League Council, 29 January 1956.
8. Mushtaq Ahmad, *Government and Politics,* p. 145.
9. *Manifesto of the Pakistan Democratic Party,* published by Ahmad Ali Mondal, Dacca, 1969, p. 1.
10. For details, see N.C. Sahni, *Political Struggle in Pakistan,* Jullundur, 1969, pp. 145–59.
11. *Keesings,* 17–24 May 1969, p. 23353.
12. *The Muslim,* 1 November 1983. See Muhammad Waseem's article.
13. *Foundation and Policy, Pakistan People's Party,* printed by Mubashir Hasan, Lahore, 1967.
14. Ferozsons, *Political Parties: Their Policies and Programmes,* Lahore: Ferozsons, pp. 216–8.
15. Ibid., p. 227.
16. *The Financial Times,* 13 August 1973. Pakistan Supplement, p. 11.
17. Ibid.

18. *The Guardian,* 6 February 1976.
19. *Pakistan Times,* 13 January 1974. For a detailed analysis of the corruption and undemocratic policies of the Pakistan People's Party's government, see Anwar H. Syed, 'People's Party in Pakistan', in Lawrence Ziring, et al., *Pakistan: The Long View,* Durham, N.C.: Duke University Press, 1967; Khalid bin Sayeed, *Politics in Pakistan,* New York: Praeger, 1980 (See chapter on 'Bhutto's Populist Movement and the Bonapartist State'); and Lawrence Ziring, *Pakistan: The Enigma of Political Development,* Boulder, Co.: Westview Press, 1980.
20. For a detailed study, see M. Rafique Afzal, *Political Parties in Pakistan, 1947-58,* Islamabad: National Commission on Historical and Cultural Research, 1976, pp. 219–22; and K.K. Aziz, *Party Politics in Pakistan, 1947-58,* Islamabad: National Commission on Historical and Cultural Research, 1976, pp. 111–14.
21. Cited in Aziz, *Party Politics,* p. 114.
22. Mushtaq Ahmad, *Government and Politics,* p. 149.
23. Sayeed, *Politics in Pakistan,* p. 123.
24. Ibid., pp. 126–27.
25. Ibid., pp. 116–17. Also see Satish Kumar, *The New Pakistan,* Delhi: Vikas Publishing House, 1978, pp. 164–215.
26. Ibid., pp. 178–215.
27. *Nawa-i-Waqt,* 27 February 1973.
28. *New Times,* 16 March 1973.
29. Asad Gilani, *Tehrik-i-Islami,* Multan, 1962, p. 30. Asad Gilani, *Tehrik-i-Islami,* Multan, 1962, p. 30.
30. Ibid., p. 30. Address by the Jamaat *Amir* in 1945.
31. Ibid.
32. Ibid., p. 34.
33. For details, see Rafique Afzal, *Political Parties,* pp. 33–36.
34. Ziring, *Long View,* p. 128; and Sayeed, *Politics in Pakistan,* p. 157.
35. *Pakistan People's Party's Manifesto,* PPP Central Secretariat, Rawalpindi, 1977.
36. See the text of the PNA manifesto in *Dawn,* 10 February 1977.
37. Ibid.
38. Ibid.
39. Ibid., 11 February 1977.
40. For details of the election campaign, see Sharif al Mujahid, 'The 1977 Elections', in Manzooruddin Ahmad, ed., *Contemporary Pakistan: Politics, Economy and Society,* Karachi: Royal Book Company, 1982, pp. 63–87.
41. Ibid., p.78.
42. Ibid., p. 79.
43. '77 Elections: An Analysis', in *Pakistan Economist,* 23 July 1977, pp. 22–23; and *Dawn,* 6 April 1977.

44. For details, See William L. Richter, 'From Electoral Politics to Martial Law: Alternative Perspectives on Pakistan's Political Crisis', in Ahmad, *Contemporary Pakistan*, pp. 92–96; and Sayeed, *Politics in Pakistan*, pp. 157–63.
45. Satish Kumar, *New Pakistan*, pp. 348–49.
46. *Pakistan Times*, 14 October 1988.
47. Maleeha Lodhi and Zahid Husain, 'Pakistan's Invisible Government', *Newsline*, October 1992, p. 30.
48. Maleeha Lodhi and Zahid Husain, 'Power play in Islamabad', *Newsline*, June 1992, p. 25; and Zafar Abbas, 'The Year of the President', *Herald*, January 1993, p. 25.
49. Zafar Abbas, 'The Final Showdown', *Herald*, March 1993, and 'Enter the Army', ibid., July 1993.
50. Mohammad Waseem, *The 1993 Elections in Pakistan*, Lahore: Vanguard, 1994, pp. 110–24.
51. *Dawn*, 7, 8, 9 and 14 September 1993.
52. Ibid., 10, 12 August and 8 September 1993.
53. Waseem, *1993 Elections*, pp. 154 and 165.
54. *Report of the Presidential Elections, 1993*, Islamabad, 1993.
55. Mohammad Waseem, 'Pakistan Elections 1997: One Step Forward', in Craig Baxter and Charles H. Kennedy ed., *Pakistan: 1997*, Boulder, Co.: Westview Press, 1998, pp. 1–16.
56. *The News*, 1 January 1997.
57. Ibid., 6 January 1997.
58. *Herald*, March 1997; and Waseem, *Elections 1997*, pp. 10–13.
59. Mushtaq Ahmad, *Government and Politics*, p. 355.

4

FOREIGN POLICY AND EXTERNAL RELATIONS

No state can live in isolation or stay totally indifferent to what is happening in the international system. The developments outside the boundaries of a state have implications for its domestic affairs and the goals it pursues at the national and international levels. A country's national interests are the overriding considerations that shape its disposition towards other states and the developments at the international level. These are the values and objectives that a state emphasizes as the primary determinants of its political disposition and policies towards the rest of the world. These national interests or primary goals stem from the historical and ideological perspectives and the major economic and geopolitical considerations.

Usually survival and security are the major objectives of foreign policy. These are coupled with securing material welfare and prosperity for the people. However, material progress marches hand in hand with moral progress and adherence to higher human values. Therefore, foreign policy of a country should aim at the realization of the national interests and aspirations within the framework of the established norms of international conduct, such as, the Charter of the United Nations which underlines peace and justice, equality, tolerance, fundamental human rights, and service to mankind as the core values for international interaction.

The foreign policy of a country, however, cannot be static. As remarked by Lord Palmerston, there can be no eternal friends nor can there be eternal enemies in international relations. The only eternal factor is the national interest. Foreign policy continues to evolve according to the changing circumstances and conditions. The principal objectives of Pakistan's foreign policy have been security and economic development. The consideration for security is related to the defence of the country and the preservation of ideology.[1] The consideration of development springs from the realization that survival can not be ensured without economic development and social justice.

The present-day world is under the sway of big powers. Every big power is keen to secure spheres of influence in different parts of the world. Therefore, these powers are always busy in protecting and advancing their interests in the international system through political and economic diplomacy and, if needed, the use or threat of use of force. Their policies of peace and war have a strong impact on the political developments in the international system. This restricts the freedom of action on the part of the smaller states, although there are instances where the latter have persuaded the former to alter their strategies and approaches to international affairs.

Pakistan has maintained a close interaction with the international community in order to protect and advance its interests and to pursue its goals. Apart from the ideological and economic considerations, the geopolitical factors have been a major influence on Pakistan's foreign policy. Pakistan had a unique geography up to 1971 in the sense that it comprised two non-contiguous parts, East and West, separated by one thousand miles of Indian territory. This became a serious security issue because of the rift in India-Pakistan relations. The serious problems in the Indo-Pakistan relations and the split of Pakistani territory in West Pakistan and East Pakistan (now Bangladesh), led Pakistan to spend more on defence as compared to other developing countries. Geographically, East Pakistan was surrounded by India from three sides. Pakistan as a whole is wedged in between three big neighbours, namely, the Soviet Union, China, and India. There is no other country in the world which has a geographical situation akin to Pakistan. 'I know of no other small country which has the somewhat dubious distinction of having three such mighty neighbours.'[2] This created serious security pressures on Pakistan and assigned importance to its relations with India.

FOREIGN POLICY 1947–76

India

It is a dismal reality that the prospects of establishing normal relations between Pakistan and India have always appeared dim. Most Indian elite continue to question the establishment of Pakistan and some of them have not yet reconciled to the existence of Pakistan.[3] These attitudes are periodically reflected in India's official policy. Defence and security against India has always been the major concern for Pakistan. 'Pakistanis cite the long-cherished belief held among the Hindus regarding the sacred unity of India, the ancient land of Hindus. India questions the very basis of Pakistan which was established on the theory that contiguous areas constituting Muslim majority would be separated from India and constitute the state of Pakistan.'[4] Pakistan was refused its due share of assets of undivided India at the time of the Partition. India practically stopped or severely restricted the flow of the river waters to the territory of Pakistan, so badly needed to irrigate the cultivable areas. There have been three major wars between India and Pakistan in 1948, 1965, and 1971. As a result, tension or a state of cold war has always existed between the two countries. These problems have led Pakistan to allocate a substantial portion of its national budget to defence. Thus, the cornerstone of Pakistan's foreign policy is defence and security against India, a country that enjoys considerable military superiority over Pakistan, and has always, spurned Pakistan's efforts to normalize bilateral relations.

Pakistan needed stable and peaceful relations with India for setting up the new administrative structure to make the state viable. However, India refused to extend any co-operation from the beginning. India did not fulfil its obligation to transfer

Pakistan's share of military, financial, and other assets of the British Indian government to Pakistan. India's decision to extract an instrument of accession from the ruler of Kashmir through dubious means and occupation of Junagadh and Hyderabad through military action spoiled bilateral relations, not to speak of the impact of the killings that accompanied the Partition process. The outbreak of war in Kashmir (1947–48) further undermined their relations and threatened Pakistan's efforts to put its house in order. In a couple of years, the two states developed problems on sharing river water, as India interfered with the supply of canal water to Pakistan, threatening Pakistan's agriculture. The ill-feelings caused by these unfortunate developments continued to haunt their relations in the later years.

Kashmir: The problem of Kashmir can not be fully grasped without viewing its historical background. The valley of Kashmir was sold to Gulab Singh, Dogra ruler of Jammu, for seventy-five lakh (7.5 million) rupees by Lord Lawrence as a consequence of the Treaty of Amritsar (March 1846).[5] Hari Singh, a descendant of Gulab Singh, was the maharaja or ruler of the state of Jammu and Kashmir at the time of the Partition of the subcontinent. According to the census figures of 1947, the Muslims constituted 77 per cent of the population. The Muslims were living in miserable conditions under the maharaja's rule. The Dogra maharajas were alien, incompetent, dissolute, and tyrannical.[6] Political agitation against the despotic rule of the maharaja had started in the early 1930s. It was in this year that the All-Jammu and Kashmir Muslim Conference was founded and a demand for basic political rights put forward. The confrontation between the ruler of Kashmir and the politically active elements continued till 1947; the political leaders were periodically arrested.

About a month before the establishment of Pakistan, Lord Mountbatten, the viceroy of India, advised the Indian princes to accede to India or to Pakistan, keeping in mind the geographical position of their states and the wishes of their people.[7] This clearly meant that accession to India or Pakistan was to be dependent on two factors namely, geographical proximity and the wishes of the people. From both these standards, Kashmir was destined to become a part of Pakistan. From the geographical point of view, Kashmir had common border with Pakistan to the extent of 902 miles, while with India it had only 317 miles of common border. The two roads which served as a link between Jammu and Kashmir and the rest of the world passed through Pakistan. The three main rivers which irrigate the land of Pakistan originate from Kashmir.[8] The predominant majority of Kashmiri Muslims was showing strong affinity with Pakistan. It was expected that as the wishes of the people had to be taken into account while deciding about the accession of Kashmir, it would go in favour of Pakistan. As the Kashmiri people revolted against the ruler immediately after the withdrawal of the British rule in India, the ruler sought India's support to cope with the revolt. The Indian government, knowing the predicament of the ruler, forced him to sign accession with India as a pre-condition for making the Indian army available in support of the ruler of Kashmir. India, while accepting the instrument of accession, promised to settle the future of the state with reference to the people of Kashmir. A similar commitment to seek the vote of the people on the future of Kashmir was made by India to the UN Security Council, a promise that was never fulfilled by India.

In January 1948, India complained to the UN Security Council that Pakistan was giving aid to the tribesmen who had invaded a part of the valley. Since then, the Security Council has met 136 times to consider this dispute between India and Pakistan,[9] but without any tangible result. On the persistent demand of Pakistan, India agreed to hold a plebiscite in Kashmir to ascertain the wishes of the people in 1948. Then it demanded the withdrawal of Pakistani troops and nationals from Kashmir. The plebiscite was never held because, according to India, Pakistan did not withdraw its troops, which was a prerequisite for holding the plebiscite. 'If an offer is made and is not accepted or not implemented, it can not stand for ever'[10] was the contention of the Indian representative in the Security Council in response to Pakistan's demand for plebiscite. Pakistan, on the other hand, demanded plebiscite in Kashmir on the basis of the right of self-determination as enunciated in the Charter of the United Nations. Pakistan always agreed to the withdrawal of its troops from Azad Kashmir if India did the same in the main valley. Whenever the proposal for de-militarization and stationing of UN forces was put forward, Pakistan always accepted the proposal but India insisted upon the complete and unilateral withdrawal of Pakistani forces only.[11] The same opinion was expressed by General A.G.L. McNaughton in 1950 in his report to the Security Council. He stated that Pakistan accepted the proposal for a simultaneous de-militarization of the territories under the control of UN, but 'India insisted upon the complete withdrawal of Pakistani forces and the occupation of the northern areas of Baltistan and Gilgit by the Indian Army.'[12]

In 1950, Sir Owen Dixon was appointed the mediator by the UN to work on the procedures for holding a plebiscite in Kashmir in consultation with the governments of India and Pakistan. This effort also failed. Lord Atlee, prime minister of the United Kingdom, presented three suggestions for the settlement of the Kashmir problem to the Commonwealth Prime Ministers' Conference in January 1951. The proposals asked for setting up of either (1) a Commonwealth force; or (2) a joint Indo-Pak force; or (3) a local force to be raised by the plebiscite administrator. Each of these proposals was accepted by Pakistan, but rejected by India. On 22 February 1951, an Anglo-American resolution was brought before the Security Council, suggesting that the Kashmir dispute be submitted to the International Court of Justice for arbitration. Pakistan showed its willingness but India again disagreed.

In 1953, Muhammad Ali Bogra, Pakistan's prime minister, held negotiations with Nehru, the prime minister of India, on Kashmir. In the first communiqué, they agreed that the Kashmir dispute should be settled in accordance with the wishes of the people of that state. The most feasible way of ascertaining the wishes of the people was fair and impartial plebiscite.[13] It was also decided that a plebiscite administrator should be appointed who would make arrangements for holding an impartial plebiscite in the state.[14]

Meanwhile Nehru came to know that Pakistan was likely to receive military aid from the USA. This gave an excuse to Nehru to delay the matter. Nehru stated, while addressing the Lok Sabha in December 1953, that India could not honour the agreement set forth in the communiqué because 'the whole context in which these arrangement were made will change if military aid comes from America.'[15] Here it should be made clear that by December 1953, Pakistan had neither received military aid from the USA nor entered into any defence pact.[16]

During the Ayub regime, the Pakistan government made all possible efforts to normalize relations with India and to settle all outstanding disputes. Ayub Khan went to the extent of proposing joint defence with India in March 1959,[17] provided India agreed to the settlement of the Kashmir dispute. But his gesture was not appreciated by the Indian leadership, and Nehru remarked: 'I do not understand against whom people talk about common defence policy.'[18] India rejected the idea, because Pakistan was receiving military aid from the USA, while at the same time India itself was obtaining weapons from abroad. However, the conciliatory gesture of Ayub Khan blew a fresh breeze to cool down the tension, and the chronic Indus waters dispute was settled by a treaty on 19 September 1960.

During the India-China conflict in 1962, the USA, the UK, and some other western governments exerted pressure on Pakistan to show morale-boosting gestures to India during this crisis. President Kennedy wrote to Ayub Khan, suggesting a message to the Indian prime minister that 'he could count on Pakistan's taking no action on the frontiers to alarm India.'[19] This move was intended to show Pakistan's friendly stance, so that India could concentrate all its strength against China. The president of the USA and other Western countries hoped that the 'painful moments which India was then experiencing would teach them how much more important the threat from the North (the communist giants) was to the whole of subcontinent', and they also assured the president of the Pakistan that the action taken by him 'in the larger interests of the subcontinent would do more in the long run to bring about a sensible resolution of Pakistan-India differences than anything else.'[20]

As a consequence, direct talks between Ayub Khan and Nehru were arranged. On 20 November 1962, a joint communiqué was issued by both the governments, which expressed the desire for a 'renewed effort' 'to resolve the outstanding differences between the two countries on Kashmir and related matters.'[21] The statement brought a ray of hope to the people of Pakistan. But the real intentions of the Indian government were soon exposed when Nehru tried to modify, in a statement in the Lok Sabha, his undertaking given in the communiqué. His statement again put the issue into cold storage. Nehru had been so swiftly changing his stand on Kashmir that it became difficult to believe his words. Bhutto, the then foreign minister of Pakistan, reacted sharply and remarked in the National Assembly, while discussing the above-mentioned communiqué that 'if one were to accept them, it would follow that the joint communiqué is actually a deception and a fraud.'[22]

As a matter of fact, Nehru had expressed his desire for renewed effort under the pressure of the Chinese attack and American persuasion, otherwise he had been insisting since 1953 that Kashmir was a settled issue. 'Within weeks of the unilateral declaration of ceasefire by China, the Indian attitude changed completely and the talks, which had never held much promise, got bogged down in procedural wrangles and academic inanities.'[23]

The foreign minister level negotiations on Kashmir between India and Pakistan were held from December 1962 to May 1963. During these talks, Pakistan demanded that the people of Kashmir should be granted the right of self-determination. But the Indian delegation proposed the re-adjustment of the existing ceasefire line in Kashmir as a method for settling the problem.[24] Pakistan rejected the Indian suggestion. The negotiations ended in failure, which did not come as a surprise to anybody in Pakistan, but this caused some embarrassment to the great powers that were instrumental in holding these talks. The attitude of the Indian government towards the Kashmir problem was best explained by Chagla, the Indian representative, who declared in the Security Council on 5 February 1964: 'I wish to make it clear on behalf of my government that under no circumstances can we agree to the holding of a plebiscite in Kashmir.'[25] Why has India persistently refused to hold plebiscite in Kashmir was explained by the former Indian defence minister, Krishna Menon, who said: 'Kashmir would vote to join Pakistan and no Indian government responsible for agreeing to plebiscite would survive.'[26] This statement revealed the ground realities as well as apprehensions of the Indian leadership.

Another painful aspect of the Kashmir dispute is the failure of the United Nations and callous indifference on the part of great powers to resolve the issue. The United Nations has discussed the Kashmir issue many times and has passed several resolutions, but it has failed to get these implemented. This has shaken the confidence of the people of Pakistan and Kashmir in the international organization. As regards the big powers, they never took the problem seriously. For many years, the Soviet Union either abstained from voting in the Security Council on the Kashmir issue or vetoed the resolutions. The obvious reason for the indifferent attitude of the Soviet Union was Pakistan's membership of the South East Asia Treaty Organization (SEATO) and the Central Treaty Organization (CENTO). The Western allies on whom Pakistan depended for help did not attach much importance to the problem and never took the initiative to resolve the dispute.

Instead of maintaining a balance in the subcontinent, the USA and its allies gave massive military aid to India after the Indo-China border flare-up in October 1962. Pakistan protested against it and expressed its apprehension that India would use this military hardware against Pakistan and that this would also make India more stubborn in its dealings. President Ayub Khan told President Kennedy during his visit to the USA, that 'arms assistance to India would only encourage her to remain in occupation of areas which did not belong to her and the prospects of any just settlement of the dispute [Kashmir] would be eliminated'.[27] Despite all these protests, arms assistance to India continued.

In August 1965, the Indian government accused Pakistan of having sent infiltrators in Kashmir; this alleged action triggered war between the two countries on 6 September 1965, which lasted till 23 September, when a ceasefire was brought into force as a consequence of a Security Council resolution. After the ceasefire, the Soviet prime minister offered to mediate between the two sides. On invitation of Premier Kosygin, President Ayub Khan and Indian Prime Minister Lal Bahadar Shastri, travelled to Tashkent to negotiate peace and normalization of relations. Kosygin actively participated in the talks, and India and Pakistan agreed to sign a peace treaty called the Tashkent Declaration in January 1966. In the Tashkent Declaration, prime minister of India and president of Pakistan expressed their determination to restore normal relations, create a good neighbourly environment, and to settle their disputes through peaceful means. As a result of this agreement, the armies were withdrawn to their original positions and diplomatic relations were restored.

As regards the settlement of the disputes through peaceful means, promised by the Tashkent Declaration, the situation remained unchanged. The optimism generated by the declaration soon faded into insignificance. The Soviet government did not show any interest in the settlement of any old disputes and problems; it was more interested in normalization of the situation after the war. The Soviets also insisted on direct talks between India and Pakistan for the settlement of their problems. With the exception of settling the immediate problems arising out of the war, the Tashkent Declaration did not contribute to resolving any of the problems dating back to the pre-war period. That was the reason that there was much disenchantment about the Tashkent Declaration in Pakistan. Though Pakistan's diplomatic interaction with the Soviet Union temporarily improved, and the Soviet Union provided a limited number of weapons to Pakistan in 1968–70, its support to India continued to be pronounced. In fact, it increased over time as the Soviet Union stepped up military supplies and economic and technological assistance to India. When India and Pakistan seriously diverged on the East Pakistan problem (1971), the Soviet Union came out openly in support of India and extended military and diplomatic support to India when the 1971 Indo-Pakistan war (November–December) broke out. Naturally, the Kashmir problem remained unresolved, and thus it is still a threat to peace and stability in South Asia.[28]

Other Problems and Issues: Apart from the Kashmir problem, the tension over the water dispute and the Farrakka Dam was also responsible for the strained relations between India and Pakistan. Indus waters dispute was solved through the efforts of the World Bank. As a result of the Indus Water Treaty, signed in September 1960, India got the right to exclusive use of water from three rivers, namely, Ravi, Sutlej and Beas; the three upper rivers were allocated for use by Pakistan, namely, Indus, Jhelum, and Chenab. A network of dams and canals was built to transfer water from these upper rivers to the lower river areas to compensate for the water of the latter lost to India.

A particularly serious situation in India-Pakistan relations developed after the hijacking of an Indian Fokker Friendship plane to Lahore on 30 January 1971. The government of Pakistan immediately instituted an inquiry which revealed that the whole drama was organized by the Indian intelligence agency for specific motives; firstly, to ban the flights of Pakistani aircrafts over Indian territory so that inter-wing communication between East and West Pakistan was disrupted; secondly, to prove that Pakistan was involved in the Kashmir situation so that justification for Indian intervention in former East Pakistan was created.

The army action in former East Pakistan in March 1971 created a wedge between the two provinces and led to a civil war. India fully exploited the situation by aiding and abetting the separatist movement in East Pakistan; it played a decisive role in the break-up of Pakistan in December 1971.[29]

It was during the crisis of 1971 that the need for a stable representative government was realized very intensely in Pakistan. The diplomatic offensive of Pakistan against India failed miserably because of the incompetence of the military leadership. This was the first severe test of Pakistan's foreign policy, which laid bare its flaws and led to the complete re-appraisal and reshaping of the foreign policy in response to the new geopolitical realities.

The Changing Pattern of Relations with the Major Powers

Liaquat Ali Khan, the first prime minister of Pakistan (August 1947–October 1851), was a staunch supporter of non-alignment movement; he shaped the foreign policy of the country on neutral lines. Opposed to any alliances, he followed an independent foreign policy. Under Liaquat Ali Khan, Pakistan was neither tied to the apron-strings of the Anglo-American bloc nor was it a camp-follower of the communist bloc.[30]

Liaquat Ali Khan was invited by Stalin to visit the Soviet Union in 1949. Reflecting over the conflict of ideologies, he let this opportunity slide. Instead, he visited the USA in 1950. The non-acceptance of the Soviet invitation has been described as a 'grave diplomatic blunder'.[31] It is said that if Liaquat Ali Khan had visited Moscow, 'Pakistan's position would have been better appreciated by America and the Russian attitude would certainly have been conciliatory.'[32]

Pakistan was in a desperate need of diplomatic support and economic assistance from the outside for coping with its socio-economic problems. By the early fifties, the USA was showing a keen interest in Asia. It had chalked out a grand programme for re-structuring the economy of war-ravaged Europe (Marshall Plan, 1947) and for extending aid to the Asian countries. 'Liaquat's visit to the USA was probably actuated by the same consideration.'[33] Since Liaquat went to the USA ignoring Stalin's invitation, deep significance was attached to his visit to

America. Despite Liaquat's non-alignment policy, it was understood that he was tacitly inclined towards the West.

During his visit to the USA, Liaquat projected Pakistan as a democratic state following an independent foreign policy. He commented on his visit, 'If we come to a better understanding of each other's point of view, my visit will stand as an event of great importance in the history of Pakistan's foreign relations.'[34] Liaquat also tried to persuade the USA to take the initiative for solving the Kashmir dispute, but he received a poor response.[35] However, as a consequence of Liaquat's visit, Pakistan received aid from the USA, free from any obligation or influence on its independent foreign policy. The records of the United Nations debates bear testimony to the fact that at times it agreed with the Western bloc, and sometimes with the communist bloc, as the merits of the case demanded.[36]

After the death of Liaquat Ali Khan in October 1951, Khwaja Nazimuddin succeeded him as the prime minister. During his tenure, Pakistan faced a serious food crisis. On his request, the US government readily granted eight million tons of grains to Pakistan. But 'his approach to the United States for assistance could not be construed as a prelude to a military line-up... neither did he carry the country into the Western camp.'[37]

The ensuing period was marked by a change in the foreign policy of Pakistan. It appeared that the United States was prepared to extend economic aid to Pakistan and that Pakistan was willing to accede to American political demands. Ghulam Muhammad, the then governor-general of Pakistan, visited the USA in November 1953, and held conferences with President Eisenhower. It is also significant that Muhammad Ali Bogra, the then prime minister, had been an ambassador in the USA. It was generally believed in Pakistan that his appointment as the prime minister was manipulated by the US government. After the visit of the Governor-General Ghulam Muhammad, an announcement was made by the US government formally informing India that a military agreement with Pakistan was under consideration.[38] Prime Minister Muhammad Ali also said that Pakistan was thinking of forging a military alliance in the Middle East.

In 1954, the Mutual Defence Assistance Agreement was signed with the United states. The military alliance with Turkey was concluded soon after. These developments evidenced Pakistan's participation in the South East Asian Treaty Organization (SEATO). The calculated object of this treaty was the containment of communism. Pakistan, by entering into this treaty, received no guarantee of collective action against non-communist attack on its soil, while it was committed to take part in any collective action against 'red' aggression. Pakistan, apparently, could not reject the treaty without losing the economic and military assistance from the US. Now Pakistan had moved from a position of qualified neutrality to one of unqualified alliance with the West, because 'it was no longer possible for it to keep aloof from the conflict between the two major blocs'.[39] In 1955, Pakistan joined the Baghdad Pact, later known as the Central Treaty Organization (CENTO). By this time Pakistan was firmly on the Western side of the fence and this brewed an impression that Pakistan was 'being taken for granted'.[40]

The entry of Pakistan into SEATO and CENTO has been justified on the grounds that due to constant hostility of India, Pakistan had to look for allies to ensure its security. 'It was obvious that Pakistani leaders, in signing these pacts, were motivated primarily by their desire to improve the defensive capacity of Pakistan against India.'[41] There was also a strong desire in Pakistan to forge closer relations with Muslim countries. Pakistan saw in the pact of CENTO a chance to establish closer friendly relations with Iran and Turkey. Another reason for Pakistan joining the Baghdad Pact was stability and consolidation of the Muslim world. Pakistan thought that the Middle East being a vulnerable area 'could become a source of conflict between the Soviet Union and the Western world. Once such a conflict started, it would spread to our borders and seriously endanger our security. It was natural that we should have been deeply interested in any arrangement for the defence and security of this area. We also hoped that through this pact we would get a certain measure of protection against Indian designs in the Middle East.'[42]

It is difficult to make an objective assessment of the advantages which accrued to Pakistan due to these pacts. Pakistan badly needed military assistance, which was extended amounting to 1.5 billion dollars, between 1954 and 1965.[43] The economic assistance extended in the shape of PL-480 and other tied grants and loans amounted to three billion dollars. Apart from material assistance, Pakistan was able to develop closer relations with Iran and Turkey through these pacts. This relationship with Iran and Turkey finally led to the establishment of the Regional Co-operation for Development (RCD) in 1964.

'An indirect and paradoxical advantage of the Baghdad Pact was that we came to realize the disadvantages and dangers inherent in any political or military alliances of a regional character.'[44] In terms of disadvantages, Pakistan lost its independence of action. Its previous image of non-alignment was shattered. But, the greatest harm was done to the cause of Kashmir. Till 1953, India had agreed that the Kashmir dispute should be settled through an impartial plebiscite. But, when Pakistan joined the Western camp, Nehru repudiated previous commitments for holding a plebiscite in Kashmir. From then onwards, Indian efforts were diverted to isolating Pakistan at the international level. Similarly, the Soviet Union which had been neutral on the Kashmir dispute, accused Pakistan of becoming a member of an aggressive Western alliance and Khrushchev declared that Kashmir was an integral part of India.'[45] Thenceforth, the Soviet Union began to subscribe to India's claim that 'no plebiscite was possible or necessary in Kashmir.'[46] Upto that time the Soviet Union had abstained from voting whenever this issue came up for discussion, but after 1955, it vetoed every resolution of the Security Council on Kashmir.

Pakistan also incurred great hostility in the Arab world. The Baghdad Pact was bitterly opposed by president Nasser of Egypt, who accused Pakistan of 'indulging in divisive activities in the

Arab world'.[47] As a corollary to this situation, the Arab world was not prepared to support Pakistan's cause of Kashmir, though Kashmir was a Muslim majority state.

Apart from the containment of communism in Asia, the US desired another advantage from these military alliances with Pakistan. During the hearings of the Congressional Committee on Foreign Relations, it was stated that 'Pakistan can be an efficacious advocate of Western policies and can exert a moderating influence on the extreme nationalism and anti-Western attitudes'[48] of other Muslim states and members of the Afro-Asian bloc. Whether the US succeeded in achieving its goal or not is a different matter, but for Pakistan, these pacts turned out to be serious liabilities. Pakistan was often referred to as a blind camp-follower of the Western powers.[49]

Pakistan's pro-West policy continued till 1958, when General Ayub came to power as the result of martial law. Meanwhile, the policy of the US had been to appease India by giving it military aid in spite of the protests by the government of Pakistan. By 1960–61, it seemed that the American policy in Asia was undergoing a change. President Kennedy came to power in 1961. By this time some of the liberal intellectuals in the US were advocating the view that 'India, being the most influential and powerful democracy in Asia, should be supported by the West in the ideological power struggle that was taking place in Asia between the free world and a communist power like China.'[50] Selig Harrison went to the extent of saying that it was not the business of the US to subside Pakistan as a permanent garrison state with a military capability swollen out of proportion to its size. The suspension of democratic processes in Pakistan in 1958 was also criticized by journalists of the US. The status of Pakistan was so reduced internationally that Vice-President L.B. Johnson urged Nehru to extend his leadership to other areas in South-East Asia. This, he said, was in accordance with the wishes of President Kennedy.

From the military point of view, the importance of these pacts had also been reduced due to the decreasing dependence of the US on military bases in foreign countries as a result of the development of international ballistic missiles. This clearly reflected the change in the attitude of the US. As long as these pacts served the purpose of the US, it gave Pakistan some support, but when they were no longer useful for it, the US policy underwent a change in favour of India.

It was at this point that a growing need for re-evaluation of the foreign policy was felt in Pakistan. The feeling was growing that the US no longer attached much importance to the military pacts 'and that the whole military thinking has become different.'[51] So, with the change of American attitude, the foreign policy of Pakistan was also gradually changing. The trends in favour of normalizing relations with two powerful neighbours, China and the Soviet Union became apparent by 1960 in the foreign policy of Pakistan. By 1962, it became imperative for Pakistan to develop a closer understanding with China, because the USA was no longer interested in the security of Pakistan and was also giving more aid to India than to Pakistan. 'In consequence, Pakistan began to find herself at variance with America and Britain, whose steady support of India in face of Chinese hostility increased her sense of isolation, causing her to draw rather closer to China.'[52]

Another factor which greatly influenced the thinking of the planners of foreign policy was the India-China border clash in 1962. Even after the clash, India exaggerated the Chinese hostility and manoeuvred to receive massive military aid from the USA and USSR. In December 1962, the US extended military aid to India worth 120 million dollars.[53] In June 1963, the US again gave substantial military aid to India. During this period, India raised its army from eleven to twenty-two divisions, and also expanded its air force and navy.[54] Pakistan expressed grave concern over tilting the balance of power in favour of India. The US response was the usual assurance that these weapons would be used only against communist China.

Pakistan's fears were best represented by former President Ayub Khan who stated: 'Having built up this enormous war machine, India's leadership would need to justify the great hardships it had imposed on the Indian people in the process. It might also want to regain face, which it lost in the fighting with China. It was possible, therefore, that India might decide to do so by throwing her massive armour against Pakistan and possibly striking that part of Kashmir which is under Pakistan control.'[55] Later events proved that the fears expressed by Pakistan were well-founded. In 1965, India attacked Pakistan and used American weapons. These events strained the Pakistan-US relations, for it was clear that the US was out to appease India and 'get her in its orbit of political influence', and 'if Pakistan did not feel happy about it, there was nothing that the United States could do.'[56] As a result, the people of Pakistan were disillusioned because 'a relationship which had been built up after a great deal of hard work during the fifties was ceasing to command respect.'[57]

The resentment against the defence pacts—SEATO and CENTO—already existed in Pakistan but these were subjected to even greater criticism during and after the 1965 Indo-Pakistan war. The war exposed the futility of these pacts for Pakistan. While Pakistan was committed to fight against communist aggression along with the US, the members of the pacts were not obliged to help Pakistan during foreign aggression against it. Meanwhile, the attitude of the US towards these pacts also changed. Consequently the pacts lost much of their original value.

On the one hand, there was disillusionment against the US and its Western allies; on the other hand, China was emerging as a great power. Pakistan's geopolitical situation was such that it could not afford to trifle with its mighty neighbour. So far, Pakistan had completely depended on the West, but now the 'change of attitude' brought it to a point where it became imperative to search for new friends and normalize relations with China. 'And then there was the People's Republic of China fast emerging as a power to be reckoned with the USA. If we would not establish normal relations with all our three big neighbours, the best thing was to have an understanding with two of them... It was on this basis that we set out to normalize our relations with People's Republic of China and the Soviet

Union. It is in this sense that our geographical location and the political compulsions inherent therein have determined the course of our foreign policy in recent years.'[58]

When Pakistan took steps to improve its relations with China and the Soviet Union, 'the reaction of the United States was that of resentment.' In spite of Pakistan's efforts to maintain a balance between its growing friendship with China and its loyalty to its Western ally, by the year 1962, the US-Pakistan relations had been subjected to great strains, and in the course of this year the United States suspended its economic aid to Pakistan and later, on the outbreak of war in 1965, it placed an embargo on the supply of military aid as well.[59]

Pakistan-China air agreement was strongly criticized as an 'unfortunate breach of the free world solidarity', which was bound to 'have no adverse effect on efforts to strengthen the security and solidarity of the sub-continent.'[60] 'The withdrawal of US offer of financing the construction of a new airport at Dacca, the cancellation of President Ayub's visit to Washington in 1965, and the postponement of the Aid-to-Pakistan Consortium meeting in July 1965, are some of the measures resorted to by the United States to pressurize Pakistan.'[61] 'Pakistan's dislike of American involvement in Vietnam also excited resentment.'[62] The high hats of the State Department of the USA 'could not reconcile themselves to the idea that Pakistan should be acting in the field of foreign affairs without their permission.'[63] The US thought that since it had given Pakistan substantial aid, the latter 'had no right to protect herself and ensure her security in whatever manner she thought fit.'[64] Pakistan made it clear to the US that its step to normalize relations with China did not mean going into the communist orbit. It was in view of its national interests that Pakistan was trying to cultivate friendly relations with China, and in no way, did it mean going away from the military alliances. But the contention of the US was that Pakistan had entered into these pacts with the implicit purpose of the containment of communist China. With the shift in Pakistan's foreign policy towards China, its commitment to the military pacts had become doubtful.

Pakistani response was that even the US attitude had undergone a great change towards the pacts and that it was extending massive military aid to a country neutral on the issue of commission and to an enemy of Pakistan, i.e., India. It was on this occasion that President Ayub remarked that the people of Pakistan were prepared to accept economic distress for the sake of the integrity of the country and that 'people in developing countries seek assistance but on the basis of mutual respect; they want to have friends, not masters.'[65]

By 1966 Washington became appreciative of Pakistan's geographical compulsions and strategic location, and this realization gave new dimension to Pakistan-US relations. Signs of warmth in Pakistan-US relations started appearing again by 1968 when many pacts for economic aid were signed between the two countries. According to one estimate, upto the year 1970, 'US aid to Pakistan (including PL-480 aid) since 1950 amounts to over 54,000 million dollars; of which aid pledged during the Third Plan amounted to over $ 521 million.'[66]

Although the US had resented Pakistan's growing friendship with China, it had to request Pakistan for arranging a meeting between Nixon and Mao. Pakistan played an important role in this regard. But the crisis of 1971 made it clear that Pakistan achieved nothing in playing host to US-China friendship, except that it further hardened the Soviet attitude towards Pakistan. As a result of the new global situation, India and the USSR came closer and finally entered into a defence pact.

India, supported by an organized propaganda campaign and a powerful political lobby headed by senators Kennedy, Bowles, and Fulbright, was successful in obtaining a great deal of economic aid from the USA. It also received tremendous military and economic aid from the USSR. On the other hand, Pakistan was ignored by the USSR and by several other countries for proclaiming American friendship. The US also did not come forward to help Pakistan in its hour of need.

There had always been a feeling in Pakistan that the US has been encouraging secessionist tendencies in East Pakistan. It was in 1962 that Khwaja Nazimuddin, former governor-general and prime minister of Pakistan, stated that a foreign power giving aid to Pakistan wanted to divide Pakistan, and was instigating the people of East Pakistan to secure secession from West Pakistan.[67] It was believed in political circles of Pakistan that the US supplied funds to the Awami League and that Sheikh Mujibur Rehman had full backing of the US government.[68] All these actions were interpreted as 'unfriendly gestures'.

When Pakistanis compare the assistance given by the Soviet Union to India during the 1971 crisis in South Asia with what the US offered to Pakistan, they feel frustrated and dismayed. Although the State Department declared on 2 April 1971 that the situation in East Pakistan was an internal matter of Pakistan,[69] it made no effort to help Pakistan in overcoming the crisis. The US administration made some cautiously worded statements leaning towards Pakistan, but the unofficial circles and important elements in the Congress were hostile towards Pakistan. The US banned the supply of military spare parts to Pakistan in May 1971.[70] It laid down a series of preconditions bearing on the actions of Pakistani troops in East Bengal for the resumption of military and economic aid.[71] These conditions placed Pakistan in a very disadvantageous position. India continued to get highly sophisticated weapons from the Soviet Union, because of the August 1971 treaty with the USSR. On the other hand, Pakistan did not receive any military equipment from the USA with whom it had defence pacts. At the height of the war between India and Pakistan, the USA sent its seventh fleet to Indian Ocean, ostensibly to evacuate American citizens. Pakistanis thought that it would also evacuate the Pakistan army in case of surrender. Its failure to do so also caused them frustration. Afterwards it came to be known that the fleet was sent to relieve the pressure on the beleaguered Pakistani forces.[72] The former President Nixon also stated that the USA forced India through the Soviet Union to ceasefire on the western front, otherwise India was contemplating seizure of Azad Kashmir and destruction of Pakistan forces.[73]

China

Pakistan's relations with China can be divided into two phases. During the first phase, extending from 1950 to 1960, Pakistan's terms with China were merely a nodding acquaintance despite friendly gestures of Pakistan. For instance, Pakistan was one of the first countries which accorded recognition to China, and the government of Liaquat Ali Khan gave forceful support to the cause of China in the United Nations. Further, when the United Nations refused entry to China on the basis that it (China) was not willing to fulfil the obligations under the UN charter, Sir Muhammad Zafrullah Khan, Pakistan's foreign minister, argued: 'There is an apprehension that the Peking government will not be willing to discharge those obligations. Even if that were to be conceded, and it is no more than an assumption, can it be denied that the government is certainly able to discharge those obligations were it so willing, and its willingness is a matter of its own choice, which it is free any time to make?'[74]

After Pakistan's participation in the SEATO, the prospects of activating relations with China were marred. For whatever Pakistan proffered as a justification for its participation in the security pacts, 'the fact could not be disguised that the Treaty was an alignment against China.'[75] Besides, there was also a feeling in China that without Pakistan's participation, the SEATO with only two original members, would not have come into existence.[76] Pakistan took active part in Bandung Conference (1955) and supported the cause of Afro-Asian countries; this was not liked by its western allies. During this conference (1953–55) Pakistan's Prime Minister, Muhammad Ali Bogra, explained to the Chinese Prime Minister Chou En-lai that Pakistan's participation in the SEATO did not mean that Pakistan was against China or that it had any apprehension of Chinese aggression.[77] As a result, China did not adopt a hostile attitude towards Pakistan. It was also thought that the United States' military aid to Pakistan was directed against Moscow and not Peking.

Muhammad Ali Bogra could not visit China and eventually an invitation was extended to his successor, Chaudhri Muhammad Ali, who also could not pay a visit due to his preoccupation with issues at home. Huseyn Shaheed Suhrawardy (prime minister, 1956–57) was the first Pakistani prime minister to visit China in October 1956, but his visit did not prove politically fruitful as expected, because of 'Suhrawardy's gaze being all the time fixed on the red signal from Washington.'[78] Chou En-lai also reciprocated by visiting Pakistan in December 1956 and was accorded an enthusiastic welcome. However, Pakistan periodically showed a negative attitude towards China. Since Pakistan did not recognize the Chinese claim to the island of Formosa, China also did not support the cause of Kashmir. From 1951 to 1960, Pakistan continued to support the Western sponsored resolutions, postponing consideration of the question regarding UN membership for communist China. But despite all this, China did not come out openly in favour of India on the Kashmir question. Contrary to the Chinese attitude, the USSR adopted a hostile attitude and vetoed several resolutions regarding the solution of the Kashmir problem. Earlier in 1959, Pakistan had taken up the matter of demarcation of the border with the Chinese government. This was an important problem for Pakistan, because the maps published by the Chinese government showed large parts of Pakistan's territory as Chinese. Pakistan also knew that China was maintaining armed forces along the Sino-Pak border, while the Pakistani side was inaccessible.[79]

The second phase of Pakistan's relations with China starts from 1960 when Pakistan started supporting the cause of China inside and outside the United Nations. While criticizing the American attitude toward China, Manzoor Qadir, the then foreign minister of Pakistan, plainly stated in a television interview in Washington that, as a matter of principle, 'what justification is there not to recognize China?'[80] In 1961, President Ayub Khan visited the US, where he supported the idea of Chinese entry into the United Nations. 'I had made Pakistan's position clear during my visit to the United States in 1961. I had publicly stated that it was only fair to allow the People's Republic of China to occupy her legitimate position in the United Nations.'[81]

It was in 1961 that the Chinese government showed its willingness to take up the issue of the demarcation of the Sino-Pakistan border. It was followed by a silence on both the sides for about a year. During this period, two incidents took place which eventually paved way for closer friendship between China and Pakistan. The first was President Ayub's daring support to China during his visit to the United States in 1961. Secondly, it was in the same year that Pakistan voted in favour of seating China in the United Nations. As a result, negotiations regarding the demarcation of the border started in 1962. In March 1963, Pakistan's Foreign Minister, Zulfikar Ali Bhutto, went to Peking and signed the border agreement. The agreement was followed by the Indian propaganda that Pakistan had surrendered 2050 square miles of the territory to China. But the facts of the case are that both the sides made concessions. The area in dispute was 3400 square miles. The final compromise gave 2050 square miles to China, while Pakistan got 750 square miles. The objective evaluation of the agreement shows that Pakistan surrendered its territory on the maps whereas China had to withdraw its frontier forces from about 750 square miles. Pakistan's contention is that the conceded territory was never under its control.[82]

The border agreement laid the foundations of cordial relations between China and Pakistan. 'Its sole purpose was to eliminate a possible cause of conflict in the future.' But, as a result of this agreement, 'the Chinese began to have trust in us and we also felt that if one was frank and straightforward one could do honest business with them.'[83]

The border agreement was followed by the establishment of air link between China and Pakistan. The Pakistan International Airlines (PIA) took initiative with the Chinese government that it should be allowed to fly to Japan through China. The Chinese government accepted the proposal of the PIA, and thus new doors leading to a long and valuable friendship opened.

Meanwhile, Pakistan showed a keen interest in the Afro-Asian affairs where the interest of the two countries coincided. This was another factor which further cemented the relations between the two countries. After this, trade and cultural delegations were exchanged. Import and export facilities were provided by both the countries. A scheme of extending scholarships to Pakistani teachers was also chalked out by the Chinese government. China also provided technical assistance to Pakistan for the building of its industries. In 1964, China extended a loan of 60 million dollars for financing imports from China. The loan was payable over twenty years by Pakistani exports. A monthly shipping service was arranged between the two countries.[84] All these factors created an atmosphere of goodwill and trust in both the countries.

Then came the historic visit of President Ayub Khan to China in February 1964. The joint communiqué covered a large area of understanding. For the first time, China pledged support to the holding of a plebiscite in Kashmir.[85] In 1965, Ayub Khan again visited China. The communiqué indicated Pakistan's opposition to the scheme of creating two Chinas, and the Chinese supported the Pakistani demand for plebiscite in Kashmir.[86]

Pakistan's advances towards China created strains in Pakistan's relations with the US. Pakistan sought 500 million dollars from the Consortium for the first year of the Third Five Year Plan which was to be launched on 1 July 1965. The US government refused 40 per cent of the required aid on the ground that the Congress had not authorized it. Pakistan criticized this decision because the US government had already pledged 940 million dollars to India well in advance of Congress authorization. The suspension of the American aid in 1965 was 'directly attributable to the shift in Pakistan's foreign policy'.[87]

The India-Pakistan war of September 1965 not only exposed the futility of the defence pacts, but also determined the future course of Pakistan's foreign policy. While the US remained neutral, China went to the extent of issuing an ultimatum to India. The unequivocal support given by China during the war would stand as a great landmark in the history of Sino-Pakistan relations. After the Indo-Pak war, China gave economic and military aid to Pakistan. The Chinese tanks and aircraft were displayed for the first time in the Pakistan Day parade on 23 March 1966. The display of Chinese arrangements was described as a proclamation that Pakistan would not hesitate to draw on Chinese resources in defending its frontiers.[88] In the same year, Liu Shao-Chi, Chairman of the People's Republic of China, visited Pakistan. He was given an unprecedented reception. He reiterated his country's support to Pakistan to resist any 'aggression without any hesitation should the aggressor dare to attack Pakistan again.'[89]

With the establishment of closer relations between China and Pakistan, the exchanges of cultural and trade delegations became frequent. China extended substantial technical and financial assistance for the building of various industries in Pakistan, which included aid for an ordnance factory in former East Pakistan and the mechanical complex at Taxila. In 1969, Pakistan and China were connected by a road known as the Silk Route. This route has a historical significance, as it is the only road that connects China with the subcontinent. The arrival of the first camel caravan carrying Chinese goods in Pakistan was hailed warmly. The completion of the Karakoram Highway between Gilgit and the Chinese border in February 1971, built with generous Chinese assistance, further strengthened the relations. This route increased China-Pakistan trade. During 1969–70, many new trade agreements were signed. In 1970, China promised assistance in the field of mining, industry, and transport, etc. In 1969, China announced a credit of 40 million dollars to Pakistan. According to the agreement; two-thirds of the credit was to be utilized for the projects and one-third for the import of Chinese commodities. Another significant friendly gesture came by the end of 1970, when the Chinese government agreed to provide an interest-free loan of 500 million Yuans (1000 million rupees), repayable over a period of twenty years, for Pakistan's Fourth Five Year Plan.

The importance of Chinese technical and economic assistance was enormous for Pakistan in view of the decreasing aid from the US and other Western countries. At the national level, the people of Pakistan supported the efforts of the government to minimize its dependence on the West. It was, therefore, expected that excellent relations between China and Pakistan would continue to contribute positively towards stability and peace in Asia. On the cultural front, Pakistan established close cultural relations with China. From September 1967 to 1971, over fifty cultural delegations were exchanged.

While China had been supporting Pakistan on Kashmir, Pakistan subscribed to the idea of 'one China', and strongly advocated China's seating in the UN. It was with the active support from Pakistan that China became a member of the United Nations in 1971.

Although China's support to Pakistan during the crisis of 1971 was not as warm as in 1965, it acted prudently by adhering to the principle of non-interference. In March 1971, the Chinese prime minister extended full support to Pakistan and its people 'in their struggle to safeguard national independence'.[90] In April, China assured support in case 'the Indian expansionists dare to launch aggression against Pakistan.'[91] Chinese support was not confined to verbal declarations, it also extended military and economic aid. Besides a loan of 88 million dollars, China offered 30 million dollars to enable Pakistan to overcome financial difficulties. China quietly advised Pakistan to find a political solution to the Bangladesh crisis. The suggestion was repeated when a Pakistani delegation visited Beijing in early November 1971, although China reiterated support to Pakistan barring military intervention. Furthermore, the massing of Soviet troops on the Sino-Soviet border restrained China from building pressure on India by troop mobilization on Sino-Indian border. Therefore, China limited its support to Pakistan to the diplomatic field, continued to extend economic assistance, and supplied military hardware during and after the Bangladesh crisis and the war with India (November–December 1971).

The Soviet Union

The emergence of Pakistan, with its size, population, and resources, was a significant development from the Soviet point of view.[92] The Soviet government had always shown keen interest in Asia for its geographical location and emerging forces of nationalism. The Soviet Union had a particular interest in Pakistan because of its desire to gain access to the warm water ports of the Indian Ocean, particularly Karachi, which also provides an outlet to the oil-rich area of the Middle East.

It was against this background that Stalin extended an invitation to Liaquat Ali Khan in July 1949 to visit Moscow. Later, the US also invited him to Washington. Though Pakistan pursued non-alignment during this period, Liaquat's decision to visit the US only cast doubts about the non-involvement policy and provided positive evidence of pro-Western leanings which was to become pronounced in later years.[93] The Soviet leadership was extremely unhappy over Liaquat Ali Khan's disregard of their invitation. This was the beginning of the distrust between Pakistan and the Soviet Union.

In 1954, Pakistan joined the SEATO and, in 1955, it became a member of the CENTO. Thus, Pakistan was firmly wedded to the West. It created great resentment in the Soviet Union. The Indian government also exploited Pakistan's membership of these pacts 'and presented us [Pakistan] to the Soviet Union as some kind of theocratic state opposed to all liberal movements.'[94] It may also be mentioned that there was a certain amount of inhibition in Pakistan as well about the Soviet Union. It was thought that contact with the USSR would encourage the growth of communism in Pakistan. In the first decade of independence, many in Pakistan argued that communism negated the basic principles of Islam. In 1950, Prime Minister Liaquat Ali Khan had asked for a guarantee from the USA against the menace of communism.[95] Pakistan also believed that 'they (Soviets) do not believe in God and cannot therefore have any morals.'[96] Prime Minister Suhrawardy blamed communism for the cold war and warned that should Pakistan become a satellite of the USSR, it would never be able to get out of control.[97] The Soviet leadership periodically described the emergence of Pakistan as a consequence of the British policy of divide-and-rule.

The Soviet resentment against Pakistan manifested in its refusal to honour the commitments on Kashmir embodied in the resolution of the Security Council. The USSR government not only supported the Indian claim that Kashmir was an integral part of India, but also extended economic and military assistance to it. The government of Pakistan can also be blamed for its persistent cold attitude towards the Soviet Union. In 1956, the Soviet government offered technical and economic assistance to Pakistan and also expressed its willingness to make available to Pakistan its technical knowledge of the peaceful uses of atomic energy. In the same year, the USSR government expressed its readiness to assist Pakistan in building a steel mill. At the same time, the first Soviet deputy premier visited Pakistan and declared that 'the problem of Kashmir should be decided by the will of the people.'[98] These were clear indications on the part of the Soviet leadership to establish cordial relations with Pakistan. But the successive governments in Pakistan were rigidly pro-West and were content with the Western aid. The result was that they did not respond favourably to the Soviet gestures of goodwill.

Due to the American economic and military assistance, the policy of Ayub's government remained unchanged towards the Soviet Union during the initial period of his rule. Pakistan had also given air bases to the US. These bases enabled United States to watch the military movements of the Soviet Union. This exposed Pakistan to hostile action by the Soviet Union. But the tension between Pakistan and the Soviet Union touched the highest point after the flight of a U-2 plane from Peshawar in May 1960. It provoked the anger of Khrushchev, the then prime minister of the Soviet Union, who threatened Pakistan with dire consequences. It has already been discussed that the Soviet Union vetoed every resolution suggesting plebiscite in Kashmir during these years.

By 1961, Pakistan was also re-evaluating its foreign policy. At the same time, the Soviet Union made an offer for prospecting oil, which was readily accepted. Under Pak-Soviet Agreement (4 March 1961) Pakistan received a loan of 30 million dollars and technical assistance for oil exploration. 'The oil deal proved to be the beginning of a series of agreements for the operation of air services, exchange of cultural delegations, assistance for the mechanization of agriculture, building of power projects, and for the promotion of technology and scientific knowledge.'[99] In 1961, the Soviet Union also offered Pakistan a credit of 530 million dollars and also offered to train Pakistani engineers. In 1964, the Soviet Union extended a credit of 519 million dollars for the purchase of heavy machinery. In 1966, Pakistan entered into barter agreements with the Soviet Union under which, for the export of rice, cotton, jute, etc., Pakistan obtained Soviet vehicles and agricultural machinery. To cap it all, assistance extended by the USSR for the building of a steel mill in Pakistan and air transport agreement were expected to play an important role in further consolidating these friendly relations.

The India-China war of 1962 accelerated the process of rapprochement between the Soviet Union and Pakistan, which had begun in 1961. First, due to the supply of Western arms to India, Pakistan gradually moved out of the Western orbit. Secondly, the Soviet Union recognized the changing trends in Pakistan's foreign policy and wanted to encourage these by making attractive offers of economic and technological assistance. Moreover, India began to lean heavily towards the West after its military defeat in the war with China. It obtained massive military assistance from the US and other Western countries, which perturbed the Soviets. The *New York Times* apprehensively wrote that Washington, by rushing arms to India, intended to force its entry into the SEATO and the CENTO.[100] Pakistan, on the other hand, was gradually adopting a neutral posture. In 1963, Sir Zafarullah Khan visited Moscow and said on his return that, 'Russia would respond to any Pakistani move for friendship.'[101]

By 1965, the ice had been broken between the two countries. Pakistan had established friendly relations with China, and was looking forward to developing similar relations with the Soviet Union and other socialist countries. By this time the Soviet Union had also adopted a neutral attitude towards the disputes between India and Pakistan. But it was not until April 1965 that Pakistan was able to establish direct contact with the USSR. It was in this month that President Ayub Khan visited the Soviet Union (first Pakistani head of government to visit the Soviet Union) 'to recover the lost links'.[102] During this visit Ayub Khan tried to remove the suspicions of the Soviet Union regarding Pakistan's alliances with the West. He told Kosygin, 'We had not joined the pacts to encourage aggression in any direction; our sole concern was our security.'[103] He also pointed out that massive military aid to India by the USSR and the US was helping it to pursue an aggressive policy. President Ayub Khan's visit covered much ground in the political spheres. Soviet neutralism became firm. During the Indo-Pakistan conflict over the Rann of Kutch, the USSR government advised both India and Pakistan not to weaken each other since only the imperialist powers would gain from such a situation.[104]

During the September 1965 war, Kosygin expressed his profound concern over the situation and offered his services for mediation. It was obviously a sign of departure in the Soviet policy which, until a couple of years back, was confined to supporting India in the Security Council. It was on the initiative of the Soviet prime minister that Pakistan and India signed a peace treaty at Tashkent, called the Tashkent Declaration, which served as the framework for normalization of their relations in the aftermath of the 1965 war.

This was followed by several exchange visits between the Soviet Union and Pakistan. The Soviet Union also agreed to sell some weapons and military equipment to Pakistan during 1968–70 despite the protests made by the Indian government. This created an impression that the Soviet Union had adopted neutralism as a principle of its foreign policy towards India and Pakistan. Although relations between Pakistan and the Soviet

Union made steady progress after 1965 for some time, the disillusionment created by the aftermath of the Tashkent Declaration could not be overlooked. The people of Pakistan had expected the Soviet Union to mediate between India and Pakistan for the solution of the Kashmir dispute. They thought that the Soviet Union was morally bound to do so. But the silence of the Soviets over Kashmir and its continued military supplies to India caused much disappointment amongst the Pakistani people who looked forward to closer friendship with the Soviet Union.

President Ayub's second visit to the Soviet Union in 1967 broadened the base for co-operation. Identity of views was expressed on major international issues, that is, Middle East and Vietnam. Ayub clearly hinted at terminating American base in Pakistan.[105]

During the years 1965 to 1970, many trade agreements were signed between Pakistan and the Soviet Union. As a result the trade between the two countries increased by about seven times since 1956–57 when exports and imports between them amounted to no more than Rs 7 million each way.[106] As regards the Soviet assistance for development projects, there were about thirty projects under implementation in 1971, for which the Soviet Union had extended loan and technical assistance. The government of the USSR also promised a credit of 200 million dollars for Pakistan's Fourth Five Year Plan in June 1970, when President Yahya visited Moscow.

Apparently this economic and technical assistance to Pakistan had brought normalcy in Soviet-Pakistan relations but the fact remained that the Soviet Union never reconciled with two major principles of Pakistan's foreign policy, that is, its defence pacts with the West and the growing friendship with China. The ideological split between China and the USSR led the Soviets to look for an ally to counter the Chinese influence in this region. The Sino-Indian border clashes paved way for Indo-Soviet friendship. India being a large and non-aligned country suited the Soviet Union. At the same time, India also exploited the situation and received massive aid both from the Soviet Union and the USA. The Soviet Union increased military and economic aid to India which was valued at 300 million dollars annually and included the most sophisticated weapons.

After the Sino-Soviet border clashes in 1969, the Soviet Union's primary concern was the containment of China. The Soviet leadership now expressed its disapproval of Pakistan's relations with China. During his visit to Pakistan in February 1969, the Soviet defence minister, Andrei Grechko, told S.M. Yousuf, the then foreign secretary, 'You cannot have simultaneous friendship with the USSR and China.' His response was, 'What is permissible for a super power is not possible for a country like Pakistan.'[107]

The Soviet Union propounded the idea of regional economic grouping, often described as the Asian Collective Security System to implement its policy of containment of China. Kosygin met Yahya on 25 March 1970, and stressed the importance of the regional grouping, but Pakistan's foreign ministry spokesman announced clearly that 'Pakistan would not join an alliance against China.'[108]

By early 1971, the Soviets were unhappy with Pakistan on two major counts: first, Pakistan's close friendship with China; second, Pakistan's rejection of the Soviet-sponsored Asian Collective Security Pact. When Pakistan decided to take military action in East Pakistan on 25 March 1971 to put down the insurgency, the Soviets got an opportunity to build pressure on Pakistan. On 2 April, the Soviet president, Podgorny, wrote a letter to Yahya Khan, criticizing Pakistan's decision to use force in East Pakistan.[109] He wrote:

In these days of trial for the Pakistani people, we cannot but say a few words coming from true friends. We have been and remain convinced that the complex problems that have arisen in Pakistan of late can and must be solved politically, without use of force. Continuation of repressive measures and bloodshed in East Pakistan will, undoubtedly, only make the solution of the problem more difficult ... do great harm to the vital interest of the entire people of Pakistan.

Yahya's reply was short and curt: 'Pakistan was determined not to allow any country to interfere in its internal affairs.' The tone and contents of this letter reflected the Soviet concern for the people of Pakistan but, the sympathy shown for the Awami League and advice for the transfer of power were distasteful to Yahya. Yahya's reply was discourteous and undiplomatic, which further alienated the Soviets. Yahya had assured Moscow that he would soon start a dialogue with the elected representatives, but the Soviets realized that Yahya had no such intention. The Soviets still continued to advise Yahya for a political solution, because it would have better served the Soviet interests.

With the signing of the Indo-Soviet treaty in August 1971, the Soviet Union's partisan policy was affirmed. 'The draft of the treaty had been prepared in 1969 in connection with the Asian Collective Security Arrangement.'[110] India and the Soviet Union felt the need for taking up the treaty issue after Henry Kissinger's secret visit to Peking via Islamabad for establishing direct relations with China; the earlier secret diplomatic exchanges that facilitated this visit had taken place through Pakistan. On 15 July 1971, the US President Nixon made the dramatic announcement of the Sino-American rapprochement. This shocked India and the Soviet Union, who felt that a US-China-Pakistan axis had been formed, which amounted to their isolation. Both wanted to take some steps to show that their diplomacy was dynamic and they could work together to deal with the implication of the Sino-US opening. Prime Minister Indira Gandhi immediately took up the Soviet ideas on collective security propounded in 1969. The two sides decided to change its form and achieve the same security objectives by giving it the form of a bilateral agreement; even in 1969, the idea of some kind of bilateral agreement was proposed, but it was not pursued at that time. Now, the changed environment led them to adapt the 1969 ideas to the 1971 situation.[111]

Article 8, 9, and 10 of the Indo-Soviet Treaty of Friendship and Co-operation, singed in August 1971, have military implications. Article stipulated 'in the event of either party being subjected to an attack or threat thereof, the high contracting parties shall immediately enter into mutual consultations in order to remove such a threat and to take appropriate effective measures to ensure the peace and security of their countries.' In accordance with the spirit of the treaty, the Indian foreign minister assured his countrymen on 29 October 1971 that India could count upon the Soviet Union for total support in the event of a conflict with Pakistan.[112]

After the conclusion of this treaty, the Soviet news media unleashed a propaganda campaign against Pakistan, laced with threats and intimidation. When hostilities broke out between India and Pakistan, Moscow held Pakistan responsible, and threatened that it would not remain indifferent, and that these developments affected its own security. Moscow also warned other countries to stay out of the war,[113] a warning which was evidently directed against China. Throughout the crisis, the Soviets openly sided with India, whereas Pakistan received only a limited assistance from the USA.

The Soviet Union's partisan role was a part of its international strategic framework, because it viewed seriously the implications of a civil war in its immediate vicinity. Its major concern was the containment of China. First, it strengthened India so as to use it in the event of a Sino-Soviet confrontation. Secondly, the Soviets also toyed with the idea of realizing their old dream of establishing naval bases in the Indian Ocean. Thirdly, with the separation of East Pakistan, the Soviet Union expected to get a firm footing in South-East Asia.

India invoked article 9 of the Treaty of Friendship and Co-operation in early November 1971 to obtain concrete support from the Soviet Union for its planned invasion of East Pakistan. This collusion proved decisive during the Indo-Pak war of 1971. The Soviet military and diplomatic assistance to India and its role in the Security Council served as an umbrella for India's successful involvement in the conflict in East Pakistan.[114] According to the revelations of syndicated columnist, Jack Anderson, the Soviet ambassador to India, Nikolai M. Pegov promised on 13 December that the Soviets could open a diversionary action against the Chinese in Sinkiang, and would not allow the seventh fleet to intervene. Besides these assurances, the Soviets provided tanks, combat aircraft, missiles, submarines, missile boats, and heavy equipment worth 70 million dollars to India.[115] In November, Soviet transport aircraft carried advanced military equipment and SAMS, accompanied by Soviet instructors, to India.[116] Even after that, more tanks, rockets, MIG-23 fighter bombers, etc., were supplied. It was also reported that the Soviet army personnel were manning Indian missile boats and flying Indian army planes during the war.[117] Russians had also consented to shift MIG-21 and TU-16 bombers from Egypt to India.[118]

In the Security Council, the Soviet Union blocked every resolution aimed at the peaceful solution of the East Pakistan problem. The Soviet diplomats in the Security Council were heard asking the Indian representative that how long would they take to reach Dacca? The Soviet Union was so concerned about the slow progress of Indian forces that it sent its first deputy foreign minister to Delhi during the war. The Soviet minister was soon convinced that the morale of Pakistani forces had been broken and that the surrender was only a matter of three or four days.[119] It was in this perspective that the Chinese accused the Soviet Union of being the 'real director of the Bangladesh farce'.[120]

In December 1971, when Bhutto came to power, Pakistan had been disintegrated and the entire nation was demoralized. The defence pact, CENTO had failed; the people felt betrayed and isolated. Bhutto, therefore, thought of a defence pact with China as a morale booster. He visited China in January 1972, but instead of a defence pact, he returned with the Chinese advice that common interests counted more than formal defence pacts.[121]

The Soviet-Pakistan relations in early 1972 were at the lowest ebb. Bhutto believed in putting into action 'preventive diplomacy to avoid global power intervention which subjected the weaker nations to suffer from punitive diplomacy.'[122] About a month before his visit to the Soviet Union, Bhutto hinted darkly that Moscow was up to 'monkey business' through its agents and propaganda, 'stirring trouble inside Pakistan all the way from North-West Frontier bordering Afghanistan down to Baluchistan on the Arabian Sea.'[123] He visited Moscow in March 1972, on a fence-mending mission. Although a 'workable equilibrium' emerged from this visit, 'isolating the area of conflict'[124] the Soviet stand on the 1971 events was most depressing for Pakistan. Kosygin clearly told Bhutto that if history was to repeat itself, the Soviets would repeat their 1971 performance, because they felt justified in doing so. However, Bhutto's visit paved way for the normalization of Pak-Soviet relations.

In February 1974, Pakistan and the Soviet Union agreed on an exchange programme in the fields of science, technology, education, art, culture, etc. Bhutto's diplomatic overtures to the Soviet allies in the Middle East and Afghanistan were also successful. However, the Kabul government, after the Daoud coup in July 1973, adopted a belligerent posture towards Pakistan. Sardar Daoud, in his first speech, revived the issue of 'Pakhtunistan', followed by an organized propaganda campaign against Pakistan. As expected, Pakistan responded in the same tone and Pak-Afghan relations deteriorated rapidly. In September 1974, Kabul warned that the 'long smouldering border dispute' with Pakistan could erupt into 'a full-scale war'.[125]

In October 1974, Bhutto again visited Moscow and expressed satisfaction over his talks with the Soviet leaders.[126] This visit resulted in more aid for the Karachi Steel Mill and expansion of trade between the two countries. In the wake of Delhi's efforts at normalized relations with Peking, Moscow felt inclined to help Bhutto in his attempts to improve Pak-Afghan relations. Bhutto, an experienced diplomat with an apparently stable position at home, was certainly able to make a favourable dent in the Soviet hostility towards Pakistan. In 1975, President Podgorny visited Kabul and emphasized the need for peace in the region. Thus, a significant change in the Russian posture was noticed. The Shah of Iran also made concrete efforts to reduce areas of tension between Kabul and Islamabad by promising economic assistance to Kabul. As a result of these developments, the Afghan deputy foreign minister, Waheed

Abdullah, did not mention 'Kabul's problems with Islamabad'[127] during his speech in the Islamic Foreign Ministers' Conference at Istanbul. It was followed by the cessation of hostile propaganda by the mass media of both the countries.

The year 1976 brought in a different pattern of diplomacy in the region. Bhutto visited China in May 1976, and noticed a major shift in the Chinese foreign policy. The Chinese prime minister, deviating from the historical approach, neither openly attacked India nor made any references to the Kashmir dispute in his speech. Premier Hua's speech clearly reflected China's new policy of actively encouraging the relaxation of tensions on the Indian subcontinent to oust the Soviet influence from the countries of South-East Asia.[128]

In June 1976, Bhutto went to Kabul and his visit was termed as an 'initiative on the road to an era of goodwill, understanding, peace and confidence in relations,' between the two countries.[129] Although Bhutto was able to cover significant ground, deep-rooted differences could not be resolved so soon. President Daoud, while sounding a note of optimism, said 'undoubtedly, a long-standing and old political difference had existed and exists... and this cannot be resolved in one or two talks.'[130] Meanwhile, the Soviet Union agreed to sell helicopters to Pakistan, besides increasing its economic assistance.

The US continued to take an active interest in the efforts of the Shah of Iran for a Kabul-Islamabad rapprochement and viewed the extension of the Soviet influence to Pakistan with concern. Dr Henry Kissinger visited Pakistan in August 1976, mainly to 'carry forward the process of reconciliation' and to consolidate the US influences.[131] He said that security, territorial integrity, and independence of Pakistan were matters of great concern for the US.[132] During his short stay at Kabul, Kissinger showed keen interest in the prospects of Pak-Afghan rapprochement and 'reportedly offered massive economic aid to Afghanistan in return for the latter's willingness to abandon or, at least, freeze the Pakhtunistan issue.'[133] Kissinger's visit to Pakistan was followed by President Daoud's visit. Referring to the political differences with Pakistan, he expressed firm hope that a 'reasonable and honourable solution would be found.' These developments gave rise to a certain amount of optimism and encouraged speculation regarding the settlement of Pak-Afghan differences. While the process of rapprochement continued, India watched these moves with concern and suffered from a sense of isolation.[134]

The negotiations with Afghanistan were interrupted with the imposition of martial law and removal of Bhutto in July 1977. General Ziaul Haq, the Chief Martial Law Administrator, visited Afghanistan in 1977 but without much success, because he required time to stabilize his own position. Hence, he was unable to negotiate with President Daoud from a position of strength. It is important to point out that the Soviet media extended complete support to Bhutto during the 1977 general elections and the subsequent opposition agitation against him. As a matter of fact, Bhutto's shrewed slogan of socialism had fascinated the communist countries and had drawn most of them into his magic circle. His removal by General Zia was, therefore, disliked by the Soviets. Moreover, Zia's commitment to Islam and his efforts to Islamize Pakistani society created apprehension in Moscow, because the Soviets viewed the Islamic resurgence movements in Pakistan and Iran with suspicion, as these were likely to have repercussions in Afghanistan and Central Asian Muslim states of the Soviet Union. To cap it all, Bhutto's execution against the Soviet advice further annoyed them.

Against this background, the coup in Afghanistan in April 1978, led by Pro-Soviet Noor Muhammad Taraki, undermined the prospects of improvement of Pak-Afghan relations. The Taraki government revived the Pakhtunistan issue and officially observed the Pakhtunistan day. In May 1978, the Soviet ambassador to Pakistan, disregarding all diplomatic niceties, warned Pakistan in a press interview against opposing the Taraki government.[135] In March 1979, for the first time, the Soviet news agency, *Tass*, accused Pakistan of training Afghan rebel groups. It was followed by Afghan artillery shelling across the Durand Line into Pakistan territory.[136] In July, the first minister in the Afghan cabinet propounded the theory that 'his countrymen retain the age-old rights to go freely into certain areas of Baluchistan and the Frontier.'[137] It was a manifestation of Afghan ambitions to extend its sway over these areas of Pakistan.

Although Pakistan left the CENTO in 1979, and joined the non-aligned movement, it did not succeed in changing the hostile posture of the USSR. The Soviet media continued its propaganda campaign against Pakistan. Even the third, Soviet-backed coup, led by Babrak Karmal, did not change the situation. The new Afghan government accused Pakistan of sending trained guerrillas into Afghanistan. On the other hand, the Afghan government tried to foment separatist sentiments among tribal Baluchs and Pushtuns. Therefore, Pakistan had to face unparalleled difficulties.

The Muslim World

From the very day of its inception, Pakistan demonstrated deeply positive sentiments towards the Muslim world based on common bonds of faith, culture, and history, and attached great importance to its relations with the Muslim states. Even before the Partition of the subcontinent, the Muslims of undivided India gave their support to the cause of Muslims everywhere in the world. They launched a movement in India in support of the Ottoman Caliphate in Turkey in the immediate aftermath of the First World War. The Indian Muslims, especially the Muslim League, enthusiastically supported the cause of the Palestinians.

After independence, Quaid-i-Azam Muhammad Ali Jinnah, the founder of Pakistan, declared that to establish close friendly relations with the Muslim countries was the cornerstone of Pakistan's foreign policy. Prime Minister Liaquat Ali Khan also firmly believed and advocated the cause of Islamic unity. But, to the great disappointment of Pakistan, it was discovered gradually that the Arab nationalists did not attach much importance to Islam. Some of them, it was later realized, even made distinctions between Arabs and non-Arabs. Gradually, the feeling grew in Pakistan that religious sentiment alone was not enough to resolve the differences with the Muslim countries and to develop close relations with them.

Afghanistan, though a Muslim country, created the problem of Pakhtunistan for Pakistan, besides making territorial claims on Pakistani territory in the provinces of the NWFP and Baluchistan. It gave financial aid to the Pakistani tribals and encouraged them to challenge Pakistani authorities. Afghanistan was the only country to vote against Pakistan's admission to the United Nations in 1947.[138] When Pakistan joined the defence pacts in 1954 and 1955, Afghanistan exploited the occasion to provoke feelings of indignation in the Middle East.

In these anti-Pakistan activities, the Afghan authorities were supported by India whose interest lay in ensuring that in the event of war with Pakistan over Kashmir, the Afghans should open a second front against Pakistan in the North-West Frontier.'[139] Despite this, Pakistan followed a policy of patience with Afghanistan. Pakistan gave Afghanistan facilities for trade and passage of goods by its railway.

Amongst the Muslim countries, Pakistan has always cherished close friendly relations with Iran and Turkey. The former Shah of Iran was the first foreign dignitary to visit Pakistan. Both Iran and Pakistan supported each other in and out of the UN.

Pakistan, Iran, and Turkey were allies in the CENTO. The heads of the three states, however, felt that economic and cultural co-operation should be initiated outside the CENTO framework. Thus emerged the idea of the Regional Co-operation for Development (RCD), which aimed at closer economic and cultural collaboration. Formed in July 1964, the RCD was designed to connect the three countries through rail, road, and air, along with collaboration in the field of shipping, abolition of visa formalities, and free movement of goods. The RCD secretariat was established in Iran. Many meetings of the heads of states, ministers, and secretaries were held. An instance of these fraternal ties was visible when both Turkey and Iran came to the help of Pakistan during the September 1965 war with India. It was alleged by India that Iran supplied oil free of cost to Pakistan and Turkey helped with the aircraft during the war. In July 1967, the Ramsar summit was held, which was attended by the Shah of Iran, the president of Pakistan, and the prime minister of Turkey. A political touch was given to the RCD at this summit. The communiqué stated that 'their designated representatives will meet from time to time to review political developments and to consider measures for collaboration.'[140]

Pakistan's relations with Indonesia have been very cordial. During the September 1965 war, Indonesia gave all-out support to Pakistan. Pakistan had concluded an agreement of economic and cultural co-operation with Indonesia, known as IPECC, on the pattern of the RCD. The Suharto coup of 1965 changed the position to the extent that the emotional and all-out support of Soekarno was no longer available to Pakistan. However, the new leadership re-affirmed its close bonds of co-operation with Pakistan.

Malaysia being a Muslim country and a member of the British Commonwealth, had normal relations with Pakistan, but during the September 1965 war, Malaysia openly sided with India. Consequently, Pakistan broke off diplomatic relations with it. Due to the efforts of some friendly countries, diplomatic relations were resumed. The hostile attitude of Malaysia continued. It was the first major Muslim country to recognize Bangladesh.

Pakistan was able to develop cordial relations with most of the Middle Eastern states. Pakistan extended vehement support to the movement for the independence of Morocco, Tunisia, and several other African countries like Somaliland and Eritrea. Pakistan had some problems with Egypt because its leader, Nasser, was very critical of Pakistan's alignment with the West. He refused to appreciate the causes that led Pakistan to enter into the defence alliance with the US. As Nasser had his own problems with the Western countries, especially the United Kingdom, he felt that Pakistan should not have gone closer to these countries. Besides, Nasser's close personal relations with the Indian prime minister, Nehru, strengthened Nasser's bias against Pakistan. However, Pakistan's relations with Egypt improved after the latter's setback in the 1967 Arab-Israeli war, and especially after the death of Nasser in 1970. While Pakistan's consistent advocacy of the cause of the Palestinian Muslims produced a favourable atmosphere in the Arab bloc the political weakness and internal schisms among the Arabs prevented the flowering of a solid bloc of the Muslim world. Iraq left the Baghdad Pact and Syria forged unity with the United Arab Republic (UAR), but a revolution reversed the tide. The Qasim Revolution in Iraq (1958) assumed an anti-Nasser posture, which was reversed only after another revolution.

Although Jordan being a small and insecure country needed the Western patronage, King Husain bravely opted to steer an independent course. Jordan gave unique support to Pakistan during the 1965 war. Its representative in the Security Council condemned the nefarious designs of India in the conflict against Pakistan. Like Jordan, Syria and Iraq also extended their support to Pakistan on the Kashmir issue. In the same manner, Pakistan offered material assistance to Jordan during the Israeli attack of June, 1967. Since then, Pakistan has stood by Jordan and has supported the Arab cause in a resolute manner. King Husain and the former Pakistani President Ayub Khan exchanged many visits, which resulted in developing closer relations between the two countries. The Pak-Jordan friendship has passed through many tests. As in the past, Jordan gave all support to Pakistan in the Indo-Pak conflict of 1971.

In September 1969, a conference of the Muslim countries was convened at Rabat, capital of Morocco. India also tried to participate in the conference on behalf of the Indian Muslims. The Pakistani delegation protested against it and walked out of the meeting. Consequently, India was refused entry and Pakistan was placated. It was described as a remarkable success of Pakistan's diplomacy. In this conference, Pakistan promised all possible support to the Arab cause and this greatly enhanced its prestige in the Arab world. In accordance with the decisions of the Rabat conference, a meeting of the foreign ministers of all the participating Muslim countries was held in Jeddah in March 1970, where it was decided to establish an Islamic Secretariat.

This was considered to be the first step towards an eventual Muslim commonwealth of nations, and marked a good beginning towards greater unity among Muslims of the world. The second Islamic Conference of Foreign Ministers, attended by twenty-three representatives, was held in Karachi in December 1970. The conference gave unanimous support to the imperative need of strengthening the Islamic front in order to undo Israel's expansionist designs. The conference also condemned the Zionist efforts to change the status of Jerusalem.[141]

As mentioned earlier, Pakistan's relations with Egypt (United Arab Republic) had not been cordial, because Pakistan found it difficult to evoke support from the UAR in the name of Islamic brotherhood. The UAR developed closer relations with India. In November 1951, the Egyptian foreign minister told an Indian journalist that Egypt expected support from India in its struggle for national liberation.[142] King Farouq ridiculed Pakistan by saying: 'Don't you know that Islam was born on 14 August 1947'.[143] Pakistan's ambiguous policy on the Suez crisis, 1956, due to Pakistan's participation in the West-sponsored military pacts further strained their relations, although the Egyptian cause enjoyed strong support at the common-man level in Pakistan. After assuming power, President Ayub Khan made earnest efforts to put the relations between the two countries on a mutually satisfactory basis, and was able to achieve some success.

In April 1960, President Nasser came to Pakistan where he was accorded a warm welcome. In November of the same year, President Ayub Khan visited Cairo where he tried to remove the misgivings of the Egyptian government. While addressing a rally of the National Union Ayub Khan said: 'Pakistan's representatives may have acted in a clumsy manner at the time of the Suez crisis, but every sensible man in Pakistan had been deeply distressed by the invasion and their sympathies were all with Egypt.'[144] He also asked whether the UAR had supported Pakistan on Kashmir. Certainly the record of Pakistan in support of the Arab cause is much more impeccable than the apathetic attitude adopted by the UAR on the Kashmir issue.

It was expected that the intimate contact between the two countries would bring about a change in the attitude of the UAR government towards Pakistan. Despite Pakistan's gestures of goodwill, the UAR abstained from voting on the Security Council's resolutions on Kashmir in June 1962. The obvious reason was its alignment with India.[145] Though the myth of Indian non-alignment had been exploded after India received massive military aid from the West, the UAR continued to support India.

During the September 1965 war, the UAR government adopted a neutral posture, while the public sentiment was pro-Pakistan. After the daring support of Pakistan to the UAR during the Arab-Israel war of June 1967, it was expected that the Pakistan-UAR relations would improve. But it appeared that President Nasser was not prepared to relax his rigid posture. The government of the UAR did not attach any significance to Pakistan being a Muslim state and treated it only as a friendly state like others. When Fauzi, the special representative of President Nasser, was asked if the brotherhood amongst the Muslims of the world had deepened after the 1967 crisis, he replied: 'Brotherhood should not be limited between the Muslims alone but between all men for good purpose.'[146] He also parried questions on the formation of an Islamic bloc and the utility of regional alliance like RCD.

The foreign policy of Pakistan during 1969–71 passed through very curious phases. In the beginning of Yahya's time it was simply bizarre. The policies formulated had lost their dynamic quality produced by the incorporation of new ideas. At one stage the approach of the career diplomats dominating the foreign office became rigid, barren, and hide bound, losing all touch with reality. But by and large, the foreign policy of Pakistan during the Yahya regime, was a continuation of the previous trends and, till the appointment of his cabinet, there was no discernible change. But this did not mean that there was no change on the part of the foreign powers. After the unexpected and unconstitutional takeover by General Yahya, in spite of his solemn declarations and the credence accorded to his promises by the people, the West European countries and the USA grew cold towards Pakistan. The so-called benign militaristic regime of Ayub Khan during the last two years had been regarded with grave suspicion, and the democratic institutions of the period, so much eulogized by the press and the politicians conforming to Ayub's views, were discredited as sham institutions. The foreign policy, perforce, came to be stagnant and static, losing all its momentum in the direction of renovation and innovation. The cordial understanding that had been affected between Pakistan and China was not maintained at the previous harmonious level and was even somewhat neglected.

For a number of reasons, Pakistan emerged from the bloody war of 1971, not only bruised, torn, and tormented but also decimated. An analytical survey of the events would not absolve India of the role it played in dismembering Pakistan. The unsympathetic and somewhat injudicious attitude shown by the Soviet Union, Great Britain, West Germany, Poland, and the USA during the East Pakistan crisis, was as much due to the diplomatic offensive or machinations of India as to Yahya's follies. Indira Gandhi's tour of European countries and the USA was meant to crown the efforts of her colleagues in isolating Pakistan, and had been especially undertaken to win these countries over to India's side, and produce a sort of justification for its involvement in the East Pakistan conflict. The public opinion in all these countries had already veered round to the Indian contention. The pity is that all this failed to awaken the Yahya regime to the realization of its neglected task. The hurried tour made by the foreign secretary as an emissary of the president achieved no dependable support for the cause of Pakistan. The debacle in East Pakistan and a humiliating defeat on the western front became inevitable. India, with the blessings of a super power, openly defied the resolutions of the Security Council and showed the same discourtesy to the resolutions of the General assembly, 104 members of which wholeheartedly supported a peaceful settlement of East Pakistan's issue.

POST-1971 PAKISTAN

The exit of Yahya from power on 20 December 1971 was bound to augur a significant change in the foreign policy of Pakistan. The East Pakistan fiasco shattered the old notion of non-alignment and brought about radical changes and drastic re-adjustments in Pakistan's relations with the major powers. The transfer of power to the Pakistan People's Party, the principal political party in West Pakistan, injected a new interest and enthusiasm in foreign affairs, a field of particular interest to its leader, Zulfikar Ali Bhutto.

The cardinal principles of Bhutto's foreign policy were 'bilateralism' and 'personal diplomacy'. He firmly believed in personal diplomacy and undertook more foreign tours during the first three years of his government than any of the Pakistani leaders. Personal diplomacy helped him in establishing personal contacts and explaining Pakistan's view abroad. Bilateralism envisaged good relations with all countries on a bilateral basis. To avoid antagonizing anyone, the strategy evolved was to set up a bilateral relationship with every one of the three big powers.[147] Pakistan was, to some extent, successful in its venture.

After the assumption of power, Bhutto vowed to pursue an independent foreign policy, free from all pressures. Some of the major steps, indicative of real change in the foreign policy, included:

(1) Withdrawal from the Commonwealth.
(2) Recognition of East Germany, the Democratic Republics of Korea and Vietnam, the Republic of Guinea Bissau, the Royal government of National Union of Cambodia.
(3) Withdrawal from the SEATO.

Bhutto undertook a whirlwind tour of twenty countries immediately after assuming power, concentrating in the first instance on friendly countries who had stood by Pakistan in times of need. A re-affirmation of support from these countries enabled Pakistan to negotiate with India from a position of strength. The desire to establish bilateral friendly relations with big powers took him to China in January, to the Soviet Union in March 1972, and to the USA in September 1973.

Negotiations with India had always been a difficult chapter of Pakistan's foreign policy, but the surrender of 1971 made it more perilous. After assuming power, Bhutto expressed his desire to normalize relations with India and offered a dialogue for seeking a just and honourable settlement. As a result, the emissaries of both the countries met in April 1972, in Murree and Rawalpindi to draw up an agenda and fix a date for a summit meeting between India and Pakistan. Consequently, the Simla summit took place from 28 June 1972, leading to an agreement on 2 July, named as the Simla agreement. The Agreement brought an end to the state of conflict and confrontation between India and Pakistan and outlined the principles for normalization of their bilateral relations, as well as for settling the problems arising out of the 1971 war. They committed themselves to the settlement of differences through peaceful means; to respect each other's national unity, territorial integrity, political independence, and sovereign equality; to refrain from threat or use of force; and to cease hostile propaganda against each other. The steps decided for gradual normalization of relations included withdrawal of forces to their respective sides and respect of the Line of Control in Kashmir, as arising out of the ceasefire after the 1971 war, although this was not supposed to prejudice the two sides' recognized positions on the Kashmir issue. The Simla Agreement was duly ratified by the National Assembly on 14 July 1972, and the instrument of ratification was delivered to India on 18 July 1972, which in turn handed over its own instrument of ratification on 1 August 1972.

Another delicate issue between India and Pakistan was that of over 91,000 prisoners of war (personnel of the military and paramilitary, and civilian internees). In response to Bhutto's request for treatment of this issue under the Geneva Convention, India took a stand that they had surrendered to a joint command of India and Bangladesh, and could not be released without the prior consent of Bangladesh. Bangladesh threatened to put at least 195 Pakistani prisoners of war on war trial—a demand endorsed by India. Pakistan opposed this and maintained that Bangladesh could not take such an action as the prisoners were under Indian custody, and therefore, it was the duty of the Indian government to protect their rights under international law.

Meanwhile, Bangladesh applied for UN membership in August 1972. The resolution calling for its admission was vetoed by the People's Republic of China. During the General Assembly session in September 1972, Pakistan took the stand that Bangladesh should be admitted only after the implementation of the General Assembly resolution of 7 December 1971, and Security Council Resolution of 21 December 1971. India and Bangladesh issued a joint declaration on 17 April 1973 de-linking the humanitarian issue of prisoners of war from the political question of recognition of Bangladesh. This was welcomed by Pakistan, but it had to file a petition with the International Court of Justice to prevent the transfer of 195 prisoners which Bangladesh wanted to try for 'war crimes', by the end of May 1973.

Talks were held between the representatives of India and Pakistan in lslamabad in the last week of July 1973, but these remained inconclusive because India could not make any commitment without consulting Bangladesh. The talks were resumed in New Delhi on 18 August 1973 and continued till 28 August, when the first Delhi Agreement was signed.

The salient features of this agreement were:

(a) Simultaneous repatriation of all Pakistani prisoners of war and civilian internees, all Bengalis in Pakistan, and a substantial number of non-Bengalis in Bangladesh.
(b) Bangladesh agreed that no trial of the 195 prisoners of war shall take place during the entire period of repatriation and, pending the settlement of the question, these prisoners of war shall remain in India.
(c) On completion of the agreed repatriations, or earlier if agreed, Bangladesh, India, and Pakistan will discuss the question of the 195 prisoners of war. Bangladesh stated that

it would participate in the meeting only on the basis of 'sovereign equality'.

(d) The government of Pakistan would initially receive a substantial number of non-Bengalis from Bangladesh who are stated to have opted for repatriation to Pakistan. The prime ministers of Bangladesh and Pakistan, or their designated representatives, will meet after the initial repatriations are completed, to decide what additional number of persons who may wish to migrate to Pakistan, may be permitted to do so.

The repatriation of Pakistani prisoners of war from India began in September 1973 and was completed in April 1974. A large number of Bengalis were repatriated from West Pakistan to Bangladesh and non-Bengalis from Bangladesh to Pakistan during the same period.

Meanwhile, important developments took place in the relations of Pakistan with the Muslim world. Pakistan's efforts to restore its prestige and revitalize its relations with the Muslim countries culminated in a decision to hold the Islamic Summit Conference in Lahore in February 1974. This conference saw Pakistan at the zenith of its glory when thirty-seven heads of Muslim states met in Lahore under the chairmanship of Pakistan's prime minister to discuss the problems facing the Muslim world. This conference and Pakistan's constant support to the Arabs greatly improved its reputation in the Muslim world. Besides Saudi Arabia Pakistan established closer relations with the UAR and Libya. These countries showed keen interest in Pakistan and extended economic aid.

It was on the eve of this conference that the government of Pakistan announced its recognition of Bangladesh. As a result, Sheikh Mujibur Rahman, prime minister of Bangladesh, came to Lahore to participate in the conference. Later, as a result of an agreement amongst Pakistan, India, and Bangladesh in April 1974, the government of Bangladesh abandoned the idea of putting Pakistani prisoners of war on trial. Bhutto visited Bangladesh in June 1974, and his visit paved the way for the restoration of diplomatic relations between Pakistan and Bangladesh. The latter raised the issue of assets, whereas the Pakistani stand was that 'assets also mean liabilities.'[148] After the death of Sheikh Mujibur Rehman in 1975, Pak-Bangla relations started improving. Pakistan despatched fifty thousand tons of rice and ten million yards of cloth to Bangladesh as a gift from Pakistan. Diplomatic relations were established in 1976, followed by telecommunication links and resumption of air services. Trade agreements were signed and delegations exchanged.

The process of normalization with India continued until India's atomic explosion in 1974. Pakistan lodged a strong protest against India's atomic explosion and its fallout on Pakistan. Pakistan believed that it would completely upset the military balance in the region. Consequently, Pakistan launched a worldwide campaign for declaring South-East Asia a nuclear-free zone and also exerted pressure on the USA for the resumption of military aid. Pakistan's efforts in this regard were crowned with success and its resolution declaring South-East Asia a nuclear-free zone was passed by the General Assembly with an overwhelming majority.

With the separation of East Pakistan and the emergence of Bangladesh in 1971, Pakistan's importance had declined, whereas India had emerged as a great power in Asia. This situation encouraged Afghanistan, a hostile neighbour, to raise the bogey of Pakhtunistan more vigorously. The Afghan government, headed by Sardar Daoud, adopted a threatening posture towards Pakistan. The Afghan delegate did not hesitate to criticize Pakistan even during the Islamic Summit Conference in Lahore.

In the past, Iran had stood by Pakistan through all crises, but during 1974, it gradually moved towards India, causing suspicion in Pakistan. The Shah of Iran visited India in October and announced that Iran 'would never assist Pakistan if it starts an aggressive war against India.'[149] Iran also promised substantial economic aid to India and concluded many agreements. Bhutto, on the other hand, stated that Pak-Iran relations were based on solid grounds and that Pakistan would maintain its friendship with Iran even if it annoyed some great powers.

However, relations among the RCD countries continued to flourish despite Iran's friendship with India. Followed by a meeting of the three heads of the states in Izmir in 1976, the Treaty of Izmir was signed by the foreign ministers of Iran, Pakistan, and Turkey in March 1977. The treaty aimed at developing the RCD region into a free-trade zone and envisaged the establishment of various institutions in the RCD countries.

Pak-Turkish relations, based on solid grounds, were steadily progressing without any fluctuations and strain. The Turkish-Pakistani joint ministerial commission signed a protocol in March 1977 for increased co-operation in the fields of trade, industry, agriculture, and technology.

Pakistan's relations with China continued to improve. Bhutto's visits to China in 1972, 1974, and 1976 were described as successful. The joint communiqué issued at the end of Bhutto's visit in May 1974 indicated that his visit had made a significant contribution to the consolidation of close relations with China.[150] China's support to Pakistan during the crisis of 1971 and afterwards, and its stand on the admission of Bangladesh to the UNO, will always be remembered by the people of Pakistan with gratitude.

China had been extending financial, economic, and technical assistance to Pakistan. The exchange of cultural, trade, and goodwill missions was a regular feature. In 1976, China agreed to extend assistance for setting up a huge paper mill at Jaranwala, which was considered to be the biggest Chinese project in Pakistan after the heavy mechanical complex at Taxila.

Pakistan's relations with the United states had been cordial during this period. The USA gave reasonably firm support to Pakistan during the crisis of 1971 and voted with 104 UN members, condemning India. Pak-US relations were based on reciprocity and mutual understanding. Even differences on various international issues were not allowed to strain the relations.

Bhutto's visit to the US in September 1973 further strengthened the friendship between the two countries. President Nixon's statement that 'the integrity of Pakistan was a cornerstone of American foreign policy' constituted a landmark in the history of Pak-US relations. His successor, President Ford also confirmed that his government was pursuing the same policy towards Pakistan.[151] After India's atomic explosion, Pakistan had been exerting pressure on the USA for the resumption of military aid.[152] During Kissinger's visit to Pakistan in October 1974, Bhutto raised the problem of the ban on the supply of American arms.[153] The arms embargo was ultimately lifted when Bhutto visited the United States in February 1975.

The Pak-US relations were strained in 1976, when the US pressurized Pakistan to abandon its peaceful nuclear programme. This process started when Pakistan decided to purchase a reprocessing plant from France after providing international guarantees. Apprehending nuclear ambitions, the US pressurized both the seller and the buyer to abandon the deal, but did not pressurize the French government to discontinue its supply of uranium to India. Bhutto, during the last days of his government, alleged that the US was funding the agitation against him and was determined to punish him for his nuclear programme. Thus, the year 1977 witnessed Pak-US relations at the lowest ebb. It was believed that Kissinger had threatened Bhutto with dire consequences if he continued with the nuclear programme.

Bhutto attached special importance to relations with the Muslim countries and devoted significant attention to building closer relations with Saudi Arabia, the United Arab Emirates (UAE), and Libya. He was successful in developing personal rapport with the heads of these states, and this was why all of them made all possible efforts to save him from execution, after the Supreme Court sentenced him to death in 1979. His execution had a cooling effect on Pakistan's relations with these countries, but it was a temporary phenomenon, and Zia was able to revitalize relations with the Muslim world.

During his regime, Bhutto paid visits to the Muslim countries which were reciprocated. Saudi Arabia and Libya extended economic assistance to Pakistan. Meetings of the leaders of these countries were held regularly to review bilateral relations. King Khalid of Saudi Arabia visited Pakistan in October 1976, and said that his visit would 'foster co-operation between us in all fields of activities'. The joint communiqué was significant in the sense that it referred to the Kashmir dispute and hoped that it would be resolved in accordance with the United Nations resolutions. During the first half of 1977, many dignitaries from the Muslim countries visited Pakistan. The Iraqi vice-president came in January and signed an agreement for trade, economic, and technical co-operation. A joint commission was set up to ensure its implementation. Libyan and Kuwaiti foreign ministers visited Pakistan in May and showed brotherly concern about the agitation. Bhutto paid flying visits to Saudi Arabia, Libya, Kuwait, the UAE, Iran, and Afghanistan in June 1977, because these countries had shown concern over the continuing constitutional crisis in Pakistan, which had erupted after the general elections. Apart from the Muslim countries, Bhutto also espoused the cause of the Third World which enabled him to maintain cordial and friendly relations with several important developing states of Asia and Africa. Pakistan also championed the cause of the removal of racial discrimination in South Africa, Rhodesia, and Nambia. Pakistan extended economic and technological assistance to a number of African countries.

FOREIGN POLICY 1977–85

Taking advantage of the unending agitation against Bhutto, General Ziaul Haq, assumed power on 5 July 1977, and imposed martial law in the country. During 1977–85, Pakistan made serious efforts to normalize relations with India. Pakistan played an active role in the Muslim world and made sincere efforts to resolve inter-state conflicts such as the Iran-Iraq war. Apart from following the principles of personal diplomacy and exchanging visits with the various heads of the Muslim countries, Zia successfully pursued 'tight-rope diplomacy', maintaining a diplomatic balance between the Soviet Union and the USA.

China

Zia visited China in December 1977, for a general review of bilateral relations. His visit was reciprocated by the Chinese vice-premier who headed a forty-member delegation and arrived in Islamabad in June 1978. The two leaders later said that Pakistan and China had complete identity of views.

In addition to heavy mechanical complex at Taxila, the biggest sheet-glass factory was set up at Nowshera in collaboration with China. Opening of the all-weather Karakoram Highway (KKH) had already enfolded the two nations into warm embrace of eternal friendship. Consequently, a large number of trade and barter agreements were signed, apart from the cultural exchange programmes. It is worth noting that after Chou En-lai's visit to Pakistan in 1965, the second visit of a Chinese prime minister (Zhao Ziyang) took place in June 1981. The Chinese prime minister, supported Pakistan's stand on Afghanistan issue. Pakistan also got some military hardware from China. However, the visit of the Chinese president in April 1984, was most significant. The Chinese president supported Pakistan's stand regarding the Soviet invasion of Afghanistan and demanded immediate withdrawal of the Soviet troops from Afghanistan.

A major achievement of Pakistan's foreign policy during Zia's regime was Pakistan's admission to the Non-Aligned Movement (NAM) in 1979. Zia led the Pakistani delegation to its summit conference at Havana (1979) and New Delhi in 1983. Unlike blocs and defence pacts, the NAM is a movement united by common ideals of peace and it reflects determination of the member-nations to avoid involvement in super powers' politics and conflicts. It was on the insistence of Pakistan that the New Delhi NAM conference took up the issue of the Soviet military intervention in Afghanistan and passed a resolution urging the withdrawal of foreign (i.e., Soviet) army from Afghanistan. In this conference, Pakistan supported the principles of self-determination, non-interference, and anti-colonialism. Pakistan also urged that South Asia should be declared a nuclear-free zone and the Indian Ocean should be made a zone of peace. Another important achievement of Pakistan was its election as a non-permanent member of the Security Council. Pakistan assumed a seat in the UN Security Council on 1 January 1983 for two years.

Afghanistan

The most important reality which went a long way in shaping Pakistan's foreign policy during Zia's rule was the Soviet occupation of Afghanistan. In 1978, curtains began to rise on the political stage of Afghanistan, and a drama of horror started. Sardar Daoud was removed by an army-backed coup in April 1978. Noor Muhammad Taraki was installed as the head of the state, who enjoyed the support of the People's Democratic Party of Afghanistan. This coup interrupted the process of reconciliation between Afghanistan and Pakistan, which was started by Bhutto. In fact, some sort of agreement on the Durand Line was in the offing and Pakistan's foreign minister, Agha Shahi, was preparing to leave for Kabul, but the coup pre-empted the whole exercise. In September 1979, Taraki was dashed down by another coup led by Hafizullah Amin. In December 1979, the Soviet forces moved into Afghanistan on a massive scale. Amin was killed and the Soviets installed Babrak Karmal in his place.

The Soviet-engineered coup in Afghanistan in December 1979, made the Soviet Union a political factor in Pakistan's calculations[154], because its military presence on the western frontier was a constant threat to Pakistan. As a result, approximately three million Afghan refugees found shelter in Pakistan, putting great pressure on Pakistan's economy and causing many socio-political problems. Soviet occupation of

Afghanistan led to a prolonged guerilla war between the Afghan Mujahideen and the Afghan army backed by the Soviets.

The Afghan war caused instability in the entire region. The Soviet Union accused Pakistan of direct involvement in the Afghan civil war and alleged that the Mujahideen were being armed and trained by Pakistan. Hence, the Soviet Union held Pakistan responsible for the continuous trouble in Afghanistan. Moscow Radio beamed anti-Pakistan propaganda. Pakistan maintained a policy of restraint in the face of Soviet threats and repeated air violations by the Afghan air force, followed by firing on Pakistani villages. In 1981, a PIA Boeing was hijacked to Kabul, which accelerated the process of deterioration of the situation in the region.

Soon after the Soviet military intervention in Afghanistan, Pakistan tried to explore the prospects of a negotiated settlement of the problem based on withdrawal of the Soviet troops, guarantee of non-intervention, and return of the Afghan refugees. Pakistan's efforts enjoyed international support including that of the US, China, and the Muslim world. Pakistan took the initiative of organizing the meeting of the foreign ministers of the Islamic countries at a conference, which condemned the Soviet action, appointed a committee comprising foreign ministers of Pakistan and Iran and secretary-general of the organization to resolve the issue. The committee could not make any headway because of the non-co-operation of the Soviet Union. The Afghanistan problem was also taken up by the UN General Assembly in January and September 1980, which passed resolutions with an overwhelming majority, calling for a peaceful settlement of the Afghanistan crisis, including the withdrawal of the Soviet troops and return of the Afghan refugees to their homes.

The Soviet Union

Pakistan's relations with the Soviet Union deteriorated after Pakistan openly opposed the Soviet military intervention in Afghanistan, demanded immediate withdrawal of its troops, and mobilized international support for that purpose. In the beginning, the Soviet attitude was threatening; it talked about teaching a lesson to Pakistan. When Gromyko met Agha Shahi at the United Nations in September 1980, 'he chided his Pakistani counterpart that you seem to want to fight a war with us.'[155]

The Soviet Union accused Pakistan of helping and training the Afghan guerrillas and of 'dancing to the tunes of the US.' It also claimed that Pakistan had given military bases to the US which was vehemently denied by Pakistan. Though Pakistan supported Afghan, resistance against the Soviet military presence in Afghanistan, and offered refuge to over three million Afghan refugees, Pakistan adopted a low-key approach so as to avoid direct confrontation with the Soviet troops in Afghanistan. For example, whenever the Afghan aircraft violated Pakistan's airspace or bombed the border areas, Pakistan air force chased them out rather than shoot these aircraft down, because these were being flown by the Soviet crew. In a couple of instances when the armed helicopters were forced to land in Pakistan, the Soviet crew was returned quickly. Pakistan also maintained diplomatic interaction with the Soviet Union throughout this period. In August 1981, Soviet deputy foreign minister, Nikolai Firyubin, visited Islamabad and discussed bilateral relations. In October 1981, Pakistan's Foreign Minister Yaqub Khan had a meeting with his Soviet counterpart at the UN headquarters in New York. He visited Moscow in June 1983. Gromyko emphasized the importance of a political settlement after the cessation of foreign interference in Afghanistan. The Soviet Union also supported the indirect talks between Pakistan and Afghanistan initiated in 1982 at Geneva through the special envoy of the UN secretary-general.

Ziaul Haq attended the funeral of President Leonid Brezhnev in November 1982 and of President Andropov in 1984. He was one of the few foreign guests who met with the new Soviet president on these occasions. These meetings were interpreted by the international media as a sign of healthy change in the Soviet attitude.[156] However, there was no change in the Soviet hostility towards Pakistan and the Soviets gave no indication of an early withdrawal from Afghanistan.

Despite political estrangement, economic ties between Pakistan and the Soviet Union remained intact; bilateral trade showed some increase during these years. A new barter trade agreement was signed for 1983–84. The Soviet Union extended technological assistance, training facilities, and credits for various projects to Pakistan. Two new oil rigs for the exploration of oil were also committed and the Soviet Union made investment in Pakistan for the production of Belarus tractors. However, the political relations remained strained, because the Soviets wanted Pakistan to stop opposing their intervention in Afghanistan. They promised to step up economic relations, and offered more economic and technological assistance if Pakistan changed its policy towards Afghanistan.

India

When Ziaul Haq assumed power in Pakistan, the Indian government was headed by Morarji Desai of the Janata Party. The two governments worked towards improving their relations. The differences over India's decision to construct the Salal Dam in Kashmir was resolved amicably, and an agreement was signed by Agha Shahi and his Indian counterpart, Atal Behari Vajpayee, on 14 April 1978. The two foreign ministers undertook exchange visits to each other's country, generating some goodwill.

The return of Indira Gandhi to power in India in January 1980 adversely affected the normalization trend. India under Indira Gandhi supported the Soviet military intervention in Afghanistan and accused Pakistan and the US of engaging in subversive activities in Afghanistan. India maintained, as the Soviet had claimed, that the Soviet forces entered Afghanistan on the invitation of the Afghan government and that these would return when the Afghanistan government asked them to do so. The Indian government was more concerned about the political and security assistance to Pakistan from the West in the context of the Afghanistan crisis rather than the Soviet military presence in Afghanistan. The sharp differences between India and Pakistan on Afghanistan became an additional cause of tension between the two countries.

Other issues that adversely affected Indo-Pakistan relations were: the Kashmir problem, India's arms build-up and nuclear capability, India's hegemonic ambitions, and India's opposition to Pakistan's nuclear programme. However, the major setback to the process of normalization was caused by the Indian propaganda and campaign aimed at dissuading the United states from supplying arms to Pakistan. India, with a much bigger size and an overwhelming military strength, viewed Pakistan's acquisition of arms as a threat to its integrity. When the Soviet defence minister visited India in March 1982, *The Economist* rightly commented that Indira Gandhi was making political capital out of an alleged threat from Pakistan, even though the military balance was heavily in India's favour and could shift even more decisively after the arms-bearing visit to Delhi by Marshal Ustinov.[157]

In view of New Delhi's apprehensions, Pakistan offered a no-war pact to India in September 1981, including proposals for reduction of arms and inspection of nuclear plants. This sincere offer was made with a view to reduce tension and to build up mutual confidence. On 27 October Indira Gandhi said that a no-war pact made no sense to her, as Pakistan was preparing for war. In an interview with the American Television Network, Indira Gandhi remarked that Pakistan could be removed from the NAM if it continued getting arms.[158] In response to India's provocative remarks, Pakistan showed restraint, which was appreciated by the international press. According to the *Washington Post,* India was losing out to Pakistan in the world perception of who is more reasonable.[159]

In January 1982, Agha Shahi visited India and held negotiations with his counterpart, but no significant development was noted. Meanwhile, the government of India offered a treaty of friendship and proposed the establishment of a joint commission to review and promote bilateral relations. In August

1982, parleys were held by the India-Pakistan foreign secretaries, but these did not lead to any substantive results.

The formal agreement to set up a joint commission was signed during Zia's visit to New Delhi in March 1983, in connection with the NAM Summit meeting. The commission was to provide mechanism for economic, technical, and cultural exchanges. Inaugural session of the joint commission, in June 1983, was marked with expressions of goodwill by both the foreign ministers.

The period beginning from August 1983, registered a downward trend in India-Pakistan relations, and exposed the hollowness of the conciliatory efforts. In August 1983, the Movement for Restoration of Democracy (MRD) launched anti-Zia campaign in Pakistan. India's prime minister and foreign minister issued undiplomatic statements supporting the MRD, thus interfering in the internal affairs of Pakistan. Indira Gandhi also addressed a letter to Zia for the release of Khan Abdul Ghaffar Khan. These moves not only embarrassed the MRD leadership, but also created tension between the two countries.

India accused Pakistan of supporting the Khalistan movement in East Punjab. Although the government of Pakistan refuted the allegation, the Indian government continued repeating its charges. Although President Ziaul Haq expressed his confidence and optimism concerning the process of Indo-Pak normalization, most of the analysts expressed pessimism about it. Even during the first half of 1984, India had been blaming Pakistan for war preparations, creating war hysteria in India. In April 1984, both the countries charged each other with border violations. In this way, in addition to the Kashmir problem, four major problems adversely affected India-Pakistan relations: differences on Soviet military intervention in Afghanistan, the supply of weapons by the US to Pakistan and India's procurement of weapons from the Soviet Union, the trading of charges of intervention in domestic affairs, and periodic hostile propaganda.

It was also during this period that the Siachen Glacier problem cropped up, when India occupied the higher elevations of this glacier hitherto the two sides had avoided stationing their troops at that level. The failure to resolve this problem also undermined their relations.

The United States

The Pakistan-US relations had started deteriorating in 1976, when the Ford administration exerted unprecedented pressure on Pakistan to abandon its deal for the purchase of a nuclear reprocessing plant from France. When Pakistan did not concede, the US persuaded France to renege from its deal which it did in 1978, giving a cause of complaint to Pakistan.

During the Carter era (1977–81), Pakistan remained a low priority for the US strategic interests, because the White House believed that 'India's hegemony in South Asia is unquestioned and must be adapted to rather than challenged.'[160] Accordingly President Carter visited India in early 1978 and bypassed its old ally, Pakistan. This confirmed the old dictum that friendship between the countries was not permanent, it was subject to their national and global interests. In April 1979, the Carter administration suspended all economic, technical, and military aid to Pakistan on the pretext that it was building an 'Islamic bomb' by secretly creating a uranium enrichment facility. In November 1979, the burning down of the US embassy by a mob in Islamabad brought the Pakistan-US relations to the lowest ebb.

However, the major developments on the international scene forced the US to revise its strategic outlook and cultivate Pakistan for coping with the fallout of these developments. The first development was the Islamic revolution in Iran in February 1979, which manifested strong anti-America disposition from time to time and, in November, took the American diplomat and other staff of its embassy in Tehran as hostages. The second development which really forced American administration to revise its policy towards Pakistan was the Soviet invasion of Afghanistan in December 1979. The Americans were now looking for a 'foothold' in the area in order to protect and promote their strategic interests. Even during the election campaign of 1980, Reagan had called for establishing American military bases in Pakistan.[161] It was a different matter that Pakistan was determined not to provide any such facility to the US. Pakistan acquired importance for the Americans due to its geographical proximity to the Gulf region and Afghanistan. American stakes in this region were very high[162] which could not be adequately protected without the support of Pakistan.

It was in this perspective that in February 1980 the Carter administration offered 400 million dollars to Pakistan as security and economic assistance. The offer was rejected by President Zia as 'peanuts', as it was likely to entangle Pakistan in super power rivalry without much improving its security. Pakistan's rejection was appreciated in the country and caused 'surprise' in Washington. In October, Zia visited the US to address the UN General Assembly as well as to meet with Carter for consultations on security matters and especially for the US economic and military assistance to Pakistan. The US assured support for Pakistan's security.

The Reagan administration that took over in January 1981, evinced better appreciation of the problem and was more forthcoming on economic assistance and military sales to Pakistan. In June, the US secretary of state visited Pakistan for settling the details of the assistance package. Later, the US offered a package of 3.2 billion dollars for economic assistance and military sales to Pakistan for six years (1981–87). Its details were finalized in the next couple of months, which were announced on James Buckley's visit to Islamabad in mid-September; in December, the formalities for making this assistance package available were completed. The assistance package was equally divided between economic assistance (loans and grants) and military sales (all loan). The US also agreed to sell 40 high-performance F-16 aircraft at the cost of about 1.1 billion dollars outside the assistance package. The changed American attitude was also reflected in the statements of the American officials. On 12 November 1981, the under secretary of state described Pakistan as 'an essential anchor of the entire

South-West Asia region.'[163] In the same manner, commander of the US Pacific fleet, who visited Pakistan, said in a congressional testimony that 'Pakistan's strategic location requires us to strengthen our security relationship.'[164] Pakistan and the US maintained a high level civil and military interaction during these years. The foreign minister of Pakistan visited the US quite frequently and American civil and military officials also travelled to Islamabad from time to time. In December 1982, president Zia visited Washington, where he was received with open arms by the US officials, including President Reagan.

The process of 're-invigoration' of Pakistan-US relations maintained its tempo[165] during 1983–84. Pakistan obtained military hardware and F-16 aircraft. In August 1983, the US promised an additional grant of about 518.5 million dollars. As usual, brisk activity was witnessed on the diplomatic front, including exchange of official delegations. Some of the important visits included those of Secretary of State George Schultz, in July 1983, followed by visits of secretary of defence, and chief of staff, US air force, in September 1983. Reciprocally, Pakistan's foreign minister visited New York and Washington many times. The US supported Pakistan's efforts to seek a peaceful settlement of the Afghanistan problem.

The Muslim World

An important feature of Pakistan's foreign policy is its brotherly relations with the Muslim countries. The concept of Islamic solidarity has been shaped in the case of Pakistan's foreign policy by a number of factors: history, geography, faith, political convergence of interests, economic ties, and the overwhelming participation of overseas Pakistanis in Muslim states' economic development.[166]

Pakistan has always been supporting the cause of the Palestinians on all international forums, as well as boldly criticizing the policies of Israel. In fact, Pakistan's strong condemnation of Israel has earned it the latter's hostility. Hence, it was not surprising that in the mid-1980s, the international press carried a report about Israeli plans for air-strikes against Pakistan's nuclear installations. During the Lebanon war (1982 onwards), Pakistan offered military assistance and sent a delegation to Syria and the Palestine Liberation Organization (PLO). Pakistan was an active member of the Organization of Islamic Conference (OIC) and other international forums supporting the cause of the Muslim countries.

Zia's fervour for Islamic countries and his contribution to their cause were acknowledged by the OIC, when it asked him in 1980 to undertake goodwill missions to Tehran and Baghdad in order to re-establish peace between the two countries who were then engaged in an armed conflict. In October 1980, Zia addressed the UN General Assembly on behalf of the Muslim world. Of course, it was an honour for Pakistan.

Pakistan actively participated in the third Islamic Summit, held at Taif, Saudi Arabia, in January 1981. The conference unanimously approved the famous Makkah Declaration, calling for *Jihad* against Israel and supporting the liberation movement of Afghanistan from the Soviet occupation. The Ummah Peace Committee, constituted to bring about peace between Iran and Iraq, included President Zia as well. The Ummah Peace Committee visited Tehran and Baghdad several times, but without success.

During the years from 1977 to 1984, President Zia visited Saudi Arabia many times. A large number of visits were exchanged at the level of ministers of both the countries. Some agreements were also signed by Saudi Arabia and Pakistan, including two security agreements signed in April 1984, relating to the extradition of criminals and exchange of information, as well as training of security personnel. Apart from extending economic assistance, Saudi Arabia had been supporting Pakistan's stand on various international issues, including the Afghanistan question. Several thousand Pakistanis are currently employed in Saudi Arabia.

Diplomatic exchanges and economic interaction between Pakistan and the Gulf states expanded in the Zia regime.

President Zia paid visits to Kuwait in 1977, 1981, and 1983. The Amir of Kuwait visited Pakistan in 1980. Zia visited Dubai, Doha, Muscat, and Abu Dhabi in 1977, 1981, and 1982. The ruler of the UAE, Zayad Bin Sultan-al-Nahyan, visited Pakistan several times during these years. These visits contributed to a better understanding between Pakistan and the UAE, Kuwait, Saudi Arabia, and other Gulf states, where thousands of Pakistanis are employed.

Zia also visited Libya in 1977 and Syria in 1982. Pakistan's relations with these countries could be described as satisfactory, lacking the warmth of the Bhutto era. With Jordan, Pakistan's relations made remarkable progress. Zia visited Jordan in 1977, 1981, and 1982. The crown prince of Jordan, Prince Hassan, visited Pakistan in 1982.

The Islamic revolution in Iran led to a polarization in the Muslim world, because Iran openly desired to export the revolution to other Muslim states. Hence, the Iranian revolution was perceived as a threat by the monarchies and kingdoms around Iran. In this polarization, Iran was backed by Syria and Libya, while Saudi Arabia was supported by Jordan, Iraq, and the Gulf sheikhdoms. Due to Pakistan's close relations with these Arab states, Pak-Iran relations were clouded with suspicion. At one time, Radio Tehran went to the extent of inciting the people of Pakistan to overthrow the military government.[167] Despite this, Pakistan did not react and maintained cordiality in its interaction with Iran. Zia visited Tehran several times in order to bring an end to the Iran-Iraq war. Pakistan's foreign minister, Agha Shahi, also visited Tehran in February 1980, assuring Tehran that Pakistan was deeply committed to Iran's independence and integrity. During 1981–82, several Iranian delegations visited Pakistan, including the Iranian foreign minister. Short-term and long-term trade agreements were signed in April 1982, leading to an increase in trade. The years 1983–84 witnessed a significant change in the attitude of both the countries. These official contacts contributed to greater understanding between the two countries resulting in expansion of trade. Iran, surrounded by hostile monarchies, now looked at Pakistan as a neutral state with friendly posture. Decision to revive RCD with a view to achieve closer unity between the three old friends was symptomatic of this change in attitude.

Pak-Turkish relations as usual remained very cordial and intimate. President Ziaul Haq visited Turkey more than once. Likewise, the Turkish president and prime minister visited Pakistan many times. There was a complete identity of views between the two countries on international issues. Meetings of the joint Pak-Turkish commission were held regularly to review the progress and to identify new areas of co-operation, including extension of the institutional framework to forge close economic ties.

On 15 November 1983, the Turks of Cyprus proclaimed an independent state under the name of Turkish Republic of North Cyprus. It was immediately accorded recognition by Turkey. The Security Council session was convened to consider the unilateral declaration of independence. As in the past, Pakistan supported the cause of the Turkish Cyprots. Pakistan's help was acknowledged with a sense of gratitude. The Turkish prime minister, Turgut Ozal, visited Pakistan in May 1984 and said that he considered Pakistan his second home. Congruence of views on all major issues was expressed. President Zia said that Pakistan and Turkey shared common perceptions on the regional and global issues. Pakistan and Turkey also signed a protocol for economic and technical co-operation. Bilateral trade was expected to expand, leading to closer relations.[168]

By and large, Pakistan maintained cordial relations with most of the Muslim countries, especially with the Gulf states. Its gradually rising prestige in the Muslim world was an important factor responsible for America's 'warmth' for Pakistan, because the US, having lost credibility in the Muslim world due to its total commitment to Israel, sought Pakistan's good offices for interaction with the Muslim countries.

FOREIGN POLICY 1985–88

The security compulsions which shaped Pakistan's foreign policy in the past significantly contributed to Pakistan's foreign policy strategies during Junejo's prime ministership (March 1985–May 1988). The major concern continued to be the problems and difficulties caused by the Soviet military presence in Afghanistan. India's traditional enmity and military pressure and its efforts to disrupt Pakistan's relations with the West were other major concerns. In addition to the pressure in the foreign policy domain, some of the external actors like India and the Soviet Union also tried to build pressure on Pakistan by engaging in sabotage, i.e., bomb blasts, and other terrorist activities through intelligence agencies or air raids across the border. These activities were intended to pressurize the people and government of Pakistan into accepting the peace terms offered by the Soviet Union at Geneva. Anyhow, Pakistan's resistance did not slack; it remained firm on its principles regarding the Afghanistan issue. Due to the convergence of Indo-Soviet interests in this region, Pakistan suspected the Indian hand playing a malicious game behind its internal problems. Hence, India-Pakistan relations were overshadowed with uncertainty. As in the past, Pakistan maintained cordial and friendly relations with USA, China, the Muslim countries, and the other South Asian countries. Pakistan continued playing its role in the UNO, the NAM, and the South Asian Association for Regional Co-operation (SAARC) with unabated zeal.

The United States

Significant improvement was experienced in the US-Pak relations, especially during 1985–86, due to their shared perceptions of the regional security environment against the backdrop of Afghanistan problem. In 1985, the American administration reiterated its support to Pakistan, and appreciated Pakistan's steadfastness against the Soviet threats. The steady implementation of economic assistance programme initiated in 1981, was followed by an offer of one million tons of US wheat, economic assistance from the World Bank, as well as assistance from the Aid to Pakistan Consortium. Another notable gesture was that the American Congress did not apply cut on the administration's aid proposal to Pakistan during 1986. In addition to some other weapons and military hardware, Pakistan received more F-16 aircrafts from the USA twenty-five in 1985 and fifteen in 1986. President Reagan also re-affirmed the American support to Pakistan under the Mutual Security Pact of 1959. When the Soviets issued a warning to Pakistan about its nuclear programme in 1986, the US government advised them to keep their hands off Pakistan.[169]

The second six-year (1987–93) package of economic assistance and military sales was negotiated during 1985–86 and approved in 1987. Its total value was 4.02 billion dollars at concessional rates of interest. Out of this allocation, 2.28 billion dollars were assigned to economic and technological assistance and the rest of the amount (1.74 million dollars) was given in the form of credits for buying weapons and military equipment. Though a close security-related co-operation continued between Pakistan and the US, they diverged on Pakistan's nuclear programme. Pakistan resisted the American pressure for abandoning this programme. India played up the nuclear issue in order to disrupt the security ties between the US and Pakistan.

The nuclear issue was raised during Prime Minister Junejo's visit to Washington in September 1987. Junejo unsuccessfully tried to convince Washington about the peaceful nature of the nuclear programme. The US delayed the release of new assistance in October 1987 in order to build pressure on Pakistan on the nuclear issue. They did the same in 1988 and 1989, but as the Afghanistan issue was still live, they did not press hard and released new aid after some delay.

Pakistan wanted to obtain AWACS aircraft from the US so that an air-borne early warning system could be established against the regular intrusion by the Afghan air force. Washington recognized the genuineness of Pakistan's need, but refused to give the AWACS aircraft. Instead, the US offered a less sophisticated aircraft which was not acceptable to Pakistan. Still, Pak-US relations continued to progress. Zia's demise on 17 August 1988 was condoled by President Reagan, and Secretary of State George Shultz, the latter visited Pakistan to attend Zia's funeral.

The Soviet Union

Pak-Soviet relations suffered from great stress due to the Soviet intervention in Afghanistan. There was no meaningful improvement in their relations, although Zia visited Moscow in March 1985 in connection with Chernenko's funeral, and had a brief meeting with Gorbachev. As in the past, the Soviet government continued employing pressure tactics to bully Pakistan. The Soviet blamed Pakistan of 'aiding and abetting' the insurgents in Afghanistan. The Soviet deputy foreign minister went to the extent of saying that Pakistan was at war with the Soviet Union.[170] It was followed by a statement of the Soviet ambassador to Pakistan in February, alleging that Pakistan was involved in an undeclared war against Afghanistan and that Pakistan had established training camps for the Afghan freedom-fighters.

However, they continued to maintain trade relations; neither any expansion was noticed nor any senior Soviet official came to attend the inauguration of the Karachi Steel Mill set up with the Soviet assistance. The assistant naval attaché of the Soviet embassy in Islamabad was assassinated by unidentified gunmen in September 1986, which provoked hostile reaction from Moscow.

With the assumption of power by Gorbachev (1985), the Soviet government reviewed its Afghanistan policy and began to give indications for showing some flexibility in this respect. Gorbachev openly admitted that Afghanistan was a bleeding wound for the Soviet Union. Therefore, the Soviet government expressed its willingness to disengage from Afghanistan and to work towards its peaceful settlement. The first step was the replacement of Babrak Karmal with Najibullah as the head of state in 1986. Another important Afghan leader, Shah Muhammad Dost, was also replaced. Later, some troops were withdrawn as a gesture, indicating a clear change in the Soviet disposition towards Afghanistan.

The most significant gesture was noticed during Gorbachev's visit to India, when he 'neither endorsed the Indian leadership's anti-Pakistan tirade nor attacked the American supply of arms to Pakistan.'[171] These developments paved way for the visit of Pakistan's foreign secretary to Moscow in December 1986, where the question of the time frame for the withdrawal of Soviet army from Afghanistan was discussed. This visit was reciprocated by the visit of the Soviet deputy foreign minister in January 1987.

The two pre-requisites for the success of the Afghan settlement were international guarantees regarding non-interference in the internal affairs of Afghanistan and a precise timetable for the withdrawal of the Soviet troops. In fact, these two issues were interlinked. The Soviets were reluctant to announce a timetable unless international guarantees were furnished, but the US refused to offer any guarantee prior to the Soviet withdrawal. During 1985, the Soviet Union reportedly insisted that the refugees issue should be tackled separately, but Pakistan stressed on an integrated action. The Soviets desired to protect the pro-Soviet government in Kabul in any broad arrangement, whereas the US wished to install a government acceptable to the Mujahideen and capable of defending the American interests. Thus, Pakistan was caught up in a grim situation; it had to face the threat directly, but could not proceed alone towards a workable solution.

As a matter of fact, the Soviet politburo was divided over the military action in Afghanistan. Andropov, who succeeded Brezhnev, belonged to the group which was opposed to the Soviet intervention. Hence, he was inclined towards concluding the agreement leading to the withdrawal of the Soviet troops. Moreover, the Soviet Union had realized the consequences of their action by 1983. They had been condemned by the world community and had been unable to establish a firm control on the Afghan territory. When President Zia visited Moscow for Brezhnev's funeral, he was received by President Andropov, which was interpreted as a healthy change in the Soviet attitude. Consequently, Pakistan-Afghanistan indirect negotiations at Geneva showed reasonable progress in 1983.

Andropov's successors were believed to be hardliners. Both Chernenko and Gorbachev adopted a tough posture on Afghanistan. During the visit of the UN Secretary General to Moscow in July 1984, Chernenko categorically stated that the Soviet Union would not withdraw its forces, unless asked to do so by the Kabul government, following international guarantees of non-interference.

Accordingly, President Zia was not received by Chernenko when he went to Moscow to attend Andropov's funeral in 1984. During President Zia's visited in March 1985, to attend Chernenko's funeral, the Soviet Union exhibited a tough attitude. It was learnt that the Soviets told the Pakistani president that they were not prepared to engage in a prolonged stalemate with Pakistan over Afghanistan. Indications were that the Soviets might opt for a long-range military solution of the situation by increasing their strength in Afghanistan, followed by increasing the pressure on Pakistan, if a diplomatic solution was not achieved soon. The Matni incident in 1985, in which several Soviet soldiers were killed, further heightened tension. This was followed by a tirade of propaganda unleashed by Radio Moscow warning Pakistan 'not to play with fire.'

Undoubtedly a negotiated political solution remained the only way out. The UN Secretary-General's representative on Afghanistan, Diego Cordovez, rightly remarked in August 1984 that 'time is running short for the achievement of a negotiated solution', and that the diplomatic process could not go on forever. Moreover, the continuous inflow of Afghan refugees into Pakistan had far-reaching socio-economic and political implications for Pakistan. As the political solution of the problem was delayed, a large majority of the refugees were expected to settle here permanently, straining the modest economy of Pakistan. Even otherwise, being well-equipped and well-trained, they constituted 'a state within the state'.

In a dramatic move, Afghanistan's president, Najibullah, with the blessings of the Soviet leadership, announced a temporary unilateral ceasefire on 1 January 1987, and offered establishment of a government of national reconciliation. But the seven-party alliance of Afghan Mujahideen rejected the Soviet-sponsored peace overtures. The Geneva-based dialogue on Afghanistan was bogged down on the issue of the time frame for the withdrawal of the Soviet forces. All the other aspects of the settlement had been agreed in principle. Pakistan insisted on a six-month deadline, while the Afghan government proposed a phased withdrawal over two years.

The eighth round of the Geneva talks was held from February to March, in which the composition of the Afghanistan government and procedure for the withdrawal of the Soviet troops were discussed. The deadlock continued on the issue of time frame. However, deliberations in Yaqub-Shevardnadze meeting in New York, in September 1987 indicated, to great relief, that the Soviets would drop the precondition of a coalition government for setting a date for the withdrawal. After the Reagan-Gorbachev summit meeting in December 1987, the Soviet foreign minister Shevardnadze visited Kabul and US under-secretary for political affairs, Armcost, visited Islamabad in December 1987 and January 1988 respectively. The period beginning 1987 to April 1988, witnessed unprecedented diplomatic activity. In February 1988, the Soviet deputy foreign minister visited Islamabad. Then Gorbachev made a dramatic announcement, yielding more ground in meeting the Pak-US terms for a settlement. He announced 15 May as the withdrawal date, in case an agreement was reached at Geneva. The final and the longest round of Geneva talks was held from March to April 1988. In the course of these talks, the leaders of Afghanistan and the Soviet Union met in Tashkent to declare that all the obstacles to the proposed peace accord had been removed.[172] Consequently, the long-awaited peace accord on Afghanistan was signed at Geneva on 14 April 1988.

The Geneva Accord comprised four agreements, namely, (i) Bilateral Agreement on the Principles of Mutual Relations; (ii) Declaration on International Gurantees; (iii) Bilateral Agreement on Voluntary Return of Refugees; and (iv) Inter-relationship for the Settlement of the Situation Relating to Afghanistan. The withdrawal of the Soviet troops was addressed in the fourth agreement, which suggested that it would begin on 15 May 1988, as announced earlier, and it would be completed within nine months, i.e., 15 February 1989. The Accord (four agreements) was signed by Pakistan's minister of state for foreign affairs (Zain Noorani), Afghanistan's minister of foreign affairs (Abdul Wakil), the US secretary of state (George P. Shultz), and the Soviet foreign minister (Eduard Shevardnadze).

The Geneva Accord was welcomed almost all over the world, because after Vietnam, this was the first time that a super power had decided to withdraw from a war to which it was deeply committed. The Geneva accord was not a treaty imposed on anyone after defeat; 'it [was] a road map to sensible destination of international understanding.'[173] The then prime minister of Pakistan, Junejo, said that 'no better agreement could be wrested in the given circumstances.'[174]

China

Sino-Pakistan relations are an excellent example of shared perceptions on important issues and dependable friendship based on principles. Both the countries have maintained regular contact over the years, adding new dimensions to their friendship. Periodic consultation has been a regular feature. In the period 1985–88, Pakistan-China friendship continued its steady march towards greater understanding and warmth of relations. Throughout this period, China extended its wholehearted support to Pakistan on the Afghanistan crisis and continued to demand the withdrawal of the Soviet troops from there. It also welcomed the Geneva Accord.

Several trade and cultural delegations were exchanged between China and Pakistan, which contributed to the expansion in trade. Prime minister of Pakistan visited China in November 1985. In September 1986, Pakistan signed an agreement with China for co-operation in the peaceful uses of nuclear energy in the field of industry, agriculture, and power generation. China extended an interest-free loan, amounting to 27 million US dollars, and also helped Pakistan in modernizing the heavy mechanical complex at Taxila in the year 1987. Negotiations were also started for setting up a small tractor-production plant in Pakistan. Under a protocol signed in May 1987, Karachi shipyard was to fabricate two heavy cargo ships for China.

Chinese prime minister, Zhao Ziyang, was given a very warm welcome when he visited Pakistan in June 1987. The communiqué reflected complete identity of views on all important issues, both international and regional. The trade, cultural, military, and diplomatic exchanges with China during 1987 outnumbered Pakistan's diplomatic exchanges with any other country.

India

Indo-Pak relations were tinged with uncertainty and involved a simultaneous pursuance of positive and negative interaction. In spite of the expression of good intentions and noble sentiments by the leaders of the two countries, they could not overcome the deep-rooted historical distrust shaped by their negative mutual interaction. That is why, excepting for a short period of the Janata rule in India (1977–79), Indo-Pakistan relations generally remained far from satisfactory.

During 1985 a large number of visits were exchanged, as well as a meeting of the India-Pakistan joint ministerial commission was held. Direct-dialling telephone system was introduced and the Sikh hijackers held in Pakistani jail were put on trial. Yet mutual bickerings continued, affecting Indo-Pak relations.

Historically, three issues were considered by the Indians to be the obstacles in the way of normalization between India and Pakistan. First, Pakistan's stand on Kashmir; second Pakistan's acquisition of the American arms; and third, Pakistan's unwillingness to accept India's hegemony in this region. Especially after the Indo-Pak war of 1971, followed by the Indian atomic explosion in 1974, India considered itself to be the 'regional super-power'. Contrary to this concept, Pakistan believes in sovereign equality.

Other differences which emerged during the last few years of this era and complicated the normalization process were the differences on how best to contain the proliferation in South Asia, the Siachen Glacier issue, and the Indian accusation that Pakistan was aiding and abetting the Sikh extremists. Indian campaign against Pakistan's nuclear programme, mounted since 1981, reached its crescendo in 1985 when Rajiv Gandhi visited the Soviet Union, the US, France, and other countries, and accused Pakistan of manufacturing nuclear weapons.

President Zia's visit to India on his way back from Maldives in December 1985 was a positive move which went a long way in easing the tension caused by the above-mentioned issues. The visit was deliberately kept low-key by India. President of Pakistan was neither accorded formal reception nor seen off by his Indian counterpart. Anyhow, Zia-Rajiv meeting produced many agreements leading to the expansion of economic and cultural relations. The most important development was an agreement-in-principle for not attacking each other's nuclear installations.[175] (This agreement was formally signed in December 1988.)

During 1986, talks and meetings between senior officials and political leaders of both the countries were held on issues relating to political relations, trade, the Siachen glacier, and the Khokarapar route across India-Pakistan border in Sindh. Apart from an agreement on co-operation in agricultural research, another accord relating to the modalities of the accord not to attack each other's nuclear installations was also signed. The optimism created by these developments proved, as usual, to be shortlived, because Rajiv's proposed visit to Pakistan was postponed, followed by the Indian foreign minister's accusation that Pakistan was involved in the Sikh trouble. India also resented Pakistan's expression of concern on anti-Muslim riots in India, in which large number of Muslims were killed. Many other complaints and accusations such as construction of airports in Azad Kashmir and the alleged involvement of Pakistan in an attempt on Rajiv's life in October 1986, were made by India and rejected by Pakistan. Pakistan also expressed its concern on India's anti-Pakistan propaganda, concentration of Indian troops on Pakistani borders, constructions of a barrage on the Wular lake (River Jhelum) and India's involvement in the troubles in Sindh. These complaints and counter-complaints only revealed deep-seated distrust between the two neighbours, which formed part of their legacy of the past. In this background, it was illogical to expect a change of hearts inspite of many visits and efforts made by Zia and Junejo, which served only as a temporary device for defusing tension.

Therefore, Junejo's visit to Bangalore in November 1986, in connection with the annual summit of the SAARC where he also met the Indian prime minister, could not create a favourable climate for the normalization process. Pakistan's Foreign Minister Yaqub Ali Khan rightly stated in the Parliament on 27 April 1987, that the impetus in the Indo-Pak contact which had generated hope for a new chapter in their relations, received a serious setback due to the unfounded doubts expressed by India regarding Pakistan's involvement in their domestic troubles. He also referred to Pakistan's proposal for a cut in the defence budget and implementation of the non-aggression agreement— the proposal made to India in response to its propaganda against Pakistan's nuclear programme. Instead of giving a favourable consideration to Pakistani proposals, India enhanced its defence budget by 43 per cent[176] and acquired more sophisticated weapons, war planes, and missiles etc., from abroad. It was interesting to note that the increase of three billion dollars in the defence budget of India for 1987–88 was higher than the total defence budget of Pakistan which stood at 2.6 billion dollars.

In January 1987, India concentrated its army on Pakistan's border under the pretext of exercises, code-named Brasstacks, which created a dangerous situation, because Pakistan also moved its troops as a precautionary measure. However, diplomatic channels were activated to defuse the tension. The dialogue at the level of defence and foreign secretaries led to a de-escalation of the tension, at least for the time being. President Zia took the initiative of going to India in February for witnessing a cricket match between India and Pakistan. The media described the visit as 'cricket diplomacy'. His meeting with Rajiv Gandhi resulted in further relaxation of the tension. These meetings and exchanges created shortlived but positive results and helped in averting the awkward situation. No long-term solutions were found to the Indo-Pakistan problems.

Rajiv Gandhi again made hard-hitting statements against Pakistan's nuclear programme during his visit to the US in 1987. The beginning of 1988 witnessed the repetition of the same old story: Rajiv Gandhi attacked Pakistan on its major foreign policy planks, especially on its nuclear programme, and accused Pakistan of supporting the Sikh separatist movement in the Indian Punjab. During his foreign tour to Syria and Germany, he alleged that Pakistan was making nuclear bomb, stockpiling arms, and encouraging terrorism in India. In his speech in the UN General Assembly, Rajiv repeated these charges.

Pakistan denied the Indian charges of encouraging the Sikh militancy. Pakistan's foreign minister, Yaqub Ali Khan, issued a strong denial of this allegation during his visit to China in June 1988, but it did not make any impact. President Zia, during his address in an international seminar in Islamabad on 28 June, also called upon the Indian leaders to resume serious dialogue with Pakistan on issues of peace and regional security. He warned that 'smaller nations do not necessarily have a smaller right to sovereignty'. But India's indignation emanated from the prospects of Mujahideen-dominated government in Kabul having friendly posture towards Pakistan. India's failure to determine the direction of Kabul government's attitude towards Pakistan which India considered to be its right being the regional power, was a source of great disillusionment for its ambitious prime minister.

The problem relating to Pakistan's support to the Sikh cause discussed at all levels between India and Pakistan, led to an agreement to start joint patrolling of the border and India's decision to install a fence on the border. Accordingly, a barbed wire-fence was erected by India.[177]

As regards Pakistan's nuclear programme, Pakistan expressed its willingness many times to sign the Non-Proliferation Treaty simultaneously with India, accept full-scope safeguards to its nuclear programme with India, conclude a bilateral agreement with India for mutual inspection of each other's nuclear facilities, make a joint declarations with India renouncing nuclear weapons, and enter into a nuclear-test ban treaty. But India refused to accept equality with Pakistan on the nuclear issue. India's attitude implied that while Pakistan renounced nuclear weapons, India would be free to multiply its bombs in the basement to a limitless extent.[178]

India's nuclear programme was way ahead of Pakistan's nuclear programme and it had more than ten functioning nuclear reactors. It was negotiating with the Soviet Union for two additional reactors. It had three reprocessing plants, heavy-water plants, and it also succeeded in obtaining 15 tons of heavy water from Norway. In fact, India aimed at becoming a world power like China. This plan was backed with a massive build-up of India's defence capability. Ratio of Pakistani forces *vis-à-vis* India varied from 1:3 to 1:7.[179] India had already sent its troops to Sri Lanka, ostensibly for peace-keeping purposes in 1987, and wanted the hegemonic supervision of its other neighbours as well as.[180] Pakistan was an eyesore for India because it was determined to resist India's hegemonic ambitions. As India and Pakistan differed in the goals of their foreign policies, their relations were not likely to improve. Pakistan emphasized the principle of sovereign equality of all states and mutual respect and mutual adjustment through dialogue, but India's agenda was ambitiously self-centered—an India-dominated South Asian power structure, where India's role would be of the guardian and gate-keeper of the region.

South Asian States and the SAARC

Pakistan had cordial relations with Bangladesh, Nepal, Sri Lanka, and the Maldives. These states adopted a posture on the Afghanistan problem which was similar to the one adopted by Pakistan. These states also supported the Pakistani demand for designating South Asia as a nuclear weapons free zone. An active diplomatic interaction was maintained with these states, including the visits of the heads of governments.

Another important development was the formal launching of the South Asian Association for Regional Cooperation (SAARC) on 7–8 December 1985 at Dhaka, where heads of states of the seven South Asian countries met for the first time for this purpose. The SAARC was established to promote greater co-operation amongst the member states in all the areas of mutual interest with the aim of promoting peace and stability in the region, to accelerate economic development, and to work towards improving the quality of life for the people. The SAARC charter subscribes to sovereign equality of member states, respect for their territorial integrity, political independence, and non-interference in the internal affairs of each other. It lays down that decisions would be taken unanimously, and bilateral and contentious issues shall not be entertained. The roots of the SAARC go back to 1980, when, the president of Bangladesh, Ziaur Rahman, proposed the setting up of a regional organization for promoting co-operation amongst the states of South Asia. Initially, the senior officials of South Asian states held several meetings to discuss the details of the proposal. In August 1983, their foreign ministers had their first meeting and decided to set up such an organization. They also agreed on a number of fields to which the organization was to give serious attention. In December 1985, the SAARC was formally launched as a regional organization for economic, technological, social, and cultural co-operation with a focus on the problems which could best be tackled jointly.

The SAARC consists of seven countries; Pakistan, India, Bangladesh, Bhutan, Maldives, Nepal, and Sri Lanka. It represents a population of over one billion, i.e. about one-fifth of the world population. The functions of the SAARC include meetings of heads of states once a year, meeting of the council of Foreign Ministers twice a year, and meeting of the Standing Committee of Foreign Secretaries, as often as required, as well as technical committees meetings for implementation, co-ordination, and monitoring co-operation in their assigned fields.

It was in 1986 that the SAARC demonstrated a throbbing of active life in the form of a large number of conferences, meetings, workshops, and training courses. Two meetings of the Standing Committee of Foreign Secretaries and council of ministers were held, followed by the second SAARC summit at Bangalore in November 1986. The summit provided an opportunity to the leaders of the member states to exchange ideas and to deliberate on social, economic, cultural, and technological matters of mutual interest. In this meeting it was decided to set up a permanent SAARC secretariat at Kathmandu (Nepal), and Abdul Ahsan of Bangladesh was elected its first Secretary-General. The SAARC declaration re-affirmed its commitment to promote peace, stability, amity, and progress in the region through strict adherence to the UN Charter and non-alignment.

The SAARC secretariat was formally opened at Kathmandu in January 1987. As usual, many meetings of SAARC foreign ministers, foreign secretaries, and other officials were held to discuss matters of common interest, and about a dozen seminars were organized. Pakistan called for the adoption of a regional approach for dealing with the problem of nuclear proliferation, and called for a dialogue on this issue under the SAARC umbrella in the foreign ministers' meeting held in June 1987. The third SAARC summit was held in Kathmandu in November 1987, which approved a convention relating to the repression of terrorism. The summit also decided to set up an emergency food reserve system and a commission to study the causes and consequences of natural disasters.

The president of Sri Lanka visited Pakistan in 1986. The visit was returned by President Ziaul Haq in December. These visits reinforced the friendship and mutual understanding between the two countries. The prime minister of Sri Lanka visited Pakistan in March 1987, and discussed the regional situation and other matters of mutual interest, including co-operation in the fields of trade and transport with the Pakistani Prime Minister, Junejo. The fourth session of Pakistan-Sri Lanka Joint Committee for Economic and Technical Co-operation, held in Islamabad in August 1987, led to an expansion of trade between the two countries. Pakistan also offered a credit of 50 million rupees to Sri Lanka.

The president of Pakistan visited Maldives in 1985, which led to the expansion of trade between the two countries. Pakistan offered a soft-term loan for the purchase of rice, wheat, flour, machinery, steel products, and medicines from Pakistan. Maldives also obtained certain training facilities. Similarly, as a gesture of cordiality, Pakistan offered a soft-term loan to Nepal for the purchase of textile machinery.

Pakistan's relations with Bangladesh continued to expand at the bilateral level. President Zia visited Bangladesh twice in 1985, and contributed a respectable amount to the relief fund for cyclone-affectees. The President of Bangladesh, H.M. Ershad, visited Pakistan in 1986, and again in 1988 to attend the funeral of President Zia. The second meeting of Bangladesh-Pakistan Joint Economic Commission, held in 1987, led to an expansion of trade between the two countries.

The SAARC enabled Pakistan to interact directly with the leaders of Bhutan. As the Kingdom of Bhutan is treaty-bound to accept Indian guidance on foreign policy, India did not allow Bhutan any direct interaction with Pakistan. With the establishment of the SAARC, Bhutan and Pakistan could interact in its meetings at various levels. The SAARC contributed to promoting a greater interaction amongst the states of South Asia, but it could not facilitate the removal of the basic political obstacles to the improvement of their relations. As a result, the SAARC could not bloom into an effective regional organization. Time and again, Pakistan, Bangladesh, and Nepal have urged the need for taking up difficult bilateral problems on the SAARC platform, but India has resisted these suggestions. As the SAARC decisions had to be taken unanimously, nothing could be done in this regard. However, the SAARC has played an important role in promoting co-operation in the less salient areas amongst the member states, and enabled their leaders to discuss their bilateral relations informally on the sidelines of the SAARC meetings. Despite its limitations and handicaps, the SAARC is a useful regional organization.

The Muslim World

'Stretching right from Morocco to Mauritania in the extreme north of the Dark continent to shiny shores of Malaysia and Indonesia in the extreme south of the Indian Ocean',[181] there is a continuous chain of more than fifty Muslim countries. Most of them are linked with each other like loops of a chain. Inspite of the ethnic diversity, these countries are bound with each other by the bond of Islamic brotherhood, faith, and culture.

From the beginning, Pakistan has tried to promote brotherly relations with all the Muslim countries. Pakistan gave them unflinching support against their common adversary, Israel. The fifth summit of the OIC, held in Kuwait in January 1987, and attended by forty-four members, re-affirmed its support to Pakistan's stand on Afghanistan, and paid tribute to President Ziaul Haq for his deep concern for the problems facing the Muslim countries. The conference also explored prospects of improving co-operation within the OIC in economic, technological, and diplomatic fields.

Historically, Pakistan had closer relations with Iran, and Turkey and these three countries set up the RCD. This relationship was disturbed after the overthrow of the Shah of

Iran in 1979. However, the three countries realized the need for rehabilitating close collaboration in the economic field, and decided to replace the RCD with a new organization, the Economic Co-operation Organization (ECO), which held the first meeting of its High Council in Tehran in January 1985. The high council discussed the scope and functions of the organization, and set up four committees to promote co-operation in the economic, technical, industrial, agriculture, education, and scientific research fields. The high council's third meeting, held in Islamabad in 1986, reviewed the progress made in different sectors and decided to expand the scope of, trade, economic, and technological co-operation amongst the member states. Pakistan imported oil from Iran and exported wheat, rice, textile products, etc. to Iran. The Iranian president's visit to Pakistan in 1986 and other exchange visits at the ministerial level added new dimensions to the Pak-Iran relations.

The Gulf states have been an area of major interest for Pakistan since the early seventies, when Pakistani labour began to be exported to these countries. The remittances made by the Pakistani labour to their families helped to improve the position of Pakistan's foreign exchange. Pakistan obtained soft-term loans and grants from a number of Gulf states like the UAE, Kuwait, Saudi Arabia, and the Islamic Development Bank. These Gulf states and Libya invested in several joint projects in Pakistan. The president of the UAE, Sheikh Zayad Bin Sultan-Al-Nahyan, gifted a modern medical complex in Lahore, and contributed to setting up Islamic centres in three Pakistani universities for promoting Islamic studies. Pakistan's relations with Libya suffered in 1985–86 because the former extended a lukewarm support to the latter in its conflict with the USA. This created a strong impression that Pakistan was not forthcoming in its support for Libya because of the influence of the conservative Arab states and the US which were providing economic assistance to Pakistan. Pakistan maintained its non-partisan posture on the Iran-Iraq war urging both sides to cease fire and to negotiate for the resolution of their differences.

Pakistan maintained its historical warmth and cordiality for Saudi Arabia. The president and prime minister of Pakistan paid several visits to Saudi Arabia during this period. Saudi Arabia extended material and diplomatic support to Pakistan in the context of the Afghanistan problem and welcomed the signing of the Geneva Peace Accord on Afghanistan.

FOREIGN POLICY 1988–90

Shortly after the signing of the Geneva Peace Accord on Afghanistan in April 1988, the Soviet troops began a slow withdrawal from Afghanistan in May, which was completed in February 1989, although the Soviet puppet government of Najibullah continued to function in Kabul until April 1992. The Soviet withdrawal was a major triumph for Pakistan. However, the withdrawal period (May 1988 to February 1989) was not trouble free. As the Mujahideen mounted their pressure on the Najibullah government, the Soviets accused Pakistan of creating trouble in Afghanistan, and many instances of border clashes in Pakistan-Afghanistan border took place. The Soviets continued to use threatening language against Pakistan. On the other hand, the US began to show signs of reducing its interest in the region as the Soviets began their withdrawal. Subsequent to the completion of the Soviet withdrawal, the US felt that it could divert its attention from Afghanistan to other areas; this also signalled the declining strategic relevance of Pakistan for the US policy makers. Within Pakistan, the significant development was the death of Ziaul Haq in a mysterious air crash on 17 August 1988. Three months later, new general elections were held in Pakistan, followed by the assumption of power by Benazir Bhutto as the head of the PPP-led coalition government on 2 December 1988.

During Zia's regime, Benazir had been critical of his policy regarding the Afghanistan problem, out of personal hostility, as an attempt to arouse people's ire against Zia. Benazir condemned the connection with Washington that had, in her opinion, exposed Pakistan to the Soviet threats. She could not appreciate the diplomatic gains the Zia government made during these years, plus the valuable American economic assistance, combined with weapons and military equipment.

When Benazir came to power, the international environment had changed. Her early statements against Washington's connection in making Pakistan a staging base for the Afghan Mujahideen did not please the American leadership that was already perturbed by the notion of the 'Islamic Bomb'. However, it was not long before she decided to strengthen ties with the US, and worked towards removing misunderstandings about Pakistan's nuclear programme.

Benazir Bhutto visited the US in June 1989, and expressed Pakistan's interest in strengthening Pakistan's ties with the US On the nuclear issue, she assured the American administration that Pakistan neither had a bomb nor it intended to manufacture one. However, she made it clear that as a sovereign nation, Pakistan had every right to pursue its nuclear programme. Though the US administration reciprocated the desire to maintain cordial relations with Pakistan and offered to sell thirty-eight F-16 aircrafts to Pakistan, it continued to entertain serious doubts about Pakistan's nuclear programme and indicated dwindling interest in supporting the Afghan resistance groups.

The Western interest was gradually shifting towards a host of global issues like population explosion, environment, refugees, trans-border migrations, narcotics trafficking, terrorism, disarmament, nuclear nonproliferation, human rights, and gender issues, etc. With such a transformed international environment, Pakistan could not sustain the oversized role it had played in the context of the Soviet military intervention in Afghanistan (1979–89). Pakistan was faced with three 'realities': its diminished strategic importance, the changing international environment marked by uncertainties, and a host of unresolved problems inherited from earlier periods which could no longer be dealt with by outdated strategies.[182]

Benazir Bhutto travelled extensively to other countries; there was hardly a month when she did not undertake a foreign trip.

As she enjoyed a good reputation abroad, especially in the West, she liked to spend more energies in visiting abroad. However, she faced a difficult situation at the domestic front. The Opposition was quite strong and assertive, and her coalition government could not pull together effectively. Shortly after she became the prime minister, Ghulam Ishaq Khan, who was closely identified with Zia won the presidential election. So was Sahabzada Yaqub Khan whom Benazir retained as her foreign minister. She also confronted a highly changing international environment, making it difficult for her to command the foreign policy.[183]

Despite the improved interaction with India and Rajiv Gandhi's visit to Pakistan in December 1988 (for the SAARC summit conference) and in July 1989, the two countries continued to diverge on most of the issues. Rajiv Gandhi often alleged that Pakistan was supporting 'terrorism' in Kashmir and in the East Punjab and was developing nuclear capability which, like a sword in a madman's hand, was a threat to the security of the region. Pakistan refuted these accusations, underlining the fact that India was trying to externalize its domestic problems. The root causes of the problems in Kashmir and East Punjab were domestic, which India was not prepared to admit. On the nuclear issue, Pakistan maintained that India, having exploded a nuclear device in 1974 and having a well-developed nuclear programme, did not have any justification for objecting to Pakistan's small-size peaceful nuclear programme. Addressing a joint session of the US Congress in 1989, Benazir made it clear that Pakistan would readily enter into agreement with New Delhi for creating nuclear-weapons-free zone in the region. It was on the eve of the SAARC summit in Islamabad on 27–31 December 1988 that the prime ministers of India and Pakistan signed an agreement not to attack each other's nuclear installations. They also agreed to an annual exchange of lists of each other's nuclear installations on the first of January.

Rajiv Gandhi visited Islamabad again in July 1989, and the two prime ministers discussed bilateral relations with the objective of reducing tension in the region. The nuclear issue was also discussed. Benazir once more publicly declared her country's interest in any arrangement that would guarantee a nuclear-free subcontinent.[184] However, India showed no interest in this proposal. Later in the year, the two countries signed an agreement for the expansion of bilateral trade and the two sides agreed to a method for resolving the Siachen Glacier dispute. However, shortly afterwards, India backed out of its commitment on the method for resolving the Siachen Glacier issue.

Pakistan rejoined the Commonwealth in September 1989 (it had withdrawn from it in 1972), as India could no longer oppose Pakistan's admission after the restoration of democracy there.

On the Kashmir issue, Pakistan continued to demand its settlement in accordance with the resolution of the UN and extended moral and political support to the insurgency that developed in Kashmir in 1989 against the oppressive policies of the Indian administration. The SAARC summit conference was held in Islamabad in December 1988 and all the heads of SAARC countries visited Pakistan. This enabled the King of Bhutan to visit Pakistan and the two countries decided in principle to establish diplomatic relations. However, no embassies could be established in each other's capitals because India is not in favour of Bhutan's direct interaction with Pakistan. Under a treaty signed by Bhutan and India in 1950, Bhutan is bound to accept India's advice on foreign policy issues. India did not advice Bhutan to set up its embassy in Islamabad.

There were significant developments in connection with the Afghanistan problem. Under the Geneva Accord, the pull-out of the Soviet troops was completed by 15 February 1989. Pakistan demanded that in place of the Soviet-installed government of Najibullah, a non-aligned interim government comprising all Afghan groups should be set up to avoid civil strife.

The government tried unsuccessfully to instal an interim government of the Afghan resistance groups who also attempted to militarily capture Jalalabad; this attempt failed miserably. However, the Mujahideen continued to fight against the

Najibullah government which carried on after the withdrawal of the Soviet troops from Afghanistan.

Pakistan's relationship with China, shaped over the past four decades, groomed into a strong factor for strengthening regional stability and global peace. What sustained this relationship was the mutual respect for each other's sovereignty and their common determination to resist and thwart hegemonic tendencies, both at the global and regional levels. The strength of Sino-Pak friendship was adequately reflected in the exchange of high-level visits between the two countries. The web of co-operative interaction between China and Pakistan covered diverse fields. During his visit to Pakistan in November 1989, the Chinese premier, Li Peng agreed to provide Pakistan with a 300 MW nuclear power plant in Chashma. This nuclear power plant, under the International Atomic Energy Agency (IAEA) safeguards, is an appropriate symbol of the strength and enduring quality of Sino-Pak relations.

FOREIGN POLICY 1990–93

New elections were held after the dismissal of Benazir Bhutto's government in August 1990. The Muslim League won the elections at the national level and formed a coalition government under its leader, Nawaz Sharif, in November 1999. He remained in power till July 1993. This section covers the foreign policy of Pakistan during his rule.

A major transformation took place in the international system during this period, first the formal ending of the cold war in 1990, and then, the disintegration of the Soviet Union in 1991. All Soviet republics became independent and in this way a number of new Muslim independent states emerged in Central Asia and the Caspian region. These developments also shifted the focus from global confrontation to the issues of domestic stability and economic development, human rights, democracy, participatory governance, sustainable development, and good governance. Above all, only one super power, i.e. the US, was left in the field. Many writers described this to be a unipolar world, although many had doubts about the ability of the US to dominate the international system. However, with the absence of a countervailing power, the American options increased in the international system. Pakistan had to review its approaches to the international and regional issues in the light of these dramatic changes.

Iraq's invasion of Kuwait in August 1990, and the war against Iraq, launched by a coalition of countries led by the US in January 1991, created a difficult situation for Pakistan. On the one hand Pakistan supported Kuwait's independence and was in favour of the American military action against Iraq, but it felt that the excessive use of force against Iraq had created difficulties for the ordinary people of Iraq and had escalated tension in the Gulf region. In the aftermath of Iraq's invasion of Kuwait, Nawaz Sharif visited Saudi Arabia and held talks with King Fahd in November 1990; he also called on the Amir of Kuwait and reiterated his government's opposition to Iraqi aggression committed against Kuwait. Pakistan also made 5000 troops available to Saudi Arabia for internal security.

On 22 January 1991, Nawaz Sharif embarked on a peace mission to Iran, Turkey, Egypt, and Syria, and urged them to take a joint stand for peace in the region, stop the action of the allied forces against Iraq, and persuade Iraq to withdraw from Iraq. Although Turkey had been very critical of the Iraqi leadership, it backed Pakistan's initiative to resolve the crisis. In Damascus, Nawaz Sharif held talks with his Syrian counterpart, Mahmood Zubi, as well as with President Hafez Al-Asad. They agreed that necessary measures by the Muslim *Ummah* were essential to put an end to all this hurly-burly. All shared the opinion that Iraq's action was detrimental to the interests of the whole *Ummah*. He reached Amman on 25 January and held an elaborate and cordial meeting with King Husain. In Riyadh, Prime Minister Nawaz Sharif had a meeting with King Fahd in which he apprised him of his peace mission. It was from Jeddah that Nawaz Sharif sent special messages to the presidents of Iran, Turkey, and Syria informing them that he had been assured that the Saudi government would not harm the territorial integrity of Iraq.

On 4 February 1991, Nawaz Sharif offered a six-point peace formula which emphasized an immediate ceasefire; withdrawal of troops from the Gulf region by Iraq and allied forces; an emergency OIC conference to work out an agreed solution; implementation of the UN resolutions on Palestine and Kashmir; posting of an Islamic force in the Gulf, and declaration of the holy places in Iraq and Saudi Arabia as 'peace zones'.[185]

An important foreign policy issue during this period was the suspension of American economic assistance and military sales to Pakistan in October 1990, when the American president refused to certify that Pakistan did not possess a nuclear device, activating sanctions against Pakistan. This was the invocation of the so-called Pressler Amendment (passed by the US Congress in 1985) against Pakistan which later adversely affected Pakistan-US relations.

Another issue that created problems for Pakistan was the ongoing Afghanistan problem. Pakistan had a troubled interaction with the Najibullah government in Kabul. After it decided to quit, the Afghan Mujahideen, despite Pakistan's best efforts, could not agree on a mutually acceptable government for Kabul. The civil strife continued unabated in Afghanistan. 'In order to demonstrate its keen interest in the negotiated settlement of the Afghanistan problem, the government announced and took initiatives in tandem with the United states and other concerned countries in order to step up efforts for a peaceful solution.'[186] The Nawaz government, in January 1992, extended unqalified support to the United Nations' five-point peace plan' which enjoyed the support of Washington and the moderate resistance groups in Afghanistan.

The removal of Najibullah by a four-member council in April 1992 marked a dramatic shift in the course of events in Kabul. Pakistan helped the resistance forces reach an accord, independent of the UN involvement, to facilitate a peaceful transfer of power. Despite strong opposition from the Hikmatyar group to certain provisions of this accord, the Pakistan government wanted to see it implemented. It was alleged that the accord was made under the US pressure, because Washington was believed to be averse to the idea of an Afghan government led by such Islamic hardliners as Gulbadin Hikmatyar.'[187] (See also the section on Afghanistan for more details.)

Pakistan maintained a keen interest in the SAARC and strove to remove mutual mistrust as a prerequisite for the effective working of the SAARC. The sixth SAARC summit, which was to be held in Colombo from 7–9 November 1991, was postponed on the Indian initiative, because the King of Bhutan expressed his inability to attend the summit for domestic reasons. In fact, India first pressurized the ruler of Bhutan not to attend the summit on account of 'domestic problems', and then started the propaganda that its prime minister, Narasimha Rao, might not be able to go to Colombo for 'security reasons'. In Colombo on 8 November, Prime Minister Nawaz Sharif, said that if India had accepted the offer of representation of King of Bhutan by his envoy, the conference would not have been cancelled.[188] Addressing the inaugural session of the sixth SAARC summit held in Colombo on 21 December 1991, Prime Minister Nawaz Sharif pleaded for fostering a better understanding among the SAARC nations to bless the region with peace and prosperity. He assured Pakistan's full co-operation and support in promoting the objectives and spirit of the SAARC.

Pakistan's relations with India were a mixed bag. A high-powered military delegation from Pakistan, headed by Lt.-Gen. Shamim Alam Khan, chief of general staff, visited New Delhi in April 1991 to firm up an agreement on non-violation of each other's border territory. The two sides completed their work on 3 April on two agreements providing for advance notification of military exercises and for preventing air space violations. The technical aspects having been considered in the foreign secretaries meeting which began on 5 April, the agreements were signed by the Indian Foreign Secretary Muchkund Dubey and his Pakistani counterpart Shahryar Khan.

Prime Minister Mian Nawaz Sharif visited New Delhi on 24 May 1991 to represent Pakistan at the funeral rites of Rajiv Gandhi, who was assassinated in a bomb blast in Tamil Nadu. 'I have come here to convey to the people of India the feelings of the people of Pakistan who are extremely saddened as a result of Rajiv Gandhi's death', he said in an airport interview, and added that 'Pakistan condemns terrorism in all its forms and anywhere'.

Nawaz Sharif held wide-ranging talks with top Indian leaders. He started his round of bilateral discussions and meetings with a call on the Indian Vice-President Shankar Dayal. Both felt the need for solving all issues through peaceful dialogues. Prime Minister Nawaz Sharif's initiative for peace with India and message of goodwill to his Indian counterpart Narasimha Rao, and Foreign Secretary Shahryar Khan's four-day trip to New Delhi from 18–21 August 1991 failed to evoke any reconciliatory gesture from the Indian leaders who were apparently not inclined to reciprocate any friendly gesture. With the Kashmir dispute, the tension between the two countries remained at its peak. Then India definitely lost its nuclear innocence after successfully testing its first medium-range missile 'Agni' and later a short-range missile 'Prithvi.' With a range from 2500 to 5000 km, Agni missile was a threat not only to Pakistan, but also to China and the Soviet Union, making India a neighbour which one can not neglect in the regional balance of power.

In the meanwhile, the insurgency in the Indian-administered Kashmir created a serious challenge to the Indian establishment there. India adopted a dual policy of despatching more troops to Kashmir to crush the insurgency and accused Pakistan of aiding and abetting the insurgency; at times claiming that Pakistani 'agents' were at the back of the agitation in Kashmir. Pakistan denied these charges and said that the Kashmir insurgency showed the failure of the Indian government to win the hearts of the Kashmiris and that Pakistan extended political and diplomatic support to the Kashmiris struggling for their right to determine their future. India continued to accuse Pakistan for the trouble in Kashmir, which adversely affected their bilateral relations. Another incident that undermined their relations was the demolition of the historic Babri mosque in Ayodhya by Hindu extremists in December 1992. Pakistan protested against this incident and there were widespread street demonstrations in Pakistan as a protest against this incident.

Pakistan's interaction with Bangladesh remained cordial and friendly during the first term of Nawaz Sharif. When a cyclone caused serious loss to human life and property, Nawaz visited Dhaka in early May 1991 to express sympathy and to gift medicine and relief goods; Pakistan also loaned three helicopters for the relief and rescue operations. In an interview, Nawaz Sharif said: 'This visit is only a mission of solidarity, a mission to reassure our brothers that in their hour of grief, they are not alone.' Accompanied by Begum Khaleda Zia, he visited the cyclone-ravaged areas. During his meeting with the Bangladeshi Prime Minister, Mian Nawaz Sharif announced a grant of 100 million rupees as relief for the cyclone-affected people and handed over to her a cheque for 20 million rupees as the first instalment.'[189] The visit of Begum Khaleda Zia to Pakistan in 1991 explored further avenues of mutual co-operation, especially in the field of industries. Nawaz Sharif again visited Dhaka on 12–13 December 1992. His visit reflected two-fold objectives: expression of solidarity with Bangladesh and manifestation of unabated support to the SAARC.

Six Central Asian Muslim republics emerged as independent states after the disintegration of the Soviet Union in 1991. These were Kazakhstan, Kyrgyzstan, Tajikistan, Uzbekistan, Turkmenistan, and Azerbaijan. Pakistan accorded diplomatic recognition to these and other former Soviet republics. An eighteen-member high-level delegation, led by the minister of State for Economic Affairs, Sardar Asif Ahmed Ali, left for Moscow and six Soviet Muslim Republics on 24 November 1991, with a view to establishing relations with 60 million Muslims in the former Soviet Union. In Tashkent the delegation called on President Islam Karimov of Uzbekistan and offered a revolving credit of 30 million dollars for the purchase of

Pakistan engineering goods. In Baku, Pakistan and Azerbaijan signed a memorandum of understanding and two protocols to establish economic, cultural, scientific, and educational ties between the two countries. Pakistan and Tajikistan signed a memorandum of understanding in Dushanbe. In Bishkek (formerly called Frunze), Pakistan and Kyrgyzstan signed a joint declaration to promote economic and cultural relations with the Central Asian Republics. A number of other agreements were also signed between the two countries to bring them closer to each other. Under the agreement signed with Kyrgyzstan and Kazakhstan, joint working groups were to be set up to explore the possibilities of linking these republics with the Karakoram Highway in northern Pakistan through the Chinese province of Sinkiang to enable these republics to have access to the seaport of Karachi.

This development opened a new vista of co-operation at inter-Islamic level. These countries were soon embraced into the fold of Economic Co-operation Organization (ECO). These six republics and Afghanistan joined the ECO in the summit conference held in Tehran in February 1992. They resolved to develop the ECO into a viable economic bloc. At the ministerial meeting in Islamabad on 28 November 1992, the ECO's promise of becoming a major vehicle for regional co-operation was translated into a reality, when these member countries agreed upon various projects envisaging enhanced co-operation as outlined in the understanding reached at the Ashkabad Summit.

A parliamentary delegation of Azerbaijan called on the Senate chairman, Waseem Sajjad as well as the president in December 1991. This was followed by the visit of the president of Kazakhstan on 23 February 1993, who held fruitful talks with Prime Minister Nawaz Sharif on bilateral relations. There were several other exchange visits between Pakistan and these states of Central Asia.

The sixth OIC summit, postponed on the request of Saudi Arabia and Egypt in view of the Gulf crisis, was held from 9–11 December 1991. The last summit had been held in Kuwait more than four years ago and since then the world situation had undergone a tremendous change. The end of East-West cold war, dismemberment of the Soviet Union, and the collapse of the communist regimes in East Europe were the major international developments that required the Muslim countries to redefine their policies towards various issues. The situation after the Gulf war presented an important topic for discussion, because it had a direct impact on the Muslim world in general, and the Arab and Gulf countries in particular.

The political committee of OIC foreign ministers unanimously adopted draft resolutions proposed by Pakistan on Kashmir, Afghanistan, and the plight of the Muslim minorities in various parts of the world. The outgoing OIC Chairman, the Amir of Kuwait, emphasized the need for the efforts to achieve greater unity, solidarity, and progress of the Muslim world. He particularly spoke of the main issues facing the *Ummah,* such as Afghanistan, Jammu and Kashmir, the Middle East, Lebanon, and the problems facing the Muslim minorities. 'Tackling of these problems needs collective efforts by the Ummah', he said, and urged the OIC to make efforts for the just solution of the Kashmir dispute.'[190]

The new chairman and Senegalese president, Abdou Diouf, said that the sixth summit was being held in an unprecedented historical context, in addition to being still marred by the Gulf crisis and its consequences for the *Ummah.* 'The summit is characterized by the hopes and fears generated by major political and economic changes which have been unfolding for sometime now', he emphasized. Pakistani prime minister, Mian Nawaz Sharif, proposed a four-point action plan for the *Ummah's* economic integration and collective security. Advocating the creation of a common Islamic market, the prime minister said that it was imperative for the realization of the aim of economic integration of Muslim countries.'[191]

Pakistan maintained an active interest in OIC. In the sixth summit held in Dakar (9–11 December 1991) Nawaz Sharif proposed creation of the common Islamic Market for a meaningful economic co-operation among the Muslim states. The Dakar declaration, whose resolutions were proposed by

Pakistan, was adopted. It was a clarion-call for a united approach by the OIC member states to banish poverty, work for prosperity, consolidate unity, take a leap towards progress in science and technology, and to strive collectively for the resolution of all outstanding political issues. The OIC endorsed the resolutions on Kashmir, Afghanistan, and Muslim minorities, which were initially forwarded by Pakistan. For the first time, the OIC expressed concern over the woeful condition of the people of Jammu and Kashmir, fighting for their right to self-determination.

An emergency session of the member states of the OIC was held in New York on 14 August 1992 at the behest of Pakistan to discuss the situation in Bosnia-Herzegovina, the emergent Muslim state in Europe. The session was attended by ambassadors of the OIC states which are also members of the United Nations. The objective of this Pakistani initiative was to chart out a unified and collective Islamic stand on the Bosnian issue for the tenth Non-Aligned Summit which was to begin in Jakarta on 1 September. The spokesman said, 'the Islamic voice at the Jakarta summit would not be a weak one out of 104 members of the NAM, forty-seven belong to the OIC.'[192]

The foreign ministers of Iran, Pakistan, and Turkey held the second round of trilateral talks under the ECO from 2–4 January 1991 in Islamabad, on various issues and considered measures for further strengthening the fraternal relations between the three countries. They exchanged views on the areas of concern, with particular reference to the crisis resulting from the Iraqi occupation of Kuwait. They decided to breathe a fresh spirit into ECO and for this purpose they agreed to convene the meeting of seven technical committees following the next meeting of the Council of ministers. They appealed to Iraq to implement the resolutions of the UN Security Council and to honour the declaration of the OIC in the spirit of Islamic solidarity by withdrawing unconditionally from Kuwait.

As a result of the efforts of the leader of Pakistani delegation, Akram Zaki, a memorandum of understanding on the establishment of an Investment and Development Bank of the

ECO and a protocol on preferential tariff arrangement was signed in Tehran on 23 May 1991, under which the three countries agreed to give 10 per cent reduction in import tariffs on the agreed list of items.

As stated above, the ECO formed initially among Iran, Pakistan, and Turkey was expanded in 1992 to include Afghanistan and six Central Asian Muslim states. The ECO objectives include sustainable economic development by promoting intra-region trade, economic liberation, privatization, narcotic control, and environmental protection. Within a short span of time, the ECO had established relations with other regional organizations, such as ASEAN, EU, SAARC, South Pacific Forums, and ESCAP, which bears testimony to its growing popularity.

Pakistan continued playing an active role in the UN during this era. Pakistan's emphasis on the need to promote regional security and disarmament was endorsed by the UN when the UN General Assembly voted overwhelmingly in December 1992 to endorse the concept of regional disarmament including nuclear non-proliferation. India was the only country to abstain from voting on this resolution. The General Assembly also extended its approval to two other Pakistani proposals—for a 'nuclear-weapon-free' zone in South Asia, and for the strengthening of 'security guarantees' to non-nuclear-weapon states. Each of these proposals received more votes than the previous year, indicating increasing support for them. These proposals reflected Pakistan's firm commitment to nuclear non-proliferation and India's opposition to the efforts directed at dispelling the nuclear threat.

Pakistan was elected member of the Security Council in January 1993. Throughout the year it played an active role in defusing tensions and promoting stability in various parts of the world regarding peace missions of the UN. Pakistan sent 500 troops to Somalia, without any political interest, to join the UNOSOM, and an efficient election team to supervise elections in Cambodia under the UNTAC.

In addition to the UN, Pakistan also played an active role in the NAM. The tenth meeting of the NAM foreign ministers was held in Accra from 4–7 September 1991 (for which Pakistan was earlier elected as the vice president). Ghana's head of state, Jenny Rawlings, called upon the members to evolve a 'new world order' in the wake of the end of cold war. A joint communiqué, called the Accra Declaration was issued which redefined goals for the future and suggested expansion of the Security Council.

A NAM ministerial meeting was held in Cyprus in March 1992 to discuss an 'action plan'; the delegates expressed concern over the tardiness and slow-paced progress of NAM. Members were, therefore, suggested to consider enrolling Azerbaijan, Turkmenistan, Tajikistan, and Uzbekistan as full members, Germany and China as observers and the Netherlands as a guest participant.

On 12–15 May 1992, the NAM foreign ministers met in Bali for a political and economic survey and for chalking out a programme for the summit conference that was to be held in Jakarta in September 1992. Pakistan's delegation was led by the minister of state for foreign affairs, who actively participated in its deliberations.

Prime Minister Nawaz Sharif led Pakistan's delegation to the tenth summit with optimism and advocated that the adherence to the basic principles of NAM had become more relevant after the collapse of the former Soviet Union. In the inaugural session of the summit, Pakistani Prime Minister Nawaz Sharif urged the Third World nations to play a vigorous role in the new world economic order.

The Muslim World

Pakistan has always maintained a special relationship with Saudi Arabia. President Ghulam Ishaq Khan paid a four-day official visit to Saudi Arabia in October 1991 to discuss matters of bilateral and regional interest, but there was no fixed agenda for the talks. President Ishaq Khan and King Fahd agreed to desist any new form of imperialism that could emerge in the formulation of a 'New World Order'. The two leaders held wide-ranging talks on 8 October on regional and international issues. King Fahd briefed the Pakistani president on the latest developments on the Middle East peace plan and hoped that the Palestinians would be able to achieve independence. President Ishaq Khan briefed King Fahd on the latest position of the political settlement of the Afghanistan issue, and on his discussions with the Iranian leaders and with the UN secretary-general during his visit to Tehran. King Fahd expressed his full support to Pakistan on these issues.

Following the visit of the Saudi minister for state and cabinet affairs, Sheikh Ibrahim Masood, to Islamabad on 23 February 1991, a special envoy of King Fahd came to Pakistan to deliver the kings's message to President Ishaq regarding developments in the Gulf war. Dr Abdullah Mohsin al-Turki, heading a seven-member delegation, called on Prime Minister Nawaz Sharif on 5 September and discussed the latest developments relating to the Afghanistan issue. He also met the leaders of Afghan Mujahideen in Islamabad and Peshawar.

A high power parliamentary delegation, led by the speaker of the National Assembly, Gohar Ayub, visited Saudi Arabia from 20-23 January 1991 to express solidarity with the government and people of Saudi Arabia against the threat of the Iraqi forces, then occupying Kuwait. General Mirza Aslam Beg, the then COAS, arrived in Jeddah on 18 February to visit Pakistani troops stationed at various places in Saudi Arabia. He met the Saudi defence minister, Prince Sultan Bin Abdul Aziz, and discussed the war situation.

Secretary-general foreign affairs, Akram Zaki called on Saudi foreign minister, Prince Khalid in Jeddah on 23 September 1991, and discussed the viable solution of Afghanistan problem, taking into account the latest developments, especially the negative symmetry announced by the USA and the Soviet Union.

On his way to the Herat Commonwealth Conference on 13 October 1991, Nawaz Sharif had a brief stopover in Makkah where he performed *Umrah*, and had some heart-to-heart talk with King Fahd. Later, the prime minister paid a special official visit to King Fahd on 23 October 1991.

Prime Minister Nawaz Sharif reached Jeddah on a private visit and was received by King Fahd on 11 September 1992 at Al-Salam Palace. They reviewed the situation in Bosnia-Herzegovina, Afghanistan, and Kashmir. President Ghulam Ishaq Khan paid a three-day official visit to Saudi Arabia from 2–4 October 1992. He called on King Fahd and exchanged views on important regional, international, and bilateral issues, besides reviewing the situation prevailing in Bosnia-Herzegovina and the Indian-held Kashmir.

Iran is another neighbouring Islamic country with which Pakistan has maintained a very cordial relationship from the beginning. That pattern continued in this period also. President Ghulam Ishaq Khan, on a four-day official visit to Tehran from 12–15 September 1991, met the Irani President Rafsanjani. Agreeing upon enhancing the scope of co-operation, they decided to constitute five committees to prepare reports, including specific targets in different areas for the expansion of the economic co-operation.

In the last week of February 1991, the Majlis of Iran speaker, Hujjatul Islam Mehdi, arrived in Islamabad, leading a sixty member delegation. Addressing the National Assembly, he condemned the role of the US and allies in the Gulf. He maintained that the Gulf countries should have a share in safeguarding the security of the region proportionate to their geographical conditions.

Later, Prime Minister Nawaz Sharif held a meeting with Iranian President Hashmi Rafsanjani on 9 December 1991 at Dakar and discussed various international and bilateral issues with him, including the Gulf crisis. The Iranian president assured Iran's unswerving support on the Kashmir issue and expressed his concern over the repression in the occupied Kashmir.

The Iranian minister for heavy industries, Nejad Hosseinian, along with a four-member delegation, arrived in Islamabad on 3 December 1991 for a five-day visit. The two countries signed a memorandum of understanding envisaging the implementation of the decisions for setting up an oil refinery and seven sugar factories in Khozestan province of Iran. Other areas and projects specified for co-operation in the first phase included, in addition to the above, the setting up of cement industries and manufacturing and exchange of automobile and tractor components. The Iranian foreign minister, Dr Ali Akbar Velayati, visited Islamabad from 28–30 July 1991 for talks on the Afghan issue. He, along with the Pakistani leadership, met the Afghan Mujahideen groups based in Pakistan and Iran, to evolve a common approach to work for a political settlement of the problem. Dr Velayati called on President Ghulam Ishaq Khan and discussed bilateral relations and regional and international situations.

As an expression of cordiality, top-level visits were frequently exchanged between Pakistan and Turkey during 1991 and 1992. Talks during these visits were reflective of identity of views and feelings on global and regional matters, including the Kashmir issue, the Cyprus question, and the Middle East problem.

President Turgut Ozal, while flying to Singapore, made a brief stopover at Karachi in May 1991 and was received by President Ghulam Ishaq Khan. The two leaders held talks on the major regional and international issues with remarkable identity of views. They also shared perceptions regarding the post-war situation in the Gulf.

Prime Minister Nawaz Sharif and Turkish President Turgut Ozal met at Dakar (on the eve of OIC Summit) on 9 December 1991 and exchanged views about various international and bilateral issues. They also discussed the methodology and experiences of the economic liberalization policy in their respective countries. President Ozal briefed Prime Minister Nawaz Sharif on the political situation in Central Asia.

President Ghulam Ishaq Khan undertook an official five-day visit to Turkey. President Turgut Ozal demanded that the sufferings of the people of Kashmir must come to end 'at the earliest'. He said that the problem of Kashmir was among the international issues which Turkey hoped to see resolved by peaceful means.

Turkish prime minister, Suleman Demirel, accompanied by a high power delegation, arrived in Islamabad on 24 October 1992. Turkey and Pakistan reaffirmed their solidarity with the people of Kashmir in the realization of their right of self-determination, and reiterated their stance for the resolution of the Kashmir problem.

The cultural exchange programme for 1993–96 was signed in Islamabad on 28 November 1992, aiming at strengthening the traditional cordial relations through the promotion of cultural ties between the two countries. The package covered fields of arts, education, publication, sports, media, and science.[193]

Pakistan's relations with other Muslim countries are based on warm friendly sentiments. The Gulf crisis was a strange mess, a brother looking daggers at another. Pakistan reacted very cautiously and prudently to the Iraqi invasion of Kuwait. Although Pakistan had despatched troops to join the allied forces, it was for the protection holy places in Saudi Arabia, and the peace efforts by Pakistan focused on the search for a peaceful settlement of the issue. Taking serious notice of the indiscriminate bombing of the civilians in Iraq by the allied planes, Pakistan vehemently demanded immediate halt of the hostile activities. As for the rebuilding of the war-ravaged Kuwait, Pakistan offered help in terms of manpower.

Similarly, Pakistan played a significant role when peace was being negotiated between Israel and the Palestinians; Pakistan emphasized the need for a solution acceptable to the Palestinians. Even after the conclusion of the peace agreement of September 1993, Pakistan did not recognize Israel, as it was, in Pakistan's view, 'the usurper of the Palestinian land'.

Afghanistan

Pakistan pursued a vigorous diplomacy to undergird a durable peace in Afghanistan through peaceful negotiations. Pakistan's strategic compulsion dictated maintenance of friendly ties with Afghanistan, Iran, and Russia. To sort out the issue, Pakistan held discussions with the Mujahideen, and finally, as a result of deliberations in which Saudi Arabia and Iran also joined, the Mujahideen agreed to send a delegation to Moscow for talks with the Russian leaders for a viable solution of the problem. On 18 March 1992, Najibullah announced that he would step down to facilitate a settlement of the conflict, that is free and fair elections under the UN peace plan. This was a silver lining in the clouds hovering since long over the horizon of Afghanistan. As a gesture of goodwill, the joint ministerial commission signed a memorandum of understanding for economic co-operation in the fields of agriculture, trade, science, technology, and culture. But darkness again overshadowed Afghanistan due to the emerging tension between Hikmatyar and Professor Rabbani. Pakistan still maintained an active interest and continued its efforts to patch up the differences, culminating in an agreement in March 1993, known as Islamabad Accord. According to this agreement, principal Afghan leaders concurred on the power-sharing formula, creation of national army, and elections within eighteen months. Unfortunately, the Afghan leaders were divided again, and Pakistan, in the grip of internal political strife, could not exercise its full influence on them.

Since the time the Soviet Union stepped into Afghanistan, Pakistan had been striving for the adoption of a rational approach to resolve the conflict, persuading the interested parties to abandon their intransigent and belligerent posture and to assemble for dialogues at the negotiation table.

In the wake of the Geneva Accord of 1988, the Najib regime offered for a shared approach on the Afghan problem but Pakistan depreciated the idea and continued to back up the efforts of the Mujahideen to establish a peaceful, acceptable, and viable framework for Afghanistan government. Pakistan also played an active role in sorting out the major differences between the various groups of Afghans after the withdrawal of

Najibullah, and used its good offices towards the conclusion of the Peshawar Accord of April 1992.

A ray of hope glimmered, after all, when the Afghan prime minister, Fazlul Haq Khaliqyar, addressing a press conference in New York on 25 September 1991 and the UN secretary-general, Javier Perez de Cuellar in his report issued to the General Assembly on 22 October 1991, made it public that President Najibullah would step down to facilitate a settlement of the conflict in Afghanistan. The Perez de Cuellar said that the situation in Afghanistan had reached a 'critical stage', but a 'unique opportunity' existed to resolve the question.'[194]

President Najibullah announced on 18 March 1992 that he was to step down from the new administration which had to arrange for free and fair elections under the UN peace plan. Pakistani minister of state for foreign affairs, Siddique Kanju said that Najibullah's announcement fulfilled the first prerequisite of Engineer Gulbadin Hikmatyar's own four-point peace plan under the Peshawar Accord, signed by all the conflicting groups prior to the fall of Kabul. Sibghatullah Mujaddedi was appointed the first president of Afghanistan for two months, after which he was supposed to hand over the presidency to Professor Burhanuddin Rabbani. But Mujaddedi backed out of his commitment ratified in the Peshawar Accord and tried instead to vest executive authority in the two government councils.

In May 1992, the Afghan president, Sibghatullah Mujaddedi, the paid his first official visit to Islamabad. Speaking at the state banquet, President Ghulam Ishaq Khan said, 'We look forward to your active participation in the regional co-operation Organization (ECO). Pakistan and Afghanistan together can play a vital role for the stability and progress of our region.' He further said: 'Pakistan desired to see a united, peaceful, stable, and prosperous Afghanistan.'

Pakistan and Afghanistan had earlier agreed to set up a joint ministerial commission to strengthen economic co-operation in the fields of trade, agriculture, science, technology, and culture. The Afghan minister for planning, Al-Sayed Muhammad Ali

Javed and the Pakistani finance minister, Sartaj Aziz, signed a memorandum of understanding to this effect in Islamabad on 8 July 1992.

As time rolled on, some complications cropped up between Prime Minister Hikmatyar and Professor Rabbani. The president of Pakistan initiated a patch-up which finally culminated into the conclusion of what was later known as the Islamabad Agreement of March 1993. Towards the end of 1993, the struggle for power inside Afghanistan witnessed a new shift, another episode in the conflict which further confounded the internal scenario of Afghanistan.

Bosnia

The heart-rending spectacle of the Muslims of Bosnia, afflicted by the atrocious brutality of the Serbs, touched chords of compassion in the people of Pakistan. The foreign minister and the president of Bosnia visited Pakistan on 8–9 August 1997 to seek consolation. As announced by the minister of state for foreign affairs in the National Assembly on 12 August 1992, Pakistan offered moral and diplomatic assistance, including a grant of 10 million dollars, loans of 20 million dollars and one crore rupees. Pakistan launched a relief fund for the Bosnian Muslims and settled about 2600 refugees in Pakistan in 1993.

At the OIC and the UN, Pakistan urged military action under article 42 of chapter VII of the UN Charter, since Belgrade continued to disdain the will of the international community. Pakistan also offered to send its troops to Bosnia as a part of the UN peace keeping force. The foreign minister of Bosnia arrived in Pakistan on 8 August 1992. He was received by the president and the prime minister who had detailed exchange of views and discussions with him on the situation in Bosnia. The foreign minister of Bosnia, addressed a press conference on 9 August and described the magnitude of the aggression and brutality in Bosnia.[195]

The United States

In October 1990, the US suspended all economic assistance and military sales to Pakistan as a retaliation against Pakistan's nuclear programme. This ban was imposed in pursuance of the Pressler Amendment which stopped the supply of military hardware, weapons, and F-16 aircraft for which Pakistan had already made the payment. This amounted to the discontinuation of the second six-year package of economic assistance and sale (1987–93). (See above for its initiation in 1987.) Pakistan, looking for an alternative source of defence supplies, sought assistance from China which did not let Pakistan down despite the American pressure for not doing so. What worried Washington was Pakistan's nuclear programme and the multilateral initiative for the creation of a larger group of states, extending from Iran to the Central Asian republics, which the Americans interpreted as the spread of Islamic fundamentalism and a threat to their interests in the region.

The US Afghan policy underwent a radical change. Pakistan had lost its front-line status, and its importance for safeguarding the American vital interests in the region no longer existed. Hence, the US kept a tight rein over the supply of military hardware and spares to Pakistan. Pakistan, however, sought assistance from China for supply of military hardware and spares, especially those spares which could fit into the US-made weapons. The United states pressurized China to desist from supplying any such thing to Pakistan, but China resisted to accept the pressure. Pakistan was rapidly improving its ties with Iran, extending it to Central Asia, something which the United states did not like.[196]

The US senator, Larry Pressler arrived in Islamabad on a two-day visit on 12 January 1991. While in New Delhi, the senator had warned that the emergence of 'a potential fundamentalist Islamic confederation' with a nuclear capability would be a threat to India. Pakistani minister of state for foreign affairs, Siddique Kanju said, 'These are personal perceptions of the senator. Pakistan cannot help it if geography has placed it at the crossroads of South Asia, Middle East, and Central Asia'. During a meeting with the Senate chairman, Waseem Sajjad, Pressler said that Pakistan's proposal for a regional approach towards nuclear non-proliferation was positive and that his statement in Delhi was reported out of context. Sajjad made it clear that Pakistan was neither making nor it wanted to make nuclear weapons.[197]

Prime Minister Nawaz Sharif held wide-ranging discussions with the US vice-president, Dan Quayle in New Delhi on 24 May 1991. He was assured that Pakistan was not engaged in the manufacturing of nuclear weapons. Prime Minister Nawaz Sharif launched a multilateral initiative to work out a regional solution to the issue of nuclear non-proliferation in South-Asia. On 6 June 1991 he proposed a five-nation conference of the United states, Russia, China, Pakistan, and India to seek an equitable and non-discriminatory solution of the nuclear problem in the region.

The US Under-Secretary of State for International Security, Reginald Bartholomew, arrived in Islamabad on 19 November 1991 on a two-day visit from Beijing on his way to New Delhi. Pakistan told the US that it looked forward to reviving its relations with the US, provided it did not cut across its principles or its national interest.

Pakistan's Minister of State for Foreign Affairs, Muhammad Siddique Kanju, visited Washington in June 1992 on a three-day mission, had talks with the Secretary of State James Baker, and drew attention to the flagrant human rights violations in Indian-occupied Kashmir.

Meanwhile, Pakistan's Foreign Secretary Shahryar Khan, visited Washington on 18 and 19 November 1992 as part of the ongoing bilateral consultations with the US administration. The US Assistant Secretary of Defence, James R. Lilly, visited Islamabad from 21–25 September 1992 for discussions with the officials of Pakistan as part of the ongoing dialogue between the two countries on issues of mutual interest.[198]

A problem in the Pakistan-US relations cropped up regarding the role of those Arab and other Muslim volunteers (described as Afghan war veterans) who were associated with the Afghan resistance groups fighting against the Soviet troops in Afghanistan. After the withdrawal of the Soviet troops from Afghanistan, they stayed on in Afghanistan and the adjacent Pakistani territory. They often returned home and resorted to violence against their governments, which they viewed as corrupt and un-Islamic. They also targeted the American interests in the Arab world and elsewhere, as they viewed it to be pro-Israel and against the Muslims. The American government was perturbed by the activities of these militant Islamic groups, described as terrorists, as they targeted the American interests and also those Muslim governments that were known to be pro-America. The US blamed Pakistan for not controlling these elements, although during the days of the Afghan war, the American CIA had encouraged them to join the Afghan war, and had worked closely with them. Now the US no longer needed them to fight against the Soviets, so they were designated as terrorists, and Pakistan was accused of letting them use its territory. In 1992–93, the US threatened Pakistan to declare it a terrorist state for allowing its territory to be used by these elements. Pakistan took some steps in 1993–94 to contain their activities and the US withdrew Pakistan from the list of the countries under observation for their alleged promotion of terrorism.

China

Pakistan-China friendship has always stood the test of time. China assured Pakistan that it would honour all its commitments, despite the improvement in its relations with India and pressure from the US; that it would continue to support Pakistan in the field of defence, and enhance its level of economic assistance to Pakistan. It was through China's co-operation that Pakistan entered the field of heavy industries. The heavy mechanical complex at Taxila and the aeronautical complex at Kamra are ever-shining examples of the co-operation between the two countries. China also extended its support to Pakistan's nuclear and missile programme.

Prime Minister Mian Nawaz Sharif left for Beijing on his first official visit from 26 February to 1 March 1991. This visit provided an opportunity for an indepth bilateral review of the economic relations as well. Both the countries had identical views on the Gulf crisis which had gained new dimension with the ground attack by the US-led allies.[199]

President Yang Shangkun of China arrived in Islamabad on 26 October 1991 on a five-day official visit. The visit gained great significance in view of the new situation which had emerged after the end of the cold war following the collapse of the Soviet communism in the region. The visiting Chinese president held formal talks with the Pakistani president on bilateral relations, comprehensively reviewing the current regional and international developments, including the Washington-Moscow agreement to cut off supply to Mujahideen in Afghanistan. Prime Minister Nawaz Sharif paid a courtesy call to the visiting Chinese President Shangkun. The two leaders exchanged views on bilateral relations as a model relationship, worthy for emulation by other states. Both the leaders agreed to expand their co-operation and exchange of visits at different levels.[200]

Nawaz Sharif went to Beijing on 6 October 1992 on a five-day official visit in response to an invitation extended by the Chinese prime minister, Li Peng. The Chinese premier said that the time-tested friendship between China and Pakistan would further develop after the visit of Nawaz Sharif. Pakistani prime minister said that China was a dependable friend of Pakistan and their mutual relations would grow with the passage of time. He said 'Our all-weather friendship has become a model of good neighbourly relations between the two states. These relations have not only greatly benefited our two peoples, but have contributed significantly to the peace and stability in the region'.[201]

Prime Minister Nawaz Sharif visited the British prime Minister John Major, in London on 16 June 1992 on a three-day official tour. The British prime minister appreciated Pakistan's commitment to democracy and human rights in laudatory terms, and paid rich tributes to the valiant role it had played in rescuing Afghanistan from the clutches of the Soviet forces. The British foreign secretary, Douglas Hurd, arrived in Islamabad on 31 October 1992 on a brief visit, and held talks with the minister of state for foreign affairs, Muhammad Siddique Kanju. The talks centred around Kashmir, Afghanistan, Central Asia, and the issue of disarmament and arms control.

Nawaz Sharif also visited Paris in 14 January 1991 on a five-day official visit. As a result of these talks, Pakistan and France settled a thirteen-year old financial dispute over the cancellation of a nuclear deal by Paris. France had agreed to pay 600 million francs (about 118 million dollars) as a compensation for not keeping its promise to supply a nuclear reprocessing plant to Pakistan in 1978. Prime Minister Nawaz Sharif had talks with President Francois Mitterrand on Pakistan's defence needs and various issues facing South Asia. The prime minister told the press reporters that he was satisfied with the talks with president Mitterrand.

Prince Akishino and his wife arrived in Karachi on 8 November 1992 on a four-day visit to Pakistan on the invitation of the government of Pakistan to celebrate the fortieth anniversary of establishment of diplomatic relations between Pakistan and Japan. Nawaz Sharif visited Tokyo on 17 December 1992 and held talks with his Japanese counterpart, Kilchi Miyazawa, who was convinced about the peaceful nature of Pakistan's nuclear programme. Prime Minister Nawaz Sharif assured the Japanese investors that all private, domestic, and foreign investments in Pakistan would remain safe. Japan offered the 27th 'yen package' to Pakistan, assuring to provide 35 billion yen (280 million dollars). A six-member JICA (Japan International Cooperation Agency) delegation, led by Hidero Maki, visited Pakistan to have a general talk on the JICA's aid activities in Pakistan. Maki said on 28th October 1991 that in 1990–91 the Japanese aid to Pakistan was 194 million dollars, which made Pakistan's ranking 8 in the list of the developing countries that were under Japan's ODA (Official Development Assistance).

FOREIGN POLICY 1993–96

Benazir Bhutto's second tenure, which lasted from October 1993 to November 1996, witnessed greater problems of political and economic management. Although she travelled abroad frequently she found it difficult to handle the various foreign policy issues efficiently. There was hardly any significant progress on the vital issues like Kashmir, Afghanistan, and the nuclear programme. India-Pakistan relations remained tense and there was little improvement in the US-Pakistan relations. This period also witnessed a rise in the terrorist activities within Pakistan, which were related to foreign policy issues. Two Americans were killed in Karachi in March 1996, the Egyptian Embassy was partially destroyed in a bomb explosion in November 1995, and the activities of Islamic militants against the US continued. India repeatedly charged Pakistan with supporting the Sikh insurgents in the Indian Punjab. In short, her period did not bring any worth-mentioning achievement in the field of foreign policy.

Three major issues dominated her government's foreign policy agenda: Kashmir, Afghanistan, and the removal of the Pressler Amendment for resumption of weapons procurement from the US. Benazir Bhutto's government achieved a modest success on these issues, but no coherent and clear priorities and strategies were evolved for coping with the post-cold war situation.

Hoping to inject a new life into the collapsing economy, Benazir Bhutto made a whirlwind tour of about thirty-five countries, costing 5 billion rupees to the Pakistani exchequer.[202] Ostensibly these extensive and expensive visits were made for two purposes: to attract foreign investment to Pakistan and to project the Kashmir issue on the international scene. These visits, however failed to produce the desired result, because of lack of sufficient homework needed to present these issues on the international forum.

On the Afghanistan problem, Benazir's government chose to operate under the UN-sponsored peace plan. The problem became more complicated with the rise of the Taliban (starting in September 1994) whose political orientation based on religious training frustrated the efforts to defuse the situation in Afghanistan. The growth, expansion, and rise of the Taliban has been phenomenal; in less than four years of their emergence they had been able to capture Kabul.[203]

Benazir Bhutto visited China and North Korea whose governments supported Pakistan's stand on Kashmir. Concerted efforts were made to project the issue on the international forum. Pakistan sent delegations to various countries of the world and raised the issue of violation of human rights in Kashmir by India's law-enforcing agencies in the UN Human Rights Commission's meetings in Geneva.

The Organization of Islamic Countries' (OIC) decision to set up a contact group on Kashmir and the passing of a resolution at the OIC summit conference in Casablanca were termed by the leaders as 'successes', but Pakistan had failed to move resolutions on Kashmir in the UN Human Rights Commission and the UN General Assembly. On the nuclear issue, the primary thrust of the Clinton administration was on capping Pakistan's nuclear programme. The US assistant secretary of state, Robin Raphel, made this clear in an interview to a correspondent of *India Today*, published on 15 April 1995:

We are working very hard right now with Pakistan to persuade them to cap their programme. We've realized that to try to get Pakistan and India to move simultaneously didn't seem to be working, so we are trying a new tack. If we can get Pakistan to cap their programme, it is very much in the interest of everybody in the region including India.

Commercial relations with the US improved modestly, but the Pressler amendment still stood as an impediment to developing any meaningful political and economic links. The US deputy secretary of state, Strobe Talbott, during his tour to South Asia in April 1995, presented a proposal to seek a one-time waiver of the Pressler Amendment from the Congress, enabling the US administration to release thirty-eight F-16 aircraft to Pakistan, in exchange for 'verifiable capping' of Pakistan's nuclear programme. Islamabad disapproved of the idea of an 'on-site inspection' of nuclear facilities.[204]

Indo-Pakistani relations remained stagnant. The seventh round of talks held in January 1994 in Islamabad proved futile. Both India and Pakistan charged each other with covert interference in their domestic affairs, leading to the expulsion of some diplomats and the closure of the Pakistani consulate in Bombay and the Indian consulate in Karachi.

Earlier, on 9 March 1995, the state and the defence departments had expressed the view that the Pressler Amendment was an obstacle to improving relations with Pakistan. The assistant secretary of state, Robin Raphael; assistant secretary of defence, Joseph S. Nye; and deputy asstistant secretary at the state department, Robert Einhorn, were unanimous in their view that the Pressler law had failed in its primary aim of checking Pakistan from pursuing its nuclear programme.

A significant 'view-point' in the US-Pakistan relations was the trip of Hillary Rodham Clinton to Pakistan on 25 March 1995, despite the murder of the two American consulate employees. The trip went on as planned. She visited Islamabad and Lahore; the theme of her visit was the role of women in Pakistan. This visit, reciprocated by Benazir Bhutto's visit to the US in early April, could be viewed as a manifestation of the public support by the Clinton administration to the Benazir government.

On 5 April 1995, Prime Minister Benazir Bhutto began an official visit to the US to negotiate on the release of thirty-eight F-16 fighter planes and military equipment for which Pakistan had made payment before the imposition of the sanctions in October 1990. President Clinton promised to support moves for removal of the sanctions imposed under the Pressler Amendment. The US house of representatives passed an amendment, called the Brown Amendment, for the release of the above equipment to Pakistan. On 28 September 1995, the US senate voted (55 to 45) to pass this amendment, making it possible for the American government to release the military equipment and weapons Pakistan had paid for before the imposition of the Pressler Amendment. This was only one-time exception; the over-all ban on the sale of weapons was not lifted. The Brown Amendment also made it possible for the US government to sell the F-16 aircraft to some other country and reimburse whatever money Pakistan had paid for these aircraft. This development removed an irritant in the Pakistan-US relations.[205] The Pak-US consultative group for regular consultation on security affairs was also revived in 1995.

Pakistan's co-operation in the arrest and extradition of Ramzi Ahmed Yousef, allegedly involved in the Trade Center bombing in New York on 7 February 1995, was greatly appreciated by US administration. But Pakistan's image was awfully tarnished when, on 8 March 1995, two employees of the American consulate in Karachi were murdered on one of Karachi's busiest streets, and, on 19 November, the Egyptian embassy in Islamabad was bombed, killing fifteen people and wounding fifty-nine others. Worse still, Mir Aimal Kansi, accused of killing two Central Intelligence Agency employees outside the CIA headquarters on 25 January 1993, having returned to Pakistan, was untraceable. The American government wanted the Pakistani government to help in his arrest. In order to build pressure, the US administration periodically threatened to label Pakistan as a terrorist state if the required help was not made available by Pakistan for controlling those engaged in terrorism.

Pakistan and India diverged on signing the Comprehensive Test Ban Treaty (CTBT) at Geneva in 1996. Instead of extending unqualified support to a comprehensive test ban, India insisted that the treaty must include a time-bound framework for the elimination of the nuclear weapons of all nuclear powers. Pakistan advocated global de-nuclearization and voted in favour of the CTBT in the UN General Assembly, but maintained that such a treaty should be applicable to all the existing nuclear powers and also the 'threshold' states. Pakistan declared in clear terms that it would not sign the CTBT if India stayed out of it. Pakistan was working on different versions of the Hatf missile, in addition to its reported acquisition of M-11 missile components from China, in view of India's superiority in conventional weapons. Following the test-firing of the short-range ballistic missile, Prithvi, tested fourteen times since 1988 and finally in January 1996, the test-firing of Prithvi-II, with a range of 250 km by India evoked bitter comments from Pakistan. Also, India had been working on an intermediate-range ballistic missile, Agni, with a range of 2000 to 2500 km.[206]

Benazir Bhutto visited New York city in October 1995 to attend the fiftieth anniversary celebrations of the United Nations. Almost 187 heads of states and foreign ministers attended the dinner, hosted by the mayor of the New York city. The Pakistani prime minister made an impassioned appeal to the world leaders to hear the groans of tortured Kashmiri people and to ensure that their right to self-determination is not denied to them. She also suggested that a United Nations conference be held in Islamabad the next year to seek 'peacekeeping and conflict resolution mechanisms'. She also made a reference to the Afghan refugees question, stating that 'although the conflict of Afghanistan is over, there are around 1.5 million Afghan refugees in Pakistan'.[207]

The UN secretary-general, Dr Boutros Ghali arrived in Islamabad on 6 September 1994 on a three-day official visit to hold talks with Pakistan's leaders on global issues and for further strengthening the relations between the UN and Islamabad. He appreciated Islamabad's contribution to the UN peacekeeping operations abroad. Addressing a press conference on 8 September, Boutros Ghali promised to play the part of an 'honest broker' between Pakistan and India on the Kashmir dispute, in view of its vital importance for the regional peace.[208]

India told the UN secretary-general that any attempt by him to play the role of a mediator between Pakistan and India on the

Jammu and Kashmir dispute would not be acceptable to New Delhi. The UN secretary-general drew the world's attention to the Kashmir dispute in his annual report to the UN General Assembly issue on 26 September 1994. This was for the second consecutive year, after a lapse of many years, that a reference was made to the Kashmir dispute in the report.

The UN General Assembly, on 17 December 1994, gave its approval to a resolution on the establishment of nuclear-weapon-free-zone in South Asia, with Bhutan, India, and Mauritius being the only negative voters. The resolution was sponsored by Bangladesh and Pakistan.

South Asia

Pakistan continued to play an active role in the SAARC. Addressing the eighth SAARC summit held in New Delhi from 2–4 May 1995, Pakistan's president said that the mistrust and unresolved political issues in the region were barriers for SAARC to achieve its objectives. 'A lasting peace can be assured only if we abide by the principles of the UN Charter and fulfil the commitments undertaken by us bilaterally and internationally.'[209]

India-Pakistan relations, inspite of several rounds of talks between the leaders of the two states, continued to deteriorate because of the uncompromising attitude of India for an amicable solution of the Kashmir issue. The charges of interference in the internal affairs, leading to the closure of Pakistani consulate in Bombay and the Indian consulate in Karachi, embittered the relations all the more. The crushing of indigenous insurgency in Kashmir by brute force and frequent deployment of Indian forces on the line of control intensified the tension. Yet efforts were made for improving their troubled bilateral relations.

President Farooq Ahmad Leghari had a meeting with the Indian Prime Minister P. V. Narasimha Rao in New Delhi on 2 May 1995 after the inaugural session of the SAARC summit. Regarding these talks he briefed the press reporters that he had discussed with Mr Rao 'the core issue of Kashmir, sharing the view that the dispute must be resolved through peaceful means and not by military means'. Yet it is quite contradictory to note that according to a UN report, India had emerged as the biggest conventional arms buyer in the Third World, spending 12.2 billion dollars over a five-year period ending in 1992.[210]

On 24–25 April 1995, the prime minister of Bangladesh, Begum Khaleda Zia, in the course of her two-day visit to Islamabad in her capacity of chairperson of the SAARC, held talks with Pakistan's president and prime minister on matters pertaining to the forthcoming SAARC summit to be held in New Delhi from 2-4 May 1995. The two countries, on this occasion, signed two memorandums of understanding pertaining to the field of reciprocal promotion and protection of investments and co-operation in agriculture.

In 1994–95 Bangladesh exported goods worth 28 million dollars to Pakistan, while imports from Pakistan stood at about 101 million dollars. To review the transactions, the sixth meeting of the Pakistan-Bangladesh Joint Economic Commission was held in Islamabad on 26 July 1995.

Pakistan also maintained close and cordial interaction with Nepal and Sri Lanka. Nepal's prime minister paid a visit to Islamabad in November 1996. The two governments agreed to set up a business council to encourage ties between their private sectors.

The Muslim World

Pakistan, as chairman of the conference of Foreign Ministers and the OIC contact group on Bosnia-Herzegovina, played a leading role in co-ordination with other OIC member states to activate the international community to take resolute action for establishing peace in Bosnia-Herzegovina. Pakistan convened a number of OIC meetings for this purpose, including the special OIC ministerial meeting on Bosnia-Herzegovina in Islamabad in July 1993, and ministerial meetings of the OIC contact group in January and April 1994 in Geneva and New York. Pakistan's proposals on the de-nuclearization of South Asia, the solidarity of Islamic *Ummah*, Negative Security Assurances, regional arms control, and military balance also received due consideration at various OIC conferences.

Deeply moved by the terrible human-rights situation in Bosnia-Herzegovina, the OIC contact group meeting in Geneva on 8 December 1994 called upon the world at large to reaffirm their commitment to supporting the political independence and sovereignty of the republic. The OIC, on 2 March 1995, urged the commission on human rights in Geneva to take notice of the grave violations of the human rights of the Kashmiri people and adopt effective measures for safeguarding their fundamental right to self-determination in accordance with the UN resolutions.

In the annual meeting of the OIC foreign ministers, which was held on 2 October 1995, Pakistan urged all its members to take a joint action during the current session of the UN General Assembly to win support for the fundamental rights of the people of Jammu and Kashmir. The Islamic foreign ministers adopted the report of the OIC contact group on Jammu and Kashmir and recommended the OIC member states to establish contacts with other countries in order to promote the just cause of the Kashmiri people at the UN and other international bodies.

The seventh Islamic summit opened in Casablanca on 13 December 1994 amid hopes that the *Ummah* would take strong stand on the issues of Bosnia-Herzegovina and Kashmir. The prime minister of Pakistan called upon the Muslim countries to become partners for peace, commit themselves not to use force against each other, and develop a system for collective security against aggression. His address concentrated on two major issues confronting the Muslim world—the Serbian aggression against Bosnia and the Indian repression in Kashmir.

The two-day third summit of the Economic Co-operation Organization (ECO) was held in Islamabad on 15 March 1995. In her opening address, Prime Minister Benazir Bhutto appreciated the collective efforts in making the meeting successful by providing a concrete framework for accelerated regional co-operation. Besides the other items on the agenda, the members signed agreements for ECO airline, shipping, trade and business, bank, and insurance company.

Pakistan maintained a keen interest in promoting co-operation in the economic relations with the Central Asian republics. Turkmenistan's president, Saparmurad Niyazov, arrived in Islamabad in August 1994 for a three-day state visit and held detailed talks with Pakistan's prime minister on bilateral co-operation and regional issues, including Kashmir and Afghanistan. A natural-gas pipeline from Turkmenistan to Pakistan was to be laid entirely by the private sector for the supply of 2 billion cubic feet gas a day at an estimated cost of 3 billion dollars. A memorandum of agreement was signed to this effect by the two sides at the conclusion of the ECO summit in Islamabad. Turkmenistan and Pakistan also agreed to use Herat-Chaman-Karachi route for transit-trade activities between the two countries.

On 12 August 1994, Azerbaijan's minister of health, Ali Binnat Oglu, visited Pakistan. Addressing a news conference in Lahore, he said that his government was keenly interested in promoting economic and trade relations with Pakistan by launching projects under joint venture in the fields of pharmaceuticals, commerce, and industry.

Kyrgyzstan's president, Askar Akayev, arrived in Islamabad on his first state visit from 10–12 December 1994. They discussed major international and regional issues, including the Kashmir dispute, Tajikistan, Afghanistan, and the situation in Bosnia-Herzegovina, besides proposing bilateral co-operation in a number of areas including promotion of trade and tourism. The two sides signed six agreements aimed at promoting bilateral co-operation in economic, commercial, political, and other fields. They also agreed to establish a joint ministerial commission.

A seven-member trade delegation from Belarus, led by Deputy Prime Minister Uladimir Gurkun met Pakistan's commerce minister on 12 January 1995, and discussed in detail ways and means for enhancing business and economic relations between the two countries. Pakistan and Ukraine stressed the need for a just and peaceful settlement of the Jammu and Kashmir dispute and the problem of former Yugoslavia through bilateral talks in the light of relevant UN resolutions. Benazir Bhutto arrived in Tashkent on a two-day visit on 22 May 1995. The two sides, Benazir and President Islam Karimov, expressed their resolute will to work for the peace and security in the region.

Benazir visited Almaty, Kazakhstan, in August 1995 and held a meeting with President Mursultan Nazarbayev. They discussed the security situation in the region, including the problem of Kashmir, Afghanistan, and Tajikistan. Four agreements were signed relating to principles of mutual co-operation, helping each other in legal cases, avoidance of double taxation, and reciprocal trips by the citizens of both the countries.

Saudi Arabia and Pakistan strengthened their bilateral relations in the fields of trade, culture, and defence. The fourth session of the Pakistan-Saudi Arabia Joint Ministerial Commission was held in Riyadh on 17 January 1995, and the progress in trade was reviewed. It was noted that the total trade between the two countries had grown by 12 per cent per annum despite the recession during the last five years. The commander of Royal Saudi land forces met the chairman joint chiefs of staff committee and the army chief and discussed matters relating to further enhancing the meaningful co-operation between the armies of the two countries. Benazir visited Saudi Arabia in August 1994, where she performed *Umrah* and held detailed talks with King Fahd on various subjects, with special reference to Kashmir and Afghanistan. King Fahd reaffirmed his country's commitment to Pakistan, a country which he described as being very close to his heart.

Because of its geo-strategic location and bonds of faith, history, and culture, Iran and Pakistan are closely linked. Frequent high-level exchanges is a regular feature that keeps the two countries in touch and well-informed about regional and international issues. The first bilateral visit of the prime minister of Pakistan abroad was her visit to Iran in December 1993, which restored vitality and warmth in the relations and allowed detailed discussions on bilateral matters. During the visit, Iran stated that the Kashmir problem ought to be settled in accordance with UN resolutions. President Farooq Leghari went to Tehran on 10 September 1994 on a three-day visit, primarily to explore new avenues of economic co-operation. Besides, further support for Pakistan's just stand on Kashmir was galvanized. Despite cordiality, Iran and Pakistan developed differences on the role of the Taliban in Afghanistan. Iran opposed their rise and supported their adversaries, the Northern Alliance. Pakistan was inclined towards the Taliban. Iran and Pakistan held frequent consultations for defusing the situation in Afghanistan and to establish a broad-based government in Afghanistan, but they did not succeed. This created some strains in their interaction, although they continued to maintain a cordial economic and cultural relationship.

Pakistan and Turkey have traditionally enjoyed ties of brotherhood and friendship, and have always stood cheek by jowl in war and peace. Turkey is supportive of Pakistan's cause for Kashmir. The prime minister of Pakistan visited Turkey in December 1993. The prime ministers of Turkey and Pakistan visited Sarajevo together in January 1994, in order to create a pleasant climate for peace and stability in the region. President Farooq Leghari went to Ankara on 21 September 1994 on a three-day official visit, and discussed with the Turkish president, Suleman Demirel, matters of bilateral interest, including ways and means of further cementing the mutual co-operation, particularly in the economic field. After attending the two-day ECO summit, attended by ten nations, the Turkish president paid a three-day official visit to Pakistan in March 1995. Pakistan and Turkey signed two agreements on promotion and protection of investments and agricultural co-operation. Several high-level visits, including those of army commanders, were exchanged between the two countries.

Pakistan felt deeply grieved at the plight of Iraqi people due to a prolonged imposition of the UN sanctions against Iraq. In

1994–95, Pakistan sent goodwill delegations to Iraq and donated medicine and rice. In September 1996, Pakistan 'regretted' the US air raids on selected Iraqi targets and expressed support for Iraq's sovereignty, its territorial integrity, and the inviolability of its borders.

Pakistan continued to extend its unflinching support to the cause of Bosnian Muslims. The Bosnian prime minister, Haris Silajdzic and the Croatian prime minister, Nikice Valentice were accorded a warm welcome when they arrived in Islamabad on 28 October 1994 for a brief stopover. The leader of the Opposition, Mian Nawaz Sharif, presented of 20 million rupees to the Bosnian President Alija Izzetbegovic in Sarajevo on 6 January 1995. President Izzetbegovic expressed his gratitude for the courtesy shown by Mian Nawaz Sharif and the Pakistani nation.

Afghanistan

The Afghanistan situation created diplomatic problems for Pakistan. President Rabbani backed out of the commitments made in the Islamabad and Peshawar accords (1992 and 1993) for creating a broad-based government. When Pakistan and the Rabbani government held talks on this issue, the latter decided to oppose Pakistani suggestions. An Afghan group, backed by the Kabul government, hijacked a Pakistani bus along with passengers; this was followed by an attack on Pakistani embassy in Kabul for alleged support to Rabbani's adversaries, i.e. the Taliban. In fact, it was the second attack on the Pakistan Embassy in Afghanistan in less than two years. The mob ransacked the mission in February 1994, protesting at the killing of three Afghan gunmen in Islamabad, who had hijacked a school bus from Peshawar. Pakistani foreign minister warned the Kabul regime on 10 September that Pakistan would not re-open its embassy in Kabul unless the Afghan President Burhanuddin Rabbani, made an unqualified apology to the government and people of Pakistan. In response, the Afghan government shrugged off the demand. Pak-Afghan relations further deteriorated when two planes violated Pakistan's air space and dropped nine bombs in the Trimengal area near Parachinar in Kurram Agency on 22 August 1995, and refused permission to PIA to fly over their territory. In September 1995, Pakistan declared thirteen members of the Afghan embassy as *personae non grata.*

In September 1996, the Rabbani government was ousted from Kabul which was taken over by the Taliban. Rabbani moved to the northern region and joined hands with General Dostam and vowed to fight against the Taliban. Rabbani and Dostam were being supported by Iran, Russia, and India. Pakistan sympathized with the Taliban, but favoured the establishment of a broad-based government in Kabul that was acceptable to most Afghan tribal and ethnic groups.

China

The prime minister of Pakistan paid a visit to Beijing in December 1993, revitalizing the Sino-Pakistan relations. China endorsed Pakistan's proposal for a five nation conference to evolve a non-discriminatory non-proliferation regime in South Asia. Five agreements were also signed for extending the scope of economic co-operation.

During President Leghari's visit to China in 1994, both the countries agreed to strengthen bilateral economic ties and to remove the existing trade imbalance between the two countries. President Leghari, in his address to the Chinese business leaders, called for Chinese investment and joint ventures in manufacturing ships, submarines, frigates, aircraft, and bridges used by the armed forces.

China and Pakistan maintained a steady co-operation in the defence and security affairs. China extended valuable help for developing the defence industry in Pakistan. China also co-operated with Pakistan for the production of K-8 jet. The senior military officers visited each other. For example, a high-level Chinese defence delegation, led by China's defence minister, General Chi Haotian, paid a six-day official visit to Pakistan in July 1994 for talks on defence co-operation and for further cementing friendly relations between the two countries. The visit was in response to two separate visits by Pakistan's Army Chief, General Abdul Waheed, and the defence minister to Beijing. Pakistan's air force chief, Chief Marshal Farooq Feroze Khan also visited China in September 1994.

China and Pakistan signed four protocols for future co-operation in steel-making, heavy engineering, and power, generation sectors in March 1995. They envisaged wide-ranging Chinese technical and financial assistance for the expansion of Pakistan Steel Mill's capacity from 1.1 million tons to 1.5 million tons. The Chinese government also agreed to train Pakistani engineers.

Pakistan and China signed a protocol in Beijing for implementing their cultural exchange programme for 1995–96. Pakistan offered six scholarships to Chinese postgraduate students each year, while China promised twenty scholarships. The Chinese leadership, while supporting Pakistan on regional issues, advised its leaders to work towards settling their problems with India through bilateral and peaceful means. The same advice was given for the settlement of the Kashmir problem.

Russian Federation

After the collapse of the Soviet Union in 1991, a number of high-level visits were exchanged in 1993–96 between Pakistan and the Russian federation, the latest being the visits of the first deputy foreign minister, Anatoly Adamishin, and the foreign minister of Pakistan to Moscow in 1994. During the visit of Pakistan's foreign minister, two agreements were signed: an agreement on abolition of visas, and a protocol on consultations between the foreign ministries of Pakistan and the Russian federation on matters of mutual interest. Despite Russia's political and economic problems, it remains a powerful and important country. Pakistan attaches great importance to its relations with Moscow for achieving mutually beneficial co-operation in all possible fields of bilateral interest. Russia and Pakistan diverged on the Afghanistan problems. The former supported the Northern Alliance, while the latter leaned heavily towards the Taliban. Russians also wanted Pakistan to contain the activities of militant Islamic groups associated with the Afghan Mujahideen, who were trying to establish a foothold in the Central Asian states. However, they agreed on the need for promoting peace in Afghanistan and the establishment of a government in Kabul that enjoyed the support of most Afghan groups.

Europe

Pakistan enjoys friendly relations with all the countries in Europe. The European Community is Pakistan's biggest trading partner. About 30 per cent of Pakistan's total exports go to the European Community and more than 25 per cent of its total imports come from the European Community. The prime minister of Pakistan paid a visit to Davos in Switzerland in January 1994 to attend the annual meeting of the World Economic Forum, and addressed the forum on her government's policies of economic reform, which had created an attractive climate for foreign investment in the country through privatization, deregulation, and removal of restrictions on foreign exchange restrictions.

Benazir Bhutto and the British Prime Minister John Major had wide-ranging and detailed talks at the foreign and commonwealth office on 28 November 1994. The discussion covered bilateral relations and regional and international issues, with special focus on the solution of the Kashmir dispute which posed serious danger to the peace and stability in the South Asian region. Benazir also called on the Queen.

President Farooq Leghari held an informal meeting with the French President Francois Mitterand in Paris in June 1994, during which they discussed bilateral, regional, and international issues of mutual concern. President Mitterand had made a special gesture of inviting President Leghari for the meeting on his way back from his unofficial trip to the United states. Prime Minister Benazir Bhutto arrived in Paris in November 1994 on a three-day official visit. She had an hour-long meeting with French President Francois Mitterand and discussed the Kashmir issue and its fallout on India and Pakistan relations. France and Pakistan signed letters of intent concerning infrastructure deals worth 3.7 billion francs (710 million dollars) in April. The deals involving a communications satellite and an underground system in Karachi, were struck after a meeting between the Pakistani prime minister and French industry minister.

The Pakistani army chief, General Abdul Waheed visited Paris in July 1995. He called on various senior defence officials and visited training institutions and defence industries there. The French chief of defence staff, Admiral Jacques Lanxade, accompanied by a four-member delegation, arrived in Islamabad as a follow-up of French defence minister's visit. He held talks with Pakistani military leaders to consider the possibility of supplying Mirage 2000-5 aircrafts.

Prime Minister Benazir Bhutto visited Bonn in April 1994 and held talks with the chancellor on a wide range of bilateral regional, and international issues. An official German spokesman told newsmen that Chancellor Kohl underlined Pakistan's importance for Germany in the bilateral and overall Asian context in the efforts to' establish closer relations with the countries of the region.

The German president, Dr Roman Herzog, arrived in Islamabad in April 1995. Herzog, during his talks with Prime Minister Benazir Bhutto and President Leghari, raised sensitive questions on the non-proliferation treaty, Pakistan-India relations, the alleged attempt to smuggle fissile material into Pakistan from Germany, human rights in Pakistan, and the change in a paragraph on blasphemy law. 'I am satisfied by the answers that I received from my hosts' was the answer given by the German president to a journalist.

Japan

Pakistan enjoys friendly relations with Japan. The two countries share identity of views on major international and regional issues. Japan has emerged as the major donor and trade partner to Pakistan. Japan maintained this relationship during this period. In fact, economic and technological co-operation further expanded. Japan pledged 350 million dollars as the twenty-eighth yen loan to Pakistan in 1994–95 apart from a sum of 100 million dollars as emergency assistance as a relief for the flood damage.

The Third World

Prime Minister Benazir Bhutto visited Pretoria in May 1994 to attend the inauguration of the new president of South Africa after the first all-race elections. During her visit, she met various heads of states and other African leaders attending the ceremony. The power was handed over to the black majority, who had remained in servile subjugation under the whites for 300 years. Nelson Mandela made it clear that all the minorities, 5 million whites, 3.5 million coloured people, and one million Asians, would merit value and esteem for their contribution to the development of the country.

Pakistan maintains embassies in fourteen of the most important African countries. The rest of the countries are covered through concurrent accreditation. Pakistan's support for African liberation movements has not gone unnoticed and, in turn, the African countries, by and large, have stood by Pakistan in the international forums in its hours of need. Pakistan is implementing a special technical assistance programme for the African countries under which technical education and training facilities are provided on completely cost-free basis, in diverse fields such as diplomacy, agriculture, civil aviation, railways, banking, human resources, management, etc. During the period 1987–1993, more than 556 scholarships have been availed by thirty-nine African countries under this programme. Pakistan also made a donation, worth 34 million rupees, of electric motors and pumps, sewing machines, rice, sporting equipment, medicines and cash assistance to a number of African countries under the Africa fund during 1991–93.[211]

POST-FEBRUARY 1997 FOREIGN POLICY: NAWAZ SHARIF'S SECOND TERM

The government headed by Nawaz Sharif that took over in February 1997, redefined its strategies and options in view of the fast changing global and regional realities. As a matter of fact, neither economic development can be achieved nor the foreign policy can be successful without internal political and economic stability. That is why the Sharif government, at the very outset, made serious efforts to attract foreign investment and to strengthen trade and economic relations with other countries. However, owing to nuclear explosions in May 1998, Pakistan had to face hardships in the wake of economic sanctions imposed by the US, other developed countries, and international financial institutions.

The month of May 1998 witnessed a drastic change in South Asia's security scenario. India made five nuclear tests on 11 and 13 May and thus, intensified the security threat to Pakistan. Overjoyed on this development, the senior members of the BJP (Bhartia Janata Party) government in New Delhi issued threatening statements towards Pakistan, asking Pakistan to change its policy on Kashmir. They also hinted at taking military action across the line of control in Kashmir. This naturally perturbed Pakistan. The international community criticized India's action, but it applied weak sanctions against India, which led Pakistan to think that India would get away with its nuclear explosions. Pakistan also sought categorical guarantees from China and the Western countries against India's possible nuclear blackmail. No such guarantee was given to Pakistan by any country. In the meanwhile, firing across the line of control started and lasted for a few days. This led the Pakistani policy makers to conclude that the international community would neither offer categorical security to Pakistan nor would it take stern action against India. This would, in Pakistan's view, embolden India who would adopt a more threatening posture towards Pakistan. In view of the changed security environment and their assessment of what was likely to happen, they felt that Pakistan's security situation would worsen in the near future. Therefore, they decided to give a 'matching response' to India's nuclear explosion and to restore the strategic balance in the region by exploding nuclear devices. On 28 and 30 May, Pakistan exploded six nuclear devices in the Chaghi hills in Baluchistan. These explosions were welcomed by the people in Pakistan who felt that this was an appropriate response to the Indian explosion and a warning to India that it should not develop any ambition for military action across the line of control or on the international border.

Pakistan's foreign minister, Sartaj Aziz, declared on 31 December 1998 that Pakistan was more secure than ever after exercising the nuclear option. The nuclear explosion also brought the Kashmir problem to the world stage; it was now being viewed as a flashpoint for a nuclear conflict in South Asia. Sartaj Aziz said that the nuclear explosion had helped Pakistan to overcome the threats India had started hurling on Pakistan after its explosions.[212]

The Sharif government was able to project Kashmir effectively at the international level. In September 1997, Nawaz Sharif presented the Kashmir case before the international community in his address to the UN General Assembly. The American President Bill Clinton also made a reference to the Kashmir dispute during his address to the UN, followed by Kofi Anan, the UN Secretary-General who mentioned the Kashmir problem in his annual report. Support of the international community for the Kashmir cause was further highlighted by President Nelson Mandela who underscored the need for the resolution of Kashmir dispute and called upon the NAM in 1998 to lend its support for this cause. In May 1998, the nuclearization of South Asia brought greater international focus on Kashmir.

However, the Afghanistan problem produced some negative repercussions for Pakistan. 'Pakistan found itself alienated from Iran, the Central Asian republics and Moscow who had been, in varying degrees, exercising their influence behind the anti-Taliban forces in Afghanistan. Since Pakistan alone had shown proclivity to the Taliban, it was rendered into a 'marginal state'. Given the Taliban's isolation—it had won recognition from three governments only: Pakistan, the UAE, and Saudi Arabia—Pakistan's policy was not expected to gain acceptance in the South-West and Central Asia.[213]

On the economic front, Pakistan faced an extremely difficult situation. The explosion of bomb was followed by an explosion of prices. Pakistan had to put its economic house in order, control high spending, trade deficit, and improve its foreign exchange reserves, as it faced the serious threat of becoming a loan-defaulter. Defaulting would undermine its prospects for attracting investment and financial support from abroad, adversely affecting its role and position in the international system.[214]

In a nutshell, the foreign policy during this period generally focused on the efforts to promote peace and order on the globe. Under the UN peace mission, Pakistan sent troops to Somalia where fifty-five Pakistani soldiers were killed. Pakistan also took part in some other UN peacekeeping missions. Bosnia was offered humanitarian assistance. The relations with Central Asian Muslim republics were further strengthened. Cordiality in Pakistan's relations with China was reinforced and efforts were made to dispel the Iranian misgivings regarding Pakistan's role in Afghanistan. The structural adjustments in the economy helped to improve the economic situation. Intra-Afghan dialogue and the need for regional consensus on the future of Afghanistan were emphasized by Pakistan as a strategy for solving the Afghanistan problem. Slowly but surely, Pakistan started emerging as a stable and peace-loving state.

South Asia

The new environment of the unipolar world was conducive to the meaningful working of the regional organizations like the SAARC, which was committed to peaceful coexistence and regional development. India advocated the idea of sub-regional co-operation within the SAARC framework. It was an attempt to exclude Pakistan from the regional co-operation process, because this sub-regional co-operation focused on all the SAARC members to the exclusion of Pakistan.[215] Pakistan, in the ninth SAARC summit held in Male in May 1997, strongly condemned the idea of sub-regional grouping, and other member states also endorsed Pakistan's view-point. Pakistan further expressed its commitment to the liberalization of trade under the South Asian Preferential Trade Agreement (SAPTA). However, economic and trade relations do not fully mature unless the required political push is available for that purpose and the member states have a shared regional security perspective. This is certainly missing in South Asia.

The tenth summit meeting of the SAARC was held in Colombo on 31 July 1998. This conference was the first direct contact between the prime ministers of India and Pakistan after the two countries went nuclear in May 1998. As expected, this one-to-one meeting between the two prime ministers did not produce any results.[216] Although the SAARC provides an important forum to the South Asian leaders to discuss problems with a view to defusing tension and promoting co-operation, their basic contradictions and divergent perceptions continue to undermine the realization of its goals.

On 15 January 1998, a tripartite trade conference involving Pakistan, Bangladesh, and India, was held in Dhaka. Prime Minister Nawaz Sharif reiterated in his address that it was important to promote both democracy and development simultaneously, as two inter-connected wheels run side by side. He said that it was imperative to adopt a common line of action to achieve the economic and commercial objectives in South Asia in the fields of communication, transportation, taxation, trade, etc. The conference decided that a 'free trade' area be established in South Asia. This was in fact an endorsement of the SAARC efforts to promote regional trade with lowered tariffs.

The dialogue between India and Pakistan was revived when, Nawaz Sharif, soon after coming to power, sent a conciliatory message to his Indian counterpart, calling for a peaceful resolution of all outstanding issues. India also showed eagerness for easing the tension, to be able to concentrate on domestic problems and economic development. This exchange of sentiments led to the meeting of foreign secretaries in New Delhi on 28-31 March 1997, followed by the second round of talks in Islamabad on 19–23 June 1997. In the meeting in June, they agreed to set up eight working groups to deal with bilateral issues of peace and security, Jammu and Kashmir, Siachen, Wuller Barrage, Sir Creek boundary, terrorism and drug trafficking, economic and commercial co-operation, and promotion of friendly exchanges in various fields. Later, India refused to set up the mechanism in the form of working groups in the above mentioned agreed areas.

Nawaz Sharif met his Indian counterpart six times: on the eve of SAARC summit in Male in May 1997, in the fifty-second UN General Assembly session in September 1997, in the Commonwealth meeting in Edinburgh in October 1997, in the trilateral business summit in Dhaka in January 1998, in the SAARC summit in Colombo in July 1998, and in New York in September 1998 on the occasion of the UN General Assembly session. These meetings, especially the one held in New York in September 1998, led to the revival of the bilateral dialogue at the foreign secretary level in October 1998 and they agreed to discuss all the contentious issues between the two countries. However, the dialogue at the senior officials level clearly showed that India was interested only in continuing the dialogue; it was not interested in settling any of the issues. On Kashmir, India agreed to talk, but there were sharp differences between India and Pakistan as to what constituted the core of the Kashmir problem. The October round of talks did not produce any positive results, although both sides reiterated their desire to work towards promoting peace and promised stability in the region and that they would continue to hold talks. It may also be pointed out that Pakistan agreed to sell electricity to India. But this deal could not go through because India offered a very low price which was not acceptable to Pakistan.

Though India agreed in the SAARC summit (May 1997) that for the implementation of SAPTA under the SAARC, reconciliation on the Kashmir issue was needed to promote an environment of trust, its obsession establishing its 'dominance' in South Asia did not dissipate. India's procurement of nuclear-specific submarines from Russia, together with sophisticated aircraft and nuclear weapons, were noted with alarming concern by Pakistan. These symbolized her 'dominance' in the region and threatened Pakistan's security. The test-firing of Prithvi-II with a range of 250 km capable of delivering war-heads, followed by the test-firing of Agni ballistic missile with a range of 2000 to 2500 km, and finally the bomb explosion in the desert of Rajasthan on 11 and 13 May 1998, sent a shockwave in Pakistan. Now, it was Pakistan's turn. Pakistan test-fired its Ghouri missile in April, and blasted six bombs in Baluchistan on 28 and 30 May. Pakistan decided to explode nuclear devices because India, after having exploded its nuclear devices, had started issuing threatening statement against Pakistan; asking Pakistan to change its policy towards Kashmir, because India was now a nuclear power. There were also reports that India was planning a pre-emptive strike at Pakistan's nuclear installation. Since no credible security guarantees were available to Pakistan, it decided to go for 'matching' nuclear explosions.

These nuclear blasts brought India from soaring ambition 'down to earth'. The Indian leaders stopped issuing hawkish statements against Pakistan and agreed for a dialogue with

Pakistan on the outstanding problems. A slow process of dialogue was initiated after a meeting between the two prime ministers in New York on the eve of the UN General Assembly session in September 1998, when they agreed to discuss all contentious issues, including Kashmir.[217] The dialogue was held in October at the senior official level; the two sides agreed to encourage travelling to each other's country, and decided to start a bus service between Lahore and Delhi. On the other hand, India and Pakistan expelled the staff members of each other's high commission in March and October 1998.

The most significant development was the Indian Prime Minister Atal Behari Vajpayee's decision to travel to Lahore in February 1999 inaugurating the bus service initiated between Lahore and Delhi. He had meetings with Pakistani Prime Minister Nawaz Sharif and discussed all the contentious issues. A high-sounding 'Lahore Declaration' was issued by the two prime ministers, reiterating their strong desire to promote peace and amity between the two countries and to settle all disputes, including the Kashmir problem, through negotiations. They also decided to tone down propaganda against each other through state media. They vowed to 'refrain from intervention and inter-ference' in each other's internal affairs and agreed to take 'immediate steps for reducing the risk of accidental or unauthorized use of nuclear weapons' and promised to pursue more confidence-building measures. In March 1999, the bus service (agreed to in 1998) was started regularly for ordinary people.

A temporary strain developed in their relations in April 1999, when India test-fired Agni-II and Trishul missiles; Pakistan responded by test-firing Ghauri-II and Shaheen missiles. Pakistan clearly demonstrated that it would not be deterred by India's growing arsenal and that it had the capability to match India's technological advancements in the defence and security field. The process of dialogue was further delayed by the announcement of new general elections in India after Vajpayee's government lost a vote of confidence in the Lok Sabha in May 1999. During this whole period, when the two sides were generally talking in a friendly tone, incidents of exchange of firing across the line of control in Kashmir continued to take place from time to time, each blaming the other side of starting the trouble. In the last week of May, India launched a ground and air offensive against the Kashmiri Mujahideen in the Kargil sector of the Indian-administered Kashmir, claiming that these militants were sent in by Pakistan. This was accompanied by an increased exchange of firing across the line of control. India's two aircraft, MiG-21 and MiG-27, entered Pakistani air space in Kashmir which were shot down by Pakistani ground-fire. The intense clash between the Mujahideen and the Indian troops in the Kargil areas lasted until July. All friendly countries advised both sides to show restraint. However, as the Indian elections were scheduled for September, the Indian government maintained a very hawkish attitude. Pakistan, on the other hand, payed deference to the advice of the friendly countries and tried to defuse the situation. Pakistan's prime minister held consultations with the US President Bill Clinton in Washington on this issue. The two leaders agreed on the need for restoring peace in Kashmir, and Pakistan offered to advise the Mujahideen to withdraw from the Kargil area. President Clinton promised his help to find a solution to the Kashmir problem. By the end of July, most Mujahideen had returned to the Pakistan area and the fighting had died down. However, India and Pakistan continued to exchange firing across the line of control in Kashmir from time to time. These developments violated the spirit of the Lahore Declaration (February 1999) and showed that the confidence-building measures (CBMs) and diplomatic courtesies alone could not improve their bilateral relations. The CBMs may be important for easing tension, but these are not a substitute to problem-solving. Unless some of the outstanding problems are actually resolved, the CBMs alone can not ensure peace and stability.

The Muslim World

The Organization of Islamic Conference (OIC) held an extraordinary summit conference in Islamabad on March 23 1997 to express solidarity with Pakistan on the fiftieth anniversary of its independence. On this auspicious occasion, the OIC vehemently endorsed the resolution for the right of self-determination to the people of Kashmir, and supported Pakistan's efforts to seek a peaceful resolution of this issue. Pakistan maintained its traditional support to the Palestine Liberation Organization (PLO) and endorsed Turkey's demand for the establishment of a bi-zonal and bi-communal federation in Cyprus. Pakistan had been supporting the Muslim government of Bosnia-Herzegovina from the beginning of the civil strife which followed the break-up of Yugoslavia. A limited number of Muslim refugees from Bosnia were accommodated in Pakistan, and in 1996, Pakistan made available 300 police personnel for service in Bosnia for one year. Since April 1997 Pakistan has been provided training to Bosnian military officers in Pakistani military institutions.[218]

In view of the special value that Pakistan attaches to its relations with the Islamic countries, Pakistan actively participated in all OIC activities. Following the extraordinary session held on 23 March 1997, the secretary-general of the OIC, Dr Azeddine Laraki, paid a visit to Prime Minister Nawaz Sharif from 13–15 September 1997. The ninth OIC summit was held in Tehran in December 1997. The Kashmiri leaders also addressed the OIC summit. The Tehran summit adopted resolutions on the Jammu and Kashmir dispute and accepted Pakistan's proposals on the questions of UN reforms and expansion of UN Security Council.

Pakistan's foreign minister also attended the OIC foreign ministers' meeting held in Doha from 15–19 March 1998. Kashmir, Afghanistan, and the Gulf situation were the main agenda items of this meeting. The foreign minister of Pakistan highlighted India's callous atrocities and massive massacre of the people in the occupied Jammu and Kashmir. The conference unanimously condemned the Indian violation of human rights and the indiscriminate massacre of the Kashmiri people by the Indian security forces.

An extraordinary Economic Co-operation Organization (ECO) summit was held in Turkmenistan in May 1997, which was attended by Prime Minister Nawaz Sharif. The outcome of the summit was the Ashkhabad Declaration on the development of transport and communication infrastructure and network of transnational pipelines in the ECO region. The declaration emphasized early completion of ECO railway and road networks to accelerate the pace of co-operation within the region.

The prime minister led Pakistan's delegation to the fifth ECO summit meeting held in Almaty (Kazakhstan) on 10–11 May 1998. The summit was preceded by the annual meeting of the ECO council of ministers. Besides reviewing the ECO activities, the events witnessed the conclusion of important agreements on regional co-operation.

The idea of the developing group of eight countries (D-8) with Bangladesh, Egypt, Indonesia, Iran, Malaysia, Nigeria, Pakistan, and Turkey as its members, was originally conceived in October 1996 by Necmettin Erbakan, the then Turkish prime minister. The D-8 focused on socio-economic development through co-operation among its members. The membership of the D-8 enabled Pakistan to interact closely with important Asian, African, and Arab countries. Each country has been allocated one or two areas of co-operation. Pakistan has been assigned the agriculture sector. Prime Minister Nawaz Sharif led the Pakistani delegation to the first D-8 Summit held in Istanbul on 15 June 1997. The Summit signed the Istanbul Declaration calling for increased co-operation in different areas including trade, industry, agriculture, joint business councils, etc.; it also approved a document on the structure and functioning of the organization.

Pakistan interacted with the Central Asian republics on a regular basis on the Afghanistan situation and for improving trade and commercial and cultural relations. Nawaz Sharif also paid a courtesy call in October 1997 to the president of

Turkmenistan who had undergone a bypass surgery. The major obstacle to developing meaningful economic and trade relations with the Central Asian states was the civil strife in Afghanistan which made the road-transit route extremely unreliable and unsafe. Pakistan and Turkmenistan were interested in having a gas and oil pipelines network laid from Turkmenistan to Pakistan via Afghanistan. An international oil consortium, headed by an American firm, Unocal, agreed to work on this project. However, this project had to be shelved due to the uncertain conditions in Afghanistan. This shows that Afghanistan's internal situation is not improved, Pakistan would miss a big opportunity for cultivating economic and trade links with Central Asia. An alternative four-partite transit trade agreement between Pakistan, China, Kazakhstan, and Kyrgyzstan was signed in November 1998, for trade with Central Asia through the Korakoram Highway to Xinjiang province of China, and then from there to Kazakhstan and Kyrgyzstan. This route became operational by the end of 1999.

Prime Minister Nawaz Sharif visited Saudi Arabia many times during 1997–99. As usual, there were periodic visits of senior officials, including the visits of Prince Salman, governor of Riyadh and the crown prince Abdullah in 1998. The latter declared Pakistan to be his second home. Saudi Arabia offered liberal support for various development projects of Pakistan.

In December 1997, the fifth session of the Pak-Saudi joint ministerial commission was held in Islamabad for the purpose of expanding the existing co-operation in the fields of economy, trade, joint ventures, manpower, narcotics control, etc. The talks in which the Saudi side was led by commerce minister, Osama Jaffar Faqih, revealed that Pakistan's two-way trade with Saudi Arabia amounted to 960 million dollars during 1997, and about 800,000 Pakistani workers in Saudi Arabia continued to make a crucial contribution to Pakistan's economy by sending remittances.

The warmth and closeness between Pakistan and Turkey was clearly visible when President Suleman Demirel came to Pakistan to attend the extraordinary meeting of the OIC summit held in connection with fiftieth anniversary of Pakistan's independence. President Demirel paid his second visit to Pakistan within one year when he came on 18–19 December 1997 for the opening ceremony of the Islamabad-Peshawar motorway. The project was awarded to a Turkish firm M/s Bayindir. The Turkish president also witnessed the signing of a canal construction project in Peshawar, awarded to another Turkish firm.

Prime Minister Nawaz Sharif visited Istanbul to attend the first D-8 summit on 15 June 1998. The prime minister's visit was followed by the bilateral visit of Foreign Minister Gohar Ayub Khan to Turkey in August 1998. The foreign minister held detailed discussions with his Turkish counterpart, Mr Ismail and also called on Prime Minister Mesut Yilmaz and President Suleman Demirel. The Turkish leadership was apprised of Pakistan's peace initiative on Afghanistan and its efforts for the promotion of intra-Afghan dialogue.

The president of Pakistan visited the UAE in May 1997, and held useful discussions with the UAE president. Pakistan has a strong presence of its nationals (about 450,000) in the UAE. The two-way trade with the UAE during 1997 was valued at 658 million US dollars, with the balance in the UAE's favour, owing to Pakistan's imports of petroleum and petroleum products. The president of the UAE, Sheikh Zayed Bin Sultan Al-Nahyan came on a private visit to Pakistan in February 1998. During his stay in Pakistan, the president and the prime minister met him and discussed various issues of bilateral interest with him.

The eighth session of the Pak-UAE joint ministerial Commission was held in Abu Dhabi from 18–19 October 1997. It was co-chaired by Foreign Minister Gohar Ayub Khan and Sheikh Hamadan Bin Zayed Al-Nahyan, minister of state for foreign affairs of the UAE. The two sides agreed, *inter alia,* to rectify trade imbalance and to finalize the proposed agreement on economic and commercial co-operation between their federal chambers of commerce and industry.

Pakistan's relations with Iran continued to face problems due to their differences on the Afghanistan situation. Iran abstained from voting on Kashmir in the UN Human Rights Commission session in Geneva in 1994. Iran was interested in a gas pipeline to Pakistan which was to be extended later to India. Initially, Pakistan responded favourably, but later it did not show much interest, which practically suspended the project at the planning stage. As Iran developed problems with Pakistan, it cuddled up with India, the arch-rival of Pakistan. Its articulation favouring Pakistan on the Kashmir issue also toned down. Pakistan recognized the Taliban's government in Kabul and Iran joined hands with Russia and India to support Rabbani, Dostam, and Ahmad Shah Masood. In this context, Moscow expanded its supply of arms and weapons to India; forty SU-30 fighters were delivered during November 1996, and in addition, two nuclear reactors were promised.

Inspite of these misgivings and divergent strategic approaches on Afghanistan, Iran and Pakistan did not let their bilateral relations to be spoiled completely. In January 1999, plans were finalized for setting up an oil refinery on the Hub coast of Baluchistan as a joint venture. Purchase of bulldozers from Iran to barter with a sugar plant was also agreed to. Prime Minister Nawaz Sharif visited Tehran to expand bilateral relations in various fields besides this. Nawaz Sharif also profited from various other meetings with the Iranian president: on the fringes of the extraordinary OIC summit in Islamabad in March 1997, the ECO summit of May 1997, the eighth OIC summit in Tehran in December 1997, and the fifth ECO summit in May 1998.

Nawaz Sharif paid a special visit to Iran on 16–17 June 1997. He briefed the Iranian government on the atrocities of the Indian forces in Jammu and Kashmir and held a detailed discussion on the Afghanistan issue. This visit, followed by various top-level visit exchanges, swept away the clouds of misgivings between the two countries. An agreement on the delimitation of maritime boundary and a cultural exchange agreement for 1997–2001 were signed. Foreign policy makers in Pakistan thus moved successfully in approaching old friends to end all reproach by expanding bilateral relations with an open mind.

The government of Pakistan had been extending diplomatic and material support to the government and people of Bosnia-Herzegovina. As a member of the Assistance Mobilization Group (AMG), Pakistan attended its meeting held in March in Doha and then in Sarajevo in June 1997. Under the training programme for 200 Bosnian army personnel in Pakistan, fifty-seven Bosnian trainees reported at different training institutions and schools in Pakistan.

Pakistan also sympathized with the Kosovars of Albanian origin when the Serbian troops started their ethnic cleansing in 1998-99. Pakistan supported the NATO air strikes against Serbia for forcing it to stop its atrocities against the Kosovars. Pakistan also supplied relief goods for the Kosovar refugees in Albania, and Pakistan's prime minister visited Albania in May 1999 to express solidarity with them and to seek views as to how Pakistan could support the just struggle of the Kosovars against Serbia.

Afghanistan

Pakistan's commitment to the restoration of stability in Afghanistan in the face of sharp antagonism from Moscow and New Delhi symbolized its valiant spirit in foreign policy. But the ensuing civil strife with potential spill over in the neighbourhood, was a new challenge. In the persisting conflict between the Taliban and the Northern Alliance, the Taliban ultimately took over Kabul in September 1996, and established their sway over a major part of Afghanistan. In May 1997 the Taliban's interaction with Ahmed Shah Masood and Karim Khalili of Hizb-e-Wahdat signified a step towards forming a broad-based government. To accelerate this process, Pakistan accorded recognition to the Taliban's government on 25 May 1997, which reflected the initial arrangement for turning the chaos into order and peace in Afghanistan. Saudi Arabia and the UAE followed suit in recognizing the Taliban regime as a foundation for political stability in Afghanistan.

Nawaz Sharif vigorously pursued, peace initiative, maintaining contacts with the Taliban and the Northern Alliance leaders, and arranging their meetings in Dubai, Kandahar, and Mazar-e-Sharif. As a result of intensive discussion, Mulla Omar, supreme leader of the Taliban movement, agreed in April 1998 to Pakistan's proposal of formation of a commission of ulema, representing both sides, to start intra-Afghan dialogue. The UN and the OIC also endorsed the proposal jointly.

The strategic compulsions impress on intra-Afghan dialogue to evolve a formula for power-sharing in Afghanistan, enjoying the support of the major Afghan groups and the neighbouring states. The US is also not indifferent to the situation in Afghanistan. It wants peace and stability there, because instability in Afghanistan has not only disturbed the bordering states, but it has also given impetus to international terrorism and narcotics trafficking.

Another reason for the US involvement in the Afghan problem is that the US views the spread of militant Islam as a threat to its interests. Therefore, the strengthening of Islamic forces (described as Islamic fundamentalists) in Afghanistan, Iran, Pakistan, and the Gulf region is considered a disturbing development for the US, which it wants to contain. With communism eliminated as the main threat to the Western world, analysts in the US and Europe began to look at the Islamic world as the next credible threat to the West's pre-eminent place on the globe. The US therefore, built pressure on the Taliban for changing their ways. It refused to recognize the Taliban government, and demanded that they relax restrictions on women. When the chief of the US delegates to the UN, Richardson, visited Pakistan and Afghanistan, he suggested, *inter alia*, that women's rights should be respected. The Taliban spurned all his suggestions. However, during October-December 1998, the UN's special envoy, Brahimi, visited Pakistan, Iran, Afghanistan, and some Central Asian states. The Taliban leaders interacted with Brahimi. In March 1999, in a meeting held in

Turkmenistan, he was able to secure an agreement between the Taliban and Ahmad Shah Masood's faction for sharing power. However, like many earlier arrangements, this one also failed to improve the situation, as no follow-up meeting could take place to settle the details of this agreement.

One point of dispute between the Taliban government and the US was the latter's alleged involvement in drug trafficking and the use of the Afghan territory by the groups and individuals who are involved in terrorist activities against the American citizens and interests. The Taliban leaders denied any connection with drug trafficking and terrorist activities, although they admitted that Osama Bin Laden was based in Afghanistan. They asked for concrete evidence of his terrorist activities before he could be expelled from Afghanistan. In August 1998, the US launched a cruise missile attack on the alleged Bin Laden training camps in Afghanistan, close to Pakistan-Afghan border. Osama Bin Laden was not there on that day, but several other inmates of the camp were either killed or seriously injured. The Talibans protested on these missile raids.

The US government also complained that Pakistan's intelligence agency, ISI, was supporting the Taliban and their military operations, although no concrete evidence was offered in support of this allegation.

The United States

In order to assert its primacy as the sole super power, the US focused its attention on shaping the new world order. Many issues were highlighted to achieve this goal. These included promotion of capitalist economy, free trade, a US-dominated international economic order, democracy and human rights, and nuclear non-proliferation. The issues of environment, good governance, terrorism, and population were also raised as sticks to beat the poor developing countries with, by pointing out deficiencies in their systems on the basis of the criterion evolved by the US and other Western countries. In fact, these themes and policy objectives were the pious veils to camouflage the American diplomatic designs for taking over the role of a global policeman. Pakistan, with its support record for the Taliban and a penchant for Islamic system, could no longer qualify as a US favourite.

Another irritant was Pakistan's unshakable ties with China. Reckoning that China would soon become a powerful actor in Asia, the US wanted to contain China. In this context, the Clinton administration cancelled the proposed 450 million dollar, deal of satellite with China as this could help the Chinese armed forces to develop very accurate long-range missiles. To contain China, the US started strengthening the security of Japan, and adopted a lenient policy towards India. At the same time, enlargement of the NATO was drawing Europe closer for building a European security and defence identity, capable of coherent military action. This strategy betrayed 'cold war thinking' against China, and spelled trouble for the Muslim states as well; especially for Pakistan, since it was close to China and influential in Afghanistan.

It was, therefore, unrealistic to hope that the US would offer military assistance to Pakistan for countering India's hegemonic designs. For the US, India was important as a potential counter-weight to China. The US not only stopped the military sales to Pakistan in 1990, but also summoned back the frigate and warships that had been leased to Pakistan. This increased the existing military imbalance in South Asia to the advantage of India. On the other hand, India received nuclear-powered submarine and conventional weapons from Russia. It had already initiated the manufacture of MIG aircraft at home. Looking for an alternative source, Pakistan could receive only some Russian-made helicopters and tanks from Ukraine. Pakistan also obtained some weapons and military equipment from China.

However, the US made a friendly gesture in April 1996, when, following the Brown amendment, it transferred military equipment worth 368 million dollars to Pakistan. Then the news that Pakistan had procured M-11 missile components and ring magnets for uranium enrichment from China, raised a shockwave in the US administration; some elements in the US engaged in China- and Pakistan-bashing. Meanwhile, the issue of signing of the Comprehensive Test Ban Treaty (CTBT) came up ; this treaty was given its final shape in 1996 and was presented to the UN General Assembly for approval. Pakistan voted in favour of the CTBT, but Pakistan made its signatures on the CTBT conditional to India's signature. Unless India signed the CTBT, Pakistan maintained, it could not sign it and undermine its nuclear weapons option unilaterally.

On the assumption of office in February 1997, Nawaz Sharif wanted to improve Pakistan's relations with the US without compromising its primary interests. It required a dialogue on the points of divergence. This process was initiated with the visits of senior officials. Following the visit of Pakistan's foreign secretary to the US, Nawaz Sharif met President Clinton in New York on 22 September 1997, where both attended the UN General Assembly session. The meeting was described as useful, as they exchanged views on all issues, including India-Pakistan relation, non-proliferation and the CTBT, and other important issues. The US under secretary of state and the US chief delegate to the UN visited Pakistan in October 1997 and in April 1998 respectively, for talks on regional and bilateral issues, including Afghanistan, regional security, India-Pakistan issues, and Kashmir.

A new and difficult phase in Pakistan-US relations began with the nuclearization of South Asia in May 1998. Soon after the Indian explosions, the US attempted to persuade Pakistan to desist from exploding nuclear devices. Senior American officials, including Strobe Talbott, deputy secretary of state, General Anthony Zinni, commander of the US CENTCOM, and Karl Inderfurth, assistant secretary of state for South Asia visited Pakistan and offered economic and military assistance. They also offered to move the Congress to repeal the Pressler Amendment for resuming economic assistance and military sales to Pakistan. Pakistan had strong reservations about the viability of the American offer, as it outlined the general principles rather than a specific package of assistance. Furthermore, any assistance to Pakistan would have required the approval of the Congress. Given the problems of the Clinton administration at that time, Pakistan was not optimistic about the capability of the Clinton administration to obtain the necessary permission from the Congress for an assistance package for Pakistan, especially when it was to include military sales. Pakistan also wanted a security guarantee, but the US was not prepared to make any such commitment.

Pakistan's decision to explode nuclear devices on 28 and 30 May 1998 was criticized by the US and it imposed economic sanctions against Pakistan, as it had done against India after its explosion earlier in May. The World Bank, the IMF, the Asian Development Bank, Japan, and Canada also suspended their economic assistance to Pakistan. In order to meet with immediate needs, Pakistan sought financial assistance from Saudi Arabia, the UAE, and the Islamic Development Bank. A dialogue was initiated with the US on the non-proliferation issues in the South Asian context. The meeting between Clinton and Nawaz Sharif in September 1998 in New York helped to bring the two countries closer on the non-proliferation issues. Pakistan declared that it did not intend to explode more nuclear devices unless the regional situation changed drastically. It also announced its commitment to not exporting nuclear weapons technology to any other country, and offered to work with India for creating a strategic restraint regime for South Asia for ensuring peace and stability in the region. (India did not respond favourably to the Pakistani offer of a strategic restraint regime.) On the CTBT, Pakistan delinked its position from that of India, stating that it would sign this treaty keeping in view its interests and in an 'atmosphere free of coercion.' This meant that Pakistan wanted the sanctions to be withdrawn as a prerequisite for signing the CTBT. However, Pakistan was not willing to sign the Non-proliferation Treaty (NPT) in its present discriminatory form. Pakistan also agreed to join the Geneva-based conference on the preparation of nuclear missile material cut-off treaty, but it did not accept the American demand of ceasing the production of fissile material immediately. Pending the finalization of the

Fissile Material Cut-Off Treaty (FMCT), Pakistan was not prepared to give up this option.

Several rounds of the Pakistan-US dialogue on nuclear issues during 1998–99 partly bridged the gap between the perspectives of the two countries. The US decided to lift the sanctions against Pakistan by not opposing approval of loans to Pakistan by international financial institutions. This came as a big relief to Pakistan whose economy was facing serious problems after the imposition of economic sanctions and refusal of economic assistance by the IMF and the World Bank.

On 1 December 1998, Nawaz Sharif visited the US again. He emphasized the lifting of the remaining sanctions against Pakistan in order to make it possible for the Pakistan government to sign the CTBT. One result of the visit was that the US reimbursed the money Pakistan had paid for the purchase of F-16 aircraft. It may be pointed out that the initial decision to return the money was made in 1995, but as the US could not sell these aircraft to any other country, no payment could be made to Pakistan then. Now the US decided to reimburse the money even though the aircraft had not been sold. Pakistan thus received 484 million dollars in two instalments (157 million dollars and 327 million dollars) and 140 million dollars were adjusted against cost of food grain that the the US promised to supply in the next two years. About 34 million dollars were deducted by the US as service charges.[219] In early 1999, the US Department of State's reports on terrorism and narcotics trafficking acknowledged Pakistan's efforts for checking these problems in the Afghanistan-Pakistan area.

The IMF approved the new loan package for Pakistan and the Aid-to-Pakistan Consortium (the Paris Club) agreed to reschedule Pakistan's debt in December 1998 and January 1999, providing a major relief to Pakistan's troubled economy. Since the early 1990s, Pakistan had accumulated a huge amount of internal and external debts due to the bad habit of over-spending. By early 1999, Pakistan's foreign debts amounted to 32 billion dollars. The debt servicing for external and internal loans has become the single largest item in Pakistan's national budget (bigger than defence expenditure). As international sanctions were imposed after the May 1998 nuclear explosions, Pakistan found it difficult to repay its debts. But for the revival of economic assistance by the IMF and the World Bank and rescheduling of its loans by the Pakistan Development Forum, Pakistan would have defaulted. This problem has been taken care of for the time being, but as long as Pakistan does not control its non-development expenditure and improve its economic management, the debt problem will continue to cast a dark shadow on Pakistan's economy, undermining its credibility at the international level.

By mid-1999, the Pakistan-US relations showed some improvement from what these were in the immediate aftermath of the nuclearization of South Asia in May 1998. Though most of the economic sanctions were in place and the US was not providing any bilateral economic assistance or military sales to Pakistan, the dialogue on the nuclear issue had shown some progress, although Pakistan and the US still diverged on some aspects of the nuclear issue. Pakistan wanted the US to play an active role for finding solutions to the India-Pakistan problems, especially the Kashmir problem. But India was totally opposed to any role by the US or any other power in solving the India-Pakistan problems. Such an Indian attitude marred the prospects of peace and stability in South Asia. Unless the major outstanding problems between Pakistan and India are resolved and India tones downs its hegemonic agenda, Pakistan not be expected to surrender its nuclear weapons programme. The nuclear programme is viewed by Pakistan as integral to its security in a difficult, if not hostile, regional environment, especially when India continues to expand its conventional and nuclear military power.

China

Pakistan-China co-operation expanded during the Nawaz Sharif era in most areas of mutual interest, i.e., the economy, commerce and trade, science and technology, agriculture and power-generation. Two-way trade between Pakistan and China crossed the one billion dollar mark. The Pak-China joint committee on scientific and technical co-operation held its fourteenth session in Beijing on 29 July 1997 and formulated the programme for scientific and technical co-operation. The cultural exchange programme between the two countries for the years 1997-99 was signed in Islamabad on 24 April 1997. The programme encompassed such varied areas as culture, arts, education, broadcasting, television, films, information, sports, etc. In December 1997, the Chinese minister of state in-charge of physical culture and sports visited Pakistan and signed two memorandums of understanding in the field of sports.

The president of Pakistan paid a two-day visit to China in April 1997. Foreign Minister Gohar Ayub Khan visited Beijing in September 1997 for bilateral consultations with Vice-Premier and foreign minister, Qian Qichen. Among the Chinese dignitaries, vice-foreign minister Tang Jiaxuan visited Pakistan in August 1997. As a special gesture of goodwill towards Pakistan, China participated in the golden jubilee celebrations of Pakistan's independence in March 1997.

Several exchange visits of delegations between the two countries for co-operation in the field of defence took place, demonstrating close Sino-Pak co-operation in this area. General Yang Bo, member of China's Central Military Commission and chief of the general political department of PLA visited Pakistan in May 1997. He was awarded *Nishan-i-Imtiaz* (Military) by the president of Pakistan in recognition of his outstanding contributions to the promotion of relations between the two armed forces. Award of *Nishan-i-Imtiaz* (Military) was also given by the president to Vice-Admiral Shi Yunsheng, Commander of the PLA (Navy) who paid a visit to Pakistan in October 1997. From Pakistan side, the chief of naval staff paid visit to China in March 1998.

Earlier, in February 1998, Nawaz Sharif paid a six-day visit to China. The visit aimed at exploring new avenues to strengthen Pak-China friendship and to seek closer economic co-operation.

During the talks China extended traditional and unqualified support on Kashmir and reiterated to resolve it according to the UN resolutions. Pakistan and China signed two agreements of mutual co-operation in economic collaboration, technical and agricultural sectors.

China accepted Pakistan's justification of its nuclear explosions that these were done in response to India's explosions. However, it advised India and Pakistan to work towards non-proliferation in the region. It also advised India and Pakistan to settle their outstanding disputes and problems through peaceful means and bilateral dialogue. China also denied having provided nuclear weapons technology to Pakistan. It claimed that China's co-operation with Pakistan in the nuclear field was peaceful and that its support to Pakistan's missile programme was within the parameters set out by the international community. The nuclear power plant at Chashma, supplied by China, is expected to go in production of electric power by the end of 1999.

Russia

Pakistan and the Russian federation maintained a regular dialogue on bilateral and regional issues, but the legacy of troubled relations during the Soviet era continued to haunt them. However, like the Soviet period, problems in the political domain did not adversely affect their mutual interaction for economic and trade links.[220]

Russia and Pakistan agreed in early April 1997 on the need of an intra-Afghan dialogue in order to create a broad-based government in Afghanistan.[221] Several high-level contacts took place and the two countries made earnest efforts to enhance mutual understanding on issues of common interest. Russian Prime Minister Victor Chernomyrdin's message of felicitations to Prime Minister Nawaz Sharif reflected the changing environment of bilateral ties. In the message, Chernomyrdin stated that Russia placed a high value on good relations with

Pakistan, as both countries had many common goals in securing international peace, co-operation, and development.

Russian deputy foreign minister, Victor Pasuvaluk visited Pakistan in June 1997 for the next round of consultations on Afghanistan. Among other things, he indicated the Russian interest in developing oil and gas pipelines in co-operation with Pakistan as well as building road and communication links from the Central Asian republics to Pakistan. He was also briefed on Pakistan's initiative for resuming talks with India.

The Russian deputy foreign minister visited Pakistan in March 1998 for a review of their bilateral relations. The two sides agreed on steps to accelerate their economic and cultural ties. They also discussed the Afghanistan problem and the two sides felt that they should work for establishing a broad-based government in Kabul for the promotion of peace and stability in the region.

The most significant development was Prime Minister Nawaz Sharif's visit to Moscow in April 1999. This was the first visit by a Pakistani prime minister after the svenenties, and reflected a strong desire on the part of Pakistan and Russia to overcome the negative legacy of the past and to improve their relations. Russian President Boris Yeltsin said that it was the time for Russia and Pakistan 'to burry the past and start a new phase of relationship on the basis of mutual trust and confidence between the two as sovereign and equal friends.'[222] The two sides had detailed discussions on various issues of mutual interest, including Afghanistan, Pak-Russian relations, the nuclear question, India-Pakistan relations, and regional peace and stability. It seems that this visit enabled the two sides to understand each other's perspectives on these issues, especially on Afghanistan. This raises the hope that they would be able to co-ordinate their efforts for the promotion of peace in Afghanistan and maintain smoother interaction on other issues. The two sides signed two agreements for improving their trade and economic ties, and granted the status of the 'most-favoured nation' (MFN) to each other for ensuring non-discriminatory treatment in taxes, customs, mothods of payment, and transfer of payments. They also decided to set up a joint ministerial commission as an official forum for deliberation on economic, trade, and culutral affairs

Japan

Pakistan enjoys friendly relations with Japan marked by strong co-operation in the economic and commercial fields. Japan is the largest donor of economic assistance to Pakistan and a leading trading partner. Two-way trade exceeds 1.5 billion dollars every year. The Japanese foreign minister's visit to Pakistan in July 1997 afforded an opportunity to the two countries to hold a detailed exchange of views on bilateral, regional, and international matters. The two sides identified areas of co-operation in various fields.

During the Japanese foreign minister's visit in March 1998, Japan pledged a loan of 250 million American dollars for Pakistan's banking sector reforms programme. Japan offered soft-term loan so that Pakistan could implement the economic reforms. After India's nuclear explosions, Japan tried to persuade Pakistan not to follow India's example. A special representative of the Japanese government visited Pakistan especially for that purpose in May 1998. When Pakistan exploded nuclear devices, Japan suspended all economic assistance to Pakistan. Later, Japan insisted that Pakistan should sign the CTBT if it wanted the economic assistance to be restored.

Great Britain

In October 1997, the prime minister of Pakistan visited Edinburgh to participate in the Commonwealth Heads of States' summit and met Prime Minister Tony Blair, and several other world leaders. Queen Elizabeth-II and the Duke of Edinburgh paid a state visit to Pakistan in October 1997 in connection with the celebrations of the fiftieth anniversary of Pakistan's independence. The Queen expressed a keen interest in Pakistan's development and praised the role of the Pakistani expatriate community in the United Kingdom. The British Foreign Secretary Robin Cook, who accompanied the Queen, held discussions with Pakistan's foreign minister who discussed, *inter alia*, Afghanistan and Kashmir. The British foreign secretary expressed his willingness to play a mediatory role for the solution of India-Pakistan problems; Pakistan accepted the suggestion, but India categorically rejected it.

Prime Minister Nawaz Sharif represented Pakistan at the Commonwealth Heads of States' meeting held in Edinburgh during October 1997. The highlight of the conference was the address of the Pakistani prime minister delivered on special invitation to mark the golden jubilee of Pakistan's independence. While at Edinburgh, Nawaz Sharif had bilateral meetings with prime ministers of Bangladesh, Canada, India, and the United Kingdom. He was also received by the Queen.

A GENERAL APPRAISAL

Foreign policy of a developing country facing economic hardships, political instability, and serious security pressures, tends to be an external projection of its internal requirements rather than a rational response to shifts in global environment. Pakistan faced internal and external difficulties from the beginning. In addition to the problems arising out of the Partition process in 1947, Pakistan faced the difficulties of setting up a state structure in the face of India's persistent hostility. It needed external support and co-operation not only for putting its economic house in order but it also needed external help to strengthen its security *vis-à-vis* a bigger, powerful, and hostile neighbour, India. These two sets of considerations have continued to shape Pakistan's foreign policy, because the survival of the state and pursuance of its national interest depended on the realization of these considerations.

Economic and political viability and external security, the two interdependent elements, form the cornerstone of Pakistan's foreign policy. Pakistan's participation in the US-sponsored security alliances in the mid-fifties can be understood only with reference to these twin goals. The participation in these alliances strengthened Pakistan's security, but there was a price attached to it. Pakistan was tied to the Western bloc and was entangled in the super power cold war. It also incurred the displeasure of the Soviet Union which retaliated by supporting India on Kashmir and all such other issue between the two countries. The US was not prepared to support Pakistan to that extent, although it made Pakistan play the role of its proxy in the region. Pakistan also developed an effective and multifaceted interaction with the Muslim countries and succeeded in obtaining their valuable diplomatic support; in the seventies and the eighties, some of the oil-rich Arab states extended economic assistance as well. Pakistan maintained an active role in various international and regional organizations in order to improve its diplomatic clout. Pakistan has always been active in the UN, the OIC, the ECO, the NAM, and the SAARC. Active diplomacy and strong defence were viewed as two interlinked strategies to cope with internal economic pressures and external security threats.

Pakistan did not hesitate to change its foreign policy strategies, when the conditions demanded such a step. In the mid-1960s, Pakistan began to distance itself from the Western camp and adopted an independent foreign policy by cultivating relations with China, the Soviet Union, and other socialist states. This change matured into the policy of non-alignment in the early seventies, and Pakistan projected itself as the champion of the socio-economic causes of the developing world. It supported the demand for a new international economic order that dealt with the developing countries in a more just and equitable manner.

The Soviet Union's military intervention in Afghanistan in December 1979 created a very difficult security situation for Pakistan. Its economy was also adversely affected with the influx of Afghan refugees and other repercussions of the Afghan war. Pakistan joined hands with the Western countries to cope with the situation, but avoided formal alignment with them, so that its autonomy in deciding about foreign policy options was not compromised. Pakistan took a great risk in spearheading the resistance to the Soviet aggrandizement in Afghanistan; the forced withdrawal of the Soviet troops from there in 1991 was a tribute to its determination to stand for the right cause. However, the fracturing of Afghanistan due to the civil strife between the various Afghan resistance groups has been a major disappointment for Pakistan. This has caused much damage to Pakistan's diplomacy, economy, and security. This problem will continue to be a drag on Pakistan's foreign policy.

The end of the cold war did not improve Pakistan's security situation. It reduced Pakistan's strategic importance for the US which no longer needed Pakistan for pursuing its agenda against the Soviet Union. The US, as the sole super power, could apply more pressure on Pakistan and other developing countries. The US demonstrated its military capability to assert its commanding position in the international system by resorting to force against Iraq in 1990. It also launched cruise missile raids on Sudan and Afghanistan in August 1998, claiming that the attacks were on the bases of Muslim 'terrorists' in these countries. Though the US projected itself as the champion of democracy and human rights; it was not prepared to take a clear position in favour of the rights of the people of Kashmir who were suffering under the oppressive policies of the Indian government. For the US, India was too important a country to be alienated for the human rights of the Kashmiris. The US periodically built pressure on Pakistan on a number of issues, i.e., transnational Islamic militant groups, narcotics trafficking, and the nuclear issue. Pakistan dealt with this pressure through diplomacy and necessary adjustments in its foreign and domestic policies.

The international trends towards global issues namely terrorism, drug trafficking, nuclear proliferation, and human rights became conspicuous in the post-cold war unipolar world. Pakistan's foreign policy oriented itself to these new priorities in the global politics. Peaceful negotiations on the Kashmir issue and intra-Afghanistan dialogues have been promoted. Pakistan actively participated in the UN peace operations in different parts of the world, and extended humanitarian assistance to Bosnia and the Kosovar refugees in Albania. Co-operation has been extended to international agencies in eliminating drug trafficking and terrorism. Some structural changes have been made in the economy in order to overcome the economic problems and difficulties. Bilateral relations have been expanded. On top of all, for the first time, India has been persuaded to resume talks on the Kashmir issue, although this does not mean that this problem will be settled soon.

Pakistan viewed the emergence of the Muslim states of Central Asia as a new opening and took steps to improve relations with these states. However, the continuing civil strife in Afghanistan has become a major obstacle to evolving a meaningful relationship with these states. If the situation in Afghanistan is not brought under control in the near future, this new opening may be lost.

Pakistan's current foreign policy focuses on self-reliance (even in defence); holding on fast to the time-tested friendship of China; promotion of regional consensus on Afghanistan; greater economic co-operation and trade with the neighbouring states; removal of Iran's misgivings about Afghanistan, establishment of bilateral relations with the US and Russia; strengthening of the OIC, the ECO and the SAARC; and above all, an early and peaceful settlement of the Kashmir problem and improvement of relations with India.

Nawaz Sharif's visits to the US (1997, 1998) and Russia (1999) are significant. These reflect a strong desire to maintain autonomy in the field of foreign policy. Pakistan supports China's efforts for creating a multipolar international order in place of a more or less US dominated unipolar international system. Pakistan's nuclear policy also shows that its leadership wants to maintain an autonomous and credible nuclear deterrence for countering the Indian nuclear threat. Pakistan makes no claim to any global role or regional leadership. In fact, Pakistan is opposed to any country's effort to create its hegemony in a region. That is why Pakistan continues to view India's nuclear and conventional military build-up as a de-stabilizing development, because India wants to use this to restrict the foreign and domestic policy options of the neighbouring states. Pakistan has resisted these trends in the past and there is every evidence available to suggest that Pakistan would continue to do that in the future.

Another major issue that Pakistan's foreign policy faces pertains to its economy. Pakistan is confronted with a number of economic problems at a time when it is restructuring its economy for bringing it in line with the changing global environment. It requires external support to cope with the economic pressures and exigencies of structural changes in the economy. Its reliance on the international financial institutions like the IMF, the World Bank, and the Aid-to-Pakistan Consortium (also called Pakistan Development Forum) have continued. These organizations also set out economic conditions while providing economic assistance and loans. Pakistan has often been handed down a set of priorities which it must follow if it wants more assistance. These conditionalities pose a major challenge to the policy-makers, i.e. how to maintain a delicate balance between these demands and the imperatives of national interests.

Experience suggests that the one-track policy of considering the US aid as panacea for all ailments, is a hazardous strategy. Time is ripe for multilateral diplomacy. India has normalized its relations with China; China has improved relations with Russia; and Russia with the US. Therefore, Pakistan must also adopt a multilateral and issue-oriented approach for extending the scope of its interaction in and around its neighbourhood and on the global level. However, the worrisome development is that Pakistan's problems in the neighbourhood have increased: Afghanistan suffers from civil strife with negative spillover on Pakistan; Pakistan continues to have troubled relations with India; Pakistan's relations with Iran have suffered a setback due to the Afghanistan problem. Pakistan is bracketed with the

Taliban, while Iran is supporting the Northern Alliance. As India is also worried about the rise of the Taliban, Iran and India appear to be moving closer to each other. In a situation like this, Pakistan should work towards demonstrating that it is not permanently linked with the Taliban and that it would be willing to support the move to create a broad-based political arrangement in Afghanistan through the UN and other neighbouring states. An active diplomacy can improve the regional situation, and Pakistan will be better placed to cope with the security pressure caused by India which continues to be Pakistan's major security concern.

The frequent meetings between the prime ministers of India and Pakistan are positive developments. The same can be said about the meetings between the foreign ministers and senior officials of the two countries. Similarly, the adoption of confidence-building measures to improve the bilateral relations between India and Pakistan is equally desirable. Peace and normalization of relations are in the interest of both countries. However, these steps alone can not provide a durable basis for peace and stability in the region. These can not be a substitute to a permanent solution of the problems. Unless these conferences, meetings, and friendly gestures produce some concrete results, that is, solve some outstanding problems, the long-term prospects of India-Pakistan relations can not improve.

To sum up, the transformed international and regional environment at the beginning of the twenty-first century calls for a re-orientation of Pakistan's foreign policy. There is a need to pursue multilateral diplomacy and promote regional economic co-operation rather than looking towards one particular powerful country. The twenty-first century is not the time for binding firmly with any one country—a policy that has created problems in the past and could spell disaster in the future. The scope of relations should be as wide as possible and should be based on mutually advantageous considerations. The US and other Western states can continue to be Pakistan's partners, but Pakistan's foreign policy options and strategies should be determined by its national interest rather than by the desire to stay in the good books of a certain country. With Russia, there is a scope for improvement of relations. Nawaz Sharif's visit in April 1999 has provided a good opening to explore such prospects. The China connection can and should be strengthened to increase the foreign policy options. It is also desirable to continue improving relations with the Muslim states in the neighbourhood and elsewhere. The new century offers new opportunities. Pakistan must avail itself of these in order to cope with the challenges of the transformed international environment.

NOTES AND REFERENCES

1. Ayub Khan, *Friends Not Masters*, p. 114.
2. Ibid., p. 117.
3. Subramaniam Swamy in *Organizer*, 13 July 1974.
4. Sayeed, *The Political System of Pakistan*, p. 262.
5. Alastair Lamb, *Kashmir: A Disputed Legacy, 1846-1990*, Karachi: Oxford University Press, 1993, p. 8; and K. Sarwar Hassan, *Pakistan and the United Nations*, New York: Manhattan Publishing Company, 1960, p. 87.
6. Ibid.
7. Sardar M. Ibrahim Khan, *The Kashmir Saga*, Lahore, 1965, p. 41.
8. Sarwar Hassan, *Pakistan and the United Nations*, p. 86.
9. Sayeed, *The Political System of Pakistan*, p. 264.
10. *United Nations Security Council Official Records, 1090th Meeting, Nineteenth year, 10th February 1964*, S/PV 1090, p. 17.
11. *United Nations Security Council Official Records, Fifth Year Supplement for September through December 1950*, Document S/II 1791, p. 36.
12. Ibid.
13. Joint Communiqué by the prime ministers of India and Pakistan, 20 August 1953.
14. Ayub Khan, *Friends Not Masters*, p. 131.
15. Nehru's statement in Indian Parliament, 23 December 1953.
16. Ayub Khan, *Friends Not Masters*, p. 131.
17. Ibid., p. 126.
18. *Dawn*, 5 May 1959.
19. Ayub Khan, *Friends Not Masters*, p. 141.
20. Ibid.

21. Z.A. Bhutto, *Foreign Policy of Pakistan*, Karachi: Pakistan Institute of International Affairs, 1964, p. 49.
22. Ibid, pp. 57, 58.
23. Ayub Khan, *Friends Not Masters*, p. 150.
24. Z.A. Bhutto, *Foreign Policy of Pakistan*, pp. 77–78.
25. *United Nations Security Council Official Records, 1088th Meeting, Nineteenth Year, 5 February, 1964*, p. 14.
26. Arthur Bemon Tourtellot, 'Kashmir: Dilemma of a People Adrift,' *Saturday Review*, 6 March 1965.
27. Ayub Khan, *Friends Not Masters*, p. 130.
28. For an in-depth study of different aspects of the Kashmir problem, see Robert G. Wirsing, *India, Pakistan and the Kashmir Dispute*, New York: St. Martin's Press, 1994; and Pauline Dawson, *The Peacekeepers of Kashmir: The UN Military Observer Group in India and Pakistan*, Bombay: Popular Prakashan, 1995.
29. For details, see Safdar Mahmood, *Pakistan Divided*, Lahore: Jang Publishers, 1990, chapter on 'Indian Involvement'.
30. *Pakistan Times*, 10 March 1951. See Liaquat's speech.
31. Mushtaq Ahmad, *Government and Politics*, p. 107.
32. Ibid.
33. Ibid., p. 108.
34. Liaquat Ali Khan, *Pakistan: The Heart of Asia*, Oxford Printing Press, 1951, pp. 15–16.
35. Ibid., p. 11.
36. *Pakistan Times*, 10 March 1951. See Liaquat's speech.
37. Mushtaq Ahmad, *Government and Politics*, p. 111.
38. Ibid., p. 112.
39. Prime Minister's broadcast to the nation, 1 October 1954. See *Dawn*, 2 October 1954.
40. Ayub Khan, *Friends Not Masters,* p. 132.
41. Sayeed, *Politics in Pakistan*, p. 269.
42. Ayub Khan, *Friends Not Masters*, p. 155.
43. *The New York Times*, 29 August 1965.
44. Ayub Khan, *Friends Not Masters*, p. 156.
45. Sayeed, *Politics in Pakistan*, p. 271.
46. Ayub Khan, *Friends Not Masters*, p. 132.
47. Ibid., p. 156.
48. *Mutual Security Act of 1958. Hearing before House Committee on Foreign Relations, 85th Congress, Second Session, 15–16 April 1958*, Washington DC, p. 1753.
49. Sarwar Hassan, *Pakistan and the United Nations*, p. 73.
50. Selig S. Harrison, *India and the United states*, New York: 1961, pp. 28–64.

51. National Assembly of Pakistan, *Debate 1*, No.12, 27 June 1962, pp. 621-22.
52. L.F. Rushbrook Williams, *The State of Pakistan*, London: Faber, 1966, p. 126.
53. Ayub Khan, *Friends Not Masters*, p. 134.
54. Ibid., p. 135.
55. Ibid., p. 136.
56. Ibid.
57. Ibid., p. 158.
58. Ibid., p. 118.
59. Rafique Akhtar, *Pakistan Year Book*, p. 102.
60. *The Round Table*, September 1963, p. 396, Quoted in Sarwar Hassan, ed., *Pakistan Horizon*, Karachi: Institute of International Affairs, p. 43.
61. Ibid.
62. Rushbrook Williams, *The State of Pakistan*, p. 126.
63. Ayub Khan, *Friends Not Masters*, p. 159.
64. Ibid.
65. Ibid., p. 158.
66. Rafique Akhtar, *Pakistan Year Book*, p. 103.
67. *Dawn*, 20 December 1962.
68. *Pakistan Times*, 8 November 1970.
69. *Dawn*, 7 April 1971.
70. Ibid.
71. *The Guardian Weekly*, 15 May 1971.
72. S.M. Burke, *Pakistan's Foreign Policy*, Karachi: Oxford University Press, 1973, p. 406.
73. Richard Nixon, 'A Report to the Congress', 9 February 1972. Also see An Interview with the president: 'The Jury is Out', *Time*, 3 January 1972.
74. *Official Records of the Fifth Session of the General Assembly*, 1950, p. 97.
75. Mushtaq Ahmad, *government and Policitcs*, p. 59.
76. Ibid.
77. Statement of Muhammad Ali Bogra, National Assembly of Pakistan, *Debate*, vol. 1, no. 12, 27 June 1962, pp. 622-23.
78. Mushtaq Ahmad, *Government and Politics*, p. 61.
79. *The Morning News*, 31 May 1960.
80. Ayub Khan, *Friends Not Masters*, p. 162.
81. *The Pakistan Observer*, 19 November 1959. See President Ayub's interview with *Daily Mail* correspondent.
82. *United Nations Security Council Official Records, 1114th Meeting, Nineteenth year, 11 May, 1964*, S/PV. 1114, pp. 11-12.
83. Ayub Khan, *Friends Not Masters*, p. 164.
84. Rushbrook Williams, *The State of Pakistan*, p. 123.

85. *Dawn*, 24 February 1964.
86. *Peking Review*, 11 March 1965, pp. 9–10.
87. Mushtaq Ahmad, *Government and Politics*, p. 63
88. Ibid., p. 64.
89. *The Pakistan Observer*, 17 April 1966.
90. *The Pakistan Times*, 25 March 1971.
91. Ibid., 13 April 1971.
92. Rafique Akhtar, *Pakistan Year Book*, p. 96.
93. Mushtaq Ahmad, *Government and Politics*, p. 50.
94. Ayub Khan, *Friends Not Masters*, p. 169.
95. *New York Times*, 13 April 1950.
96. *Dawn*, 31 March 1954
97. *Dawn*, 10 December 1956.
98. Mushtaq Ahmad, *Government and Politics*, p. 51
99. Ibid., p. 52.
100. *New Times*, no. 50, 1962.
101. *Dawn*, 26 June 1963.
102. Ayub Khan, *Friends Not Masters*, p. 169.
103. Ibid., p. 171
104. *Pravada*, 9 May 1965.
105. G.W. Chaudhury, *India, Pakistan, Bangladesh and Major Powers*, New York: The Free Press, 1975, p. 57.
106. Rafique Akhtar, *Pakistan Year Book*, p. 100.
107. Ibid., p. 61.
108. *The Pakistan Times*, 11 July 1969.
109. Robert Jackson, *South Asian Crisis: India-Pakistan-Bangladesh*, London: Chatto and Windus, 1975 p. 39.
110. Ibid., p. 71.
111. J. A. Nik in his book, *Russia, China and Bangladesh* has discussed the background to this treaty and its character.
112. *Asian Recorder*, 1971, p. 10501.
113. *The Daily Telegraph*, 7 December 1971.
114. *The Sunday Times*, 9 December 1971. See Henry Brandson's report.
115. *President Nixon's Foreign Policy Report to the American Congress*, 9 February 1972.
116. *The Times*, 6 November 1971.
117. *Dawn,* 10 December 1971. Also *Daily Telegraph*, 28 December 1971.
118. *The New York Times*, 31 March 1972. Also the *Herald Tribune*, 17 January 1972.
119. Kuldip Nayyar, *The Distant Neighbours*, p. 181.
120. The PCNA Commentary, *Dawn*, 12 December 1971.
121. *International Herald Tribune*, 14 February 1972.
122. Z.A. Bhutto, *The Myth of Independence*, Karachi: Oxford University Press, 1969, p. 13.

123. *International Herald Tribune*, 14 February 1972.
124. *The Pakistan Times*, 20 December 1972.
125. *Kayhan International*, 30 September 1974.
126. Bhutto said: 'We achieved still greater mutual understanding. We hope opportunities have been created for further improving Soviet-Pak relations'. *The Christian Science Monitor*, 6 November 1974.
127. *Patriot*, 28 May 1976.
128. Ibid.
129. *The Kabul Times*, 7 June 1976.
130. Ibid., 12 June 1976.
131. *The Hindu*, 2 August 1976.
132. Ibid.
133. *Dawn*, 6 August 1975.
134. *Patriot*, 15 August 1976.
135. *The Hindu*, 2 August 1976.
136. *Nawa-i-Waqt*, 9 May 1978.
137. *The Guardian*, 24 March 1979.
138. *General Assembly Official Records, 92nd Plenary Meeting*, 30 September 1947.
139. Ayub Khan, *Friends Not Masters*, p. 174–75.
140. Safdar Mahmood, *International Affairs*, p. 234.
141. Rafique Akhtar, *Pakistan Year Book*, p. 113.
142. Cited in Burke, *Pakistan's Foreign Policy*, p. 67.
143. *Dawn*, 27 September 1956.
144. Ayub Khan, *Friends Not Masters*, p. 155.
145. Mushtaq Ahmad, *Government and Politics*, p. 72.
146. Safdar Mahmood, *International Affairs*, p. 233.
147. Burke, *Pakistan's Foreign Policy*, p. 360.
148. Zahid Malik, ed., *Pakistan After 1971*, Rawalpindi: 1974. Also see Agha Shahi, *New Dimensions in Foreign Policy*, p. 22.
149. See Press conference of Prime Minister Z.A. Bhutto, *Pakistan Times*, 27 December 1974.
150. *All India Radio*, 4 October 1974.
151. *Dawn*, 15 May 1974.
152. *The Morning News*, 11 August 1974.
153. *The Jang*, 23 September 1974.
154. *The Muslim*, 21 February 1983.
155. *The Muslim*, 15 September 1981. See article by Mushahid Hussain.
156. *The Muslim*, 19 February 1983.
157. *The Muslim*, 15 September 1981. See article by Mushahid Hussain.
158. *The Muslim*, 19 February 1983. See article by Mushahid Hussain.
159. *The Muslim*, 9 April 1984.
160. *The Economist*, 27 March–April 1982.
161. *Dawn*, 16 July 1982.

162. *The Washington Post*, 3 December 1981.

163. Lawrence Ziring, 'South Asian Tangles and Triangles' in Ziring, ed., *Subcontinent in World Politics*, p. 24.

164. *The Muslim*, 19 February 1983. See article by Mushahid Hussain.

165. *The Muslim*, 20 February 1983. See article by Mushahid Hussain.

166. *Dawn*, 5 April 1983.

167. Ibid.

168. Quoted in M. Raziullah Azmi, 'Pakistan-US Relations', *Pakistan Horizon*, 3rd quarter, 1983, pp. 43–44.

169. Ibid.

170. *The Muslim*, 1 January 1984. See article by Hasan Askari Rizvi.

171. *The Muslim*, 20 February 1983.

172. Radio Tehran Broadcast, 2 September 1980.

173. *The Muslim*, 14, 15 May 1984.

174. *The Muslim*, 2 January 1986, 'Pakistan's Foreign Policy in 1986'.

175. Ibid., 15 May 1988, 'Geneva Accord: Fears Overshadow Hopes'.

176. *The Nation*, 30 May 1988.

177. *The Muslim*, 12 June 1988.

178. Ibid., 15 April, 1988 See article by Gulbadin Hikmatyar in special supplement on Geneva Accord.

179. *The Nation*, 17 April 1988. Also see statement by Syed Hashim, former Vice-Chancellor, Kabul University.

180. *The Muslim*, 3 January 1986. See article on Foreign Policy.

181. Rafique Akhtar, ed., *Pakistan Year Book, 1987-88*, Karachi: East and West Publishing Company, 1988, p. 267.

182. Hasan Askari Rizvi, 'Pakistan and the Post-Cold War Environment', in Craig Baxter and Charles H. Kennedy, eds., *Pakistan: 1997* Boulder, Co.: Westview Press, 1997, pp. 38–39.

183. S. M. Burke and Lawrence Ziring, *Pakistan's Foreign Policy*, 2nd edn., Karachi: Oxford University Press, 1990, p. 463.

184. Burke & Ziring, *Pakistan's foreign Policy*, p. 470.

185. Rafique Akhtar, ed., *Pakistan Year Book: 1991–92*, 19th edn., Karachi: East and West Publishing Company, 1992, p. 246.

186. *The News*, 9 April 1991. *The Nation*, 5 April 1991. *The Muslim*, 5 October 1991.

187. M. Raziullah Azmi, ed., *Pakistan-America Relations: The Recent Past*, Karachi: Royal Book Company, 1994, pp. 92–93.

188. Rafique Akhtar, *Pakistan Year Book*, p. 219.

189. Ibid., p. 236.

190. Ibid., p. 238.

191. Ibid., p. 239.

192. Rafique Akhtar, *Pakistan Year Book: 1992–93*, 20th edn., Karachi: East amd West Publishing Company, 1993, p. 280.

193. Ibid., p. 332.

194. Rafique Akhtar, *Pakistan Year Book: 1991–92*, p. 235.
195. Ibid., pp. 279-80.
196. Ibid., p. 279.
197. Ibid., p. 285.
198. Rafique Akhtar, *Pakistan Year Book: 1992–93*, p. 259.
199. Rafique Akhtar, *Pakistan Year Book: 1991–92*, p. 221.
200. Ibid., p. 222.
201. Rafique Akhtar, *Pakistan Year Book: 1992–93*, p. 296.
202. The statement of a senior official of the ministry of finance. See Saeed Shafqat, *Civil-Military Relations in Pakistan: From Zulfikar Ali Bhutto to Benazir Bhutto*, Boulder, Co.: Westview Press, 1997, p. 245.
203. For an incisive and informative analysis on the Taliban rise and possible involvement of Pakistan, see, Ahmed Rashid, 'Road to Disaster,' *The Herald*, November 1996, pp. 74–77. Also see Ikram Sehgal, 'Among the Taliban,' *The Nation*, 19 November 1996.
204. Tahir Amin, 'How to Resolve Kashmir Issue', pp. 145–146.
205. *The Nation*, various issues from 18 October to 30 October 1995.
206. Ibid., pp. 40–41.
207. Rafique Akhtar, *Pakistan Year Book; 1994–95*, 22th edn, Karachi: East and West Publishing Company, 1995, p. 265.
208. Ibid., p. 268.
209. Ibid., p. 274.
210. Ibid., pp. 287–288.
211. Pakistan Ministry of Information and Broadcasting, *Pakistan: 1995: An Official Handbook*, Islamabad: Directorate General of Films and Publications, 1995, pp. 31–32.
212. Sartaj Aziz, 'Pakistan More Secure than Ever Before', *Pakistan Times*, 1 January 1999, p. 1.
213. *Dawn*, 6 January 1999, p. 13.
214. Hasan Askari Rizvi, *Pakistan and the Post-Cold War Environment*, p. 57.
215. See on sub-regional co-operation, Maqbool Ahmad Bhatti, 'foreign Policy Imperatives', *Dawn*, 3 March 1997.
216. 'Press Review', Defence and Media Publications, August 1998, p. 5.
217. Mahdi Masud, 'India Factor in Foreign Policy', *Dawn*, 8 January 1998. 'To delink Kashmir from other areas of co-operation, as suggested in certain quarters, would be to shelve Kashmir indefinitely, in line with India's diplomatic objectives. Popular movements and democratic struggles cannot be switched on and off like a mechanical contrivance'.
218. Hasan Askari Rizvi, *Pakistan and the Post-Cold War Environment*, pp. 55–56.
219. For details, see *Dawn*, 20 and 30 December 1998.
220. Hasan Askari Rizvi, *Pakistan and the Post-Cold War Environment*, p. 49.
221. Ibid., p. 50.
222. *Dawn*, 22 April 1999.

5

THE DILEMMA OF DEMOCRACY

The philosophical foundations of democracy rest on the notions of popular sovereignty, participatory governance, and rule with consent. The power to form and change a government lies with the citizens who elect their representatives for setting up a government. Such a government is accountable to the people through their representatives who have the ultimate power to change it. Democracy also calls for equality of opportunities and protection of law for all citizens irrespective of caste, creed, region, and religion. It allows freedom of expression and a right to set up political and other organizations within the framework of law and respect for dissent. The often-quoted classical definition of democracy as the 'government of the people, by the people, and for the people' attaches much importance to participatory governance and political management. This definition implies that the state should be governed by the people or their representatives for serving them. A government that is unable to reflect the apsirations and collective will of the people can not be described as democratic. The will of the people is ascertained in a democratic system through a participatory and electoral process as set out in the constitution of the country concerned. The constitution of a democratic state is based on the general consensus of the people and is said to represent their shared aspirations for the future. A constitution that fails such a criterion can hardly serve as the foundation of a democratic system. A democratic government remains in power as long as it enjoys the confidence and trust of the parliament and the electorate. In other words, power is trust of the people with the government which has to be exercised within a defined democratic and constitutional framework. The principle of the government's ultimate responsibility to the people is the characteristic feature of a democratic polity. However, these principles are given a concrete shape in a particular socio-economic and political environment of a country. Therefore, the institutional manifestion of democracy may vary from country to country, but it must reflect the basic principles and spirit of democracy.

Democracy, Genius of the People, and Islam

The failure to establish viable democratic institutions and frequent constitutional breakdowns in Pakistan have led many to argue that democracy has failed, and that it does not suit the genius of the people of Pakistan. Many authors held the 'selfish, corrupt and incapable' leadership of Pakistan responsible for the debacle of democracy. Some writers, especially those from the West, argued that Islam which was the sheet anchor of the Pakistani political system did not encourage democratic values. 'Islam has not encouraged systematic opposition,' writes Keith Callard who also maintained that 'the vision of good government possessed by many Muslims [was] that of a people united under a strong leader and confident in the possession of certain truth.'[1]

The logic of the first argument that democracy does not suit the genius of the people is open to debate. Certainly, there is no inherent defect in the people that makes them unfit for democracy. In the past, the people were completely involved in political movements provided these movements reflected their aspirations. Though the electorate was limited during the British period, the Muslims participated in the electoral process, especially in the 1945–46 elections which the Muslim League contested with an agenda for the creation of a separate Muslim state of Pakistan. But, after the creation of Pakistan, the people were virtually excluded from active participation in the political process since political party incorporated their will and aspirations in their programmes. Their opinion was hardly ascertained on national issues. The political scene of the country was dominated either by the bureaucrats or by the politicians who were not willing to be subjected to the restraints of the democratic process. Later, the military emerged as the dominant political force. The military-bureaucratic elites manipulated politics and often destabilized the elected governments and, thus, subverted the democratic process.[2] These power elites avoided holding elections for one reason or another. The way the affairs of the state were conducted in the fifties and the sixties could, in a way, be described as democratic. It was a bureaucratic-military rule which concentrated power in the hands of a few at the top, i.e., the governor-general, the governor, and the top bureaucracy, supported by the military. The system of goverment that gradually evolved in Pakistan neither allowed the democratic values to flourish, nor did it impart political training to the masses on democratic lines.

The ideal of democracy is not questioned by most people in Pakistan. It is accepted as the desired and final destiny of the nation. The ideology of Pakistan envisaged a democratic system of government based on the tenets of Islam like equality, social justice, participation of people in the affairs of state, consultation, and accountability of the rulers. The assumption that democracy has failed in Pakistan is, therefore, not justified. In fact, democracy, in the real sense of the word, was never introduced in this country. The people never developed a sense of participation in the government. General elections to the national legislature were not held until 1970. The people were deliberately kept out of government which had become an exclusive domain of a privileged elite. Politics was nothing more than a power struggle amongst the self-seeking leaders hankering after offices. In these circumstances, how could the genius of people be tested?

There can be no disagreement on the fact that the politicians, with a few honourable exceptions, were corrupt and the political parties suffered from serious organizational problems. They did not strike roots among the masses. The self-styled leaders reduced parliamentary institutions to a farce. Eventually, their intrigues, changing loyalties, and floor-crossing created the conditions that led to the collapse of parliamentary government in Pakistan. If general elections had been held at regular intervals, most of these political leaders would have been eliminated from the political landscape and the rest would have been left with no option but to amend their ways. Democracy lays down certain principles such as equality, accountability, justice, liberty, and responsibility, for the governance of a country. Any form of government, whether parliamentary or presidential, based on these principles, can be called democratic. If these principles are thrown overboard by the leaders, the people can not be declared unfit for democracy.

As for the attribution of problems of democracy to Pakistan's identification with Islam and the argument that there are contradictions between Islam and democracy, it seems these contentions are based on certain misunderstandings. Islam expounded the concept of an elected ruler, governance with consultation, and accountability of the ruler. These basic notions of an Islamic system are recognized by all. If the people in power failed to create institutions and processes that reflected these values, their incompetence at managing the affairs is to be blamed rather than Islam as a set of principles and a value system. Islam is not a hinderance to creating a democratic and participatory system. The people in power in Muslim states may have their power motives to establish personalized and authoritarian or dictatorial regime but still claim to subscribe to Islamic values. In reality, they are violating the tenets of Islam so far as governance and political management is concerned.

Democracy can still be rehabilitated in Pakistan provided political institutions are allowed to flourish freely. The socio-economic conditions in India were not very different from those in Pakistan at the time of the partition of the subcontinent. If the Muslim League established an undisputed rule in Pakistan, the Congress became the undisputed master of India. Then, how is it that the parliamentary form of government has worked successfully in India, while it met a tragic fate in Pakistan? The answer to this lies in a comparative study of the leaderships and the political processes of the two countries.

Major Problems and Issues of Democracy

The poor track record of democracy and the difficulties the parliamentary system of government faced in Pakistan can be attributed to a host of factors including the void of leadership after the demise of Quaid-i-Azam Muhammad Ali Jinnah, the lack of character among the political leaders, decline and degeneration of the Muslim League that had led the independence movement, weak and disorganized party systems which lacked clear-cut programmes that could inspire people, the domination of the political process by the feudal and other traditional elite who had little faith in democracy, unnecessary intervention of the head of the state in the day-to-day affairs of the state, the rise of the bureaucracy and the military to power, imposition of martial laws, and the absence of fair and free elections. One will have to examine Pakistan's political history in order to understand how these factors adversely affected the prospects of democracy.

The Constituent Assembly of Pakistan (1947–54, 1955–56) performed two major functions, that is, constitution-making and serving as a legislature under the parliamentary system; it was responsible for setting up a government. It failed badly in performing these functions. It took a long time, probably the longest, in producing a constitution, which could have been done in a year or so. By avoiding direct elections, the Constitutent Assembly lost its legitimacy and was unable to assert its role in the political system. 'Having rendered itself unrepresentative through lapse of time, the governments it supported in office were not responsible governments. Control of the majority in the House was not secured through popular policies and programmes, but by bestowing ministerial offices and pecuniary benefits on the members... That nearly one-third of the ministers between 1947 and 1954 were drawn from outside the Assembly indicated the poverty of talent in the Assembly'.[3] The members took little interest in legislative work and were more interested in enjoying the benefits of power. 'Sixteen of the twenty-eight ministers became ambassadors, governors and governors-general in the lifetime of the Assembly, only half a dozen of them continued to be in politics, one of whom (Sardar Amir Azim Khan) had an astonishingly unbroken record of cabinet membership from the day he was made a minister in December 1953, up to 7 October 1958, save for a brief interlude of a few months.'[4]

Quaid-i-Azam Muhammad Ali Jinnah, who led the Muslim League and the movement for the establishment of Pakistan, had a firm faith in democracy. As early as 1943, he remarked that 'democracy is in our blood, it is in our marrows'.[5] The Muslim League was a weak organization until 1936 when Jinnah took its control after returning from England. He put a new life in the Muslim League and his devotion to the Muslim cause won him a unique place in Muslim history. The demand for the separate state of Pakistan infused a new spirit in the League which emerged as the most influential Muslim party in India. During this period, the Muslims were resisting opposition from two fronts, that is, the Hindus and the British imperialists. This was hardly a time for imparting political training to the people. The Muslim masses, who were mostly uneducated, but were infused with the spirit of freedom, began taking active part in politics. They had absolute faith in the League and the leadership of the Quaid-i-Azam. A large number of Muslim leaders joined the League quite late and only when they became sure of the establishment of Pakistan. Their commitment to the Muslim League was not deep rooted; they wanted to make best use of the opportunities the new state of Pakistan was to offer. They did not have the necessary commitment or experience so essential for running a parliamentary system of government. In the absence of a committed and experienced leadership and vigilant public opinion, a shadow was cast at the very outset on the future parliamentary system.

Jinnah became the first Governor-General and played an active role in running the state affairs. He presided over the cabinet meetings and his advice was, for all practical purposes, considered binding by the cabinet members. He enjoyed such a popularity and confidence of the people that he was, remarked Keith Callard, 'the personification of the state'.[6] He did not derive this authority from the office of Governor-General but from his popularity among the people and from his role as the Father of the Nation. He kept the people of East Pakistan silent over the question of national language and even the separation of Karachi from Sindh could not provoke any agitation'.[7] His sudden death on 11 September 1948 created a void which could not be filled. He was a firm believer in democracy. Had he lived, the democratic institutions would have grown and flourished under his patronage. 'If he had not died then, but lived for another ten years... almost certainly Pakistan's bad years—the period between 1952 and 58 would not have shaped themselves as they did.'[8]

Before the emergence of Pakistan, the Muslim League had a lofty mission and a positive programme. It rallied the Muslim masses and mobilized their energies for the achievement of their common goal. After the establishment of Pakistan, the League became the ruling party. Gradually, it lost touch with the common man and got deeply involved in power politics. Since there was no leader or a common programme to keep the party united, it was soon divided into different factions. Their internal feuding created great mistrust and frustration amongst the people. The League was rightly criticized for snapping its ties with the people.[9] 'Yet this mighty movement sank into limbo after liberation.'[10] Had the League kept itself in touch with the people and gained their support to implement its programme, it would have sustained its support and educated public opinion on national issues. But the League discouraged political activity and placed restrictions on political freedom. As a result, positive political traditions like freedom of the press, speech, a healthy opposition, and vigilant public opinion could not develop, and the ruling elite isolated themselves from the electorate. As no credible political organization was encouraged to function, 'the death of the Muslim League marked the end of the political process.'[11]

Democratic traditions which play an important role in the working of a parliamentary system were rarely encouraged in Pakistan. The Quaid-i-Azam set a democratic precedent by stepping down as president of the League when he was elected the governor-general of Pakistan. He said that as the head of the state, he should not have affiliations with any political organization because he had to look after the interests of all sections of people.[12] The idea was to maintain the neutrality of the governor-general and to allow the Muslim League to pursue its political activities independently and without official interference. It was also decided that the ministers should not hold offices in the organization of the League. It was expected that the Muslim League, being an independent body, would keep a check on the activities of the parliamentary party and the ministers. This practice would have served as a great restraint on the activities of the politicians, but Liaquat Ali Khan, who was elected president of the League after amending the party's constitution, discontinued this practice.[13] This step retarded the growth of an autonomous party organization and undermined the democratic values. Gradually the Muslim League became a handmaiden of the government and its image as an independent party faded.

The weakness of the League encouraged the governor-general to import leaders from outside the country and to impose them on the party. The League always accepted them with open arms. Muhammad Ali Bogra, who was the ambassador of Pakistan in the USA, was appointed prime minister by Governor-General Ghulam Muhammad, and was readily elected its leader by the Muslim League. Likewise, Chaudhri Muhammad Ali accepted leadership of the League after his appointment as the prime minister. This was entirely against the spirit of a parliamentary system of government. The essence of the parliamentary system is that the leader of the majority party is invited to form the government. But, in Pakistan, the prime minister was usually appointed first; he was then owned by the majority party. The members of the League Parliamentary Party were always ready to join any cabinet. Since the prime minister in some cases was not an elected representative, he was not answerable to anybody. In that situation, he could enjoy neither the blessing of the people nor could he command support of the party behind him. Thus, he was no more than a nominee of the governor-general. He could remain in office during the pleasure of the head of the state, and had to resign when the latter manipulated to deprive him of the support of the party. These practices hampered the development of democratic concepts in the country and brought about political instability, which ultimately led to the failure of the parliamentary system.

Jinnah's successors lacked not only his stature but also political neutrality. Ghulam Muhammad and Iskandar Mirza both dabbled into power politics and played the part of kingmakers. Both of them rose to this elevated position from the ranks of government service. They lacked parliamentary spirit. In a democratic country where political parties are well-organized and are endowed with capable leadership, civil servants rarely hanker after high political positions. But in Pakistan, quite a number of civil servants became political leaders and filled the political vacuum created by the general incompetence of politicians and dearth of capable leadership. The bureaucrats-turned-politicians, with the exception of Chaudhri Muhammad Ali who did not try to cling to power, had litttle, if any, respect for democratic principles. The notion of representative government was an anathema to them, and their authoritarian personalized political management undermined whatever prospects existed for democracy in Pakistan. Ghulam Muhammad dismissed Prime Minister Khwaja Nazimuddin in 1953 though the latter had successfully piloted the budget in the Assembly. Ghulam Muhammad had such a strong hold on the ruling party, the Muslim League, that his nominee was readily accepted by its parliamentary group as its leader, while Nazimuddin was still the president of the party. According to the norms of the parliamentary system, the governor-general could not dismiss the prime minister as long as he enjoyed the support of the majority in the Assembly; Nazimuddin had demonstrated that by having his budget approved by the Assembly before his dismissal. Thus, by dismissing the prime minister without reference to the parliament, the governor-general flouted the established norm under the parliamentary system. 'The price of the governor-general's coup was high', remarked Keith Callard. 'Three major conventions of cabinet government had been destroyed or "gravely weakened". First, the tradition of the impartiality of the Governor-General had been demolished. Second, the convention of cabinet and party solidarity had been disregarded. Third, the role of the legislature as the maker and sustainer of governments had been impugned.'[14]

Ghulam Muhammad further undermined the foundations of the parliamentary system by dissolving the Constituent Assembly in October 1954. He dissolved the Constitutent Assembly when it was about to finalize and approve a new constitution which would have stripped the head of the state of effective powers. This delayed the formulation of the constitution for another seventeen months. It seemed that the governor-general was unhappy with the Assembly because it had passed constitutional and legislative measures for restricting the powers of the governor-general in September-October 1954; the governor-general therefore decided to get rid of the Assembly. This was a thoroughly unconstitutional step taken by the governor-general to protect his agenda of personalized rule. A head of the state is not expected to behave in such an irresponsible manner. He was not content with only this; he dismissed the government of Muhammad Ali Bogra to form the cabinet again. During the closing years of his life, Ghulam Muhammad was physically incapacitated due to prolonged illness, yet his lust for power did not diminish. He neither had regard for democratic values nor did he understand the parliamentary spirit. Like other politicians of Pakistan, he endeavoured to cling to power at any cost.

The parliamentary system faced similar problems in the provinces. The dismissal of provincial governments and the frequent imposition of governor's rule in the provinces did not leave scope for development of democratic traditions. There was too much interference of the central government in the affairs of the provinces. In West Pakistan, politics was a preserve of landlords who had secure constituencies. They were mostly ill-educated and had no interest in the welfare of the people. They were not loyal to any one party. Their only aim in life was to remain in power. Thus, there was ceaseless tussle for power among different groups led by Daultana, Noon, Mamdot, Dasti, Qizalbash, and Gurmani in Punjab; by Khuhro, Pirzada, Talpur, Fazlullah, and Rashid in Sindh; and by Qayyum Khan, Pir Manki Sharif, Sardar Rashid, Dr Khan Sahib, and Bahadar Khan in the NWFP. These feudals and Khans struck blow after blow at democracy and provided an unmistakable proof that feudalism and democracy could not coexist.

The soil of East Pakistan was fertile for democracy but certain groups of politicians, supported by religious minorities and leftists, created a situation which was not conducive to the growth of democracy.[15] The scramble for power between rival factions turned so ugly that, in September 1958, the speaker and the deputy speaker of the East Pakistan assembly were assaulted by the members; the deputy speaker received serious injuries and later died in the hospital. The political situation in East Pakistan had been so uncertain since April 1958 that two ministries were overthrown by the legislature in less than a week. The Sarkar ministry did not last for more than three days. As a consequence, parliamentary government was suspended and the president's rule imposed. 'But, did it necessarily mean,' remarked G.W. Chaudhry, 'that the scroll of democracy should be rolled up in Pakistan? Were there by such serious challenges and threats to democracy as to make it unworkable? Before we answer these questions, it must be borne in mind that the ways of democracy are often slow'.[16] Democracy is always a slow process and 'people can not bring democracy into being by a sudden change of attitude. Democracy attains its fuller development after many experiments, some of which may be abortive,'[17] but it should not cause disappointment.

In the centre, Maj.-Gen. Iskandar Mirza, another bureaucrat with an army background, who succeeded Ghulam Muhammad as governor-general in 1955, was no better as far as his attitutde towards representative system of government was concerned. He was a strong advocate of 'Controlled Democracy'[18] for ensuring order and stability in the polity. It was not therefore surprising that he flouted parliamentary conventions and, like his predecessor, tried to dominate and manipulate the political process. He was an expert in palace intrigues and played one political faction against another. During his tenure (1955–58), the civil service attained great ascendancy and corruption increased manifold. Again, it was mainly due to his efforts that the Republican Party emerged overnight as a rival to the Muslim League in the Centre and in West Pakistan. Iskandar Mirza was determined to keep Dr Khan Sahib in power as the chief minister of West Pakistan despite his dubious political career. It cannot be doubted that the creation of Republican Party by Dr Khan Sahib was a direct consequence of Iskandar Mirza's intrigue, with the collaboration of the provincial governor, Mushtaq Ahmad Gurmani.[19] Strangely enough, the Republican Party was never tested in an election. It was a child of palace intrigue and remained in power with the blessings of the president who never hesitated to use unconstitutional means to support Dr Khan Sahib. The report of the constitution commission, instituted in 1960 by the former President Ayub Khan, also took the view that one of the reasons of the breakdown of the 1956 constitution was interference by the head of the state in the political proces.[20]

Iskandar Mirza wanted to perpetuate himself in power and, for the achievement of this purpose; he indulged in all types of intrigues. The National Assembly consisted of eighty members who were divided into nine political parties. None of the parties had a clear majority. In these circumstances, there was no alternative but to form a coalition government. But history bears witness to the fact that a coalition government in a country where political parties are not well-organized invariably tends to be weak. As a result, swift change of government becomes a permanent feature of such a political setup. Chaudhri Muhammad Ali (prime minister, 1955–56) had to make many compromises for framing the constitution at the cost of democratic traditions. He supported Dr Khan Sahib in West Pakistan against the mandate of his party, appointed Fazlul Haq as the governor of East Pakistan to prolong the life of the Sarkar ministry, and allowed the United Front to remain in office in East Pakistan for a whole year without facing the assembly.[21] All this can not be conceived in a truly democratic country. Anyhow, he could not stay as prime minister for more than a year because he developed differences with the Muslim League. Suhrawardy who succeeded Chaudhri Muhammad Ali in 1956, had to resign after a year, because the Republican Party withdrew its support to him.[22] Chundrigar became the next premier in 1957 but his government could not last more than a few weeks due to the betrayal of the Republican Party. Then the Republican Party came to the helm of power under Malik Firoz Khan Noon in December 1957. He increased the strength of his cabinet to twenty-six in a house of eighty members to make his position secure, but it remained uncertain. He was the leader of a party which had never contested an election or gained the confidence of the people. Iskandar Mirza thus took full advantage of the weakness of the parties. The only way to eliminate this uncertain situation was to hold general elections. Several unrepresentative parties would have been removed from the political scene through this democratic process. But Iskandar Mirza and the prime ministers who rose to power between 1956 and 1958 delayed the elections for one reason or another. The nation demanded general elections but Iskandar Mirza continued to postpone it. Meanwhile, Khan Qayyum Khan was elected president of the Muslim League. He was given a historic welcome when he visited Gujrat in an election campaign. On the other hand, Suhrawardy was planning to forge an alliance between major groups in East and West Pakistan. He had promised his support to Firoz Khan for the post of president after the general elections.[23] The growing popularity of the

Muslim League and the prospects of an alliance between the Awami League and Punjabi groups meant that there was no possibility of Mirza's re-election as the president. This was not acceptable to him. He conspired with the commander-in-chief of the army, General Muhammad Ayub Khan, and declared Martial Law on 7 October 1958. With one stroke of his pen, Iskandar Mirza turned the whole country into a graveyard of the dream of establishing democracy in Pakistan. What Iskandar Mirza proposed for himself, God disposed. He had to quit on 27 October 1958, and General Ayub Khan assumed presidency.

The Constitution of 1956 was abrogated on the plea that it was based on compromises and generated instability. As regards the first part of this statement, the geopolitical realities of the country are such that no constitution can be framed here without making compromises. Nor is there any harm in it. For that matter, the constitution of any country has to be based on compromises. Turning to the second part of the statement, it can be said that the 1956 Constitution was not responsible for the instability of governments. Its germs could be found in the lack of character amongst the politicians, the unrepresentative nature of political parties, ineffective public opinion, ascendancy of bureaucracy to power, and delay in holding the general elections. These factors, and not the 1956 Constitution, generated instability. The constitution, in fact, was neither worked nor seriously followed by the politicians. Khalid Bin Sayeed has rightly remarked: 'Now that Pakistan had produced a constitution, one could see that the basic weakness of its political system was not the lack of a constitution but the absence of national political parties without which no democratic system could function.'[24]

Ayub Khan rightly diagnosed the major causes for the instability in Pakistan in his broadcast to the nation on 8 October 1958.

Ever since the death of the Quaid-i-Azam and Liaquat Ali Khan, politicians started a free-for-all type of fighting in which no holds were barred. They waged ceaseless and bitter war against each other regardless of the ill effects on the country, just to whet their appetites. There has been no limit to the depth of their baseness, chicanery, deceit, and degradation. Having nothing constructive to offer, they used provincial feelings, sectarian, religious, and racial differences to set a Pakistani against a Pakistani... The result is total administrative, economic, political and moral chaos in the country.[25]

Ayub's diagnosis was that the politicians were no better than demagogues. He, therefore, disqualified the old politicians under the Elective Bodies Disqualification Order, 1959 (EBDO) and barred them from associating with the activities of a political party up to 31 December 1966. The Ayub regime also amassed enormous powers under martial law (1958–1962) and under the 1962 constitution to suppress the freedom of the press and to control political activities effectively.[26] This further undermined the prospects of democracy.

Ayub spoke of a democracy, which could suit the genius of the people. His concept of democracy found expression in the shape of Basic Democracy, which, in fact, was more basic than democratic. Under this system, a limited number of basic democrats decided the fate of the nation. They elected the president and the members of the provincial and national assemblies, which made it easy to 'bribe and buy' the voters. The common man could develop no sense of participation in the country's affairs. The political leaders and parties were not obliged to keep in touch with the masses. No wonder, the gulf between the government and the people further widened.

Under the system of Basic Democracy, the president seemingly attained stability and security. In fact, Ayub Khan went further and established an autocratic rule in the country with the help of the civil service. In the presidential election of 1965 there are instances to prove that the whole administrative machinery helped him against Fatima Jinnah. Through threats and intimidation, the district officers captured votes for Ayub Khan and his followers. On the other hand, he imposed restrictions on the press, on political activity, and on freedom of expression. For quite a long time, fundamental rights were denied to the people. The 1962 Constitution virtually made Ayub Khan a dictator. Contrary to all democratic principles, this constitution was never put to a referendum. Thus, it left no scope for democratic institutions to flourish.

By the end of 1968, the public resentment against the undemocratic rule of Ayub Khan touched the boiling point. The people came out in the streets and launched a mass movement against his government. Demonstrations and agitation engulfed the whole country. Law and order broke down and the government was practically paralyzed. Ayub Khan offered some political concession as a compromise, i.e. not to seek re-election, resotration of the parliamentary system of government, and direct elections. However, it was too late and the political forces were not prepared to accept anything less than the resignation of President Ayub Khan. After having failed to calm down the political situation, Ayub Khan decided to step down on 25 March 1969, but he handed over power to the army chief, General A.M. Yahya Khan, rather than following the procedure laid down in the constitution he himself had given to the country.

The major cause of the mass agitation against the Ayub regime was the absence of a sense of participation amongst the people in governmental affairs. Although the country had made good progress on the economic front, the people gradually realized that they had been deprived of political freedom. The result of the 1965 presidential election in favour of Ayub Khan convinced the people that there was hardly any possibility of change of leadership or of restoration of the parliamentary system of government under the existing arrangements. Gradually, alienation mounted and reached a level towards the end of 1968 that Ayub Khan's system could not withstand the pressure. As it was not geared to cope with popular pressure, an attempt was made to contain it through the use of state apparatus, but it backfired. Ayub Khan's system collapsed altogether.

General Yahya Khan who succeeded Ayub Khan, ruled this country for more than two years (March 1969–December 1971) under the cover of martial law. In all, the country remained under army rule for more than thirteen years out of twenty-five years. Had the politicians been sincere, Pakistan would have escaped army rule.

Looking back at the political balance sheet, it can be concluded that democracy in the real sense of the word was never introduced or practised in Pakistan. For most of this period, the country was under a 'bureaucratic-cum-parliamentary' rule or under a military rule. Though Jinnah had made it clear in 1943 that there would be adult franchise in Pakistan[27], the elections were delayed unnecessarily and a system of controlled democracy and indirect elections was introduced. Democratic institutions were never allowed to grow freely. From 1947 to 1958 not a single national election was held because most of the politicians knew that the electorates would disown them. Between 1958 and 1968, two indirect elections were held which were not free from official interference. Thus, the people were deliberately kept out of the political process. They never got an opportunity to decide their fate. It is, therefore, not justified to blame them for the debacle of democracy. They still cherish the ideal of democracy and have persistently revolted against undemocratic regimes.

For the first time in the history of Pakistan, general elections on the basis of adult franchise were held in 1970. There was no doubt that the election took place in a democratic atmosphere. The people showed keen interest and took active part in the political activity, which confirmed that they believed in democracy. Like other advanced democratic countries, the people of Pakistan listened to the political leaders on radio, television, and in public meetings with great interest. Even in the rural areas where most of the population was uneducated and was still the victim of the feudal system, great political activity was witnessed. In short, the fact that the people on the whole took active interest in politics proved that they considered themselves to be fit for a democratic system.

As regards political parties, all of them issued manifestos and made all possible efforts to propagate their programmes. The leaders toured every corner of the country and tried to establish direct contact with the masses.

The People's Party had emerged as the majority party in West Pakistan (post-1971 Pakistan) with clear majority in Punjab and Sindh. It is interesting to note that the Muslim League, the oldest party which was also supported by the feudal lords and industrialists, could not capture more than a few seats. On the other hand, the People's Party, which represented the political left and stood for socialism, emerged as the majority party. Most of its candidates were from the 'black horses', middle class families and without any prominent political background. Like all other advanced countries, the people in Pakistan voted for the programme and leadership of the party rather than for familiar candidates. In this way, the first general elections broke the old chains of feudalism and class system in Pakistan. The people of Pakistan displayed great political maturity which proved that they were capable of running political institutions. So the responsibility for the failure of democracy prior to 1970 lay with the political leaders who imposed the system which suited their interest, not with the masses who were never given the chance to express their will. If free elections were held at regular intervals and democratic institutions were allowed to function, the future of democracy in Pakistan would have been as bright as in other developing countries.

The break-up of Pakistan in 1971 once again underlined the importance of a democratic system for keeping the diversified societies intact. The root cause was the the sense of depriviation that developed in East Pakistan over time due to non-availability of opportunities for political participation to the Bengalis in policy making at the national level. Their under-representation in all sectors of administration, economic deprivation, and the suppression of the democratic process excluded the Bengalis from the decision-making process, which created much frustration and alienation among them. In a country like Pakistan, no region or section of population should be neglected by the power elite; all should be provided with equal political and economic opportunities to become part of the national mainstream. It is only in a democratic system that these goals become realizable. People from different regions and sections develop a sense of participation only if they are adequately represented in the national institutions, especially the national legislature. The absence of such opportunities contributed to the separation of East Pakistan. Even for the future, all the regions and sections of population should have equal opportunities to take part in the political process and the state must work towards overcoming economic disparities and social and economic under-development so that the people of all regions of Pakistan develop a strong sense of attachment with the state and the political process.

With the separation of East Pakistan on 16 December 1971, General Yahya Khan was left with no choice but to hand over power to the Pakistan People's Party (PPP) which had, as stated above, captured the largest number of seats in West Pakistan (now Pakistan) in the National Assembly and a clear majority in the Provincial Assemblies of Punjab and Sindh. At first, an interim constitution was approved by the National Assembly which replaced martial law on 21 April 1972. Within one year, a new constitution was unanimously adopted by the national assembly which became operative from 14 August 1973; this is referred to as the 1973 Constitution. The 1973 Constitution introduced the parliamentary system, guaranteed fundamental rights, and envisaged independence of judiciary. It also provided sufficient provincial autonomy to the provinces and created a framework for participatory governance. The return of Pakistan to democracy engendered much hope that it would soon overcome its problems and create a viable and democratic system. However, these hopes were soon dashed to ground.

The constitution was not allowed to operate in accordance with its spirit. It was flouted by the leadership and the party that was mainly responsible for piloting it in the National Assembly. The constitution's democratic character was compromised by introducing amendments (fourth, fifth, and sixth) which restricted political freedom and independence of judiciary. Furthermore, the government adopted an intolerant attitude towards dissent; the Opposition was harrassed and their leaders were periodically arrested; the freedom of the press was also restricted. In short, democratic traditions and political institutions were not allowed to grow.[28] As a result, the People's Party's government degenerated into a personalized dictatorship which resorted to undemocratic practices time and again. The political forces in the NWFP and Baluchistan were alienated because of the central government's frequent intervention in the provincial affairs. As tribal resistance developed against the federal authority in Baluchistan, the federal government despatched the army to suppress the challenge; this step resulted in loss of life and resources on both sides. The army brought the situation under control but the use of coercion alienated the provincial forces which felt that the federal government did not respect provincial autonomy as guaranteed in the constitution. By 1977, the government had alienated a large section of the populace in all the provinces. As the new elections were announced for March 1977, political floodgates were opened and the government faced a serious challenge from the Opposition alliance, the Pakistan National Alliance (PNA), set up in January 1977. There were serious complaints about the government's interference with the electoral process which led the PNA's decision to launch a movement for holding fresh elections with a guarantee for their transparency. As the PPP government resisted the demand, the movement for re-polling changed to a movement for resignation of Zulfikar Ali Bhutto and introduction of an Islamic system of government for ensuring socio-economic justice and fair administration. The anti-government agitation was so widespread and intense that the government was unable to cope with the situation and called out the army to re-assert its authority. This further eroded the credibility of the government. The Opposition and the government engaged in negotiations for resolving the political crisis and agreed to hold fresh elections. However, they were unable to settle the modalities for the new elections and the interim arrangements for the run up to these elections. Furthermore, some of the Opposition leaders gave clear indications that they would not oppose the overthrow of Bhutto by the military. The senior commanders took advantage of the inability of the political leaders to clinch a political arrangement to stage a coup on 5 July 1977. Martial law was proclaimed and the 1973 Constitution was suspended. Once again, the democratic experiment failed due to the misdeeds of its architects, the inability of the political leaders to manage the political crisis, and their personalized and narrow-based approach.

The repeated assumption of power by the army was a setback to the democratic process. The political governments failed one after another for varying reasons discussed above. Many analysts have concluded from this that the people of Pakistan are not capable of running the democratic process, that they lack the capabilities and the will to run such a delicate system of governance. Such a perspective is not supported by the history of Paksitan, although one can not deny that the democratic process often ran into trouble and the military rule and martial law was imposed more than once.

The people did not get adequate opportunities for political participation through the electoral process at the national level during 1954–70. The first direct general elections at the national level were held in December 1970, although provincial elections or indirect elections to the national and provincial assemblies were held in the past. In the 1970 general elections, the people voted in favour of relatively unknown candidates, rejecting the traditional leadership consisting mainly of feudal and local influentials. These votes were cast in favour of the party and its egalitarian manifesto and not in favour of personalities. Doubtless, the people voted for the PPP to achieve Islamic *musawat* (equality) and socio-economic justice. These were the signs of political maturity. Although the nation did not have a previous experience of a national general election, it showed political insight by voting for the new leadership and the party programme.

It was, of course, difficult to anticipate the future course of events. But, when the PPP flouted its own manifesto, resorting to undemocratic policies, the very same people launched a movement against the People's Party government. The ordinary people had, in the earlier elections, given proof of their political awareness by dislodging the traditional politicians and electing educated young men of middle class background. However, they were betrayed. This was unfortunate, but not unusual. It is part of the process of development of democracy. It is a learning experience for the poeple who become politically more mature and vigilant by going through the electoral process and by coping with all types of leaders and political parties.

In the 1977 general elections, the incidents of rigging shocked the people who wanted it to be a genuine opportunity to pass a judgement on the performance of the existing government and to elect a government for the future. As they felt betrayed by the rigging, they came out in the streets on the call of the Opposition leaders. Although one can not be oblivious to the fact that a number of other factors also caused this movement against the government, the violation of the sanctity of the electoral process proved to be the immediate and the most potent cause. The movement was so strong and vibrant that Bhutto's PPP, police, the Federal Security Force, and even the army could not suppress it. Several hundred people were killed or got seriously wounded in the course of the agitation. Is it not unfair to consider such a nation that is so conscious of the sanctity of elections, as incapable of democracy?

The bureaucratic-military elite who rose to power often complained about the lack of political maturity of the people and argued that they were not fit for the western democratic process. It needs to be noted here that the Quaid-i-Azam Muhammad Ali Jinnah, the founder of the state, never expressed such views; he held the people in high esteem and had confidence in their sense of judgement. He refused to accept Pakistan without consulting his people. The point in reference is the Quaid's reply to Mountbatten when the latter offered him Pakistan and wanted the Quaid to accept it immediately. Quaid's reply was that he could not accept it without prior approval of the Muslim League. Then Mountbatten said, 'You might lose your Pakistan in that case.' But the Quaid insisted on going back to his party and the people for consultation. Neither the first Prime Minister, Liaquat Ali Khan, nor any of his successors expressed any doubt about the political judgement and democratic capability of our masses.

If we go back to the freedom movement, we find that despite strong opposition from the Congress and a number of Muslim organizations and leaders, the Muslim League succeeded in establishing Pakistan because it had the support of the majority of the Muslim masses. It was this close relationship with the people and the faith of the Muslim League leadership in the ability of the Muslim masses to make the right judgement that mobilized them to such an extent that all opposition to the idea of Pakistan was neutralized. On the one hand, the Muslim League had to contend with the Congress which was well-disciplined, influential, equipped with effecitve propoganda machinery, and had the blessings of the alien ruler. On the other hand, the Muslims lacked internal cohesion and a number of Muslim groups were opposed to the Muslim League. In addition to the opposition by the Red-Shirt regiment of Khan Abdul Ghaffar Khan in the NWFP and the Congress-connected ulema, some other Islam-oriented leaders and parties were opposed to the partition of India and the establishment of Pakistan. They supported an independent but united India. If the emotional appeal of religion could influence the Muslims, then there was an army of well-disciplined intellectuals and religious scholars available to the Congress ranging from the Ahrars to Congressite Muslims led by Maulana Abul Kalam Azad. There was not a single orator of the calibre of Attaullah Shah Bokhari, the Ahrar leader. Even he had to admit that the Muslims lent their ears to him but voted for the Muslim League. The question arises, why did the Muslims respond to the clarion call of the Muslim League, rejecting the Khaksars, the Ahrar, the Jamaat-i-Islami, the Red Shirts, and the Congressite Muslim leaders? The answer is that the Muslims of India were convinced that the Muslim League was the only party that could secure their political future and lead them to independence from the British and the un-sympathetic majority community led by the Congress.

The Muslim masses fully understood the message of the Quaid. A large number of people in the rural areas had not seen the Quaid but they responded enthusiastically to his call for the establishment of Pakistan. They had developed complete confidénce in him. It was a confidence, spontaneous and extempore, which sprouted from the seeds of understanding. Will it be fair to term such Muslim masses as politically incapable? Those who, in this critical period of the history of the subcontinent, gave their verdict in favour of the Muslim League, after rejecting all other political parties, can not be considered incapable of electing true leadership. How could the Muslim League carve out an independent homeland without the popular support? If the Muslim League had not won the 1945–46 elections in the provinces and in the Centre, the British would not have recognized the Muslim League as the only party representing the Muslims of the subcontinent. Who could say that these popular decisions were emotional and erroneous? History has proved that the popular verdict in favour of Pakistan reflected political insight and maturity.

What went wrong in Pakistan was the failure of the political leaders and the political parties to shoulder their responsibilities which the democratic process bestowed on them. They failed miserably as they engaged in brute struggle for power in total disregard for the principles of democracy. The political parties were unable to perform their primary job of interest articulation and aggregation and were unable to present alternate policy framework to the people. The elections were avoided for one reason or another and the welfare of the people was neglected. All this caused much alienation among the people whose dream of a secure and better life in Pakistan did not materialize. The failure of the political leaders to play their role enabled the bureaucracy and the military to expand their role and dominate politics. Their authoritarian and centralized management gave very little attention to the need of creating a participatory system for a diversified country like Pakistan. Their emphasis was on control and management rather than political participation and responsive governance. Three martial laws (October 1958–June

1962, March 1969–April 1972, and July 1977–December 1985) further undermined the development of democracy in Pakistan and strengthened the political circles that did not favour democracy.

The military take-over by General Ziaul Haq in July 1977 was initially projected as a ninety-day operation for holding general elections. As the General consolidated his position, he changed his mind and expanded the goals of the coup. As a result, his military rule turned out to be the longest in Pakistan's history, which cast dark shadows on the political and social landscape of the country, intensified internal cleavages, and polarized the society. However, this did not erode the demand for the restoration of constitutional and democratic rule; the major political parties and other leaders of public opinion, including non-political organizations, supported this demand. The military government decided to gradually revert to the democratic process in a manner that a return to democracy did not disrupt its policies. A step-by-step policy was announced for the replacement of military rule with an elected system. At first, General Ziaul Haq got himself elected as president for five years (1985–90) through an uncontested referendum in December 1984. It is interesting to note that Ziaul Haq did not directly seek the vote of confidence. Rather, the people were asked to endorse the process of Islamization which was interpreted as the people having mandated Ziaul Haq to stay on as the elected president for five years. The official results showed a high turn-out of 62 per cent. But independent estimates were around 10 to 20 per cent, because the response of the electorate was visibly lukewarm. After having secured his future, General Ziaul Haq decided to hold non-party general elections in February 1985 and transfered power to these elected representatives in March 1985.

Pakistan's Democratic Transition

The year 1985 is an important year in Pakistan's history as it initiated the restoration of the democratic process. Since these elections were held on non-party basis, major political parties decided to boycott them. However, this did not discourage the people from the contesting elections in their individual capacity. Over twelve hundred candidates contested for the 207 National Assembly seats for the Muslims.[29] In the absence of political parties, the candidates focused on local issues and highlighted their personal qualities, including their piety and commitment to Islam. The turn-out was impressive, with 52.9 per cent casting ballots in the National Assembly poll and 56.9 per cent in the provincial elections.

However, an interesting aspect of the campaign was that most of the elected members had identifiable political affiliations with various political parties. The Jamaat-i-Islami had nominated sixty-one candidates and the Pagara League extended support to over ninety candidates. According to an estimate, approximately 120 candidates had been associated with the parties belonging to the Movement for the Restoration of Democracy (MRD); seventy of them were known for their Pakistan People's Party (PPP) background.[30] As against the 1984 referendum, the level of people's participation in the general elections was much better. It was a reaction to the deprivation of their right to vote for a very long time. The widespread response of the masses to the election process, despite the MRD call for boycott, demonstrated their keen interest in the electoral process and their deep desire for the restoration of the democratic system.[31] Subsequently, the MRD parties realized their misreading of the political situation and suffered from a feeling of having 'missed the bus'. Opinion polls conducted by an independent agency revealed that 'the general public is taking the parliament seriously and they look quite favourably upon its performance.'[32]

On 2 March 1985, a couple of days after the elections, President Zia introduced many amendments in the 1973 Constitution. These amendments gave overriding powers to the president by diluting the original character of the 1973 constitution. It was followed by the revival of the Constitution Order, according to which the amended constitution was enforced from 10 March 1985. Over sixty amendments in the constitution retained the parliamentary system but the president was given enormous powers to command the system; the position of the prime minister was weakened. The president was given the power to nominate the prime minister, to appoint provincial governors, services chiefs, judges of the Supreme Court and the High Courts. Above all, the president enjoyed the power to dissolve the National Assembly at his discretion.

In fact, the Eighth Amendment of 1985 has altered the powers of the president *vis-à-vis* the prime minister. Now the president possesses complete control and power to take any step, which he deems fit, on the plea of safeguarding national integrity. The amendments ensured that the validity of anything done by the president at his discretion can not be called in question. Only a few analysts could anticipate the far-reaching repercussions of these amendments on the future course of Pakistan's history. Although these amendments were introduced to create a balance between the president and the prime minister, athese have decisively tilted the balance in favour of the president'.[33]

Junejo as the Prime Minister: The first session of the newly elected parliament was held on 23 March, when Ziaul Haq took oath as President for five years, i.e., 1985–90. He nominated Muhammad Khan Junejo, a political leader from Sindh, as the prime minister, as well as appointed provincial governors who, in turn, appointed provincial chief ministers. Subsequently, Junejo was given a unanimous vote of confidence by the National Assembly. Thus, he had a good start. Elected government was installed with these steps, though the overall cover of martial law was retained. The smooth transfer of power from the army to the civil authority generated a lot of optimism about the democratic prospects of Pakistan and helped to improve Pakistan's image in the world.

The National Assembly elected on non-party basis was soon divided into an Independent Parliamentary Group (IPG), consisting of about forty members, and an Official Parliamentary Group (OPG), which included the supporters of the government. Gradually, the National Assembly started asserting itself on the constitutional and political front. It demonstrated its independence by electing Fakhar Imam as its speaker against Zia's candidate.[34] Parliament, on the whole, served as a useful forum for ventilating national grievances and demands as well as for discussing national issues. In a short period, the National Assembly proved beyond doubt that it was not going to be a rubber stamp.

The Parliament soon faced the dilemma of credibility, because the country was still under martial law. Therefore, the National Assembly and the Senate passed resolutions demanding removal of martial law. Three provincial assemblies, the NWFP, Sindh and Punjab, followed the move. Consequently, Prime Minister Junejo announced on 14 August, that the martial law would be lifted on the last day of 1985. The announcement had the prior approval of President Zia. It provided a sense of relief to the people who had suffered under the martial law for more than eight years.

Before the withdrawal of martial law, the parliament adopted, with some modifications, the changes brought about by General Zia in the constitution in March as the Eighth Amendment to the constitution, thereby putting a stamp of approval on the enhanced powers of the president. The Eighth Amendment also incorporated a blanket indemnity to all the actions, laws and orders, and judgements of military courts passed during the period of martial law. The provision of indemnity to the martial law regime is a usual practice as its decrees and decisions need a legal cover. These become a part of the constitution and the legal system unless repealed or amended by a competent authority. But the 1985 indemnity extended unqualified and absolute cover to all martial law regulations and orders, including the judgements of the military courts. However, the parliament was able to secure some changes in the original draft of the March amendments. For example, the proposed National Security Council which was meant to give representation to the military in policy-making was scrapped. Some powers of the president were also reduced by allowing the National assembly to elect a prime minister from March 1990, and the provincial assemblies could elect their chief ministers from March 1988. It was made obligatory for the president to appoint provincial governors in consultation with the prime minister. The year 1985 witnessed violent ethnic conflict and inter-provincial tensions in the polity. Different provinces expressed strong dissatisfaction about the manner in which the federal government treated them. It was considered to be a legacy of the martial law regime. Another manifestation was the establishment of the Sindhi Baloch Pushtun Front in London, by, among others, Hafeez Pirzada, Mumtaz Bhutto, Fazal Bangash of the MKP, and Baluch leader Sardar Attaullah Mengal. The Front stood for a confederation. The government and the Opposition condemned this proposal. Inter-provincial differences also cropped up on the proposed construction of the Kalabagh Dam project for power generation. While Punjab favoured its construction, the government of the NWFP rejected the proposal. Later, the Sindh government also joined the NWFP government in opposing the project.

As the deadline for the withdrawal of martial law approached, the military authorities decided to take some steps to regulate political parties in the post-martial law period. The Political Parties (Amendment) Act was enforced with the approval of the Parliament. The new law provided for a cumbersome procedure for the registration of political parties with the election commission. There was a provision for banning political parties also. Unregistered parties were not allowed to contest election. martial aw was withdrawn on 30 December 1985 and the constitution was fully restored.

By the beginning of 1986, Junejo could proudly claim that martial law had been lifted, emergency had been withdrawn and the fundamental rights had been restored. Junejo also promised complete freedom of expression, freedom of the press, and a true democratic society. No doubt, he fulfilled these promises. He succeeded in creating a semblance of the participatory system, in spite of the powerful position of the president. Gradually, the credibility and popularity graph of the Junejo government rose, with President Zia deliberately keeping away from the political forefront. However, the Junejo government was caught in a paradox. It required President Zia's blessings and support to face the extra-parliamentary political forces. On the other hand, it was expected to maintain a distance from the president in order to establish its credentials as an independent democratic government. The situation led to misunderstandings and tension between the president and the prime minister, which ultimately proved fatal to the latter's government.

As the parliamentary system started operating, the need for political parties was felt more intensely, since political parties form an integral part of parliamentary system. Therefore, Junejo assumed presidentship of the Muslim League with the blessings of the Pir Pagara, hitherto president of the party. A large number of the members of the National Assembly, belonging to the OPG, joined the Muslim League. Thereafter, Junejo began to work for extending the support base of the ruling Muslim League by mobilizing support all over the country. With the help of provincial chief ministers, who became provincial presidents of the Muslim League, the party structure was sought to be anchored at the grassroots level. Muslim League offices were opened, members were enrolled, and party elections were held. As a result, the Muslim League was organized as a national political party; it was better organized in Punjab as compared to other provinces of the country. Prime Minister Junejo announced his five-point programme aiming at development, improvement of literacy rate, elimination of corruption, and improvement of the common man's lot. Members of the provincial assemblies were allocated funds to undertake development work in their constituencies. As a result, a lot of development work was carried out, especially in the rural areas. Launching of seven-and-three *marla* schemes, followed by state-owned media projection, further strengthened the political base of the party. However, the party suffered from personality rivalries and factionalism and the members often demonstrated poor discipline.

The first jolt to the independence of the Parliament came when Fakhar Imam, Speaker of the National Assembly, was removed through a vote of no-confidence in 1986. This incident had a background. First, the speaker had admitted a privilege motion against the president for making a statement assailing the National Assembly. Secondly, the prime minister and his ministers pressurized the members of the parliament and the provincial assemblies to join the Muslim League before its registration with the Election Commission, 'as required by law, which rendered them liable to disqualification as they had joined an unregistered party'.[35] Independent members in the house raised the issue. The speaker referred it to the Election Commission for adjudication. It caused great panic in the government circles. The prime minister sought help from the president who, in turn, issued an ordinance setting it aside with retrospective effect. Thus, Junejo retaliated by arranging a vote of no-confidence against Fakhar Imam. Although the move was quite constitutional, it revealed the frailty of the system and intolerance of the prime minister. It caused a serious setback to the gradually improving image and strength of the newly created political order, because Junejo and his government owed their survival to the president's intervention.

The second serious setback to Junejo government was a clash between the police and the People's Party workers when the latter held a public meeting in Lahore on 14 August 1986, as a follow-up of Benazir Bhutto's return to Pakistan in April, when she was accorded an emotionally charged reception at Lahore. The August clash resulted in four casualties. However, the MRD, headed by the PPP workers, did not succeed in securing their demand for mid-term elections due to various reasons. First, the demand, for mid-term elections did not attract the masses as general elections were held in 1985. Secondly, the opposition parties lacked unity due to ideological differences, mutual jealousies, and clash of leadership. It also lacked an organizational base. Moreover, the Tehrik-i-Istaqlal did not support the movement and Khan Wali Khan had gone abroad. On the other hand, the movement was tackled well by Punjab government and therefore it petered out sooner than expected. The most threatening problems facing the Junejo government were the ethnic clashes, riots, bomb blasts, sabotage activities, and emergence of what had been christened as 'Kalashnikov culture'. Since then it seems to have found some base in Pakistan, posing serious danger to the country's integrity. Bomb blasts and clashes took hundreds of life. The worst affected area was the province of Sindh. The use of sophisticated weapons, including rocket-launchers and missiles, was considered to be an offshoot of the Afghanistan problem. In addition, another legacy of the martial law regime, which the Junejo government had to face, was heavy expenditure on defence and the growing budgetary deficits.[36]

While Junejo encouraged political freedom, President Zia kept his grip tight on power by retaining the position of the Chief of the army staff. Unlike Ayub Khan, Zia did not take off the military uniform. He ensured his strong links with the army, and believed that army and ulema constituted his basic constituency. Hence, he genuinely looked after their interests. In spite of the restoration of the elected government, Zia continued to direct defence and foreign policies, especially relating to Afghanistan and India. Consequently, the system that evolved gradually in Pakistan after 1985 could, at best, be described as a power sharing arrangement between the army and the elected representatives, using the 1973 constitution as a cover.[37] While addressing the joint session of the Parliament on the eve of withdrawal of martial law, Zia, declared that the new system did not represent departure from the policies of the martial law government. 'It is no rival or adversary of the outgoing system. It is, in fact, the extension of the system in existence for the past several years', he declared.[38]

Junejo tried his best to raise a credible political structure for sustaining him in power, autonomous of President Zia. Unfortunately, Junejo suffered from many handicaps. First, as a nominee of the president, Junejo appeared to be an extension of the military regime. As a result, he could not emerge as a democratic leader in spite of his repeated claims that he was a product of the democratic process. Second, Junejo was never known to be a political figure of national stature before his nomination as the prime minister. Third, he could become an important political force only with a powerful party machine behind him. He tried to activate his political party, that is, the Muslim League, all over the country, but the infant organization needed time to grow and become a real political force. Fourth, since the Junejo government had come into power through non-party elections, other political parties refused to recognize its credentials. The Parliament also could not gain its proper stature, as almost all the political stalwarts were absent from the house. Fifth, the ruling party suffered from indiscipline as most of the elected members were time-servers without a clear concept of party loyalty. Sixth, Junejo depended heavily on provincial chief ministers for maintaining law and order and organizing the Muslim League in their provinces. In the process, some of the provincial chief ministers became too powerful for the prime minister. Thus, the power-sharing system suffered from inherent weaknesses of a serious nature. In the ultimate analysis, the prime minister had a weaker position than the president.

It was thought that the president would not actually exercise those powers which he managed to get through constitutional amendments on the plea of creating a balance between the president and the prime minister. Pakistan's experience suggests that whenever powers were shared equally between the president and the prime minister, it led to conflict between the two. The basic reason for this situation was the absence of well-organized political parties and strong democratic institutions, which could moderate such tensions and serve as a source of strength for the system.

By the beginning of 1988, strain between the president and the prime minister became apparent; Ziaul Haq who had wielded absolute power for eight years, was not mentally prepared to share it with anybody else. Some blame has to be shared by Junejo who unnecessarily annoyed the president on trivial matters. Ignoring the fact that he was only a partner in the power sharing system, he exceeded his limits by stretching his official authority. Contrary to parliamentary practices, the president continued criticizing the parliament for its failure to enforce Islam and produce a better system for the common man. He went to the extent of issuing an indirect warning to the National Assembly on these matters in his address to the Parliament. Zia was also allergic to political parties and often criticized them on what he perceived to be their lapses.[39] The political leaders, especially the members of the Parliament and the provincial assemblies often retaliated by engaging in bitter criticism of the the martial law policies introduced under Ziaul Haq. This led to a polarization between the president and the prime minister and other political forces, and created doubts about the viability of the political process. Never in the history of Pakistan were such attacks exchanged between the president and the Parliament, especially when the former was the architect of the restored democratic system. Differences were strongly denied by both sides, which added to confusion and distrust. Despite these uncertainties, the restored democratic system was working fairly satisfactorily. The Opposition, led by the MRD and the PPP, had come to the conclusion that they would not be able to force mid-term elections on the government. The new elections were expected to be held in 1990, after the expiry of the full term of the government. Elections were expected in 1990.

Despite the denial of a conflict between the president and the prime minister, their relations soured by April 1988, as Ziaul Haq felt that Junejo was subtly 'conspiring' against him in order to undermine his position in the polity. In order to protect his position *vis-à-vis* the perceived political threats, the president dissolved the National Assembly and removed the prime minister on 29 May 1988 under the article 58-2-b of the Constitution which empowered him to do so at his discretion. This was a most unexpected dismissal decision and was termed as a constitutional coup by the press.[40] It reminded people of the dissolution of the assembly by Ghulam Muhammad in 1954, a step for which the nation had to pay a heavy price. While announcing the dismissal of the prime minister and dissolution of the National Assembly, the president blamed the members of the National Assembly and the government of corruption and failure to enforce the Islamic way of life. It was followed by an organized campaign for character assassination of the ruling party. The provincial assemblies were also dissolved. All the chief ministers, excepting that of Punjab (Mian Nawaz Sharif), were replaced.

The inside story is not known but, according to speculations and press analysis, some important developments widened the gulf between the president and the prime minister, precipitating the 29 May action. Some trusted government servants, including General Arif, chief of the army staff, and General Rahimud-Din, chairman joint chiefs committee, were not given extensions by the prime minister, contrary to the wishes of the president. Secondly, Zia was extremely unhappy about the repeated criticism of the army by the members of the Parliament. Junejo also made sarcastic remarks about senior commanders in the budget debate in 1987 by referring to the generals as the royal people and saying, 'we will put them in Suzuki cars' (small size economy cars).[41] Thirdly, an important cause, which added to the distrust, was Junejo's decision to convene an all-parties conference on Afghanistan. It was taken as a show of strength on the part of the prime minister. The president considered himself to be the architect of Pakistan's Afghan policy. He had played an important role in shaping the Afghanistan policy, and even after the restoration of the democratic government, he continued to dominate the foreign policy through his trusted colleague, Lt.-General Sahibzada Yaqub Khan, who served as Junejo's foreign minister. In late 1987, Junejo replaced him with a political leader from Karachi, Zain Noorani, which offended the president. Now, the attempt of Junejo to call an all-parties conference to decide on the issue of signing the peace treaty on Afghanistan completely turned off Ziaul Haq. The latter felt that a delay in signing the peace treaty would enable Pakistan to extract better terms, including the setting up of an interim government in Kabul. Junejo wanted an early resolution of the Afghanistan problem in view of its negative implication on Pakistan's domestic situation. The last factor, which accelerated the decision, was Ojheri Camp explosion in

Rawalpindi, in which hundreds of citizens died and numerous houses were destroyed. This tragic incident created resentment against the army, followed by the growing demand for accountability of the officers responsible for this tragedy. This was coupled with the calls for reduction in defence expenditure.[42] According to some reports, the Junejo government was considering taking action against some senior army officers in connection with the Ojheri camp. In incident a function at the Defence College in Rawalpindi, President Zia said, 'we need patrons and not prosecutors.'[43] During these days of tension, a clash took place in Rawalpindi between young officers of the army and Bashirul Hassan, an MPA, along with his followers. It added fuel to fire, and Ziaul Haq decided to dismantle the political arrangements in order to reassert his centrality to the political process. The fact of the matter is that the political system evolved by Zia and headed by Junejo envisaged a subordinate role for the prime minister. Contrary to Zia's expectations, Junejo started asserting his constitutional role. Gradually, he began to earn the status of a credible national leader. This was not the intention of Zia who wanted him to perform a subordinate role. When Junejo came back excited after his successful tour of the USA in 1987, Zia remarked: 'I hope this visit does not go to his head.'[44]

The Opposition political parties welcomed the dismissal of the government and dissolution of the National Assembly, as it amounted to acceptance of their demand for an early election. The political parties demanded elections within ninety days, while the president's interpretation was that the constitution required announcement of the election schedule in ninety days while elections could be held later. Meanwhile, the Supreme Court declared the law about the registration of political parties as unconstitutional, thereby abolishing the distinction between the registered and non-registered parties, the latter were not allowed to contest elections under the law set aside by the Supreme Court. General Zia wanted to hold the new elections on non-party basis, as he had done in 1985. The political circles were opposed to this proposal, but he insisted on this. However, in another judgment delivered after the death of General Ziaul Haq, the Supreme Court held that non-party elections were against the spirit of the fundamental rights guaranteed by the 1973 Constitution.

The dismissal of the elected government by the president caused a setback to the democratic process initiated in 1985. Zia's own image suffered as he began to be perceived to be so power-oriented that he could not work with a representative leadership. It also had some other implications and consequences. First, the decision generated a wave of sympathy for Junejo who emerged as a '*muzloom*' (the oppressed). Secondly, it gave a new life to the People's Party which was otherwise losing its support. The Junejo government was gaining the support of large sections of the politically active populace. However, with the dismissal of the government, the PPP was able to regain its position. The Muslim League was temporarily divided into pro-Junejo and pro-Zia factions.

Though the plans were announced to hold new elections, Ziaul Haq toyed with the idea of either holding non-party elections or using the referendum provision of the constitution to postpone the elections for the sake of re-structuring the political system in the name of Islam. The political leaders expressed the fear that Ziaul Haq might impose martial law to contend with the political circles that would oppose his efforts to re-structure the polity. Such apprehensions began to appear credible after the meeting of the Muslim League held in Islamabad on 13 August 1988; it ended in heated exchanges between the opposing factions, i.e. the supporters of Zia and Junejo. This added to political confusion in the country; no one was sure if the announced elections would be held on schedule. While Ziaul Haq and the political leaders were planning their next move, the former died in an air crash on 17 August, changing the political situation altogether.

The military could easily take over power after the sudden death of Ziaul Haq but the senior commanders, under the leadership of General Mirza Aslam Beg, who succeeded Ziaul Haq as the hief of the army, decided to let the constitutional provision take effect. Accordingly, Ghulam Ishaq Khan, chairman of the Senate, was sworn in as the acting president who promised to hold the elections in accordance with the already announced plan. The top brass of the military endorsed this statement and announced their support for the constitutional and democratic procedures for governance.

The sudden death of Zia in the Bahawalpur air crash presented a fresh opportunity to put Pakistan back on the rails of true parliamentary democracy. The non-party, controlled, and guided political process that Zia had started in 1985 could no longer be sustained. Both the Junejo supporters and the Opposition parties wanted free and fair party-based elections, but Zia was opposed to them. Now, these became a possibility. The Supreme Court also came out in favour of party-based elections in a judgement, setting the stage for elections with full participation of the political parties.

Before 17 August 1988, neither the political parties nor the general public trusted the words of Zia that elections would be held in mid-November. There were strong doubts about the continuation of the post-1985 political arrangements. Many thought Zia would pull another surprise and postpone the elections. The political atmosphere changed when Ghulam Ishaq Khan, the Acting President and General Mirza Aslam Beg, the army chief, assured the political parties that elections would be held and that they would ensure that the administration was impartial in conducting the elections.

With such assurances, the political activity picked up in the country. The PPP in particular never trusted Zia and had always feared that elections would be rigged or the electoral process would be tampered to keep its leadership out of power. For the first time, in nearly fifteen years, the party regained confidence that it could win the elections and form a government. These were the first elections after 1970 in which political parties were allowed to field their candidates. Since the political parties had been banned and there were restrictions on their activities for nearly eleven years, the growth of healthy political traditions and institutions of the civil society had remained stunted in the country. Under an act promulgated by late Zia in 1979, later approved by the Parliament in 1985, the political parties were required to register themselves in order to contest elections. The constitutionality of this requirement was challenged in the Supreme Court, which declared it illegal in 1988. The High Court (later endorsed by the Supreme Court) declared that the presidential action of dissolution of the National Assembly and dismissal of the government was unconstitutional, but it refused to restore the National Assembly on the grounds that new general elections had been announced. This further increased the confidence of the parties in the evolving the democratic order.

The PPP decided to off-load its political allies with whom it had launched the Movement for the Restoration of Democracy (MRD) in the early eighties. Two factors influenced its decision: first, over-confidence in the strength of its support-base, which it thought was still intact; second, it did not trust the leaders of other parties. On the other hand, the Muslim League demonstrated greater maturity and better understanding of the ground realities by first reuniting its two factions that had developed after the dismissal of the Junejo government, and then opting for a broadly-based coalition of political parties, including the right wing Jamaat-i-Islami and the National People's Party of Ghulam Mustafa Jatoi. Some minor religious political parties were also made part of this alliance named as the Islami Jamhoori Ittehad (IJI). Twenty-five other political parties put up their candidates for the National Assembly. A total of 1302 candidates for the 207 Muslim seats of the National Assembly contested the elections. Remarkably, more than 54 per cent or about 705 candidates ran as independents or without any party affiliation.[45] This could be attributed to the long interval during which political parties were not allowed to function freely and elections were not held periodically. In fact, the first general elections in Pakistan were held in 1970, followed by the 1977 elections, which were rejected by all the Opposition parties on account of massive rigging. The 1985 elections were held on non-party basis. Naturally, the political parties could not organize themselves at all levels and throughout the country. Though there was a large number of independent candidates and many parties were in the arena, the real contest was between the IJI and the PPP. Both the parties had almost similar manifestos and programmes, but their campaigns revolved around their leaders who were pitched against each other. It was a clash of personalities as well as a manifestation of political polarization, since both the groups represented two different legacies. Those who had had a close association with late Zia led the IJI, and the PPP sought to carry on with the political legacy of Z.A. Bhutto.

Benazir Bhutto's First Term: The November 1988 elections produced a divided mandate. None of the parties won a majority in the National Assembly. The PPP emerged as the single largest party by securing ninety-four seats in a 217 seat National Assembly (excluding twenty reserved for women). It was followed by its rival the IJI which captured 55 seats.[46] In the elections to the provincial assemblies, the PPP got a clear majority in Sindh, whereas the IJI emerged as the majority party in Punjab, the largest province. The other two provinces presented confused pictures as none of the parties had a clear majority. No doubt, the PPP could proudly claim to be the only national political party having secured seats from all the provinces, as against the IJI which could not win a single seat from the province of Sindh.

By the logic of numbers in the National Assembly, President Ghulam Ishaq Khan invited Benazir Bhutto, chairperson of the PPP, to form a government at the Centre. Since the PPP did not have a majority of its own, it obtained the support of smaller parties and independents to create a working majority. Benazir Bhutto became the first woman prime minister of Pakistan when she took oath of her office on 2 December 1988. The PPP also formed its government in Sindh and became a major coalition partner with other parties in the NWFP and Baluchistan. In the Punjab, the IJI, led by Nawaz Sharif, formed the government with the support of 151 members, against ninety-nine members belonging to the PPP in a house of 260 members.

The IJI led the largest parliamentary opposition in the National Assembly, ever put together in Pakistan. And it emerged as a dominant political force in Punjab, the real power base of the country. The emergence of two main parties and two young leaders raised hopes that Benazir Bhutto and Nawaz Sharif would put behind them the political legacy of confrontation and make a fresh start in the politics of reconciliation. The political mess left by the distortions in the 1973 Constitution required greater understanding and spirit of co-operation among the political leaders to develop a new political consensus. Most observers of Pakistani politics did not see any serious ideological differences between the two leaders, and they noted that the support-bases of these two leaders were fluid. Also, they apparently shared an interest in strengthening the parliamentary democracy, free-market economy, de-regulation, and denationalization of industries and financial institutions. Nor were there any strong differences on the core issues of foreign policy. Initially, Benazir Bhutto and Nawaz Sharif created the impression that they would evolve a working relationship in the interest of democracy and the country.

However, it was not long after that the two leaders and their respective political affiliates embarked on bitter confrontation. Considerations of power and personal rivalry, more than any real differences on the national policy or political ideology, defined their antagonism. The bitterest confrontation developed between the federal government headed by Benazir Bhutto and the Punjab government headed by Nawaz Sharif. The federal government built unjustified pressure on the Punjab government. The latter retaliated, engaging in open defiance of the federal government, challenging the federal authority on each and every issue. In the past, Pakistan's polity and its social structures were polarized for a long time due to the feudal political culture, authoritarian rule, and the degeneration of the political institutions that could mediate such conflicts among the political elite. But the polarization between Bhutto and Nawaz Sharif during 1988–90 took this bitterness to new heights. They began organizing campaigns against each other by buying off the loyalties of the members of national and provincial assemblies. A new culture of corruption was introduced in which huge sums of money, mainly from the state, were given to legislators to switch sides to undermine the parliamentary majority of the rival. This vitiated the political atmosphere of the country and dimmed the hopes of economic revitalization under the democratic leadership.

More responsibility rested with the central government of Benazir Bhutto in promoting political stability. Unfortunately, she became fixated on capturing power in Punjab through bribes, intimidation, and misuse of the authority of federal government institutions. This attempt to remove Nawaz Sharif from power in Punjab backfired. Most of the Punjabi politicians were enraged by the high-handedness of Benazir and preferred to unite behind Sharif than to capitulate to the pressures of the central government. In the process, Benazir's image and policy agenda suffered gravely. Generally, the enlightened sections of the society and military, bureaucratic elite thought that she was corrupt, inefficient, and incapable of promoting the interests of the country. Although, in the beginning, she made compromises with the president and the military realizing that the balance of authority was heavily tilted in favour of them on account of the eighth amendment, she utterly failed to establish a genuine rapport with any one outside her political circle. Both Benazir and the Opposition pushed the country into a new phase of uncertainty. The political deadlock crippled the economy in a way that sent shock waves through the business community and the military establishment. The president decided to remove her from office on 6 August 1990, using his constitutional power of dissolution of the National Assembly at his discretion. This ended the deadly stalemate in the country and paved the way for new elections.[47]

Before we move on to the IJI victory in the 1990 elections and its government, it would be appropriate to briefly examine the factors that led to the removal of Benazir Bhutto. We have already alluded to the widespread corruption, mismanagement of the economy, and the inability of Benazir to create a team spirit amongst her colleagues. The PPP suffered from organizational decay, as Benazir Bhuto hardly paid any attention to its organization; she dominated the party in collaboration with a small group of loyalists, coming hard on difference of opinion. Ideologically, the PPP moved away from mixed socialist economy to free market because of the changes in the global system and due to the strong realization that the nationalization policy of the early 1970s had adversely affected the economy. The change in the ideological position of the PPP alienated some of the old stalwarts who continued to harp on the traditional notion of the control of means of production by, the state. The federal government's inability to develop a working relationship with the provincial government of Punjab also undermined the political process. In the case of Sindh, law and order situation worsened due to the growing ethnic violence and inability of the government to find a satisfactory solution to this problem. The Benazir government was not able to put its hands firmly on the economy or on the issues pertaining to political stability in the country. Obviously, Benazir Bhutto cried foul and accused the president of partiality for her dismissal.[48] But the Supreme ourt of Pakistan upheld her removal as constitutionally valid.

The 1990 Elections and Nawaz Sharif's First Term: The country went to second elections in less than three years. Many of the political leaders who were opposed to the style of PPP governance decided to form an electoral alliance with the IJI, which was itself a broad political coalition of diverse political elements. The ANP and the MQM were convinced that only an electoral strategy of fielding common candidates against the PPP would ensure success. The PPP had won plurality of seats in the National assembly in the 1988 elections because votes of the anti-PPP groups were divided among their competing candidates. This time they wanted to work together as they shared the common hatred of the PPP. Moreover, the president and some elements of the military played a critical role in bringing these anti-PPP elements together in a broad-based electoral understanding. Having removed Benazir Bhutto, the president and the military could not accept her back soon afterwards. Therefore, they extended support to the IJI and others who were opposed to her.

The IJI's electoral strategy of forging coalitions earned it a simple majority in the National Assembly in the elections held in October 1990. The IJI also retained its majority in Punjab. It increased its share of the popular votes from 30.6 per cent in the previous elections to 37.27 per cent, capturing 106 seats against PPP's forty-five seats in the National Assembly.[49] Nawaz Sharif, the leader of the IJI, emerged as the national leader, winning seats in all provinces. The most important achievement of Nawaz Sharif was to build a strong base in Punjab. His political influence in the largest province has been the main factor in his political success at the centre and in other provinces. In addition to his hectic and spirited campaigning, two other factors contributed to his party's success. First, the PPP supporters were demoralized, as Benazir was very defensive during her election campaign. Second, Nawaz Sharif was able to project himself as the likely winner and a more credible leader for delivering a better governance and restoring the falling health of the economy. As he came from a business and industrial background, the modern sector of the economy, electorates generally reposed confidence in him that he would bring the country out of the economic crisis and put it on the path to recovery.

Nawaz Sharif assumed prime ministership in the first week of November 1990 with the backing of the IJI, some other groups, and a few independent members. The new government concentrated on improving the economy that the ill-advised policies of the ousted Benazir government and widespread corruption by her close associates had ruined. Some of Nawaz Sharif's steps like liberalization of investment and lessening of bureaucratic control over sanctioning new projects considerably restored the confidence of the domestic and international investors. All the macro-economic indicators for the year 1991 showed a remarkable progress. The GDP registered a growth rate of 6.9 per cent, inflation remained below 10 per cent and the investment increased by 17.6 per cent.[50] The IJI government took some important initiatives to resolve the outstanding problems among the provinces, like apportioning the shares of federal finances. An effort was made to sort out differences over equitable distribution of Indus water.

The IJI's performance during its first two years was better than any previous political government in Pakistan. But despite the fact that the IJI enjoyed majority in the house and economy was set on the path of recovery, the president dismissed the government in April 1993, exercsing his discretionary powers. This amounted to reverting Pakistan back to the decade of 1950s when the governor-general appropriated and exercised arbitrary powers to remove prime ministers at will. In the specific case of removal of Nawaz Sharif in April 1993, personal factors played more important role than any apparent wrong-doing by the prime minister while he was in office. He had started coming out of the shadow of President Ghulam Ishaq Khan, who, in the tradition of patron-client relationship, wanted to supervise, guide, and control the political process.[51] Ishaq Khan saw in the increasing independence of Nawaz Sharif a threat to his own ambitions for power. The two leaders developed serious differences over appointment of the chief of army staff, posting of ambassadors abroad, economic liberalization, and relationship with other parties.

A number of other factors also contributed to this situation. The IJI's partnership with the ANP and MQM ended in about two years. The federal government launched a military action in Sindh in 1992 to clear the province of dacoits, anti-social elements, and ethnic terrorists. It seems the president and the army chief had deliberately kept Sindh out of the control of the IJI government, and had taken decisions which were not part of the normal political process, under the pretext of national security. The law and order situation in the country did not improve much. The collapse of the co-operative societies in

Punjab in which depositors lost more than seventeen billion rupees tarnished the clean image of the some of the stalwarts of the IJI. The most crippling blow to the government however came from shift in the inter-personal relationship among the members of troika and Benazir Bhutto. Benazir, it is suspected, launched train marches in the fall of 1992 in connivance with some elements of the armed forces. The conflict reached the point of no-return when Nawaz Sharif, in his address to the nation on 17 April 1993 accused President Ghulam Ishaq Khan of conspiring against his government. Ghulam Ishaq Khan retaliated by dismissing his government with the support of the army chief. In examining the political developments and the democratic process in Pakistan, one can not ignore the nature of civil-military relations. These episodes prove that in the post-Zia period, the military remained a powerful element behind the political changes in the country.

In removing Nawaz Sharif's government, President Ghulam Ishaq Khan presented the same legal and constitutional justification of his act as he had done before against Benazir Bhutto.[52] But this time the Supreme Court in a historic judgment, declared the dissolution of the National Assembly and dismissal of the Sharif government as unconstitutional, restoring Nawaz Sharif to power.[53] Meanwhile, the president, mainly through state agencies and palace intrigues, brought about a change in Punjab, replacing supporters of Nawaz Sharif. This episode of induced rebellion in Punjab in 1993, which was one of the worst in the political history of Pakistan, showed how members of the legislature changed loyalties overnight for bribes offered both in money and public offices. And when the Punjab Assembly tried to oust Manzoor Wattoo through a vote of no-confidence, he managed the dissolution of the Punjab Assembly by the governor. He did not stop there. He did it again within fifteen minutes after the High Court restored the Assembly. The message from the president and his henchmen was clear: they were not going to allow Prime Minister Nawaz Sharif and his government to function any more. The confrontation cost the country heavily. The crisis was resolved through the intervention of the chief of Army Staff General Abdul Waheed Kaker, on the basis of an agreement by which both the president and the prime minister resigned and new elections were arranged under a caretaker administration headed by Moeen Qureshi.

Pakistan went through another electoral exercise in October 1993. This time, the masses did not show the enthusiasm that they had demonstrated on similar occasions in the past. A state of cynicism and helplessness gripped the ordinary electorates who seemed to have been fed up by the stories of corruption, mismanagement of the economy, and personal rivalries of the leaders of all parties. Moin Qureshi's caretaker administration encouraged public discussion on corruption and all kinds of reforms in the society. Publication of the list of loan defaulters and those persons whose loans had been written-off further increased distrust in the minds of the people for the politicians. It was not surprising that the majority of the electorates preferred to stay home on the election day. The low turn-out began to affect the legitimacy of the frequent electoral exercises, which eroded faith in the ability of the political leaders to fulfil their promises.

Benazir Bhutto's Second Term: The elections, once again produced a divided mandate. Going by the percentage of popular votes polled by the main contenders, there was no significant change in their support-base. The PPP secured about 37.9 per cent, very close to what had been its previous vote bank. The strength of Muslim League, led by Nawaz Sharif was significantly reduced in the National Assembly; it also lost majority in Punjab. However, its share of popular vote increased by 2 per cent, raising it to 39.9 per cent. The third party candidates this time paved the way to the electoral victory of the PPP, though marginally. The Jamaat-i-Islami and some other parties that had contested 1990 elections as a part of the IJI, now put up their own candidates. All efforts to put together an alliance of anti-PPP groups failed, dividing their votes to the advantage of the PPP. Some sections of the Muslim League also wanted to off-load the Jamaat and other right-wing groups to restore the centrist image of the party.

Benazir Bhutto established a coalition government at the federal level in October 1993 and governments in two provinces: in Sindh where the PPP had a majority, and in Punjab where it shared power with a faction of the Muslim League (the Chattha faction) and a few others, including independent members. In case of the NWFP, the Muslim League-ANP government, installed in October 1993, was dislodged in April 1994, and a PPP government headed by Aftab Sherpao was installed. Benazir Bhutto managed to have Farooq Ahmad Khan Leghari, a PPP stalwart, elected as the president, to secure her government against the exercise of the discretionary powers of the president. In another move, she got Sajjad Ali Shah appointed as the Chief Justice of the Supreme Court, ignoring the seniority of two other judges. She made a host of other administrative changes, including the replacement of the heads of the ISI and the IB, in order to establish a firm grip over power. Benazir Bhutto began her second term as a more secure prime minister than was the case when she assumed the office for the first time in 1988. However, it was not long after that she began to falter. Her political and economic mismanagement created one crisis after another and the government's economic policies suffered heavily, causing much confusion in the polity. In her authoritarian style she picked up confrontation with the superior judiciary and began to build pressure on Chief Justice Sajjad Ali Shah, when he asserted the independence of judiciary. Her confrontation with the Chief Justice was coupled with the sharp differences she developed with President Leghari on political and economic management. What greatly undermined her government were the stories of corruption and misuse of state resources by her and her busband, Asif Ali Zardari; similar stories of corruption and kickbacks in the government deals involving senior members of the government undermined the reputation of the government and alienated the people. Benazir Bhutto and Asif Ali Zardari were known for amassing a vast fortune in the country and abroad.[54] The government was unable to manage the law and order situation in the country in general and in Sindh in particular; there were serious complaints of excessive use of coercion by the law-enforcing authorities, including a number of cases of the accused being killed in police custody, described by the press as extra-judicial killings.

Corruption was one of the charges that President Leghari levelled against Benazir in dismissing her government in November 1996. The question is how President Leghari, the party loyalist for more than two decades, turned against the PPP government? And why did Justice Sajjad Ali Shah, who was handpicked by Benazir, sided with Leghari? The answer to these questions lies partly in the inability of Benazir Bhutto to maintain a working relationship with persons of stature who showed some degree of independence, and partly in the feudal tradition of intrigues, shifting alliances, and the personalized nature of Pakistani political culture. Both the Chief Justice and the president, wanted to maintain the autonomy of their institution which brought them in conflict with Benazir Bhutto who wanted to override the political system and all of its institutions. The law and order situation in Sindh, the extra-judicial killings, unending ethnic strife in Karachi, and daily stories of large-scale corruption were factors that brought down the Benazir government the second time. The Opposition, led by Nawaz Sharif, was engaged in a relentless struggle to pull down the PPP government. It was the second opportunity for Benazir Bhutto to establish her credentials as a skilful, able, and efficient leader, but once again she failed miserably. Doubts in the public mind about her dishonesty and lack of integrity turned into belief when scandals after scandals broke out in the national and foreign press describing how Benazir and her cronies were systematically milking the country. There was a sigh of relief when she was removed. Generally, the public hailed President Leghari's action and the Supreme Court endorsed it. Her government was replaced with a caretaker government headed by a former PPP leader, Malik Meraj Khalid.

New elections, the fifth in twelve years, were held in February 1997. The election campaign and the voters turn-out showed that there was hardly any excitement among the masses about this exercise. The percentage of electorate who cast their votes was the lowest in the history of Pakistan. The main reason was that the people appeared to be fed up with the same leaders and parties dominating the electoral scene. The only change was a new party, Tehrik-i-Insaf (Movement for Justice) that the cricket legend Imran Khan launched in 1996. He ran on the plank of a clean, efficient, and good government and against the backdrop of serious charges of corruption against the leaders of the two leading political parties. The Tehrik-i-Insaf did not win a single seat in the national and provincial assemblies, which showed how well-entrenched the traditional political elites of the country were. The remarkable thing about the Tehrik-i-Insaf's support-base was that it comprised mostly of the young, educated people. The electoral failure, which was expected because of the short time available, has not deterred Imran Khan. The important point is that the political order of Pakistan or the power arrangements are facing increasing challenge of legitimacy on the basis of corruption and poor performance, and may face new social and economic forces that Imran Khan claims to represent.

The 1997 elections saw a decisive defeat of the religious political parties. This should debunk the fear that Islamic parties have a vast popular base in the country and they present a real threat to parliamentary democracy. The most remarkable outcome of the polls was that, for the first time, the Muslim League swept the polls all over the country, wining over two-thirds majority in the National Assembly. In contrast to the Muslim League, the PPP lost its support in all provinces except in Sindh, the home province of the Bhuttos. Even in Sindh, the support base of the PPP receded to the rural areas, where the feudal families dominated the electoral politics.[55]

The MQM, once again, captured most of the seats from Karachi for the National Assembly and the Sindh Provincial assembly. The Muslim League candidates captured two seats in Karachi, which showed some changes in the attitude of the voters toward the political parties. If we compare the voting percentage of the MQM in 1997 elections with its percentage in the previous elections, we see a decrease in its vote bank.

Nawaz Sharif's Second Term: The electoral results were so decisive and clear that no element in the power structure of the country could think of denying the Muslim League the right to form a government at the Centre and in Punjab. The new government at the federal level, headed by Nawaz Sharif, was installed in February 1997. The Muslim League also formed coalition governments in all the four provinces. It created a sense of optimism that the leaders from different political parties will work together for coping with the political and economic problems and will give endurance to the slowly emerging consensus for democracy. The optimism was, however, misplaced, because seldom in the history of Pakistan have the political leaders put national interests before personal interests. The Muslim League's partnership with other political parties broke down in 1998. The MQM and the ANP pulled themselves out of the partnership as they developed grievances against the ruling Muslim League. The coalition government in Balochistan, led by Akhtar Mengal, was forced out of office because the coalition partners could no longer pull together; the members belonging to the Muslim League and the others revolted.

The federal government faced tremendous difficulties in managing its relations with the MQM which refused to disassociate itself from its terrorist elements. Extortion, intimidation, and elimination of rivals from the political scene continued unabated. There was faint hope that with sharing power with the MQM and through provision of hundreds of millions of rupees to the parties for the rehabilitation of the families who had lost their loved ones in the ethnic conflict, the leaders will be persuaded to change their policies. The MQM complained that the government had not implemented the agreement it had signed with the MQM in February 1997, and sidelined it over time in Sindh. The MQM often threatened to withdraw support to the Muslim League government in Sindh and, on one occasion, its ministers did resign. However, the government persuaded them back into the government. Such a hide-and-seek interaction between the government and the MQM came to an end after the killing of Hakeem Muhammad Saeed, the former governor of Sindh and one of the most recognized philanthropists of the country, allegedly by the terrorist wing of the MQM. The federal government imposed the governor's rule in Sindh in October 1998.

The break-up of the coalitions and the inability of different poltical parties to work together for ensuring effective political and economic management shows that the democratic politics in Pakistan has not yet matured and the politicians are not sensitive to each other's genuine needs and interests. Democracy can not function smoothly if the competing interests and groups are not prepared to accommodate each other. Absolute claims or non-negotiable agendas are the anti-thesis to democracy. Like all politics, democratic politics is about compromises and accommodation, give and take, and mutual respect. This takes us back to one of the main themes of the chapter, i.e., the crisis of leadership. The poverty of good leadership is more than evident from the egotistic pursuit of selfish interests in the making and breaking of political alliances, both within and outside the assemblies. In mature democracies, political coalitions rest on common policy agendas, not on the convergence of personal interests of the party stalwarts. If the elections continue to produce divided mandates in the provinces or in the centre, the leaders may learn the virtue of political co-operation. Our experience with the democratic politics is limited by any standard and the leaders of different political parties have not been exposed sufficiently to the rigours of consensual politics.

The Muslim League government has used its parliamentary majority to make two fundamental changes in the post-Zia political system. It introduced two significant amendments (thirteenth and fourteenth) in the constitution. It was a rare occasion that the Muslim League, the PPP, and all the regional parties co-operated in making these changes immediately after the 1997 elections. The thirteenth amendment restored the parliamentary character of the constitution by limiting the powers of the president to that of a nominal head of the state. His power to dissolve the National Assembly at his discretion was done away with, and the role of the prime minister was increased for some key appointments like the services chiefs. The fourteenth amendment related to the problem of floor-crossing, which had been the main source of political instability in the past. Under the amendment, the party leader could unseat its party member to the assemblies on grounds of changing the party or for violation of the party-directive or for engaging in any activity that went against the interest of the party. These changes shifted the balance of power in favour of the prime minister, and the political arrangements that Zia had fashioned were discarded. As we have discussed above, the political intervention and intrigues by the president had reduced the parliamentary system to a farce. However, those who contend that some checks and balances are necessary in the system to restrain the power of the executive argue that the new system has given too much powers to the prime minister or the party leader, enabling him to establish his control over the assemblies and the members. In our judgement the Pakistani political system under the Eighth Amendment did not bring about any stability and it rested on the notion of the old viceregal order of controlled democracy. The frustration and disappointment of all the political parties with that system was marked by the unanimity with which they effected changes in the constitution in 1997.

By the writing of these lines in the early months of 1999, the Muslim League government had completed first two years of its tenure. The record of its performance was mixed at best. There were many systemic and structural constraints that it faced, which troubled its leaders, and pushed them from one crisis to another. It had inherited an economy that was on the verge of collapse; a political culture of corruption; and ill-defined relationship among the executive, the judiciary, and the president. The economy gained some confidence during the first year and it was set on the course of recovery, but the decision to conduct nuclear tests in May 1998 after India had taken the lead resulted in the imposition of sanctions. The scandalous agreements with the Independent Power Producers that the Bhutto government entered into with sovereign guarantees forced the government a detailed review of these arrangements. This further complicated Pakistan's relations with the international financial institutions and with some foreign governments, which had serious repercussions for the economy. International recession and economic crises in South East Asia have also adversely affected the economic conditions of Pakistan. A decision to freeze foreign currency accounts worth fourteen billion dollars undermined the morale of both investors and account holders. Other structural problems of the economy that have a bearing on the performance of democracy include huge domestic and foreign debt, budget deficit, defence burden, unpaid loans, and inability of the state to collect taxes or mobilize domestic resources. We must keep in mind that democracy and its institutionalization depend on how efficient, productive, and equitable the economic system of the country is. Economy is the key indicator according to which the stability, performance legitimacy, and popular support for an elected government has to be judged. At the time of this writing, the economy was slowly coming out of the danger zone but it had a long way to go before it could be described as stable and secure.

Some of the structural constraints like the Eighth Amendment have been removed. The president is no longer constitutionally empowered to dissolve the National Assembly or dismiss an elected government. The loopholes in the floor-crossing laws have been plugged by the fourteenth amendment. There is a trend in shifting the balance of power in favour of the representative government. But the military still looms very large over the political horizon of Pakistan. It continues to play a significant role behind the scene. Since 1998, the military has aided the development of democracy in Pakistan, although it retains the capability to stall the democratic process. It could do so during the November 1997 conflict between Chief Justice Sajjad Ali Shah and Prime Minister Nawaz Sharif. The crisis resulted from the unsettled issue of checks and balances in the political system. But such a quest became enmeshed with personal egos and palace intrigues. No one would disagree with the contention that an independent and assertive judiciary is fundamental to the working of democracy. But suspension of constitutional provisions, which a three-member bench headed by Justice Sajjad Ali Shah did in 1997, was beyond the constitutional limits within which all branches of the government have to function. Deliberate inaction by President Leghari on certain important legislations and his unwillingness to act above political considerations exposed him to allegations that he was a party to the whole crisis, and was not happy with the passage of two amendments in the constitution by the Muslim League government. The eruption of such crisis is a strong reminder that a system of checks and balances has yet to find its place in the politics of Pakistan.

Ethnic terrorism in Karachi and sectarian violence in Punjab, though somewhat controlled, has kept all the democratic governments preoccupied with the law and order problem. The subject deserves separate treatment, but that would be deviation from the main theme of the book. These are two symptoms of the collapse of authority, politicization of administrative machinery, and lack of good governance. If we take any sector of the state, governance and political management has deteriorated considerably after the restoration of democracy. The root cause is not the democratic system but the individuals, groups, and institutions that practise it, and the inability of the political leaders to cope with it in an effective manner. Their personal and partisan considerations have often given a fillip to civil violence and terrorism. Democracy never functions in the ideal mode, it faces intrinsic and extrinsic problems, both in established democratic system and in developing democracies.[56] However, these challenges are more acute in the developing societies.

Democracy allows various types of freedoms but it also expects the leaders and the people to exercise these freedoms and rights with responsibility and that they respect the right of others to enjoy the same opportunities. Furthermore, accountability of those in power is another important aspect of democracy. Both these essential attributes of democracy have not taken roots in the political culture of Pakistan. Today, governance in Pakistan is more about day-to-day crisis management rather than long-term or sustainable development of the society or institutionalization of the exercise of political authority. In the feudal tradition, Pakistani leaders have attempted to establish personal rule instead of working for the rule of law. The imperative of rule of law includes constitutional guarantees for the fundamental rights, independent judiciary, efficient administration, and responsive political leadership. The development of democracy and growth of these institutions reinforce each other.

Unfortunately, the growth of civil society in Pakistan has been slow and has often been disrupted by imposition of military rule or by the authoritarian style of many politcal governments. The quality of any democratic system can be judged from the role the institutions of the civil society play in ensuring institutional and social controls over the elected officials of the government.[57] The political parties, media, universities, professional associations, non-governmental organizations, think-tanks and independent policy forums have been weakened and their growth has been stunted by the authoritarian tradition and governmental controls. A civil culture based on citizens' participation in the political process, over and above the casting of votes in general elections, is still in the early stages of formation. Whatever the structural flaws of democracy in Pakistan, there is a growing consensus in the country that the democratic process must go on. It should be reformed in areas where reforms are necessary and possible. Democratic cultures take generations to shape new mindsets and to change the disposition of people. We are confident that democracy as a political system and as a social norm would promote the values of tolerance and mutual accommodation. It would encourage individuals and groups to pursue their interests and goals within the confines of constitution and law. It needs to be remembered that democracy is not a fixed or static system. Rather, it is an evolving process. A complex combination of social, economic, institutional, and cultural factors shape its operationalization. Personal training and qualities of leaders who run the system matters in pushing the democratic agenda forward. With all the difficultues and pitfalls, Pakistan is decidely better off under a democratic system than being without it.

NOTES AND REFERENCES

1. Callard, *Pakistan,* p. 125.
2. See Syed Nur Ahmad, *From Martial Law to Martial Law: Politics in the Punjab, 1919-1958,* Craig Baxter, trans., Boulder, Co.: Westview Press, 1985.
3. Rupert Emerson, *Represetative Government in South-East Asia,* Harvard: University Press, 1955, pp. 6-12.
4. Mushtaq Ahmad, *Government and Politics in Pakistan,* p. 162.
5. Quoted in Muhammad Khalid, *Welfare State of Pakistan,* Karachi: Royal Book Company, p. 126.
6. Callard, *Pakistan,* p. 120.
7. Khalid, *Welfare State,* p. 129.
8. Ian Stephens, *Pakistan,* London: Ernest Benn, 1963, p. 230.
9. Safdar Mahmood, *Pakistan Muslim League Ka Daur-e-Hakoomat.*
10. Z. A. Suleri, *Politicians and Ayub,* Rawalpindi: Capital Law and General Book Depot, 1964, p. 11.
11. Ibid.
12. Safdar Mahmood, *Pakistan Muslim League,* p. 137.
13. Ibid., p. 63.
14. Callard, *Pakistan,* p. 137.
15. Chaudhury, *Constitutional Development,* p. 260.
16. Ibid., p. 257.
17. R. M. Maciven, *Web of Government.* Cited in ibid., p. 257.
18. Herbert Feldman, *A Constitution for Pakistan,* Karachi: Oxford University Press, 1955, pp. 23–66.
19. Feldman, *A Constitution,* p. 17.
20. Ibid., p. 18.
21. Mushtaq Ahmad, *Government and Politics,* p. 165.
22. Republican Party was a creation of Iskandar Mirza. It was born as a result of palace intigues. It had no programme nor did it ever face the electorate.
23. Sayeed, *The Political System of Pakistan,* pp. 90–91.
24. Ibid., pp. 82–3.

25. *Morning News,* 9 October 1958.
26. Sayeed, *The Political System of Pakistan,* p. 215.
27. Khalid, *Welfare State,* p. 126.
28. Mushtaq Ahmad, *Government and Politics,* p. 126.
29. For details, see chapter on Political Parties.
30. William L. Richter, 'Pakistan in 1985', *Asian Survey,* February 1986, p. 208. For analysis of the election results, see article by Hassan Askari Rizvi in *The Muslim,* 7 January 1986. Also see the *Pakistan Times,* 23 February 1986. According to its analysis, 157 candidates belonged to the PPP.
31. Richter, *'Pakistan in 1985',* p. 208.
32. *The Muslim,* 31 December 1985. See article by Ijaz S. Gilani.
33. *The Muslim,* 1 January 1985.
34. *The Muslim,* 16 January 1986. See article by Maleeha Lodhi. Also see Richter, *'Pakistan in 1985',* p. 209.
35. *The Muslim,* 30 December 1997. See Hasan Askari Rizvi, 'The Civilian Order'.
36. *The Muslim,* 8–9 January 1988. Maleeha Lodhi writes: 'It was in the economic sphere that one of the most striking consequences of the military rule were manifest. The long period of unrepresentative rule had meant economic decision-making without constraints or accountability. There had been an unbridled growth of military expenditure which fuelled growing budgetary deficits, while the rise in the military imports contributed to the country's increasing foreign debt. The largest fiscal deficit recorded in Pakistan's history in 1987 was legacy of this kind of financial indiscipline. It was, however, the civilian administration of Junejo that was left to grapple with it.'
37. A few months before the general elections of 1985, General Zia said that he would share power rather than transfer it to the elected representatives. *The Muslim,* 1 November 1984.
38. *The Muslim,* 31 December 1985.
39. President Zia's interview in *Quami Digest* (Urdu) May 1985. He claimed that there was no need for political parties in Pakistan. *Jang,* 18 March 1986.
40. Abbas Rashid, 'Implications of the 29 May coup', *The Muslim,* 8 June 1988.
41. *The Pakistan Times,* 13 June 1987. Also see, Rasul B. Rais, 'Pakistan in 1987', *Asian Survey,* February 1988, p. 131.
42. For a detailed analysis, see Maleeha Lodhi's 'News Analysis', *The Muslim,* 4 June 1988. Also see 'Implications of the Constitutional Coup, *Nation,* 4 June 1988.
43. *The Muslim,* 12 June 1988, quoted in 'Zia's Constitutional Coup and its Likely Fallout'. Also see Rais, *'Pakistan in 1987',* p. 130.
44. Mushahid Hussain, 'News Analysis', *The Nation,* 2 June 1988.

45. *Dawn*, 13 November 1988. See an article by Sultan Ahmad.
46. *Dawn*, 29 November 1988. See the article by Shameem Akhtar.
47. *The Muslim*, 7 August 1990.
48. *Time*, 20 August 1990
49. *The Herald*, November–December 1990, pp. 8–9.
50. *Economic Survey* 1991–92, Islamabad: Government of Pakistan, 1992.
51. Rasul Bakhsh Rais, 'Elections, Regime Change, and Democracy', in Rasul Bakhsh Rais, ed., *State, Society and Democratic Change in Pakistan*, Karachi: Oxford University Press, 1997, pp. 255–76.
52. For the analysis of Nawaz Sharif's removal, see, Anwar H. Syed, 'The Ouster of Nawaz Sharif in 1993: Power Plays within the Ruling Establishment,' in Rais, *State, Society and Democratic Change in Pakistan*, pp. 45–75.
53. On the Supreme Court's role, see, Charles H. Kennedy, 'Presidential-Prime Ministerial Relations: The Role of the Superior Courts,' in Charles H. Kennedy and Rasul Bakhsh Rais, eds., *Pakistan: 1995*, Boulder, Co: Westview Press, 1995, pp. 17–30.
54. See a detailed investigative report in *New York Times,* 11 January 1998.
55. Mohammad Waseem, 'Pakistan Elections 1997: One Step Forward,' in Craig Baxter and Charles H. Kennedy, eds., *Pakistan: 1997*, Boulder, Co.: Westview Press, 1998, pp. 1–17.
56. Philippe C. Schmitter, 'Dangers and Dilemmas of Democracy,' *Journal of Democracy*, vol. 5, no. 2, April 1994, pp. 57–74.
57. Holly Sims, 'Democratization and the Revitalization of Civil Society,' in Rais, *State, Society and Democratic Change in Pakistan,* pp. 204–19.

APPENDIX 1

Objectives Resolution moved by Prime Minister Liaquat Ali Khan in the Constituent Assembly of Pakistan on 7 March 1949.

In the name of Allah, the Beneficent, the Merciful;

Whereas sovereignty over the entire universe belongs to God Almighty alone and the authority which he has delegated to the State of Pakistan through its people for being exercised within the limits prescribed by Him is a sacred trust;

This Constituent Assembly representing the people of Pakistan resolves to frame a constitution for the sovereign independent State of Pakistan;

Wherein the State shall exercise its powers and authority through the chosen representatives of the people;

Wherein the principles of democracy, freedom, equality, tolerance and social justice, as enunciated by Islam, shall be fully observed;

Wherein the Muslims shall be enabled to order their lives in the individual and collective spheres in accordance with the teachings and requirements of Islam as set out in the Holy Quran and Sunnah;

Wherein adequate provision shall be made for the minorities freely to profess and practise their religions and develop their cultures;

Whereby the territories now included in or in accession with Pakistan and such other territories as may hereafter be included in or accede to Pakistan shall form a Federation wherein the units will be autonomous with such boundaries and limitations on their powers and authority as may be prescribed;

Wherein shall be guaranteed fundamental rights including equality of status, of opportunity and before law, social, economic and political justice, and freedom of thought, expression, belief, faith, worship, and association, subject to law and public morality;

Wherein adequate provision shall be made to safeguard the legitimate interests of minorities and backward and depressed classes;

Wherein the independence of the judiciary shall be fully secured;

Wherein the integrity of the territories of the Federation, its independence and all its rights including its sovereign rights on land, sea and air shall be safeguarded;

So that the people of Pakistan may prosper and attain their rightful and honoured place amongst the nations of the World and make their full contribution towards international peace and progress and happiness of humanity.

Source: Constituent Assembly of Pakistan, *Debates, Official Report*, vol. v, no. 1, 7 March 1949, Karachi, 1949, pp. 1–2.

APPENDIX 2

1997 GENERAL ELECTIONS

Summary of Statistics for the National Assembly

The following table depicts the pattern of voting for election to the National Assembly of Pakistan on 204 Muslim constituencies:

Province/Area	Number of Registered Muslim Voters	Total Number of Votes Polled	Percentage of Votes Polled to Registered Voters
Federal Capital	228,605	105,264	46.05
Punjab	30,865,590*	12,534,915	40.61
Sindh	12,066,875	3,777,892	31.31
NWFP	6,390,704**	1,846,371	28.89
Baluchistan	3,044,548	705,604	23.17
FATAs	1,593,212	536,809	33.69
Total	54,189,534	19,506,855	35.99

* Excludes registered votes of two constituencies, i.e., NA-121 and NA-143.
** Excludes registered votes of one constituency, i.e., NA-1.

The party position on 3 February 1997 for the National Assembly is given in the following table:

Sl. No.	Name of Political Party	Number of Seats Won
1.	Awami National party (ANP)	09
2.	Baluchistan National Party (BNP)	03
3.	Haq Parast Group (HPG)	12
4.	Jamiat Ulema-e-Islam (Fazal-ur-Rehman Group) JUI (F)	02
5.	Jamhoori Wattan Party (JWP)	02
6.	National People's Party (NPP)	01
7.	Pakistan Muslim League (Nawaz Sharif Group) PML (NL)	135
8.	Pakistan People's Party (PPP)	18
9.	Pakistan People's Party (Shaheed Bhutto Group) PPP (SB)	01
10.	Independence (IND)	21
	Total	204

Summary of Statistics for the Provincial Assemblies

The following table depicts the summary of statistics relating to the four provincial assemblies:

Province/Area	Number of Registered Muslim Voters	Total Number of Votes Polled	Percentage
Punjab	31,177,690*	12,557,804	40.27
Sindh	11,997,274**	3,671,582	30.60
NWFP	6,479,968***	1,876,104	27.90
Baluchistan	2,957,769****	673,041	22.75
Total	52,612,701	18,778,531	35.69

* Excludes registered votes of two constituencies, i.e., PP-17 and PP-174.
** Excludes registered votes of one constituency, i.e., PS-55, due to uncontested election.
*** Excludes registered votes of two constituencies, i.e., PF-19 and PF-20.
**** Excludes registered votes of one constituency, i.e., PB-26, due to uncontested election.

The Province-wise statistics of each Provincial Assembly are given in the succeeding paragraphs.

Punjab

There are 240 Muslim seats for the Punjab Assembly and total voting strength, i.e., number of registered Muslim votes in Punjab was 31,483,112. However, polling was held on 238 Muslim seats as proceedings were terminated in two constituencies, i.e., PP-17 Chakwal-II and PP-174 Khanewal-I. The total number of votes cast were 12,557,804 which was 40.27% of the registered Muslim voters in 238 constituencies of the province of Punjab.

Party Position

The number of candidates fielded, and the seats won by political parties and Independents in the Punjab Assembly is as follows:

Sl. No.	Name of Political Party	Number of Contesting Candidates	Number of Seats Won
1.	Pakistan Muslim League PML (N)	235	210
2.	Pakistan People's Party (PPP)	191	3
3.	Pakistan Muslim League (Junejo) PML (J)	28	2
4.	People's Democratic Party (PDP)	10	1
5.	Muslim Itthad Party (MIP)	4	1
6.	Independents	926	21

The result shows that Pakistan Muslim League (Nawaz Group), made a clean sweep in the Punjab Assembly polls by winning 210 seats on 3 February 1997, which is an absolute majority—unprecedented in the electoral history of the country. Pakistan People's Party could win only 3 seats while Independents secured 21 seats in the Assembly.

Sindh

The provincial assembly elections held on 99 Muslim seats were contested by 1,272 candidates out of which 559 belonged to different political parties while 717 contested in their independent capacity. Total registered voters for the Sindh Assembly were 12,066,875. As one candidate from PS-55 Thar-I (Old Tharparkar-VI), was returned uncontested, the number of registered voters stood at 11,997,274 for the remaining 99 seats in the Assembly. The number of votes polled in this province was 3,671,582, which is 30.60% of the total registered voters for 99 constituencies.

Party Position

The number of seats won by political parties, and the candidates nominated in the Sindh Assembly remained as follows:

Sl. No.	Name of Political Party	Number of Contesting Candidates	Number of Seats Won
1.	Pakistan People's Party	95	34
2.	Pakistan Muslim League (N)	82	15
3.	Pakistan People's Party (Shaheed Bhutto)	73	01
4.	Haq Parast Group	57	30
5.	United National Alliance	39	01
6.	National People's Party	10	03
7.	National People's Party (Workers Group)	01	01
8.	Independents	717	15

Pakistan People's Party emerged as the single largest party in Sindh Assembly by winning 34 seats. However, none of the parties could win simple majority. Haq Parast group won 30 seats while 15 seats were won by Pakistan Muslim League (Nawaz Group) and 15 Independents got a slot in the Assembly. Among smaller parties Pakistan People's Party (Shaheed Bhutto) won one seat. The United National Alliance also got hold of only one seat. National People's Party and NPP (Workers Group) won three and one seat respectively.

North-West Frontier Province

Total registered Muslim voting strength for 80 seats of the NWFP Assembly was 6,651,672 out of which 1,876,104 votes were polled for 78 seats as election proceedings were terminated in two constituencies, i.e., PF-19 and PF-20. Due to exclusion of these two constituencies the number of registered voters for 78 constituencies stood at 6,479,968. The percentage of votes polled to registered votes remained 28.95. A total of 619 candidates were in the run of which 326 belonged to various political parties and 293 contested in independent capacity.

Party Position

The break-up of number of seats won, and the candidates sponsored by political parties and Independents in the NWFP Provincial Assembly is as follows:

Sl. No.	Name of Political Party	Number of Contesting Candidates	Number of Seats Won
1.	Pakistan Muslim League (N)	55	32
2.	Awami National Party	49	28
3.	Pakistan People's Party	43	04
4.	Jamiat Ulema-e-Islam (F)	27	01
5.	Pakistan Muslim League (Junejo)	08	02
6.	Independents	293	11

In the NWFP Assembly, Pakistan Muslim League (Nawaz Group) emerged as the single largest political party by winning 32 seats. Awami National Party, which had adjustment of seats with Pakistan Muslim League (N) won 28 seats. The two parties were allies in the Provincial set-up of the NWFP. Pakistan People's Party, which had a strong backing and support in the province, could not perform impressively and won only 4 seats. Pakistan Muslim League (Junejo), an ally of PPP, won 2 seats. Jamiat Ulema-e-Islam (Fazal-ur-Rehman Group) could win 1 seat, while 11 seats were won by the Independents.

Baluchistan

Total registered Muslim voters for 40 Muslim seats of the Baluchistan Assembly were 3,044,548. Due to uncontested return on one constituency, i.e., PB-26 Jhal Magsi, the number of registered voters stood as 2,957,769 for remaining 39 seats. A total of 673,041 votes were polled and percentage of votes polled to total registered voters was 22.75. A total of 39 Muslim seats of the Baluchistan Assembly were contested by 382 candidates of which 257 were sponsored by political parties and 125 were Independents.

Party Position

The break-up of seats won, and of candidates sponsored by political parties and independents is as follows:

Sl. No.	Name of Political Party	Number of Contesting Candidates	Number of Seats Won
1.	Pakistan People's Party	30	01
2.	Baluchistan National Party	10	09
3.	Jamiat Ulema-e-Islam (F)	27	07
4.	Baluchistan National Movement	23	02
5.	Pakistan Muslim League (N)	22	04
6.	Pukhtoon Khwa Milli Awami Party	14	02
7.	Jamhoori Wattan Party	15	06
8.	Pakistan Muslim League (J)	06	01
9.	Independents	125	08

As is evident from the above table, none of the political parties could emerge as a clear winner and the result was a split mandate. However, largest number of seats, i.e., nine was won by Baluchistan National Party (BNP). Jamiat Ulema-e-Islam (Fazal-ur-Rehman) and Pukhtoon Khwa Milli Awami Party won 6 seats each, Jamhoori Wattan Party won 6 while 8 Independents were elected.

Voter Turnout

Following table shows the turnout of voters since 1985 including that of the 3 February 1997 General Elections:

Year of Election	Percentage of total votes polled to registered voters	
	National Assembly	Provincial Assemblies
1985	53.69	57.37
1988	43.07	43.20
1990	45.46	46.10
1993	40.32	42.76
1997	35.99*	35.69

* For 204 National Assembly constituencies

Comparative study of the results of elections since 1985 shows that there has been a gradual decrease in the voter turnout. Declining turnout of voters is a matter of serious concern and an indication of people's apathy or their disbelief in the electoral process, due to time and again dissolution of assemblies on account of one or the other charges. Therefore, it is imperative not only to strengthen the democratic electoral process in the country but also wage a campaign to motivate the electorate to use their right of franchise.

The final position of main political parties and independents in the National Assembly of Pakistan and in the four provincial assemblies is given hereunder in five different tables:

I – NATIONAL ASSEMBLY OF PAKISTAN

Name of Political Party	Number of contesting candidates	Valid votes polled	Percentage of valid votes polled by parties to total valid votes	Number of seats won
PPP	163	4,215,505	21.90	18
BNP	08	125,440	0.65	03
JUI (F)	35	327,683	1.7	02
PTI	132	315,316	1.64	—
PPP (SB)	67	378,867	1.97	01
HPG	51	764,212	3.97	12
ANP	20	383,296	1.99	10
PML (J)(Chattha)	17	511,765	2.66	—
PML (N)	178	8,844,816	45.95	137
NPP	04	82,581	0.43	01
JWP	09	66,128	0.34	01
Independents	896	2,682,116	13.93	21

II – PUNJAB ASSEMBLY

Name of Political Party	Number of contesting candidates	Valid votes polled	Percentage of valid votes polled by parties to total valid votes	Number of seats won
PPP	191	2,484,026	19.94	03
PML (J)	28	270,275	2.16	02
PML (NL)	235	6,638,907	53.29	212
PDP	10	50,026	0.40	01
MIP	04	27,378	0.22	01
PTI	123	211,504	1.69	—
Independents	926	2,568,089	20.27%	21

III – SINDH ASSEMBLY

Name of Political Party	Number of contesting candidates	Valid votes polled	Percentage of valid votes polled by parties to total valid votes	Number of seats won
PPP	95	1,014,962	27.64	34
UNA	39	91,694	2.49	01
PPP (SB)	73	307,852	8.38	01
HPG	57	771,609	21.01	30
NPP (WG)	01	26,183	0.71	01
PML (N)	82	594,692	16.19	15
NPP	10	101,890	2.77	03
JUI (F)	28	57,592	1.56	—
Independents	717	631,436	17.19	15

IV – NWFP ASSEMBLY

Name of Political Party	Number of contesting candidates	Valid votes polled	Percentage of valid votes polled by parties to total valid votes	Number of seats won
PPP	43	202,275	10.46	04
PML (J)	08	39681	2.05	02
JUI (F)	27	52,758	2.72	01
ANP	49	397,230	20.54	29
PML (N)	55	583,352	30.16	33
PTI	50	67,241	3.47	—
PPP (SB)	30	21,948	1.13	—
Independents	293	511,825	26.46	11

V – BALUCHISTAN ASSEMBLY

Name of Political Party	Number of contesting candidates	Valid votes polled	Percentage of valid votes polled by parties to total valid votes	Number of seats won
PPP	30	44,013	6.54	01
BNP	19	118,098	17.55	09
PML (J)	06	10,875	1.62	01
JUI (F)	27	93,918	13.95	07
BNM	23	66,787	9.92	02
PML (N)	22	73,226	10.88	04
PKMAP	14	46,853	6.96	02
JWP	15	60,879	9.05	06
ANP	13	9,282	1.38	—
JQM	07	9,866	1.46	—
Independents	126	114,923	17.07	08

Source: Election Commission Reports.

BIBLIOGRAPHY

PRIMARY SOURCES

Official Reports and other Documents:

The Constitution of the Islamic Republic of Pakistan, 1956.
The Constitution of Islamic Republic of Pakistan, 1973.
The Constitution of Pakistan, 1962.
Constituent Assembly of Pakistan, *Debates*, 1949 and 1962.
Foundation and Policy, Pakistan People's Party, Lahore, 1967.
General Assembly Official Records, 92nd Plenary Meeting, 30 September 1947.
Government of India Act, 1935, with Independence Act, 1947, as Adapted in Pakistan by (Provisional Constitution) Order, 1947 (and Amended upto April 1955).
Legal Framework Order.
Manifesto: The Pakistan Democratic Party, Dacca, 1969.
Manifesto: Pakistan People's Party, Rawalpindi, 1977.
Mutual Security Act of 1958: Hearing before House Committee on Foreign Relations, 85th Congress, Second Session, Washington D.C. 15–16 April 1958.
Twenty years of Pakistan. Islamabad: Ministry of Information, 1967.
Official Records of the Fifth Session of the General Assembly.
Ministry of Information and Broadcasting. Pakistan: 1995, An Official Handbook. Islamabad: Director General of Film and Publications, 1995.
President Nixon's Foreign Policy Report to the American Congress, 9 February 1972.
Proceeding of the Pakistan Muslim League Council, 1956.
Report of the Presidential Elections, Islamabad, 1993.
Report on Indian Constitutional Reforms, Montagu-Chelmsford Report, 1918.
United Nations Security Council Official Records, 1088th Meeting, Nineteenth Year, 5 February 1964.

United Nations Security Council Official Records, 1114th Meeting, Nineteenth Year, 11 May 1964.

Books and Collected Works:

Afzal, M. Rafique, ed. *Selected Speeches and Statements of the Quaid-i-Azam Mohammad Ali Jinnah.* Lahore: Research Society of Pakistan, 1966.

Ahmad, Jamil-ud-Din, ed. *Speeches and Writings of Mr. Jinnah.* Lahore: Sh. Muhammad Ashraf, Vol. 1, 1968, Vol. 2, 1976.

Ahmad, Sir Syed, *The Present State of Indian Politics: Speeches and Letters.* Intr. Farman Fathepuri. Lahore: Sang-e-Meel Publications, 1982.

Ahmad, Waheed, ed., *Quaid-i-Azam Mohammad Ali Jinnah: The Nation's Voice; Speeches and Statements, March 1935–March 1940.* Karachi: Quaid-i-Azam Academy, 1996.

Aziz, K.K., ed., *Muslims under Congress Rule, 1937–39.* Islamabad: National Commission on Historical and Cultural Research, 1978.

————, *Party Politics in Pakistan, 1947–58. Islamabad:* National Commission on Historical and Cultural Research, 1976.

Gandhi, M.K., *An Autobiography.* London: Penguin, 1982.

Iqbal, Allama Muhammad, *Letters of Iqbal to Jinnah.* Lahore: Sh. Muhammad Ashraf, 1968.

Khaliquzzaman, Chaudhry, *Pathway to Pakistan.* Lahore: Longmans, 1961.

Mansergh, Nicholas, et al., eds., *Constitutional Relations between Britain and India: The Transfer of Power, 1942–47,* 12 Vols. London: Her Majesty's Stationery Office, 1970–83.

Pirzada, Syed Sharif-uddin, ed., *Foundations of Pakistan: All-India Muslim League Documents, 1906–1947,* 2 Vols. Karachi: National Publishing House, 1969.

Shamloo, ed., *Speeches and Statements of Iqbal.* Lahore: Al-Manar Academy, 1944.

SECONDARY SOURCES

Books and Articles:

Afzal, M. Rafique, *Party Politics in Pakistan, 1947–58*. Islamabad: National Commission on Historical and Cultural Research, 1976.

Ahmad, Jamil-ud-Din, *The Final Phase of the Struggle for Pakistan*. Lahore: Publishers United, 1968.

Ahmad, Manzooruddin, ed., *Contemporary Pakistan: Politics, Economy and Society*. Karachi: Royal Book Company, 1982.

Ahmad, Mushtaq, *Government and Politics in Pakistan*. Karachi: 1978.

Ahmad, Waheed, *Road to Indian Freedom: The Formation of Government of India Act, 1935*. Lahore: Caravan Book House, 1979.

Akhtar, Rafique, ed., *Pakistan Year Book*. Karachi: East and West Publishing Company, 1988, 1992, 1993, 1995, annual.

Ali, Chaudhri Muhammad, *The Emergence of Pakistan*. New York: Columbia University Press, 1967.

Ambedkar, B.R., *Pakistan or the Partition of India*. Bombay: Thacker and Co., 1946.

Ashraf, Muhammad, *Cabinet Mission and After*. Lahore: Sh. Muhammad Ashraf, 1946.

Ayub Khan, Mohammad, *Friends Not Masters: A Political Autobiography*. New York: Oxford University Press, 1967.

Aziz, A., *Discovery of Pakistan*. Lahore: Ghulam Ali, 1957.

Azmi, M. Raziullah, 'Pakistan–US Relations', in *Pakistan Horizon*, 3rd Quarter, 1983.

_____, ed., Pakistan–*America Relations: The Recent Past*. Karachi: Royal Book Company, 1994.

Bhutto, Z.A., *Foreign Policy of Pakistan*. Karachi: Pakistan Institute of International Affairs, 1964.

_____, *The Myth of Independence*. Karachi: Oxford University Press, 1969.

Burke, S.M. and Lawrence Ziring, *Pakistan's Foreign Policy*. 2nd edn. Karachi: Oxford University Press, 1990.

Callard, Keith, *Pakistan: A Political Study*. London: George Allen & Unwin, 1957.

Choudhury, G.W., *Constitutional Development in Pakistan*. London: Longmans, 1957.

_____, *India, Pakistan, Bangladesh and Major Powers*. New York: The Free Press, 1975.

Coupland, Reginald, *India: A Restatement*. London: Oxford University Press, 1945.

Dawson, Pauline, *The Peacekeepers of Kashmir: The UN Military Observer Group in India and Pakistan*. Bombay: Popular Prakashan, 1995.

Feldman, Herbert, *A Constitution for Pakistan*. Karachi: Oxford University Press, 1955.

Gilani, Asad, *Tehrik-i-Islami*. Multan, 1962.

Gopal, Ram, *Indian Muslims: A Political History*. Bombay: Asia Publishing House, 1959.

Hali, Altaf Hussain, *Hayat-i-Javed*. Lahore: Academy Punjab, 1957.

Hamid, Abdul, *Muslim Separatism in India*. Lahore: Oxford University Press, 1967.

Harrison, Selig, *India and the United States*. New York: 1961.

Hassan, K. Sarwar, *Pakistan and the United Nations*. New York: Manhattan Publishing Company, 1960.

Hunter, W.W., *The Indian Mussalmans*. Calcutta: Comrade Publishers, 1945.

Jackson, Robert, *South Asian Crisis: India—Pakistan—Bangladesh*. London: Chatto and Windus, 1975.

Johnson-Campbell, Allan, *Mission with Mountbatten*. London: Hamish Hamilton, 1951.

Keesing's Contemporary Archives, 1939.

Kennedy, Charles H., 'Presidential-Prime Ministerial Relations: The Role of the Superior Courts', in Charles H. Kennedy and Rasul Baksh Rais, eds., *Pakistan: 1995*. Boulder, Co.: Westview Press, 1995.

Khalid, Muhammad, *Welfare State of Pakistan*. Karachi: Royal Book Company.

Khan, Liaquat Ali, *Pakistan: The Heart of Asia*. London: Oxford Printing Press, 1951.

Khan, Sardar Ibrahim, *The Kashmir Saga*. Lahore, 1965.

Kumar, Satish. *The New Pakistan*. Delhi: Vikas Publishing House, 1978.

Lamb, Alastair, *Kashmir: A Disputed Legacy, 1846–1990*. Karachi: Oxford University Press, 1993.

Mahmood, Safdar and Javaid Zafar, *Founders of Pakistan*. Lahore: Publishers United, 1968.

————, *Muslim League Ka Daur-e-Hakumat, 1947–54*. (Urdu). Lahore: 1972.

Mahmood, Safdar and Javaid Zafar, *Pakistan Divided*. Lahore: Jang Publishers, 1990.

Malik, Zahid, ed., *Pakistan After 1971*. Rawalpindi, 1974.

Mary, Countess of Minto. *India: Minto and Morely, 1905–1910*. London: Macmillan, 1934.

Menon, V.P., *Transfer of Power in India*. Princeton: University Press, 1957.

Metcalf, Thomas, *The Aftermath of Revolt*. Princeton: University Press, 1962.

Mosley, Leonard, *Last Days of British Raj*. London: Weidenfeld and Nicolson, 1961.

Noman, Muhammad, *Muslim India: Rise and Growth of the All-India Muslim League*. Allahabad: Kitabistan, 1942.

Pakistan Historical Society, eds., *A History of the Freedom Movement*. Karachi: Pakistan Historical Society, 1963.

Prasad, Rajendra, *India Divided*. Bombay: Hind Kitab, 1946.

Qureshi, Ishtiaq Hussain, *A Short History of Pakistan*. Karachi: University of Karachi, 1967.

_____, *The Struggle for Pakistan*. Karachi: University of Karachi, 1965.

Rais, Rasul Baksh, 'Elections, Regime Change, and Democracy', in Rasul Baksh Rais, ed., *State, Society and Democratic Change in Pakistan*. Karachi: Oxford University Press, 1997.

_____, 'Pakistan in 1987'. *Asian Survey*, February 1988.

Richter, William L., 'From Electoral Politics to Martial Law: An Alternative Perspective on Pakistan's Political Crisis', in Manzooruddin Ahmad, ed., *Contemporary Pakistan: Politics, Economy and Society*. Karachi: Royal Book Company, 1982.

_____, 'Pakistan in 1985'. *Asian Survey*, February 1986.

Rizvi, Hasan-Askari, 'Pakistan and the Post-Cold War Environment', in Craig Baxter and Charles H. Kennedy, eds. *Pakistan: 1997*. Boulder, Co.: Westview Press, 1997.

Sahni, N.C., *Political Struggle in Pakistan*. Jullandhar: 1969.

Sayeed, Khalid bin, *Pakistan: The Formative Phase, 1857-1947*. London: Oxford University Press, 1968.

_____, *Politics in Pakistan: The Nature and Direction of Change*. New York: Praeger, 1980.

_____, *The Political System of Pakistan*, Karachi: Oxford University Press, 1967.

Schmitter, Philippe C., 'Dangers and Dilemmas of Democracy'. *Journal of Democracy*, Vol. 5, No. 2, April 1994.

Shafqat, Saeed, *Civil–Military Relations: From Zulfikar Ali Bhutto to Benazir Bhutto*. Boulder, Co.: Westview Press, 1997.

Sims, Holly, 'Democratization and the Revitalization of Civil Society', in Rasul Baksh Rais, ed. *State, Society, and Democratic Change in Pakistan*, Karachi: Oxford University Press, 1997.

Suleri, Z.A., *Politicians and Ayub*. Rawalpindi: Capital Law and General Books Depot, 1964.

Syed, Anwar H., 'The Ouster of Nawaz Sharif in 1993: Power Plays within the Ruling Establishment', in Rasul Baksh Rais, ed., *State, Society and Democratic Change in Pakistan*, Karachi: Oxford University Press, 1997.

Symonds, Richard, *The Making of Pakistan*. London: Faber and Faber, 1957.

Twenty Years of Pakistan. Islamabad: Ministry of Information, 1967.

Waseem, Mohammad, *The 1993 Elections in Pakistan*. Lahore: Vanguard, 1994.

_____, 'Pakistan Elections 1997: One Step Forward', in Craig Baxter and Charles H. Kennedy, eds., *Pakistan: 1997*. Boulder, Co.: Westview Press, 1998.

Williams, Rushbrook, *The State of Pakistan*. London: Faber and Faber, 1966.

Wirsing, Robert G., *India, Pakistan, and the Kashmir Dispute*. New York: St. Martin's Press, 1994.

Zaidi, Z.H., 'Aspects of the Development of Muslim League Policy, 1937–47', in C.H. Philips and Mary Doreen Wainwright, eds., *The Partition of India: Policies and Perspectives, 1937–1947*. London: George Allen and Unwin, 1970.

Zaman, Waheed-uz, *Quaid-i-Azam Mohammad Ali Jinnah: Myth and Reality*. Islamabad: Committee for Birth Centenary Celebrations of Quaid-i-Azam Mohammad Ali Jinnah, 1976.

Ziring, Lawrence, et al., *Pakistan: The Long View*. Durham, NC.: Duke University Press, 1967.

_____, *Pakistan: The Enigma of Political Development*. Boulder, Co.: Westview Press, 1980.

JOURNALS/MAGAZINES

Asian Survey (Berkeley)
The Economist (London)
Herald (Karachi)
Journal of Democracy (Washington D.C.)
Newsline (Karachi)
Organizer (Delhi)
Pakistan Horizon (Karachi)
Qaumi Digest (Lahore)
The Round Table (London)

NEWSPAPERS

The Civil and Military Gazette (Lahore)
The Daily Telegraph (London)
Dawn (Karachi)
The Eastern Times (Lahore)
The Financial Times (London)
The Frontier Post (Peshawar)
The Guardian (London)
Herald Tribune (Paris)
The Hindu (Madras)
The Jang (Rawalpindi)
Kayhan International (Tehran)
The Morning News (Karachi)
The Muslim (Islamabad)
The Nation (Lahore)
Nawa-i-Waqt (Lahore)
The News (Islamabad)
The New Times (Rawalpindi)
The Pakistan Observer (Dacca)
The New York Times (New York)
Paisa Akhbar (Lahore)
The Pakistan Times (Lahore)
Sadaqat (Karachi)
The Sunday Times (London)
The Times (London)

INDEX